EMOTION, IDENTITY

Emotion, Identity, and Religion

Hope, Reciprocity, and Otherness

DOUGLAS J. DAVIES

OXFORD
UNIVERSITY PRESS

OXFORD
UNIVERSITY PRESS

Great Clarendon Street, Oxford OX2 6DP

Oxford University Press is a department of the University of Oxford.
It furthers the University's objective of excellence in research, scholarship,
and education by publishing worldwide in

Oxford New York

Auckland Cape Town Dar es Salaam Hong Kong Karachi
Kuala Lumpur Madrid Melbourne Mexico City Nairobi
New Delhi Shanghai Taipei Toronto

With offices in

Argentina Austria Brazil Chile Czech Republic France Greece
Guatemala Hungary Italy Japan Poland Portugal Singapore
South Korea Switzerland Thailand Turkey Ukraine Vietnam

Oxford is a registered trade mark of Oxford University Press
in the UK and in certain other countries

Published in the United States
by Oxford University Press Inc., New York

© Douglas J. Davies 2011

British Library Cataloguing in Publication Data

Data available

Library of Congress Cataloging in Publication Data

Data available

Typeset by SPI Publisher Services, Pondicherry, India
Printed in Great Britain
on acid-free paper by
MPG Books Group, Bodmin and King's Lynn

ISBN 978–0–19–955152–1 (Hbk.)
978–0–19–955153–8 (Pbk.)

1 3 5 7 9 10 8 6 4 2

Preface

The study of emotions has become of increasing significance across a spectrum of the arts, humanities, and social sciences in recent years and has interested me a great deal because one of the enduring themes of my own work has been the human embodiment of cultural values, their emotional tones, and the question of how the human drive for meaning might generate a sense of salvation. The current resurgent interest in emotions, paralleling the late-nineteenth-century interest in religious experience and mysticism, but driven by innovations in cognitive science and evolutionary biology, prompted my own more focused interest in emotion and the ensuing writing of this book, something fostered by an Arts and Humanities Research Council-funded Network on Emotions, Identity, and Religious Communities based at Durham University's Department of Theology and Religion, which I gratefully acknowledge. I also take this opportunity to thank members of that Network for their participation, especially Dr Chang-Won Park, for help in its organization and management.

While emergent psychological studies of emotions often focus on lists or classification of emotions, with historical and ethnographic studies also providing invaluable documentation of specific contexts, this volume offers an eclectic body of material drawn from those and other sources to provide an integrated account of special relevance to theology and religious studies, but also with application to a general trans-disciplinary readership. Though this approach on the nuanced patterning of emotions in diverse groups and contexts offers many willing hostages to critical fortune, the risk is worth taking in an attempt to show something of the complexity of those nuances created by religious traditions as they manage human emotions, identity, and core cultural values. Still, many of the following chapters reveal iceberg tips of my more previous and more detailed anthropological and theological studies on death, funerary rites, Mormonism, and the Church of England.

In bringing the present form of this study to good shape I am grateful for the original dialogue with The Delegates of the Oxford University Press and for later critical comment from their anonymous reader; these proved to be invaluable. Thanks also go to Tom Perridge and Elizabeth Robottom for their initial and subsequent editorial support and patience. Finally, I thank the University of Durham and its Department of Theology and Religion for supporting my research, and the Academy of Social Sciences for admitting me as one of their Academicians in 2009. These two institutions, in their respective ways, continue to foster the conversation across boundaries that makes thinking a pleasure.

Douglas J. Davies

Durham
May 2010

Contents

Introduction

This study describes how different religious traditions prefer certain patterns of emotion, fostering and managing them at individual and community levels of identity. It will show how beliefs and doctrines interplay with human feelings to generate a sense of embodiment, that complex but valuable concept describing how cultural values become second nature to our sense of ourselves. As human beings we are deeply aware of how we feel at different times and places, as emotions or moods come and go in ways we do not always understand. We are also alert to the equally obvious fact that different societies and religious groups emphasize some part of the wide spectrum of possible human feelings, framing it with nuances of their own moral value and undertaking to cultivate and control it for the good of their community.

The processes that combine such emotions with ultimate values to produce self-identity underlie all aspects of life, though they often become most explicit in what we call religion. Though a 'religion' may or may not involve beliefs about supernatural entities, it always involves some core values and some attempt at managing them and the emotions associated with them in terms of some framing of destiny. In secular contexts, too, where some may prefer to speak of ideology, ethics, or even spirituality as the foundation of identity, the management of emotions in relation to values remains crucial to community life. One way of thinking about these emotions and values is to see them as being appropriated by individuals in nuanced ways that help to develop the identity of those individuals. This is not to say that each person becomes a puppet of society, simply dancing to the tunes of social values and expressing a group's preferred emotions. Far from it. One of the real theoretical issues of the social and human sciences, including philosophy and theology, as well as literature and music, involves the creativity that certain individuals bring to their social world. This applies not only to the great thinkers and religious innovators but to every person as he makes his own mark on the way he lives in terms of personal aesthetics. Even so, sociology and anthropology tend to think less of individuals and more of group profiles, just as theology and philosophy often think in notably abstract and not individual ways about life and its meaning. This study, however, will at least try to mix theoretical perspectives from different traditions without losing sight of life at its ordinary level. In particular, the idea of identity will run throughout this study as a prime means of understanding ourselves as self-conscious and social animals. Though it is an extremely complex idea, we will take identity to be the intersection point of self-understanding, of the views others have of us, and of a society's preferred values and associated emotions.

Given our concern with religion, we will also draw attention to 'otherness', a concept that will be a constant reminder of the relatedness of persons, whether to others in society, to the environment itself, or to the supernatural influences of which many religions speak. We will, inevitably, say much about beliefs and religious doctrines as part of the values of a society, and will be especially interested in how sacred texts, rites, and celebrations associated with beliefs become embodied in human feelings, whether in powerful but quickly passing emotions or in influentially enduring moods.[1] This triggering of emotion and the parallel management of moods in tandem with the beliefs or core values of a society provide our focus on religion. Our overarching assumption about these beliefs and emotions will be that each tradition favours a particular repertoire, syndrome, pattern, or gestalt of emotions and moods as the medium for expressing its world view. It will often be possible to identify images or scenes that capture this pattern and help focus the character of a particular tradition, as, for example, in the iconography of a seated Buddha and a crucified Christ, where the mindfulness of Buddhism's middle way meets the tortured extreme of human blood sacrifice. Such images help trigger the emotions of devotees, influence their ongoing moods, interplay with the philosophies and theologies of world religions, and direct their ethical living. They also extend into folk beliefs, art, music, and sacred narratives, all within the enormous world of emotion-fed identities. Similar images capture the transformed insight of Muhammad and Guru Nanak, the conversion of Augustine and Paul, and the experiences of thousands of other devotees and reformers, not to mention local moments of emotional power brought by shamans, healers, mediums, and revivalists across the world. Such images are explored in this study, especially in Chapter 2, through the concept of paradigmatic scenes.

---

[1] Darwin ([1872] 1998: 83). See Paul Ekman's Introduction: 'Emotions are brief and episodic lasting seconds or minutes.'

REFLEXIVITY AND OTHERNESS

Still, these issues of experience and identity pose a real challenge, because they involve studying ourselves. It often seems odd, for example, when studies of human beings speak of 'them', or of 'humans' rather than of 'us', as though they were separate entities from the scholar. While such an objectivity is easy in, say, scientific accounts of the blood supply, it becomes problematic for issues of identity. This has led many scholars to speak of 'reflexivity', of the need to consider one's own standpoint, aware of the way perception is influenced by who we are.[2] Our readiness to engage with theories about people and religion is almost inevitably related to our own starting point and to the things we view as precious, not least our commitment to or antagonism against religion as we have experienced it. Here our emotions interplay with our thoughts in ways that may not be predictable, but to which we ought to be alert if we think that there is some wisdom to be gained by studying the complex issues of emotion, identity, and religion. At the same time, however, it is wise not to let the issue of reflexivity become an end in itself, resulting in a self-absorption that can easily paralyse.[3]

Unlike some anthropologists who would 'reject the very idea of otherness', believing that it expressed a superiority or imperialism over 'others' as the objects of analysis, this study accepts 'otherness' in a more philosophical sense and existential sense as something inescapable when taking a wide view of ourselves as human beings with emotions and identities and social worlds of our own.[4] Otherness, as it interests us, has been used of a variety of human experiences that, for example, give a person a sense that he is not alone because he senses God being with him or, perhaps, because he senses a deceased relative as present. Otherness can also be used to refer to other people who influence our lives. Moreover, even when thinking about ourselves, we can sometimes feel a stranger to ourselves or gain a sense of there being 'another' aspect of ourselves that we cannot quite apprehend. These various aspects of otherness that frame our life and pervade our awareness as emotional sensations may also foster a certain kind of 'inwardness', a sense of

---

[2] Argyrou (2002: 1–27) valuably analyses 'otherness' and 'sameness' applied to anthropologists as they view 'other' cultures while being a member of a culture themselves.
[3] Lindsay Jones (2000: 206–8).   [4] Evens (2008: 118–24).

some inner place where we are able to commune with ourselves[5]—that inner place being one that some believers would also see as a meeting place between one's self and otherness. A related feature of experience that underlies this study is that of 'power', whether understood as the physical force available for self-defence or aggression or as the sense of being acted upon by invisible agents or spiritual powers. The precise way in which 'power' is qualified by context and tradition will emerge, chapter by chapter, often with a sense of its religious nature. Even so, that 'power' needs to be related to our nature as human animals evolved within hierarchical primate groups and experienced through actual or assumed reciprocal relationships in ways that foster a sense of otherness.

KEY CONCEPTS

We can now bring this idea of otherness into a wider framework of ideas that will help structure much of this study. From the many concepts that could drive our study of human concerns over the depth and significance of life, seven have been chosen as interlinked leitmotifs of this study, ordered in a threefold layering. The first three—emotion, identity, and religion—set our overall subject, though each is much debated within and between academic disciplines. The middle two—meaning and hope—qualify each other and provide a direction for the first three, with the final pair—otherness and reciprocity—adding key concepts that help interpret human awareness and social behaviour.

> Emotion – Identity – Religion
> Meaning – Hope
> Otherness – Reciprocity

While the concepts of the first-ranked triad are always influenced by a society's historical culture, with much debate over their definition, this study adopts a general approach to them.[6] Accordingly, we take 'emotions' to be focused feeling states of limited yet intense duration, but we acknowledge that scholars name types of emotion and question their universality while

---

[5] McMahon (2008: 19–37).

[6] It is hard to exaggerate the complexity of definition and diverse opinion surrounding all seven of this study's guiding concepts. Volumes exist on each one of them.

arriving at slightly different lists from each other.[7] This study will also explore terms that appear neither above nor in various other lists, but that seem unavoidable when considering complex issues of religious piety and worship.[8] As for 'identity', it is viewed as a negotiated sense of self developed over time through the emotions and moods that characterize feelings people have of themselves in relation to core values of their group. Above all, it must be noted that this analysis emerges within an early twenty-first-century British academic context and against an intellectual backdrop as described in the Preface: claims to any extensive extrapolation are very limited. Life circumstances, including ageing itself, influence the dynamics of our identity to a great extent, with people's experiences changing as new opportunities, challenges, and conflicts emerge.[9] Furthermore, some scholars would speak of 'identity' as a single entity as being quite problematic.[10] Finally, in 'religion', we have a concept that refers to clusters of symbolic rituals that enshrine the prime values and beliefs of a group and intensify their associated emotions. Religion will, however, always need contextualizing within different kinds of society, whether traditional and small scale, with a pervasive religious presence, or modern, complex, and highly differentiated, possessing both tradition-like groups of intense religiosity and others that are markedly secular.[11]

The second-layer concepts highlight the importance of 'meaning' approached not only in terms of the ideas that shape our world view but also as a bridge between the doctrines of a religious tradition and the emotional life underlying people's sense of identity. Meaning often takes the form of explanatory ideas in the form of myths, philosophy, science, and theology, but always being pervaded by distinctive moods. 'Hope' is one such mood, and is singled out in this study as especially important for the way meaning affects identity. Our aligning of hope and meaning also highlights the bio-cultural nature of emotions as explored in this study, with an emphasis on the 'cultural'. For, while hope is seldom found in psychological lists of emotion, it is a valuable notion for understanding how religions generate a sense of

---

[7] e.g. Andrade (1995: 218), who cites variations from two to ten basic responses.

[8] Goldschmidt (1990: 243): 'Love, hate, jealousy, despair, empathy, fear, joy, satisfaction, elation, depression, and sentiment that do not even appear in our lexicon become entangled in human activity'—an important caveat that affects many parts of this study.

[9] A good example is Kunin's account (2009) of Crypto-Jews in New Mexico and his notion of *jonglerie* or juggling identities according to context.

[10] Craib's criticism (1998: 63) of sociologist Anthony Giddens for oversimplifying the social world is an apt reminder for a study such as this, especially given the complexity of individuals.

[11] Cf. Guest (2007: 188), who even describes group identity as an 'affirmation of internal diversity'.

meaningful identity in individuals and groups. Much the same could be said for 'trust'. Indeed, the subtle interplay of hope and trust affects all the notions listed above, often with trust having an emphasis on present activities and hope referring to future events. One might even say that 'trust' is the present and 'hope' the future mood of 'identity'.

The third-layer motifs of 'otherness' and 'reciprocity' express something of the interactive processes by which meaning and hope are generated and expressed. Otherness and reciprocity as the final key concepts for our study can allude to supernatural, social, or self-references, with reciprocity also referring not only to the give and take underlying all aspects of daily life but also to those notions of sacrifice, offering, merit, grace, and salvation that underpin many religious phenomena and experiences.

The seven concepts arranged in these three layers have been chosen as a group of elements that, together, help us create a general approach to the way many people live. They need to be seen in the light of the fact that, just as the late nineteenth and early twentieth centuries produced stimulating explorations of religious experience, so the late twentieth and early twenty-first centuries have witnessed a wave of studies of emotions, prompted largely by developments in cognitive psychology and evolutionary biology.[12] Drawing from these sources, as well as from anthropology, sociology, philosophy, and theology, and from music, literature and the arts, this study will show how religious groups create and sustain their preferred types of identity. It would also be possible to frame this discussion, as Roy d'Andrade does, in terms of 'schemas' that frame the motives and experiences people are encouraged to possess and may actually have in different societies, an approach that lays importance on the appraisal process in a society that influences how people engage with their socially identified emotions. For simplicity's sake in this study, however, we will remain with the less sophisticated idea of a preferred pattern or syndrome of managed emotion held by religious groups and related to their core values.[13] Although we will, occasionally, look in more detail at some selected scholars and their theories of religion in relation to this, our study will not provide the kind of analysis of society and religion

[12] e.g. William James (1902); Heiler ([1918] 1932); Otto ([1917] 1924); Leeuw ([1933] 1967); Csordas (1994); Whitehouse (2004a); Corrigan (2000a, 2000b, 2008); Elliot (2005); Wynn (2005); Properzi (2010).

[13] But always cognizant of Andrade (1995: 248–50, emphasis in original) and his caution over the complexity of cultural elements and the problem of wanting to establish any overly fixed '*grammar* for each culture'.

that circles around philosophical discussions of social science and its relationship to theology.[14]

Expanding the motifs

One valuable focus on religious experience that helps contextualize otherness as one of our key elements is that of Joachim Wach and his 'four formal criteria' of religious experience: namely, 'a response to what is experienced as ultimate reality', 'a total response of the total being' to that apprehension, a sense that this is 'the most intense experience of which man is capable', and finally 'an imperative' or 'commitment which impels man to act'. He describes the root of this response to ultimacy as 'an awareness of apprehension' that does not lack a 'cognitive aspect' but is not defined by it. For him it is the sensing or apprehending of something 'powerful' that is crucial, exemplified in Rudolph Otto's notion of a sense of awe (*sensus numinis*), and Paul Tillich's of 'ultimacy'.[15] Drawing from William James, he makes the following point that is directly relevant for this study.

It is as if there were in the human consciousness a sense of reality, a feeling of objective presence, a perception of what we may call 'something there', more deep and more general than any of the special and particular 'senses' by which current psychology presupposes existent realities to be originally revealed.[16]

It is precisely this reflexive 'awareness of apprehension' or of 'something there' that is captured in 'otherness', itself a sense of alterity open for interpretation by secularists as the outcome of cognitive processing of the environment and by theists as the 'sense of God'.[17]

These clustered motifs create a perspective for our study of emotions, ensuring that no idea stands alone as sufficient to cope with the complex world of ancestors, gods, spirits, and inner sensations that motivate human lives and create emotional worlds in which to live. However, they allow us to see how groups manage preferred feelings through general moods of life and their intensified spots of emotional sensation. Though there is, inevitably,

[14] As in Mellor's valuable volume (2004). More like Daniel Bell ([1980] 1991: pp. xix–xx), however, I view society as possessing 'diverse realms' with their 'different rhythm of change'.

[15] Wach (1951: 32–5).

[16] William James (1902: 58).

[17] As Bowker argued (1973, 1978). McCauley and Lawson (2002: 8) adopt the abbreviation 'CPS' to represent 'culturally postulated superhuman' agents.

some vagueness surrounding these motifs, we are encouraged by Ohnuki-Tierney's view that there is 'a functional advantage in defining phenomena vaguely' when 'the intellectual and emotional content of a phenomenon is only dimly perceived' or viewed as embodied in people, fostered and controlled as preferred ways of feeling, acting, seeing, and even smelling.[18]

This study assumes that patterns are generated between the values, beliefs, or doctrines of a group and the way associated experiences are directed, named, and valued. Religion is taken to be a major means of creating and managing emotion, with particular traditions constituting emotional syndromes, patterns of relatively integrated world views in which experience and explanation, feeling and the naming of feelings, forge a focused way of life. Within Christianity, for example, the disciplined silence of a Quaker Meeting differs a great deal from a Charismatic worship meeting with its singing, movement, and periodic speaking in tongues or other exclamations, and is likely to be matched by differences in theological outlook.

Emotional syndromes

To think of emotions, identity, and religion as a syndrome providing a repertoire of response is to see them as constituting a relatively integrated configuration of elements that come to form more than the sum of their parts.[19] This means that, when explanations are given of the value of particular feelings and of how to develop them, both the doctrinal explanations and the feelings gain in importance. The doctrine adds value to the feelings gained, and the feelings rise in importance because of what they mean. Human feelings of positive excitement, for example, assume added significance if they are understood as a worshipping encounter with the divine and interpreted as joy, just as a negative sense of depression gains a meaningful basis if apprehended as a sorrow shared by God.

This perspective on emotional syndromes and patterned spirituality aligned with a religious configuration of identity is rooted in Max Weber's sociology of religion, which described how ritual activities might generate 'a devotion with a distinctive religious mood' and argued, theoretically, that in

---

[18] Ohnuki-Tierney (1981: 157, 149). Cf. Rappaport (1999: 304–12) on 'deutero-truth' for higher-order terms defying precise definition but allowing for shared assumptions. Also Davies and Guest (2007: 37–8, 178–80) for the 'vagueness factor' as an adaptive feature in Anglican leadership.

[19] Godfrey Lienhardt (1961: 161) describes how a deity name 'recreates for the Dinka the whole syndrome of experiences of . . . natural phenomena as they touch directly upon human life'.

some traditions 'the religious mood is the true instrument of salvation'.[20] This understanding of emotions and moods allows for comparison of groups, and encourages different traditions to appreciate each other but always with a caution, lest facile stereotypes are simplistically adopted.[21] This perspective is also a reminder that theological doctrines or even philosophical theories exist not as abstract statements but as ideas embodied by individuals and practised in private and ceremonial life as part of the *habitus*[22] or regular mode of being of a person within a culture, and being liable to change over time.[23] Here, the whole realm of ritual and symbolism bursts upon the scene of emotion and identity, making it clear that religious identity emerges and is sustained through action. It is this very integration of ideas, feeling, and behaviour that underpins this study and needs stressing before we even start talking about the misleading oppositions between thinking and feeling, thought and action, doctrine and ritual or the like.[24] This is especially important as we consider how religious teachings pervade and shape human feeling in the creation of distinctive spiritualities. The swirling dancing of Islamic Dervishes relates to individual teachers and their instruction of how one may call God to mind in ways that differ from the morning prayers of a Sikh pursuing his path of dwelling on the name of God or the Catholic devotedly receiving the body of God by eating the consecrated host at the Mass. What such examples highlight is the complex way in which human feeling is directed, prompted, and managed in and through teachings that are inseparable from rituals and symbols that express and intensify them, as Chapter 2 will show. Another key influence on ritual and belief is the anthropologist Roy Rappaport. His magisterial *Ritual and Religion in the Making of Humanity* identifies both the 'ultimate sacred postulates' or beliefs created by human beings, and

---

[20] Weber ([1922] 1965: 151). The 'sociology of emotions' emerged later. Cf. Craib (1998: 105–15).

[21] A. H. Keane, once Vice-President of the Royal Anthropological Institute, wrote an entire account of the world's peoples, including their 'mental character', and could, for example, describe the French as 'somewhat defective, as seen in the love of show and glory which is certainly stronger than their sense of duty' (1908: 353).

[22] Weber ([1922] 1965: 161). Though Weber's use of *habitus* to describe a 'pattern of life' (Parsons 1965: p. xlii) acknowledges emotion, its dominant emphasis is upon regulated patterns of action. *Habitus* is more often associated with Pierre Bourdieu's 'systems of durable, transposable *dispositions.... principles of the generation and structuring of practice*' ([1972] 1977: 72–87).

[23] See Thompson ([1963] 1968: 403) for 'emotional and spiritual paroxysms' of early Methodism.

[24] Cf. Baal and Beek (1985: 187) for the need to integrate 'rational process . . . action and feeling in religion'.

the foundational role of ritual in enacting them.[25] The following chapters will not, however, cite Rappaport at any length, because practically every topic addressed could be furnished with a theoretical comment from his work and it would be wise for those unfamiliar with his work to read it in its entirety. Another valuable background to this study may be identified in sociologist Daniel Bell's approach to 'culture' as a broad frame for human life in general and its ritual activity in particular, one with a strong existential dimension.[26] For Bell, the 'starting point in understanding culture is not human nature (as in Greek thought), nor human history (as in Hegel and Marx), but the human predicament', central to which lies the 'understanding of death', the 'nagging sense of mortality', and 'the very search for meanings that transcends one's own life'.[27]

SUMMARY

This broad approach to the field of religious studies will, then, draw material from the social-scientific worlds of psychology, anthropology, and sociology as well as from the humanities as they explore literature, music, art, and theology. This risky task acknowledges the technicalities of each discipline and religious tradition as well as the subjective nature of our own experiences. It is an approach that takes seriously the fact that, while all plant and animal life may be characterized in terms of a certain sensitivity to environment, the evolutionary development of humans has enhanced the development of self-conscious awareness evident in language, in different cultural ideas and practices, and in the time we spend thinking about ourselves. This leads us, in the following chapters, to speak of a human drive for meaning as a kind of human instinct. We are born with a capacity to explore the world and into a society that presents us with names for many things and with mythical, religious, philosophical, and scientific theories explaining their significance. Alongside these formal 'explanations' that answer our desire to know, we also encounter practical actions such as play, movement, singing, poetry, and art

---

[25] Rappaport (1999: 263–5).

[26] Some might find value in Gorringe's theological and literary perspective and carefulness over defining kinds of 'high', 'popular', and 'folk' culture (2004: 47–66). This is felt unnecessary for this book's social-scientific approach to culture, which absorbs all of these, much as in Daniel Bell, in the text.

[27] Daniel Bell ([1980] 1991: 333, 336, 352).

that also help us 'understand' our world and relate to it and its eventualities. Here subtlety of observation is encouraged through the interdependence of scholars. When an art critic writes of how El Greco develops within the subjects of his paintings a 'feeling of intense and silent communication, a plunging into one another's eyes' rather than depending upon 'the much more obvious rhetoric of gesture', we begin to appreciate a quality of emotion and relations that otherwise would elude us.[28] It is just such a drawing of attention that we seek through many sources.

The plan of this study is as follows. Chapter 1 will develop the key concepts outlined above in relation to some theories of emotion. Chapter 2 will then focus on ritual and symbol as key media for cultivating selected emotions and moods. In Chapter 3 the complex idea of identity is analysed in relation to the ways in which this sense of ourselves may be strengthened or depleted. Chapter 4 will explore human feelings surrounding grief and the desire for intensive living that sometimes overtakes people, and it will also offer some nuanced thoughts on the charisma sometimes encountered in religious leaders. Chapter 5 will ask how male and female gender has influenced religious identities and will also explore aspects of the complex idea of ritual purity. Then we turn to a series of chapters that itemize groups of feelings that religious traditions have often emphasized and sought to manage in distinctive ways. So, Chapter 6 looks at love and joy, while also contributing something to a theory of humility, while Chapter 7 deals with the universal theme of merit and its various manifestations in the phenomena of grace and pardon. Then, Chapter 8 analyses the realm of despair and hope and introduces my own theory of moral-somatic relationships as a way of understanding the link between social life and individual human feelings. Chapter 9 then takes up the characteristic religious phenomena of revelation, conversion, and spirit possession to see how these help to manage emotion and foster identity, all before Chapter 10 brings such experiences into the context of physical surroundings in a discussion of sacred place, the ritual of worship, and the role of music within emotional life. Chapter 11, in providing a final retrospective view on how religious traditions manage emotion

---

[28] Bronstein (1991: 13). Cf. Prideaux (2005: 37) on Edvard Munch, famed for his painting of *The Scream*, and whose 'portraits of the sane avert their gaze', an aversion normally retained when depicting madness. However, when painting Laura—eyeball to eyeball—'he looked straight into the eyes of the family insanity'.

repertoires, will also consider the implications of studying religion, on the one hand, and being religious, on the other, an issue already implicit in what we have already said about 'reflexivity and otherness', and which is often of personal importance to religious believers as well as to others interested in the study of religion.

1

Dynamics, Feeling, and Meanings

The Introduction proposed the theme of a human drive for meaning as one key feature of this study, and it is to a variety of complex forms of meaning-making in relation to religion, emotion, and identity that we now turn in this chapter. 'Meaning', of course, embraces a whole spectrum of human activity, from philosophical logic and scientific experimentation through the intuitions that underlie our recognition of other people, their faces and behaviour, to the way music sometimes seem to 'speak' to us and 'answer to' some joy or sorrow in our lives. For some, meaning involves some special place, perhaps their home or country or some location carrying deep religious significance, whether in their local temple, a world site such as Jerusalem, Mecca, or Salt Lake City, or some anticipated otherworld such as Paradise. Many of these contexts of meaning will be considered in this and following chapters, but always in terms of their associated emotions and moods, with hope and the part it plays within religious identity of devotees the world over often leading the field.

But, of course, this very study also involves its own form of search for meaning.[1] This is a complicated process, because it involves making assumptions about how people, themselves, pursue meaning and find it to some extent through the interplay of their religious values and emotions and the sense of identity that arises from that process. Sometimes our assumptions involve ideas that differ from those we are studying, especially if we try to find the processes underlying what people say or do in ways alien to them,[2] 'invisible processes' that work without our knowing it and deeply influence

---

[1] Cf. Fernandez (1995: 36–8) on anthropologists and their own search for meaning and the nature of 'anthropology as conversion'.

[2] Argyrou (2002: 60–91) explores the 'sociocultural unconscious': the assumption of being able to 'go underneath the symbol to the reality it represents and which gives it its meaning' (citing Durkheim [1912] 1976: 2–3).

how we view the world and certain crucial aspects of it.[3] Drawing not only from anthropology and sociology but, more especially, from evolutionary biology and cognitive science, this perspective argues that there are mental processes underlying the self-aware consciousness stressed in the last paragraph on meaning-making and typified by Pascal Boyer as 'the mistake of intellectualism', which assumed the human mind to be 'driven by a *general* urge to explain'.[4] Boyer emphasized *general* because his own view stresses not 'a general' but 'many different, specialized explanatory engines', engines, processes, or systems that are characterized as 'inference systems' that operate 'completely unnoticed, in parts of our mind that conscious introspection will not reach', but that are 'intuitions driven by relevance'.[5] These include a moral-emotional system, a verbal communication system, an intuitive psychology system, a social exchange system, a Person-File system.

Further 'invisible' influences would be put forward by other schools of psychology, especially psycho-dynamic theories originating in Freud, to whom we return below. The very term 'psycho-dynamic' speaks of the energies reckoned to be at work within the psyche or self, and it is wise to recognize the 'internal battle to maintain an identity against a disruptive emotion', since 'the relationship between emotion and identity' is as likely to be 'always in a contradictory flux' as to be in some sort of clear orderliness.[6] Many traditional religions recognize this and strive to bring order to the perceived unruliness of human emotional desire.[7] Some key Christian views have done this through motifs of spirit being opposed to flesh, just as core Buddhism sees the disruptive role of desire as opposed to the goal of its cessation. To such themes we return in the final chapter of this study.

All such endeavours to develop a preferred identity occur within cultural worlds produced by societies over many years. Religious ideas, philosophical, scientific, and social-scientific theories, the architectural and artistic heritage of a people and their musical traditions all come together as an environment of meaning. Also important to a people are those individuals and groups that have spearheaded new developments or have defended traditions in time of conflict, confusion, and change: heroes, heroines, prophets, reformers, and

---

[3] Boyer (2001: 56).   [4] Boyer (2001: 18).
[5] Boyer (2001: 19, 38, 362).   [6] Craib (1998: 115).
[7] Much fiction also deals with such emotional flux and social order. Classically, in Aldous Huxley's *Brave New World* the drug 'soma' could deliver 'all the advantages of Christianity and alcohol; none of their defects', allowing one to, 'take a holiday from reality whenever you like and come back without so much as a headache or a mythology' ([1932] 1994: 46).

revitalizers, all may become cultural heroes. In recent times many societies have also made celebrities of athletes, sportspeople, and musicians of many kinds. All of these bring some meaning to us, and add fresh features to a country's way of life or to some identifiable group that may encompass many countries.

So, the key aspect of meaning-making underlying this study concerns identity, that sense of self and of who we are in relation to others, that characterizes human life in its bridge of communication between the individual and society, a relationship typifying social science. Just how we speak of the individual–society relationship is, itself, an instructive task.[8] To speak of a 'bridge' is to indicate something of a two-way passage and not of a bond, or of individual identity as a 'product' of society. Individual identity is more of an ongoing process of relationship between individuals with themselves and with their society, one that is grounded in language as much as in processes of reciprocity; indeed, language is a prime mode of reciprocity. George Steiner, on whose work, especially on otherness, we draw in later chapters, typified this in his own philosophical-literary fashion when describing how identity comes as we not so much 'speak to ourselves as speak ourselves'.[9] But there are limits and constraints, just as there are degrees of freedom in a society for fostering what we often call individuality. Indeed, our very notion of what constitutes a 'society' is important here as a background for ideas of identity. Some societies and the religious traditions that often frame them appear very large and monolithic, with strictly imposed standards of speech, dress, and many kinds of behaviour, including who may marry whom or what may be eaten. Other societies seem much more fragmented or at least made up of numerous small and distinctive groups. In many contemporary societies people sharing certain ethnicities often live in proximity to each other and furnish an awareness of identity fostered by a protective sense of safety against the wider world. In all these contexts we encounter the interesting human fact of life that people have names that indicate identity.[10] In many traditional societies the name indicates family structure, position within a group of siblings, or a distinctive relation with the deity. In many modern societies names are much more free and may even be fanciful or created to attract attention to the individual

---

[8] Heath (2003: 80) sees 'relational empathy' as a rare though valuable part of experience underlying his atheistic nihilism.

[9] George Steiner ([1968] 1972: 72).

[10] This underlies anthropology's long-term commitment to analysing kinship systems.

rather than to the group of which he or she is part. Some people even change their names, a custom long established by actors, a fact that highlights the issue of personal identity, for an actor is one who assumes many identities over a career and may leave the public wondering who or what the 'real' person is or is like. In religious terms some groups give new names to religious devotees or initiates, showing how identity may be related to the ancestors or deities.

EMOTIONAL REPERTOIRES AND
PERSONAL AESTHETIC

It is quite obvious, however, that names are given not only to people but to an enormous number of 'things' in the world, as each society catalogues its world and organizes things into various categories.[11] This kind of cultural classification is of particular importance in this study, because 'emotions' can be approached as the 'names' a society gives to certain kinds of 'feelings'. The way a particular society or group names its feelings offers an important means of understanding how it views the world and directs its members in their approach to their environment.[12] Emotions are socially named feelings used by human groups to help stimulate, direct, and control 'feelings'. Indeed, one of the major tasks of human society as a meaning-making process has come to lie in managing human feelings as part of the total programme of making meaning. Human diversity being what it is, we find different societies engaged in such naming and management of feelings in a great variety of ways. What we can expect is that each society or group will possess what we might call a repertoire of emotions within its available syndrome. Part of the process of successful socialization of children lies in their acquiring a competence in the emotional repertoire of their culture, in knowing which to draw upon and 'perform' in any given context. This also applies to people such as religious converts who move from group to group. But it is not easy to acquire such a cultural competence in emotional syndrome and repertoire when developing one's identity in new contexts, for this takes time and is

[11] George Steiner ([1968] 1972: 72): 'Our identity is a first-person pronoun.' He speaks of Monotheism as 'that transcendental magnification of the image of the human self'.

[12] Coleridge ([1810] 1907: 352) alludes to this: 'the analysis of our senses in the commonest books of anthropology has drawn our attention to the distinction between the perfectly organic, and the mixed senses.'

acquired rather than formally learnt. Moreover, some achieve this more readily than others, given the variation in capacity to empathize evident, for example, in extremes of autism.

One of the tasks of social and human sciences is to consider the way social or group values and emotions play into, and are appropriated by, individuals. We have already alluded to this in the Introduction, but can now take it further by balancing the influence of social experience on the very categories of our thought, as argued in Durkheim's sociological theory of knowledge,[13] with what Daniel Miller has called the 'aesthetic' evident in individual and family life. Miller's detailed study of a London street with its households of families, partners, and individuals reveals an important empirical and theoretical approach to ordinary lives. He uses the term 'aesthetic' to describe a 'combination of ordering principles', 'a synthesis of memory and order', 'a kind of logic' by which individuals organize their home and live in it.[14] Miller's work is also important, because it is realistic and not bound by formal theories of socialization that assume that society makes its members in some strictly formulaic way. As he says, 'there is no evidence that people end up becoming "fully formed" at some point in their lives'.[15] Still, it is very likely that considerable differences exist between those who simply get on with living, guided by their own 'aesthetic', and others who are deeply embedded within a religious group and strongly influenced by its emotional repertoire and value scheme. Nevertheless, even religious devotees may develop their own nuanced aesthetic of participation as life experience changes over time. As Miller says of one of his individuals, 'as in the case of Peggy and Cyril, the most significant influence of all can occur when one is in one's sixties and all previous influences become completely re-configured in order to fit better with a new and now determining influence on one's life'.[16] One factor framing such continuity or change is that of place, residence, or site of influencing experiences, and, for that reason, Chapter 10 will explore the theme of place and sacred space.[17]

---

[13] Durkheim ([1912] 1976), in the preface to his *Elementary Forms*.
[14] Miller (2008: 220–1, 256).
[15] Miller (2008: 291).
[16] Miller (2008: 291).
[17] See Edgewater (1999: 153–81) for an application of this issue to music and its effects.

Core-values, core-feelings, and embodiment

All such integrated meaning-making processes engage directly with the 'core values' of a group, be it a nation state, family, club, sport, church, job, hobby, or some other network, through which life is made meaningful and a sense of identity gained. The closer people relate to such core values and their associated emotional syndrome, the more intense becomes their sense of identity; conversely, they are likely to suffer a depletion in their sense of identity if less intensely involved. Over the life course, however, individuals are likely to vary in their degree of attachment or may switch from one value set to another.

As for 'feelings' and 'emotions', this study uses 'feelings' for the many sensations and experiences that individuals have each moment of their life, while 'emotion' is retained for the names a society gives to selected feelings. Not all the feelings that we experience each day have names given to them by our society, nor do all the sensations that we have come to be regarded as 'emotions'.[18] Most people, for example, experience optical sensations that are given colour names that serve well for communicating with others, but those names do not cover every quality of colour received from the world around us. Still, societies divide experience into workable chunks that are named and learned. Similarly with sounds, touch, and words relating to these feelings. But we may, sometimes, hear a sound or touch a surface and gain a feeling that we cannot quite describe, and we cannot do so because we have not been given a word for that precise event. Smell, however, presents a distinctive example of a genre of experience that is difficult to name; indeed, while human societies have found it relatively easy to create names for colours, they have not created smell names. Instead, people speak of something smelling 'like' some other thing or being good or bad or sweet or the like. There is a complexity of personal experience and memory that presents us with smells in a way that is different from how the environment presents us with colours.

This complex picture becomes more complicated still when we appreciate that not all our feelings are prompted by the world around us but rather by the world of our own bodies. If we visit the doctor with some ailment, we may be asked to describe what we feel or what 'the pain' feels like. We may have only rough guides to inform our answer; is it a 'sharp' or a 'dull' pain, for

---

[18] Aristotle (1963: 36) notes absence of description of an exceedingly courageous man who has no fear.

example? Many aspects of our feelings connected with the basic functions of eating, excreting, and sex, for example, do not carry detailed names. This division between personal and social experience is important and changes as a society becomes more concerned with aspects of life that it may previously have ignored. The rise of medical and psychiatric interests, for example, often brings more detailed focus on feelings as symptoms of illness. This is also of deep importance for 'religion' and has further relevance as issues of 'spirituality' develop either alongside 'religion' or in its perceived declining shadow, for traditional and emergent traditions often name, cultivate, and control different forms of feeling. Taking a cue from Kieran Flanagan, this study also ensures that more ordinary and sometimes ignored aspects of religious life, mood, and emotion are considered, while some of 'the more dramatic aspects of experience' are not ignored.[19]

Such body-based themes of feeling and culture-based issues of named emotions unite in a general embodiment theory, as discussed in terms of various scholars in the following chapters. I also explored this theme of embodiment some years ago as an approach to religious experience and the ritual activity of churches, identifying it as involving 'both rational and emotional sets of awareness' in order to emphasize 'the role of emotion in the growing sense of embodiment' in a person.[20] Then I noted the importance of religious experience in the work of William James and Rudolph Otto, and was keen to speak in terms of 'mood-memory' under the assumption that we could, somehow, recall and re-experience previous emotion under the combined power of imagination and memory.[21] Now it is more psychologically and sociologically apparent that this approach needs correction to see current awareness as an outcome of one's present emotional life shaping memory to create a present 'experience'. Just as Maurice Halbwachs described 'our imagination' remaining 'under the influence of our present social milieu', we can also speak of our imagination as being ever under the influence of our present psychological milieu.[22] My earlier approach was intended to encourage an understanding of Christian spirituality and practice in terms of the acquisition of symbolic knowledge and the nature of

[19] Flanagan (1991: 236). He noted here the 'fledgling' nature of 'the sociology of emotions'.

[20] Douglas J. Davies (1986: 21–30). Charles Taylor (2007: 771) has more recently and philosophically emphasized embodiment in criticizing some Christian tendencies to 'excarnate' or shift the focus from the body to the mind or being 'in the head'.

[21] William James (1902); Otto ([1917] 1924). Cf. Schechner ([1977] 1988: 263), for discussion of performance theory and expression of emotions and Konstantin Stanislavski's 'emotion memory'.

[22] Cf. Halbwachs ([1941, 1952] 1992: 49).

emotional experiences that pervade the ritual contexts in which religious symbols are employed. My assumption was that rituals developed and expanded human experiences, enabling us to speak in a theological way of the 'salvation of the imagination' as a form of 'redemption of human embodiment'.[23] Much of this independently derived approach resembles Thomas Csordas and his anthropologically based 'embodiment paradigm'.[24] The important issue is to highlight the idea of embodiment as a way of talking about being human set amid the complex reality of our biologically animal and socially cultural way of life, all framed by the unique possibilities created by the distinctive internal mental environments of memory and personal creativity, on the one hand, and by changing physical and cultural environments, on the other.

In this picture of embodiment and of the naming of feelings as emotions, one issue of obvious significance is the relationship between the individual and society. From our earliest moments our feelings are tuned into the feelings of our mothers and others who care for us, and their feelings have already been influenced by their society's classification of emotions, even to the extent of advising or controlling how pregnant women should behave. In other words, the management of emotion surrounds us and offers one clear way of viewing the relationship between the individual and society. Many avoid this approach to the individual–society link because of its complexity, but it remains unavoidable, and we will work on the assumption that, while 'embodiment theory' accepts that individual existence can be only partially explained by the emotions route, it should be accepted as a positive approach to the ongoing process of meaning-making and identity construction.[25]

Social benefit

Society depends upon the collaboration of its members, requiring that they accept its classification of emotions and allow their own feelings to be socially managed. This intimacy of individual and society, which in practical terms means the relationship between an individual and his family, neighbours, and workmates, can be extremely difficult, for individuals sometimes have

---

[23] Douglas J. Davies (1986: 22–4).

[24] Csordas ([1990] 2002: 58–87). Cf. Svasek (2005: 13) for brief evaluative comment.

[25] Cf. D. Harvey (2000: 97–9), who discusses the body 'as porous' in relation to the ' "self–other" relations (including the relation to "nature")', and sees embodiment theory as a result of 'loss of confidence in previously established' theoretical perspectives.

thoughts and feelings that they know are unacceptable or unintelligible to others. This potential rift becomes visible, for example, in the context of some suicides, when people feel themselves at an absolute inability to explain what may have caused the death, an observation marking the fact that we do not always know what others feel and think. However, the more complex societies become, the more difficult it is for them to manage emotions on a large scale to ensure maximum cooperation of all members. This is where respect and trust become fundamental attitudes of mutuality that facilitate social cooperation through reciprocity and underpin the dynamic significance of hope that religious traditions frequently help generate.

The process of socialization and of the engendering of hope is one in which individuals adopt, internalize, and appropriate the classification of feelings presented to them by others. Some sociologists speak of individuals becoming a kind of microcosm of society, but to think of how societies propagate themselves is an intriguing issue, demanding a high degree of compliance on the part of people who have the potential to disagree. Small-scale, traditional, societies need to have a high degree of conformity in order to survive, while large-scale societies have the capacity to tolerate and even to benefit from higher degrees of dissent. Deviance from a normal range of behaviour includes deviance over issues of emotional expression. Both medical–psychiatric and legal services play their part in controlling conformity and deviance and often employ punitive measures against individuals or groups that fail to follow accepted bands of behaviour, as we see below in Mary Douglas's theory of grid and group. The degree of variation between societies can, of course, be considerable, and is often expressed in stereotypes. Within Europe, for example, some might describe the Italians as emotionally expressive people and the Finns as restrained. Similarly, within the British Isles some English middle-class groups are described as possessing a 'stiff upper lip' and some Scots as dour, marking an emotionally controlled and undemonstrative character, while the Irish and Welsh are depicted as more emotionally expressive.[26] All this shows just how important the emotional profile of individuals and groups is to others, serving to map the social world and give people some sense of the way things are. This general background is important for religion, especially if we identify a major function of historical religions as involving the management of human emotions in the face of life's

[26] See Keane (1909: 347–8) for classic stereotypes offered quite unreflectively, e.g.: 'Perhaps enthusiasm "super-exaltation" is the dominant note in the Welsh character ... seen in the difficulty you find in getting a Welshman to look facts straight in the face.'

sorrows and joys and with an eye to humanity's destiny. Here, again, hope becomes an inescapable attitude that helps orient people towards their future activity by bringing a sense of significance to their current endeavours. But here, too, we remind ourselves of the complexity of individuals, of the limits of popular stereotypes and sociological ideal types, and of the need for 'a sense of modesty' when approaching these complex areas.[27]

POWERS: SUPERNATURAL AND NATURAL OTHERNESS

This study describes a wide variety of such management procedures, embracing deities, ancestors, powers, and principles that frame identity and destiny and explain why the theme of otherness is accorded a fundamental place in this study.[28] Even though relatively small groups in more recent centuries have questioned, doubted, or denied these religious worlds, many millions continue to embrace them. Secularized domains also have to manage human emotions in relation to their preferred political principles, and these, too, will need some later attention. But why should human animals speak so extensively of such beings and forces lying beyond ordinary observation? At least two broad kinds of explanation exist.

First, it could be because there are entities lying beyond the realm of ordinary sense. We might argue, for example, that, just as modern science has indicated the presence of many phenomena that ordinary senses cannot apprehend, as with radio waves or kinds of light and sound, so there are 'supernatural' phenomena lying beyond ordinary perception that are 'caught' or indicated only by religious apprehension. Particular individuals might be understood as having special abilities in accessing and communicating these domains to others. Indeed, the differences between religions could be interpreted as being due to the cultural contexts in which each religious leader lived and made contact with those other powers. Whether in religious founders, reformers, or their devotees, such 'revelations' have often been described as having a quality of reality about them, such that they cannot be denied: revelation and conversion become self-evident as their own

---

[27] Craib (1998: 156). Cf. his 'rules for theorizing' (1998: 140).

[28] Cf. Wood (2007: 66), who avoided offering any 'theoretical hostage to fortune' by defining religion but stressed the importance of both 'non-personified energies' and 'personified supernatural entities' in understanding contemporary forms of spirituality.

proof that deities exist. John Bowker, for example, spoke of human religiosity as just such an engagement with ultimate sources, arguing for a kind of interaction between the cosmos and human perception that produces an increasingly realistic understanding of the ways things are. For him, religions are meaning-generating systems, not simply as a result of human imagination but as a creative response to the environment. Two of his major books include the phrase 'The Sense of God' in their titles, indicating the place he gives to an objective reality of God within the human environment.[29]

Second, however, is the long tradition of seeing such 'powers' as the outcome of human imagination, as in references by Ludwig Feuerbach (1804–72) and Sigmund Freud (1856–1938) to the human process of projecting human ideas on to an imaginatively constructed deity almost as a kind of screen for human thought. Others, as discussed later, have approached the human creation of supernatural ideas from an evolutionary perspective in two ways. In the nineteenth century early anthropologists spoke of the growth of religious ideas from simple to more complex forms on an evolutionary model of growth in complexity of organisms. So, E. B. Tylor (1832–1917) could talk of a primitive 'animism' developing into beliefs in ancestors and then in gods, while James Frazer (1854–1941) saw attitudes to the dead as underlying the imagined world of an afterlife replete with supernatural beings. In functional terms, William Robertson Smith (1846–94) and Emile Durkheim (1858–1917) identified the adaptive significance of religious belief and practice as making devotees 'stronger', giving them confidence to face life's hardship by lifting them out of themselves through a sense of participating in a greater whole than met their eyes. A. M. Hocart (1883–1939) pursued further the role of religious ritual in simply 'fostering life', while Thomas Maschio has developed M. Leenhardt's 'feeling of plenitude' into a sophisticated account of how people use a variety of emotional and ritual means in achieving 'superabundance'.[30] More philosophically, Charles Taylor has argued something similar for the notion of 'fullness', while recent evolutionary approaches have focused on human psychology as favouring certain perceptions of the world and the adaptive advantages inherent within them.[31]

---

[29] Bowker (1973, 1978).   [30] Maschio (1994: 33).
[31] Charles Taylor (2007: 5–12).

Emotional patterns, meaning, and salvation

One feature of religious patterning of meaning and emotion relates to a certain heightening of the sense of identity that may be classified as salvation. This problematic yet inescapable topic will recur as we ask how the human drive for meaning-making sometimes becomes a process of salvation.[32] The significance of this question lies in the fact that many of what are often called the world religions are also called 'salvation religions', making the idea of salvation one that demands some critical analysis, especially since 'salvation' involves a redefinition or a restructuring of individual identity, with corresponding shifts in the way allied feelings are named as emotions and are given theological explanation. While salvation is often aligned with processes or events in which meaning becomes intensified by reference to the otherness of ancestors, deities, or powers, it can also be given a general yet vague reference, as in the Alcoholics Anonymous movement with its commitment to an acknowledgement, if not a belief, of a 'power greater than ourselves'.[33]

The meaning metamorphosis

This transformation process is best interpreted in terms of the sociology of knowledge, an account of the way children are socialized, acquiring information about their society and a practical sense of how to behave as adults within it. This growth into a 'universe of meaning' embraces various sub-universes and, at an implicit level, includes an acquisition of how to view, classify, and relate to the world. All this becomes embedded within sets of emotional attitudes and forms of responses such that social values and attitudes come to be, as we say, second nature to us. Moreover, there is a depth of understanding that comes to people as they age and encounter the buffetings and succour of emotional knowledge. Indeed, it is valuable to think of a culture as a collection of idea-related emotions that are patterned and preferred by particular societies and are experienced in and through social events, circumstances, and places. This complex theme can also be pictured in terms of some individuals entering fully and deeply into the experiential ideas of their society through its cultural life, while others may

---

[32] Douglas J. Davies (1984a: 1–28), where I first raised this as a theoretical issue for religious studies.

[33] Galanter (2005: 6).

remain more marginal. Here ideas of alienation run alongside the potential choices open to people in terms of how they want to live, always alert to the fact that economic poverty may severely restrict such choices. Accordingly, Chapter 2 will consider rites of passage and rites of intensification as means of socially embedding people, Chapter 9 will consider religious conversion as another form of identity change, and Chapter 11 will pinpoint 'wisdom' as a quality of participation in and appreciation of the core values of a group.

Emotions contested

At this point, however, we need to focus more directly on approaches to emotion, noting that scholars frequently 'list' them in differing ways. Loyal Rue's summary-style book on the evolution of religion—itself defined as a process fostering individual well-being within an integrated community—finds it necessary to offer several schematic lists of emotions derived from the primary research of others. From Paul Ekman he takes a core group of six emotions deemed to typify basic facial responses to emotion-triggering situations: namely, happiness, sadness, fear, disgust, surprise, anger. By contrast, Robert Plutchik offers eight basic emotions: acceptance, disgust, fear, anger, joy, sadness, surprise, expectation, while Nico Frijda has ten basic forms of human response to events: desire, fear, enjoyment, interest, disgust, indifference, anger, surprise, arrogance, humility.[34]

Others rank emotions as primary, secondary, or even tertiary, with Daniel Fessler, for example, distinguishing between primary and second-order emotions, with a choice of primary emotions being those of fear, disgust, anger, and desire, with the possible additions of happiness and sadness.[35] He is unsure of the latter two because he thinks happiness and sadness may be 'follow-on' emotions, or the feelings following the achievement or failure to achieve goals associated with the four primary emotions. As for secondary emotions, he provides an extensive list but notes how difficult it is to classify these items, since they may be given different values in different cultures: he ranges them from 'interest' and 'affection' to 'wonder' and 'humility'. This part of his argument pivots around matters of cultural difference and the way in which humans come to appraise themselves as social beings. We will return

[34] Rue (2005).   [35] Fessler (1999: 75–116).

to it at the close of this chapter and revisit the issue of the subtler naming of feelings in different religious traditions as this study proceeds.

Certainly, care is needed when utilizing any particular classification of emotion, with a firm eye kept on the context involved. Rue suggests, for example, that certain 'tertiary emotions' are states that emerge 'from the coping process', with many 'so-called religious emotions' such as a sense of unity with the divine, or of grace and forgiveness, being properly classified as 'tertiary feeling states'. In this context he speaks of 'emotional virtues' that emerge within a culture in a process of 'moralizing the emotions' that has the aim of achieving personal wholeness and social coherence. These 'emotional virtues' he defines as the 'most distinctive yet most elusive feature' of human experience.[36] So, to speak of emotions and their being moralized is to highlight their bio-cultural nature and the subtlety needed in any analysis of religious experience. And, fundamentally, we can never ignore the fact that each human being is a 'moral' person precisely in the sense of being 'social'. This was the key behind Emile Durkheim's basic idea of humanity as *Homo duplex*, with people being 'double', not in the sense of duplicity and falsehood but in combining personal and social modes of existence. This double nature lies at the heart of human emotions, fanning out into many other aspects of life, from the self-forgetting service of love that some show to others to the utter self-serving negative duplicity that works against society: Durkheim aligned the social commitment with 'religion' and the selfish-centricity with 'magic'. This double nature will recur, especially in Chapters 4 and 10, when we ponder the otherness that people may experience in religious worship. Crucial to all such analysis is the cultural context of an emotion's operation and, within that context, the narratives that frame experience. Indeed, this narrative frame is integral to Rue's discussion, as it is to this study. Indeed, Rue's definition of an emotion is valuable here precisely for its intrinsic emphasis upon narrative: *'An emotion is a temporary feeling state that acquires narrative content and leads to a predisposition to act.'*[37] Here 'narrative' and action hold a firm and complementary profile. Underlying all religious endeavour for Rue is the fundamental nature of narrative, with humans as 'narrative beings' and cultures as 'narrative entities'.[38] Pascal Boyer also argued that 'we know that human minds are narrative or literary minds'.[39] This is an invaluable perspective for religious studies, in that narrative allows

---

[36] Rue (2005: 121).   [37] Rue (2005: 82).
[38] Rue (2005: 86, 126).   [39] Boyer (2001: 233).

for a theological, doctrinal, or mythical format in which the narrative brings a 'cognitive appraisal' to a feeling to yield an emotion. This narrative core is, he thinks, driven by some root metaphor, by 'God as person' as far as the Abrahamic traditions are concerned, a metaphor regularly supported by 'ancillary strategies' that include rituals. This we will explore more fully in Chapter 2, when developing the role of particular narratives and images that constitute 'paradigmatic scenes' enshrining core beliefs and commitments.[40]

HISTORICAL BACKGROUND

The history of human reflection upon these life values and their narrative matrices is practically limitless, with roots in ancient philosophies, in religious and artistic practices of all cultures. Instead of highlighting Durheim's *Homo duplex*, for example, one might adopt a more philosophical approach with Plato's reflections upon the threefold nature of a person, consisting in reason, desire, and social attitude.[41] Or one might note the more vernacular descriptions of the calculating faculty of reason and the more instinctive appetites of desire expressed in terms of 'head' and 'heart'. This might then, for example, leave the third category open to being labelled as 'enterprise' or 'ambition'.[42] Such a definitional 'problem' over identifying 'self-assertion . . . self-respect' and 'our relations with others' would, itself, be valuable for highlighting a level of reality that emerges from the interplay between emotional forces and mental self-awareness. Still, as many parts of this study will show, there is an integrity that belongs to social categories that cannot be reduced to lists of emotions but that are related to emotions and the way the thoughtfulness of cultures develops them.

Local examples of human labelling are inevitably legion.[43] One may be drawn almost at random from the eminent founder of modern botanical science, Linnaeus. His inaugural lecture at Sweden's great University of Uppsala was rooted in the convictions that 'all human knowledge is built on two foundations: reason and experience' and that 'experience ought to go

---

[40] Augé ([1998] 2004: 50) speaks of the 'paradox of religion'—namely, that it 'would like its narrative development to suppress its mythical origin'.

[41] Here Plato's notion of soul or *psyche* represents 'person'.

[42] Plato (1974: 207).

[43] See Strathern (1980: 174–219) for critical discussion of the often, and problematically, deployed distinction between 'nature' and 'culture'.

first; reasoning should follow'.[44] His unusual lecture focused not on botanical issues but on the importance of travelling within one's own country. Despite his European travels, he emphasizes the need to observe and gain deep knowledge of local contexts rather than of exotic places. He wondered, for example, how many of his distinguished audience knew of the petroleum to be found in parts of Sweden. His emphasis on the interplay of experience of the world and of local knowledge alerts us to our own world and to the recognition that exotic phenomena are 'normal' in their own place, not least as far as emotions and religion are concerned.

Approximately a century after Linnaeus, Charles Darwin was observing human and animal emotions both within his domestic circle and from exotic parts of the world, even though his findings were not published until 1872. As scholars studied human societies, much as Linnaeus studied plants, they inevitably encountered the complex fact of human self-awareness and how it is affected by different social circumstances. Here Thomas Dixon's stimulating volume *From Passions to Emotions* has shown how 'the category of emotions' as such 'is a recent invention'. He takes the period 1800–50 as one in which authors no longer spoke of 'the passions of affections of the soul, nor the sentiments', but rather of 'the emotions'.[45] This shift he links with what he calls a 'secularization of psychology', as accounts of human nature shifted from theological and belief frameworks to a newer and more psychologically informed vocabulary. It is, for example, quite a different thing to speak of 'The Passion of Christ' rather than of 'The Emotion of Christ', for the former invokes numerous theological ideas of suffering and self-sacrifice while the latter is ideologically neutral. Dixon emphasized how former theological ideas and cultural attitudes helped generate more modern psychology, while showing how difficult it is to find an agreed definition of 'emotion' and deciding to leave it as a broad field. He even thinks it wise to ponder 'good emotions' and 'bad emotions' rather than to see 'emotions' as some totally neutral notion.[46] In a valuable analogy he describes how some psychologists and philosophers approach a spectrum of potential meaning of emotion on a kind of continuum from being 'like a sneeze' to being 'like a crime'—the sneeze indicating an uncontrollable biological response while the crime is an act motivated by something known to be socially unacceptable. Following that line, this study will also refer to biological and cultural aspects

---

[44] Linnaeus, 17 Oct. 1741.
[45] Dixon (2003: 3).   [46] Dixon (2003: 247).

of emotion without having to assert the dominance of one over the other in any particular context. But, what is important is the notion of 'cultural classification' that will appear many times in the following chapters as we ponder the labels used by societies or groups for pinpointing 'experiences'.

MEANING: A BIO-CULTURAL APPROACH

Our approach, then, follows meaning-making in terms of embodiment theory leading to a notion of identity. This strong bio-cultural approach uses emotion to access the 'links between the body and social world'.[47] As already indicated above, the link between the human body and the society within which a person lives was fostered by the social scientists associated with Emile Durkheim. In offering a shorthand way of highlighting both the biological individuality and the social values that meet in and forge the identity of a person, their focus on the *Homo duplex* nature of people was another way of treating the most basic issue of social science—namely, the relationship between individual and society. Durkheim worked out his version of this idea in two rather different ways, one focusing on religious ritual, which we explore in Chapter 2, and the other concentrating on suicide, which we consider in Chapter 8. Certainly, Durkheim's study *The Elementary Forms of the Religious Life* was significant in arguing that the ritual arena of collective action helped establish social bonds in and through the emotional experience of the event. The 'Introduction' to that book was radically significant in arguing that the very categories of thought by which people function were themselves derived from social experience and that the theory of the social origin of the categories of thought offered a foundational study of the dynamics of human life.[48] This is evident in the work of Robert Hertz, Durkheim's nephew; Hertz made an early contribution to the historical development of embodiment theory in his theory of death, where he spoke of society as incarnating itself in its members.[49] This led him to argue that in funeral rites the identity of the deceased was transformed into that of ancestors or into some other status of relationship with the living. He saw

---

[47] Lyon and Barbalet (1994).

[48] His sociological theory of knowledge, part of the *Elementary Forms* that is easily bypassed, remains a crucial text, even if his detail on Aboriginal religion in later chapters remains highly questionable.

[49] Hertz ([1905–6] 1960).

funerary processes as social acts paralleling the changing emotional-psychological states of the bereaved. Despite Hertz's early contribution, it is Marcel Mauss, another 'Durkheimian', who is often best remembered for his work on 'techniques of the body', as a prime root of interest in the social significance of the human body and its behaviour. Mauss also became invaluable for his theories of gift-giving and reciprocity, processes that have, more recently, been identified by some evolutionary psychologists as possibly being grounded in brain organization that is genetically ordered to favour collaborative behaviour, behaviour that might even prompt an emotional response when a failure in appropriate reciprocity is noted.[50]

In the later twentieth century Mary Douglas's anthropology developed this general approach, showing how social values became intimately embedded within human behaviour and the use of the body, as we will demonstrate in Chapter 2.[51] Others also explored what we might call the cultural education of feeling, which, in all its complexity, involved the emergence of a particular pattern of behaviour in each society or subgroup, a pattern related to a blueprint of preferred values. In groups where religious factors are strong, it is, perhaps, easier to speak of doctrines or beliefs rather than values, but these are, for our purposes, much the same thing. Among numerous other anthropologists following this perspective, Clifford Geertz is especially valuable for the way he links beliefs and behaviour in his well-known cultural definition of religion, one that remains of considerable use.

Religion is a system of symbols which acts to establish powerful, pervasive and long-lasting moods and motivations in men by formulating conceptions of a general order of existence and clothing these conceptions with such an aura of factuality that these moods and motivations seem uniquely realistic.[52]

Despite various critics, this definition continues to serve well in drawing attention to the link between the conceptual domain of thinking and the mood-based realm of feeling manifest in ritual processes. This definition is crucial within religious studies, because it introduces the sense of critical distance from beliefs that some religious persons find difficult to achieve. Some students, for example, find the phrase 'seem uniquely realistic' difficult

---

[50] Mauss ([1925] 1969); see also Rolls (2005: 446). Rolls cites several psychological possibilities and authors discussing 'generous "tit for tat"' versus a 'strict "tit for tat"' scenario in human life.

[51] Douglas (1966).

[52] Geertz ([1966] 1973: 4).

or unacceptable, because they take Geertz to mean that such beliefs are actually untrue and only 'seem' to be realistic. What must be remembered, however, is that this is a 'cultural theory' of religion derived from a social-scientific perspective and not from a theological or faith-based position. It must deal with quite different religions that would often be deemed by one set of devotees to be untrue and vice versa. The fact of the matter is that most devotees of a tradition do 'experience' their religion in and through a series of symbols set in ritual that engender 'moods' sensed as 'real'.

Pierre Bourdieu, though without any reference to Geertz, also gave an account of the 'sense of reality' to describe 'the correspondence between the objective classes and the internalized classes, social structures and mental structures', and goes so far as to name this 'sense' or 'experience' as *doxa*.[53] This general Greek term for 'opinion, sentiment, or judgement'[54] serves him well to identify the taken-for-granted world, what phenomenologists would describe as the life world.[55] He also uses *doxa* to differentiate such a taken-for-granted world from the 'field of opinion' when self-conscious debate differentiates between orthodoxy and heterodoxy, an issue to which we will return in this study's Conclusion.

For most of this study, however, our concern lies more with Geertz's form of analysis, because it is more obviously mood and emotion related. Certainly, like Geertz, my concern in this study will be to show the importance of such moods and to see how the beliefs allied to them express particular patterns of doctrine expressed in patterns of behaviour. What is worth exploring is the interplay of a preference for certain values and the behaviours and contexts that foster them. Conversely, much is learned through contexts that are avoided or forbidden. This sense of affinity of a group for both forms of belief and behaviour will prove valuable in later chapters. To speak of 'beliefs' in terms of readily identified 'religions' is relatively easy, but it will often be necessary to deal with values and aspects of human life that are less easily defined as religious but are clearly connected with strong values related to a depth of human existence underpinning human identity and giving meaning to life: for these the difficult terms 'spiritual' or 'spirituality' will sometimes serve a useful purpose.

---

[53] Bourdieu ([1972] 1977: 164).
[54] Liddell and Scott (1861: 178).
[55] See Douglas J. Davies (1984a: 22–8) for the '*epoche* of the natural attitude' of Alfred Schutz.

COGNITION, EMOTION, AND NUANCED NAMING

We have stressed the idea of embodiment while seeking to avoid speaking in terms of thought and feeling as separate elements. The time is now right to draw on another approach to the study of emotions, one that is deeply embedded in psychology and in the study of how the brain relates to the body at large. Here we refer to Edmund Rolls's important work, which asks why humans and other animals have emotions at all. His answer, essentially evolutionary, argues that emotions are states of feeling that arise in association with desired goals that are allied with 'rewards and punishers' because they produce either a positive or a negative feeling in people. He stresses the idea that the evolution of our genetic constitution did not take a path resulting in a whole set of fixed responses to particular stimuli or situations but, instead, produced people adapted to respond in a wide variety of ways, as we may see fit in particular contexts, ways that produce emotional states. Accordingly, emotions are not feelings that immediately respond to some trigger mechanism; they are the feeling states that arise when we act in a particular way in relation to rewards and punishers. He locates 'emotions' along one axis of intensity that indicates degrees of the active achievement of a reward or experience of a punishment, with the other axis of intensity dealing with the non-delivery of a reward or the non-delivery of a punisher. In one case, for example, we can think of someone moving from a neutral starting point on to a degree of pleasure, then to elation and on to ecstasy. The delivery of a punisher, by contrast, would take a person from the neutral position to one of apprehension, then to fear, and on to terror. Again, starting from the neutral position, the non-delivery of a reward might take someone from frustration to anger to rage, while the non-delivery of a punisher would simply produce relief.[56]

Two other important aspects of Rolls's work concern language and emotional intensity. He shows how language can influence the internal operation of the brain when creating emotions, indicating how 'high level cognitive processing can reach down into the emotional systems and influence how they respond'. This leads to the more technical issue of ethics and philosophy, when he argues against the naturalistic fallacy that 'what is right is what is natural'. He does this precisely because he sees the human system of rational

---

[56] Rolls (2005: 14).

thought as having positive causal influences.[57] We return to this in Chapter 2 on the role of narrative within ritual processes and the development of religious identity. A further relevance of Rolls's work, albeit apparently counter-intuitive, is that humans may have much more intense emotional experience than other animals precisely because of their capacity for rational thought. The examples he uses are of blood loss and grief. Faced by a bleeding wound, someone might faint or be rendered useless rather than leaping to control the blood loss, a reaction caused by the fact that the person knows the importance of blood and is overwhelmed by the thought of its loss in an accident.[58] In the case of grief, he speaks of how a bereaved person is able to remember all the times spent with the departed but is also able to anticipate all the times he would now have to spend without the now-dead individual. In other words, the conceptual ability associated with memory and imagination makes the present moment of loss all the greater, as these strong human capacities intensify emotion.[59] To speak of language and thought in this way sets our discussion firmly within the interplay of emotion and culture in creating human identity through our life as socially and biologically embodied persons.

Interestingly, this interplay of factors echoes Sigmund Freud's definition of religion, but brings new resources to its understanding. 'Religion is an attempt to master the sensory world in which we are situated by means of the wishful world which we have developed within us as a result of biological and psychological necessities.'[60] Freud argued that 'strictly speaking there are only two sciences; psychology, pure and applied, and natural science', with sociology being nothing other than 'applied psychology'.[61] Against that background it is easy to see how he justifies his approach to religion's 'three functions' of 'instruction, consolation and requirements'. It achieves this by 'satisfying the human thirst for knowledge'; of soothing 'the fear that men feel of the dangers and vicissitudes of life' by assuring a 'happy ending and

---

[57] Rolls (2005: 451, 446).

[58] Otto ([1917] 1924: 127) sees responses to flowing blood in terms of both 'disgust' and 'horror', but otherwise explains emotions of 'disgust' as a 'natural, self-protective endowment', while 'horror' is framed by civilized life and ultimately comes to share in a response to the 'numinous', a category unique to itself and not derived from anything else.

[59] In terms of 'embodiment', bereavement can pinpoint aspects of the dead in the very body of the bereaved. Cf. Gail Stanley's poem (2008): 'I have his feet, her hands ... I have their loss, my grief. The cruelty of genes to remind me.'

[60] Freud ([1964] 1977: 204).   [61] Freud ([1964] 1977: 216).

comfort in unhappiness'; and issuing 'precepts, prohibitions and restrictions'.[62] The background against which these functions are achieved lies in the 'unshakable biological fact that the living organism is at the command of two intentions, self-preservation and the preservation of the species'. For Freud, this located his study firmly in 'biological psychology', in 'the psychical accompaniments of biological processes'.[63] Nevertheless, his approach to the energies that interplay between these levels of mental operation—the super-ego, ego, and id—is a firm reminder of the dynamic nature of human lives and their frequent troubles. What is important in appreciating Freud's intent is that he wished to develop psychoanalysis as a therapeutic approach different from medicine and certainly different from religion. Goldschmidt notes that the standard English terms for basic Freudian categories, as just used above, are potentially highly misleading and shift attention from 'dealing with spiritual malaise to treating mental disorder'. For Freud's German spoke not of the Latin 'id' but of *das Ich* (the I), not of the 'ego' but *das Es* (the it), and not of the 'super-ego' but of *das Über-Ich* (the over-I): so, too, Freud's *Seele* (soul) is frequently rendered as 'mind'.[64]

Disquiet and peace

Pervading Freud's work, then—and this is echoed in many religions—is the phenomenon of disquiet within human life. Indeed, most major religious traditions possess the key objective of coping with a deep sense of the inadequacy of life's meaningfulness. Not only do they provide clear indications of the nature and source of these perceived flaws in existence, but they also furnish the means of transcending them. This is one reason why major traditions have often been described as 'salvation religions', where 'salvation' can mean any kind of answer to the issue of 'evil'. But it is not only religions such as Judaism, Christianity, Islam, Hinduism, Buddhism, or Sikhism, for example, that present forms of evil and corresponding processes of salvation. The many small-scale societies described by anthropologists have also had their own traditional forms of dealing with life's ills and disruptions, whether in shamanist-like consultations for healing, in exorcism of troublesome powers, in matter-of-fact rites concerning ancestors, in sacrifices for breaches

---

[62] Freud ([1964] 1977: 197).
[63] Freud ([1964] 1977: 128).
[64] Goldschmidt (1990: 65), citing Bettelheim (1982: 64).

in social rule, or in the singing and dancing accompanying celebrations that enhance life's stability.

Lists and phrases

Because of this, the following chapters will not only consider various positive models of the human self used by religious traditions when cataloguing emotions and managing them to achieve a religious identity but will also explore the negative themes of divided selves and inner conflict, as well as conversion processes that sometimes mediate these. These negative forces that constrain developing human identity will range from the apparently more dramatic forms of spirit possession by 'external' forces to the conflict-ridden pressures of doubt-pervaded thinking minds. A basic task is to consider religious catalogues of feelings in relation to psychological and sociological approaches to emotions. This will not involve any simple acceptance of the lists of emotions cited above as some complete inventory of feeling states; indeed, from what has been said about the bio-cultural nature of emotions, it will be obvious that many words, phrases, characteristic idioms, and depictions all play a part in the creation of nuanced identities and the management of allied emotions in different communities. It is not the case that a small number of 'emotions' create identical human beings. Indeed, individuals often distinguish themselves from others in many ways, even when following conventional rules. One of the intriguing aspects of human identity lies in the way individuals navigate their way through life, adopting and sometimes abandoning cultural values as they age, encounter, and manage new experiences.[65] Nevertheless, the challenge for any group or society is to elicit cooperation or some degree of compliance from its members by fostering shared core values and agreed modes of interaction. One of the means of achieving this goal lies in the unified activities of what we call ritual. Roy Rappaport has, above most other social theorists, provided an extensive analysis of this human activity in his *Ritual and Religion in the Making of Humanity*, where he draws attention to the 'nameless and unnamable feelings' that may be evoked in collective rites.[66]

---

[65] Miller (2008: 291): 'There is no evidence that people end up becoming "fully formed" at some point in their lives.'

[66] Rappaport (1999: 387). Taking the idea of 'sentiments' from Radcliffe-Brown ([1922] 1964: 40 ff.), he defines them as 'emotion-laden but nevertheless socially approved attitudes concerning material, social or metaphysical objects'.

SUMMARY

It is with explicit psychological lists of emotions set alongside Rappaport's 'sentiments' that 'stand at one remove from emotions' in mind that we can see why this chapter has engaged with a wide variety of scholars. It is through their diverse forms of knowledge and insight that we are able to view the scope of those topics that do stand at a remove from immediate emotions. In this use of varied thinkers from the social sciences, arts, and humanities, whether ancient or contemporary, this chapter marks this study's intentionally multidisciplinary approach to the complex interface of emotion and religious identity. Indeed, many scholars will be invoked in the belief that each helps us stand back and look at things from his perspective, always mindful that we each come to the poignant themes of this study with our own initial views, identities, emotions, and particular academic expertise. And this is the point, perhaps, at which to strike a note of caution and say that, while this study will pursue a strong bio-cultural approach to emotions and identity, and while it is grounded in a firm anthropological-sociological view of human life, its broader perspective is deeply eclectic. One reason for this lies in the sense that, while all knowledge is 'one', it is often wise not to succumb to some single interpretative scheme that reckons itself as transcending its local roots.[67] So, it will not be the intention of succeeding chapters to engage in technical discussions of method or of theory of knowledge, and certainly not to try and provide any formal unified theory of emotion, identity, and religion, even though we will posit some particular ideas for partial explanation of aspects of human life and religious activities. If one word will help explain the tone of the forthcoming study, it is that of 'nuance'—the nuanced way emotional syndromes are fashioned by religious groups and by individuals within them, as well as the nuances brought to movements over time and to individuals with ageing. It is with such nuanced interplay in mind that we now turn to a major chapter on the nature of ritual as a prime arena of embodied engagement of emotion with the generation of identity.

---

[67] Even in the form of postmodern accounts of plural interpretations and narrative fluidities. Theological studies, too, are especially prone to the unified field approach, often justified through the confessional basis of a tradition-rooted commitment.

2

Ritual, Values, and Emotions

Ritual, by bonding a group's core values with its preferred emotions in response to life's reciprocal obligations and opportunities, fosters identity by giving meaning and hope to life. Such ritual processes often include a background sense of otherness,[1] a term that broadens Victor Turner's description of 'mystical beings or powers' associated with 'formal behaviour prescribed for occasions not given over to technological routine'.[2] What we often call religions have traditionally played a significant role in managing people's emotional repertoires through such rites from birth to death, with the idea of rites of passage now commonly used to describe these transitions in social status. Less familiar, but as important, are the daily and periodic rites of intensification that reinforce core values within individuals and sustain trust within a people's disposition. 'Intensification' is, itself, a significant theme enabling a distinction to be made between the stronger triggering of emotion in periodic rites and the background fostering of long-standing moods through daily activity. Plato, for example, saw the potency of daily experience when arguing that the education of leaders or 'guardians' of society should, itself, be guarded against contact with ugliness in works of art lest, like cows grazing daily in bad pasture, they do themselves 'cumulative psychological damage'.[3] Closely linked with both rites of passage and rites of intensification is the theme of sacrifice and the giving and taking of life force as a medium for dealing with both the core values and emotions of a community. All are considered in this chapter in association with the theme of reciprocity as devotees bring their needs to appropriate 'others', be they people with earthly power to help or, more often, the deities.

---

[1] While 'otherness' is largely used in this book, we will also speak of 'alterity' (Latin *alter*, other), as in George Steiner's work (1989: 3), to which we will also refer. Otherness does not demand the notion of God as 'a necessary possibility' for understanding human life and creativity.

[2] Victor Turner (1992: 18–19).

[3] Plato, *The Republic*, 401. Here 'psychological' refers to the 'soul' or *psyche* (Plato 1974: 162).

RITUAL: INTENSIFICATION OF EMOTION

Although emotions and values, as the two driving forces of human life, interplay at all times in creating and maintaining human identity, they gain distinctive significance in periodic, repetitive, and shared ritual activities often 'concentrated' in selected times, places, or persons.[4] Here it is important to stress the fact that ritual is but one form of interpersonal relationship, albeit one that is specially demarcated and given a prime social focus. In this chapter we will also stress the positive nature of many ritual events as they help create and sustain people's identity in a world that can often be problematic, an issue to which we return at the close of this chapter.

In terms of ritual, rites of passage represent a well-known category of activity, but less familiar are the equally important rites of intensification, and here we will sketch their significance in terms of each other.[5] Arnold van Gennep spoke of 'rites of passage' as the way society, as it were, takes people by the hand and moves them across various thresholds from one social status to another. Drawing on the Latin word for threshold, *limen*, he described these changes as pre-liminal, liminal, and post-liminal phases.[6] Examples might be a child separated from his parents, taken away and taught both emotional and conceptual facts of existence along with duties expected of him in the future, before being returned to society as an adult or someone prepared for marriage. Or, again, a person might be separated from lay status, be set apart and educated and 'formed' as a priest before being ordained in a new status in the world. Although van Gennep's emphasis on social status and identity did not concern itself very much with psychological factors, it will be important for our purposes to bring such elements of identity into the picture in various forms of gaining human experience.

As for rites of intensification, we will take this valuable term of Chapple and Coon that describes rites that reinforce community values, and emphasize its emotional dimension.[7] To this we could add that participants are also likely to foster and enhance corresponding experiences, moods, and emotions

---

[4] In Halbwachs ([1941, 1952] 1992: 222–3), 'concentration' resembles 'intensification'.

[5] Goldschmidt (1990: 175) thinks any distinction between the two to be 'false', and notes that neither has anything to do, for example, with other rites, such as rites of 'curing'.

[6] Gennep ([1908] 1960). Psychologists used *limen* when describing the 'subliminal' process of communicating a message below the level of conscious awareness.

[7] Chapple and Coon (1947). Cf. Coon (1950: 583).

that surround the rite and its symbolic expression of prime values. The daily, weekly, or periodic worship of groups provides such opportunities. A great deal could be said about the relationship between elite priesthoods and the laity over such repetitive rites, as opposed to less frequent ritual or to the rites of passage undergone by each category of religious devotee. For our purposes it is sufficient to identify the existence of rites of intensification and to stress that such an intensification may apply as much to ideas as to experiences.

More recent anthropologists, such as Victor Turner and Maurice Bloch, have tended to dwell more upon rites of passage than rites of intensification, perhaps because they are more obviously notable. Turner developed van Gennep and used the notion of *communitas* to describe the feelings associated with being in a liminal state.[8] He distinguished, for example, between the 'spontaneous' communitas of an unexpected triggering of emotion within a group and 'normative' or 'ideological' communitas in later forms that reflect it as institutionalized 'repeats' or, perhaps we might say, as moods. His communitas refers to a sense of unity or bonding with others, often a sense of shared fellowship under hardship in relation to those guiding the rite of passage, one that may foster an ongoing sense of mutual commitment among that peer group. Maurice Bloch stressed the existential dimension even more, arguing that rites of passage change a person in existential ways and not simply in social status.[9] He developed his idea alongside the notion of 'rebounding conquest' or 'rebounding violence', the essence of which involved this change of life perspective that could lead people to seek to effect similar change in others. The overall impact of van Gennep, Turner, and Bloch is to highlight both the social and the psychological dynamics of changes that occur as children and adults mature within a consolidated society.

Here it is also worth extending the Introduction's note on Roy Rappaport's concern with 'ultimate sacred postulates' and ritual, to highlight not simply his emphasis upon the importance of ritual for social integration but also his ethical concern over 'the preservation of the world's wholeness in the face of pervasive fragmenting and dissolving forces'. His grasp of potential ecological catastrophe, for example, takes him beyond any simple description and analysis of different cultures to a more engaged consideration of whether new rituals or liturgies ought not to be sought to sanctify commitments to

[8] Victor Turner (1969).
[9] Maurice Bloch (1992).

sustaining the world. All this is underpinned by his sense that 'humanity...
is not only a species among species. It is that part of the world through which
the world as a whole can think about itself.'[10] His approach to ritual fully
sustains this study's commitment as one that 'embraces the somatic as well as
mental processes' and explicitly acknowledges the 'emotion-laden' 'sentiments' that are sometimes 'rather specific', as with 'sadness, joy, solemnity'
and 'certainty', as well as the 'much subtler and more complex but nameless
and even unnameable feelings' that may be invoked in ritual.[11]

Rites of passage and of intensification interplay

One fundamental aspect of ritual behaviour dealing with core values is the
way rites are often associated with a sense of ultimacy as values mobilize an
individual's and a group's emotional repertoire. Religions do this by invoking
ideas of ancestors, deities, famous religious founders or leaders, or even some
ultimate principle by which the cosmos works.[12] Reflecting previous themes,
such ritual is fundamental to intensifying meaning by engaging with ideas of
salvation or ultimate destiny in a multiplicity of symbolic ways that engage
human embodiment as sight, sound, touch, and taste combine with ideas of
truth, mystery, beauty, and other cultural motifs to yield moments of pain,
pleasure, sociability, and isolation.

To speak of rites of passage or of intensification is, of course, only to use a
theoretical lens to bring some analytical sense to human behaviour.[13] A
wedding ritual conducted in a religious context, for example, could be
analysed in terms of both forms of ritual. For the married couple this is,
primarily, a rite of passage. They have, for some time, probably been in a
phase of separation from the single state as such, whether as engaged or as
living together. Through this actual rite, often involving much financial
expenditure, two families and groups of friends are brought together to
witness a legal status change by which two persons now elect to be spouses.
The day will probably activate a spectrum of emotions in relation to

---

[10] Rappaport (1999: 460–1).   [11] Rappaport (1999: 387).

[12] McCauley and Lawson (2002) have generated a complex theory on this rather obvious point;
they emphasize the role of 'sensory pageantry' as a broad ritual-symbol band of stimulation of the
senses that may explain why some rites engender more intense emotion than others.

[13] Baal and Beek (1985: 129) ask if the 'rites of passage' concept is interpretative with explanatory value or simply descriptive and aiding classification of actions.

appropriate core social values. Though there is a degree of status change for many others present, especially the partners' parents and siblings, for many others the event may become one of intensification as they acknowledge and sense again their own previous wedding day or as they affirm the values now expressed in the vows taken by the focal pair. What is a rite of passage for some is one of intensification for others. This could be repeated in the initiation rites of many groups. In Christian contexts, for example, while baptism clearly changes the status of those baptized there and then, it also challenges the rest of the congregation to recall their baptism and, in a sense, to affirm their own baptismal vows. The same might happen at ordinations for the other priests surrounding the newly ordained. Similarly at a Jewish *bar-mitzvah* or a Sikh baptism, cultural values and emotions are evoked and celebrated.

In such contexts, memory interplays with the immediate emotions of the rite as future life is anticipated. This is one reason why changes in traditional forms of rites tend to be slow or to retain key features, for they speak to several generations at once. Nevertheless, debates sometimes emerge over what rites mean and how they may change, as, for example, when traditional weddings between men and women have become models for the civil unions of homosexual partners. Can these rites be a 'wedding' or not? In the long preliterate history of humanity, convention and emotional stimuli would have been significant in perpetuating values and adherence to them. The advent of writing and the rise of elite priesthood groups, with all the political power play associated with them, provided distinctive opportunities for debates over the meaning of rites, as, for example, in the eighth–ninth-century Christian controversies over the use of icons in worship, which led to the abolition of these visual images in worship for some fifty years before a new accommodation was reached on their suitability within religious behaviour. With the advent of the printing press and the widespread growth of literacy, combining as it did in the West with the Protestant Reformation, ritual itself became an arena for debate, and often violent disagreement focused on the theological meaning of the Mass.[14] This is one of the most focused debates in world history as to the meaning of one particular rite. Did the bread and wine of this rite really, in their essence, become the body and blood of Jesus, or were they symbols or signs of them? Was the rite a

---

14 Cf. Dillenberger (1986: 243–4) for the 'quantum leap' inaugurated by literacy in religious awareness and in the role of the visual sense.

re-enactment of the crucifixion or a memorial of it? The vigour of these disagreements, which in their origin also involved intense power politics, are still evident in some Catholic–Protestant circles where pivotal rites activate deep emotions and contribute to an ongoing mood of spirituality that undergirds personal and group identities. Once pitched at abstract theological levels, such ideas can become a focus of hope that people wish to defend, even if that means harming others in the process, as Chapter 8 will show.

NARRATIVE AND PARADIGMATIC SCENES

The history of such debates easily becomes part of a total narrative of a religious tradition with Catholics, Orthodox, and Protestants, for example, all justifying their positions and opposing the others by selective use of history guided by their particular sources of authority. And the same applies to factions within these denominations and within other religions whose popular hagiographies and local myths draw on the power of stories that is native to human nature. Whether in their extreme or anodyne form, stories of all sorts consume much daily energy in communication, gossip, and talk about others and in rehearsing personal events. History, too, takes the form of elaborate storytelling, as does much literature and drama, as well as sacred texts. Sacred narrations are especially important, for they not only embed teachings within stories of supernatural persons and faith heroes but also often describe their emotions. Learning such stories of faith becomes part of devotees' self-development, for they read themselves into their faith literature and develop their own identity in close relation to it. In ritual events, too, believers find it easy to interpret their own biography as a genre of testimony, and to anticipate the future in the light of these sacred narratives of the past.

Successful narratives compress complex ideas into easily remembered storylines and poignant symbolic motifs that become a paradigm, a model of and for that world view. In Victor Turner's language, such an image would constitute a 'root paradigm', a term describing some allusive symbol that emphasized 'group survival over individual survival' and might well motivate some form of self-sacrifice in the process.[15] The power of such images and

---

[15] Turner (1974: 68).

symbols intensifies the overall story by focusing prime values in a single event and by evoking emotions that provide opportunity for people to ponder an event in such a way as to empathize with it. Myths and sacred narratives offer many examples, with Robert Alter, for example, borrowing the notion of a 'type-scene' from classical scholar Walter Arend to pinpoint the literary stylistic convention of repeated patterns of composition in biblical material.[16] The anthropologist Rodney Needham used the phrase 'paradigmatic scene' itself to frame some narrative event able to communicate an emotional message embedded within a culturally recognizable event.[17] His specific example of Peter's betrayal of Jesus, with his threefold denial heralded by the threefold crowing of a cock and its triggering of Peter's tears, typifies the experience of betrayal.[18] As Needham expressed it: 'How little we need to be told that the disciple, going outside, "wept bitterly"'. We will return to this theme of betrayal. Other technical terms for this kind of example include de Souza's 'paradigm scenarios' used to describe gang warfare,[19] and Jon Abbink's use of D. T. Langer's 'cultural scenario'[20] as a description of behaviour anticipated in the 'performance' of certain social values.

This notion is also reflected in Theodor Haecker's term 'heart-word' (*Herzwort*), which reveals 'the invisible, individual spirit of a people'. He used this notion when studying Virgil's *Aeneid*, and its value remains when emphasizing the emotional resonances that 'sound from the heart, which betray to us where the individual heart is most inclined, what is its greatest care, what its grief, its longing, its passion, its joy and its pleasure is'.[21] Haecker reminds us of the difficulty surrounding the translation of heart-words and prefers to leave them untranslated, a practice often adopted by anthropologists when retaining indigenous concepts in italics unless they have gained widespread acceptance. An excellent example of direct relevance to this study lies in Michelle Rosaldo's ethnography of the Ilongot of the Philippines, where she identifies key indigenous words that depict emotions and values, all within a strong theory of embodiment. In a double sense as far as Haecker's heart-word is concerned, Rosaldo focuses on the Ilongot notion of *rinawa* or 'heart', which is 'at once a physical organ, a source of action and

---

16 Alter (1981: 50–1). He derives it from Arend (1933).
17 Needham (1981: 89).
18 Mark 14: 66–72.
19 De Sousa (1990: 182), deployed by Maschio (1994: 191).
20 Abbink (2000: 84); Linger (1992).
21 Haecker (1947: 110). I am indebted to Louth ([1983] 2003: 79) for this reference.

awareness, and a locus of vitality and will'. She shows how, in different contexts, 'heart' can be equated with words for 'life' (*biay*), for 'shade' or 'spirit' (*beteng*), for 'breath' (*niyek*), 'knowledge' (*beya*), and 'thought' (*nem-nem*). Similarly she analyses other words that link emotion and value such as *liget*, which refers to 'energy, anger, passion' and which is evident in 'violent men but also in striving youths and energetic hunters'.[22] My colleague Charlotte Hardman has, likewise, provided detailed ethnographic accounts of emotions among the Lohorung Rai of Nepal, showing their complexity and context relatedness, as in the notion of *Saya*, whose appropriate use 'can express the state of a person's health, fortune, and relations with the ancestors'.[23] For British liturgical contexts, Martin Stringer has argued persuasively for the way the narrative stories of Christian theology interplay with the stories of a person's individual life, all as part of an empathetic understanding and what he sees as an empathetic merging of such stories.[24] His concern echoes my own interest in the power of an affinity that devotees may sense between their own lives and, for example, the life of Christ.[25]

SACRIFICE, LIFE, AND BLOOD

Within Sikhism, for example, 'Guru' might be just such a heart-word, one reinforced by paradigmatic scenes that still sustain a folk history, as in the narrative of Guru Gobind Singh and his establishment of the Khalsa as a pure and identifiable community in 1799. Here Turner's point that root paradigms often involve some form of self-sacrifice for the good of the ongoing community is valuable, for the tale tells how this Guru called for devotees to volunteer their lives for the cause. One did so and was led into a tent from which the guru appeared with blood-stained sword only to ask for another volunteer. The sincerity of potential volunteers was, obviously, challenged, yet four more came forward. Then, these five beloved ones, *punj pyare*, previously secluded, were brought from the tent dressed as Sikhs, thereafter to hold prime symbolic status in Sikh iconography and ritual, symbolizing and evoking moods of courage asked of all Sikhs. Today this sense of

[22] Rosaldo (1980: 36–7, 22).
[23] Hardman (2000: 257).
[24] Stringer (1999: 106).
[25] Douglas J. Davies (1986: 27–9).

community pride is manifest in the rite of initiation of those who 'take *amrit*', the sugar water symbolizing the sweetness of divine truth. Here it is worth noting this sensory description of 'sweetness' as a symbolic marker of engagement with 'truth', for religions seldom leave 'truth' in isolated abstraction but embody or materialize 'it' before engaging with it ritually so as to 'feel' it. Underlying this Sikh example is the wide theme of sacrifice, which has at its heart the complex interplay of life force and group values. As important in this Sikh ritual construction of identity is a complex political process by which some Sikhs set out on a concerted plan to establish a Sikh identity distinct from Hinduism, a process that occupied the later decades of the nineteenth century and prepared this Indian tradition for its twentieth-century encounter with the partition of India in 1947 and the group's subsequent expansion into numerous Western societies, in all of which a distinctive status was advantageous.[26] Oberoi convincingly demonstrates that 'between 1880 and 1909 the body was made a principal focus of symbolic concern and a central means of projecting ideological preoccupations'.[27] This applied as much to dress as to preferred ritual behaviour. The dual motif of 'saint–soldier' became valuable in later, twentieth-century, Sikhism as a way of combining a meditative dwelling upon the divine presence typified in the first Guru, Guru Nanak, with an active, militarist, defence of the Guru's teachings characterized in the tenth Guru, Guru Gobind Singh. This combined sense of self-sacrifice for the truth echoes an age-old perspective in which life itself becomes the medium for asserting and defending truth and for focusing emotions of fear, contested in courage, and loyalty, manifested in love.

Indeed 'life' and 'truth' are foundational complements for understanding emotion, religion, and identity. To sacrifice one's own life or to sacrifice some animal or plant life in its place is to deploy the very idea of life and its cessation as a means of asserting the value of some particular idea, such as patriotism or divine revelation. Here the 'bio-social' interplay makes its own appearance in the most direct way with 'life', the very dynamic force underlying existence, representing the 'bio' part of the expression, and 'truth' the social value making existence meaningful and worthwhile.[28]

---

[26] Oberoi (1997: 304–417).
[27] Oberoi (1997: 344).
[28] Greek *biotos* (life) equating with Latin *vita* (life) and *vivo* (to live).

Blood

One extensive bio-social symbol in many cultures is blood. Stanner, for example, provided subtle analysis of blood-anointing of initiates of Australia's Murinbata people. Drawn from participating kinsmen, it echoed bloody episodes in the rite's associated myth as it expressed something of the 'gainful transaction between men and their divinities' that typifies sacrifice.[29] More familiar are Jewish and Christian blood symbolism and sacrificial ritual. Its dramatic root lies in the story of Abraham's obedience to God that called him to sacrifice his only son, Isaac, an act miraculously prevented at the last minute as the boy is replaced by a ram.[30] Christians often interpret this as a partial prefiguring of the sacrificial death of Jesus as the Son of God whose shed blood is a means of the removal of sin. Blood also became a symbol of covenant between God and the people of Israel and is retained to this day in the act of circumcision of the infant's penis, which involves some symbolic bloodshed. Another root of Israelite blood sacrifice lies in the Passover rite, which takes the form of a memorial meal of sacrificed lamb, echoing God's deliverance of his chosen people from Egyptian captivity.[31] The biblical story records the killing of a lamb, whose blood marked the door of Jewish families who were 'passed over' by the power of God that killed the first-born sons of the Egyptians. This was the last of the 'plagues' that befell the Pharaoh for not releasing God's people.[32] The emotional-sensory base of this rite is reflected in its use of bitter herbs to mark the hardship of the people's experience, just as the use of unleavened bread symbolizes their state of preparedness when awaiting the act of deliverance. Today, the rite often takes place within the family or some other group of Jews, with the youngest asking the leading question of why they are doing what they do, prompting the explanation that dwells on the deeply problematic past of the people. The rite also uses wine and, in the Jewish diaspora, now ends with the expressed desire that next year it will be held in Jerusalem. Yet another notion of blood was rooted in Jewish rites of animal sacrifice and its development within the Hebrew temple cult, where a key concept emerged that life was 'in the blood', and people were

---

[29] Stanner (1960a: 108).
[30] Genesis 22: 1–19. Some scholars see this as indicating an earlier practice of child-sacrifice.
[31] The symbolic similarity between the Abraham–Isaac incident and the Passover is considerable.
[32] Exodus 12.

explicitly forbidden to eat or drink that blood precisely because it was the medium of life.[33]

Circumcision apart, Christians developed many of these Jewish blood motifs aligned with ideas of covenant, deliverance, atonement, and life, especially within the bread and wine ritual of what came to be called the Eucharist, interpreted by some as a development of the Passover meal that Jesus held with his disciples, often known as the Last Supper.[34] Though this Christian rite came to be frequent and not annual, its sense turns on being a memorial of Jesus as a divine sacrifice for sin, often interpreted as his being 'the Lamb of God' sacrificed upon the cross. It, too, involves a sense of hope for the future, symbolized in the idea that Jesus will 'come again' as a part of the divine plan of destiny. This rite has developed in a wide variety of ways and, depending upon context and time of the liturgical year, can serve as a vehicle drawing different emotions from the Christian emotional repertoire. When celebrated annually on Maundy Thursday, it echoes its symbolic day of origin at the 'Last Supper' in which the Christ of St John's Gospel gave the new commandment to love another as he had loved his disciples.[35] In a kind of moral paradox, however, this event notes that the rite was instituted, as one liturgy expresses it, 'in the same night that he was betrayed'.[36] The emotion here is often that of a solemn dwelling on the nature of the betrayal of love. By sharp contrast, the Eucharist of Easter Day celebrates belief in the resurrection of Jesus from the dead with appropriate emotions of joy and hope. Something of a combination of both negative and positive emotions is evident in the traditional Requiem Mass, a Eucharist associated with a funeral, which paradoxically combines elements of sorrow of bereavement, encouragement through the total fellowship of the living and the 'dead', and a sense of hope in life after death.

In these rites we find paradigmatic scenes from sacred texts serving as organizing foci for a group's emotional repertoire. The same can be said for the Islamic *Hajj* or pilgrimage to Mecca, in which pilgrims engage in physical movement between sacred sites that carry distinctive religious meaning and echo aspects of the life of the prophet Muhammad. In journeying to the

---

[33] Leviticus 17: 10–14. Additional political factors of religious development were involved in the ideal that all animal slaughter should be associated with an appointed sacred place that enhanced the status of the priests of that place.

[34] This is a disputed identification.

[35] 'Commandment' is *mandatum* in Latin, whence the word 'Maundy'.

[36] *Book of Common Prayer* of the Church of England.

centre of their faith in Mecca, the devout fulfil one of the faith's basic requirements and gain an emotional sense of having done so. Part of the event involves the sacrifice of a sheep, which again focuses life concerns in a powerful medium.

SCHOOLING EMOTIONAL REPERTOIRES

Some insight on how such paradigmatic scenes of enacted sacred texts help school the emotional repertoire of a tradition, and integrate aspects of cultural activities, is evident in Edmund Rolls's psychology of emotions. He thinks that one reason why people 'find drama, novels and poetry so fascinating' is because they give us opportunity to explore the emotional lives of others, even though they may be fictional. Such stories help us understand our own emotional lives and the way they interface with the emotional lives of others and he thinks it 'may be important for us to find it attractive to engage in this type of processing because of its potential adaptive value'.[37] This suggestion raises the crucial issue of the overlap between everyday behaviour and the behaviour we often isolate as 'religious'. Rolls's notion that interest in the emotional lives of others offers an understanding of how they impact upon our own life concerns has obvious significance for religious stories as motives for ethical living or, for example, for ideas of life after death. If stories have an impact on aspects of survival in ordinary life, then it can at least be anticipated that sacred stories may have an impact on issues of survival in the extraordinary or supernatural domains of an afterlife. The interplay of emotions on what we might see as a fear–anxiety–hope continuum assumes added significance if we heed Rolls's previous suggestion, discussed in Chapter 1, that cognitive abilities may influence the very dynamics of emotional experience. Sacred stories, especially when they become part of a ritual in which people participate today in 'real time', have great potential for prompting and schooling appropriate emotions and allowing individuals their own nuanced appropriation of them. This is precisely where the issue of religious formation comes into play, as members of a tradition develop what sociologists have called *habitus*, a term that has theological roots in the very idea of religious 'formation', and refers to the

[37] Rolls (2005: 451).

body as a medium of and for expressing core values.[38] In theological language, for example, Jean Borella emphasized the importance of a 'supernatural *habitus*' developing within those individuals possessing 'an inward orientation of the will' towards the means of salvation of their tradition.[39]

It is as bodies that devotees experience rites, play out afresh the acts of the founders and heroes of their faith, and develop their own religious lives through practices that pass on established values while evoking allied emotions in successive generations. Sacred texts also play their part in combining a wide variety of genres in hymns of praise to the divine through stories of events in the lives of religious founders, in portions of their teachings, in commentaries and in many forms of devotional hymns and poetry, as well as in stories of saints and other martyr or saintly figures of each tradition. The talks and sermons that are often associated with ritual events regularly take up elements of the tradition and present them to the listeners, who encounter them for the first time as children or new converts and develop increasing familiarity with them over a lifetime. Narratives, with paradigmatic scenes at their heart, implant core values in the mind and, if Rolls is right, may exert a deeply formative influence on the very structures of feeling of a tradition.

Just as episodes of daily life easily transform into soap opera or formal theatre, so they can be incorporated into ritual drama, thereby prompting emotions associated with the narrated episode. Christian liturgies, for example, regularly detail aspects of the life of Christ and seek to bring the emotions of devotees into some kind of sensory alliance with Christ. The period before and surrounding Easter documents numerous emotions in Jesus. He weeps before entering Jerusalem as potential Messiah, with crowds celebrating his arrival, on Palm Sunday; there follow days of deliberation before the Last Supper with his disciples, as discussed above, leads on, through all its pledging of allegiance come what may, to Christ's 'agony' in the garden of Gethsemane and his betrayal with a kiss.[40] His arrest is followed by his trial, his scourging, and his sorrowful walk to the place of crucifixion. His emotions on the cross are detailed prior to his death and, days later, his disciples are shocked by his appearance as a resurrected being and appear to gain a newfound energy in their own preaching of his resurrection to the world at large. In all of this, local Christian traditions have generated many

[38] Weber ([1922] 1963: 158–9) used the idea, but Marcel Mauss in 1934 is credited with its developed use. See Douglas J. Davies (2000: 108–11) for application to Mormonism.
[39] Borella ([1996] 1998: 108).
[40] e.g. Luke 19: 41 ff.

hymns, rites, and festivals evoking many emotional responses. Rites such as carrying palm leaves in imitation of Christ's entry into Jerusalem, the Maundy Thursday washing of the feet, and the Stations of the Cross, in which the faithful are called to empathize with their Saviour's feelings during his passion: all prompt an emotional alliance with Christ.

In all such cases the biblical narrative is used to bring the doctrinal ideas of the text to bear upon an aroused contemporary feeling system in the believer, one that is activated by music, silence, and hymns, as well as by bodily posture, movement, and sacred places, and by fasting and celebratory eating and drinking. So, for example, the Spiritual 'Were you there when they crucified my Lord', or the original children's hymn 'There is a Green Hill far away without a city wall, where the dear Lord was crucified, and died to save us all', serve as powerful means of triggering a contemporary emotion of sadness and grief tinged with a certain nostalgia. In a similar way, the Christmas celebrations can be understood as basic human responses of joy, hope, and togetherness, associated with mother, newborn child, family, and community, all taken and managed as doctrinal ideas of the Incarnation of the Son of God. The power of the emotions evident in 'Christmas' are so strong that, even when separated from the prime Christian message, they still work in alliance with the myths and rites of Father Christmas and 'festive spirit'. In such contexts it is easy to think of general emotions being aroused by the natural prompts of response to pain, suffering, death, and grief, all fashioned by teachings appropriate to the season.

The sacred-textual framing of these events turns 'ordinary experience' into 'religious experience', intensifying it in the process. For Rue such religious experience is vital and may 'leave a permanent mark on the memory systems'.[41] From his perspective this presumably means it is an event whose recall is invested with a high feeling state. Memory is important here. As he says, 'you cannot store a feeling in memory but you can store images that produce feelings . . . they may be recalled to participate in the construction of new mental objects . . . and evoke something very like the original experience'.[42] This important point is worth pondering. His argument is, and others support it, that memory consists primarily in retaining images from the past; images that when activated today are given energy by our present-day feeling systems. But how are those memories recalled? It can be in terms

<hr/>

[41] Rue (2005: 134).   [42] Rue (2005: 94).

of a mental picture of a place or person, of a smell, of the narrative form of a story, or of music knowledge as in Christmas carols. Rue's view is that, whatever the form, the recalled phenomenon is brought to emotional life by our present-day feeling system, an approach suggesting that our present-moment cognitive functions influence which emotional force is summoned to animate the memory. This process is important when we think of religion furnishing its members with emotion-embedded sacred narratives and providing settings of worship for their contemporary evocation. In saying this, it is important not to overload these notions of religion and narrative with excessive or even with distinctive emotions, for there are, doubtless, many aspects of ritual performance that are perfunctory and satisfy the mundane necessity of custom without evoking profounder degrees of emotion. Maurice Halbwachs (1877–1945), a younger contemporary of Durkheim, certainly argued that opportunities for engaging with other persons could foster memories of previous gatherings through present activity and 'the localization of memory', but he also saw that religions are 'orientated towards what is properly collective in human thought, that is, towards ideas and concepts'. He also thought that such abstraction also prompted in some 'a need to become initiated into more intense forms of religious life, in which a larger place was reserved for feeling'.[43]

PRIME VALUES

To speak of ritual contexts of emotion also inevitably recalls Durkheim's emphasis on group activity in stimulating feelings that helped create a sense of community and made individuals stronger through their experience of 'social effervescence'. Later scholars sometimes downplayed this psychological aspect of feelings of transcendence because Durkheim had, for theoretical reasons, quite intentionally stressed that his work was sociological and not psychological.[44] What he meant, however, was that his thinking began from society and moved towards the individual; it did not start from the individual and move to the social. This made his thinking sociological and not, as in the case of Sigmund Freud, psychological. This social focus was

---

[43] Halbwachs ([1941, 1952] 1992: 118) relates to my notion of 'superplausibility', to be discussed in Chapter 9.
[44] Moscovici (1993).

reinforced in Durkheim's thinking by William Robertson Smith's 1889 book *The Religion of the Semites*, which catalysed Durkheim's thought on religion and will be considered in Chapter 7 on sacrifice. For Smith, religious believer as he was, collective ritual gave people a sense both of power and of unity with their ancestral totems. Durkheim, as a secular Jew, retained Smith's notion of ritualized social cohesion and the idea that people might sense a transcendent power but did not think that transcendence lay in some supernatural source: the 'otherness' of transcendence was nothing more and nothing less than 'society' itself. Society experienced itself in ritual.

Thomas Csordas, one of Durkheim's critics over 'otherness', speaks of this 'major error of reductionism', as 'society mystifying and worshipping itself and thereby establishing morality and social solidarity', an interpretation he thinks abolishes 'the sacred as a category sui generis for anthropological theory'. Csordas dislikes such reductionism, because he wants to stress the perception of 'otherness' as, itself, 'a characteristic of human consciousness'. For him the 'paradigmatic significance of embodiment' lies in the way social science may find and describe 'instances of this otherness' and, in so doing, enable 'a study of the sacred as a modality of human experience'.[45] At the heart of this approach is the individual's capacity to have a sense of something other than itself. Just how that 'other' will be defined will depend upon local contexts, ideologies, and the belief of the scholar concerned. Here we have one of the most fundamental aspects of embodiment theory and of an approach to both emotions and identity—namely, the feeling of an 'other', the cultural naming of it, and its role in establishing the identity of the human beings who sense themselves in relation to it. As many parts of this study show, such an 'other' may be conceived of as anything from an ancestor to an entirely supernatural deity; in Chapter 4, for example, we will see how the theologian Friedrich Schleiermacher engaged with 'otherness'.

Another scholar of Durkheim and Robertson Smith was Mary Douglas. Her influential *Purity and Danger* noted Smith's influence over Durkheim, set Smith apart as a founder of social anthropology, and marked his influence on Sigmund Freud, whom she regarded as having taken the study of religion into a dead-end.[46] Although Douglas is similar to Smith and Durkheim in focusing on sociological and not psychological factors and, in that sense, does

---

[45] Csordas ([1990] 2002: 82–3). From one physicist's perspective, 'consciousness is a basic phenomenon that is part of the natural outworking of the laws of the universe' (Paul Davies 1995: 85).

[46] Douglas (1966: 10).

not speak of emotions as such, she nevertheless places a tremendous emphasis upon the human body as an arena of symbolic action. Recalling what was said in Chapter 1 about Hertz and Mauss, we find Douglas, too, emphasizing the body as a social microcosm, proposing that 'the body is a model which can stand for any bounded system'.[47] One important aspect of her work is captured in her idea of 'the purity rule',[48] which is a way of dealing with the relation between a community's ideology and practice in relation to social behaviour and human bodies. The purity rule speaks of the degree of control exerted over an individual by his society and of the paralleling degree of control the individual exerts over his own body. In contemporary and colloquial English, for example, we might speak of the difference between 'uptight' and 'laid-back' forms of bodily behaviour and ask how these postural attitudes of lifestyle reflect the values of the group concerned. We can equally ask how the values influence feelings. Douglas's purity rule argues that the greater the degree of social control a group exerts over an individual the greater the degree of control the individual exerts over his or her body. Control is the key feature. Douglas focuses her interests on two dimensions of control: control over ideas (or beliefs) and control over behaviour. She then analyses social groups and their members in terms of the variation of control over ideas and over behaviour expressed as a fourfold scheme: (i) high control of both ideas and behaviour, (ii) low control of both ideas and behaviour, (iii) high control of ideas but low control of behaviour, (iv) low control of ideas but high control of behaviour. Additionally, by using the notion of 'Grid' to refer to control of ideas, and 'Group' for control of behaviour, she provides a means of analysing groups, activities, and phenomena that might not otherwise be anticipated.

This included hair style, clothing fashions, speech, and physical movement. She sometimes spoke as though one might view 'society' as a series of concentric circles where the power of a society was more intense at the centre and less at the periphery. Whereas both Robertson Smith and Durkheim took sacrificial ritual as the focal point of ritual that helped generate and maintain society, Mary Douglas adopted a wider approach that allows many other contexts to function as a 'centre' of social values. But those 'centres' would always have an effect on bodily behaviour and therefore upon

---

[47] Douglas (1966: 115).

[48] A slightly misleading phrase whose focus is not on 'ritual purity'; we discuss this in Chapter 10.

emotional control. That 'centre' might consist of a person—say, the Queen of England, the American President, the Pope, or some film, music, or sporting celebrity. It could be a parent in a family or the leader of a commercial enterprise, or could consist of a place or event, indicating the significance of sacred places or festivals, for example. Similarly we can take occasions such as births, weddings, or funerals as events that focus on core values and that prompt appropriate behaviour. Sacred narratives might also function in this way. Indeed, many of these elements might combine to produce highly influential sacred phenomena. Douglas's perspective can, then, easily be understood in terms of core values related to core persons or events within a society, with her analysis following the line that, the closer someone is to the centre, the more controlled his bodily behaviour becomes. In this she was deeply influenced by Franz Steiner's work on Taboo, which was grounded in the notion that people express their 'relation to values ... in terms of danger behaviour'.[49] Her work carries obvious consequences for the naming and schooling of human feelings within a society's emotional repertoire and ongoing mood base. Some examples will make this clear.

High grid and high group: Mormon examples

Using this grid–group analysis we take two examples from the Mormon Church, one concerning missionaries and the other the place of laughter. Mormon missionaries, aged about 19–23, are familiar across the world, as they spend two years, less for women, in voluntary evangelistic service of their religious organization. Theirs is a clear example of a high-grid and high-group situation with an overall sense of control that is important as a public presentation of the ideals of Mormonism. Rising early in the morning, they shower, study their scriptures, and pray, before venturing into the public world with their minds and bodily behaviours under relatively high control. Their hair, clothing, and even tone of voice follow a standard pattern, as does their message. The young missionaries are under the direction of an older local and regional leader, and the very fact that they work in pairs also brings its own immediate degree of mutual control. This extends to their sexual behaviour, and during the period of mission these young adults are usually not married, and are strongly primed not to engage in any sexual activity,

---

[49] Franz Steiner ([1956] 1967: 147).

including that of masturbation. Purity of mind as well as of body and doctrine is sought, with Mormon terminology speaking not in terms of control but rather in terms of obedience. The church expects individuals to control themselves in the light of its teaching on faith and morals. Being a missionary brings with it a very clear sense of identity, which demands a high level of obedience, which missionaries expect of themselves, but also brings with it a social status within the Mormon world that complies with that community's expectations. It is here, too, that trust and responsibility have an opportunity to grow together. These expectations frame and influence Mormon moods.

The missionary is, symbolically speaking, the embodiment of the core values of Mormonism and stands, as it were, at the centre of the Mormon value scheme. It is of real interest that the title of 'Elder', by which a missionary is known, is otherwise restricted to top-level leaders in the church hierarchy, even though all holders of the Melchizedek Priesthood, and that means most Mormon men, actually hold that title. This suggests a symbolic similarity between the young missionaries and the top leadership, a similarity grounded in the fact that they all stand as prime examples of core values. This involves their being treated with a degree of respect as befits their office and places them under considerable obligation to behave appropriately.

The degree of emotional control expected of such leaders is closely rooted in the belief that obedience is an act of will following the idea of 'agency' as a key feature of Mormon theology. This adherence to agency, as the freedom each person possesses to act as he will, avoids the wider Christian idea of the Fall of humanity and stresses both the necessity of and the capacity for obedience. Here the role of rational control is highly prized, and runs parallel with a preference for a cognitive theory of emotions in relation to individual identity.[50] This exemplifies the affinity between group organization, particular theologies, moral theories, and understanding of emotion. Mormonism possesses an affinity with cognitive theories of emotion because it believes that individuals can and should make clear acts of decision on how to live. The very word 'obedience' frames emotions for Latter-day Saints. Theologically this is expressed in the obedience shown by Christ, who so proactively engages with evil in the Garden of Gethsemane that he sweats blood.[51] Mormons have taken this as a paradigmatic scene of obedience that informs

---

[50] See Properzi (2010).
[51] Luke 22: 44: 'as it were great clots of blood'.

their own ethical attitudes towards discipline and obedience. It has been accorded a familiar place within Mormon art, where 'Gethsemane' becomes 'the name' that 'evokes feelings of reverence and awe at what the Savior faced in this place'.[52] It is notably absent from much other Christian art and theological reference, as evident, for example, in the renowned *Seeing Salvation* exhibition in London's National Gallery, February–May 2000, which showed many paintings of Christ's scourging, crucifixion, and death but nothing on this particular Gethsemane episode.[53] Each religious tradition places its art—often of its paradigmatic scenes—where its favoured emotions lie, and they are intimately entwined with its core theological beliefs. When John Constable—eminent among artists of sky and land, with cultural vignettes between them—said that 'painting is but another word for feeling', he also depicted many devotees' practical apprehension of the nature of their tradition's art.[54]

Laughter and controlled exuberance

Art, then, may also play its role in expressing core values and evoking allied emotions. As might be expected for any high-grid and high-group context, the control of emotions, as part of the development of personal identity, will be evident across social life, including, for example, attitudes towards that spectrum of emotional expression ranging from a gentle smile to loud laughter.[55] Young missionaries, for example, are likely to be typified in Western societies as having a warm and friendly smile, but are not likely to be heard engaged in raucous laughter, and, historically speaking, there are reasons for this within Mormon culture. For the LDS notion of the ideal person—the Mormon *Homo religiosus*—includes laughter in its moral appraisal.[56] Schooled by culture, laughter offers a bodily activity integrated with preferred social values: it exemplifies the embodiment of values in a particular emotional repertoire.

For Mormons, laughter carries a certain ambiguity, being potentially positive and negative in effect.[57] It is positive if it is not too loud or if it

---

[52] Brown, Holzapfel and Pheysey (2006: 63).
[53] Finaldi (2000:104–91).
[54] Constable (1968: 77–8), cited in Stevens (1992: 9).
[55] See Douglas (1966: 172) for comments on the 'controlled smile of Christian Scientists'.
[56] Douglas J. Davies (1987: 131–6).
[57] See Douglas J. Davies (2000: 125–7) for laughter in Mormonism.

belongs to someone who can otherwise be described as a worthy Mormon: in any event, it should not be raucous. The positive expression of joy is thought to be appropriate for people who believe they possess a special revelation from God and the means of acquiring salvation in the afterlife. But this very community of Latter-day Saints, which is, normally, a positive and life-affirming place, is also an authoritative hierarchy that controls access to praised social status at the local level and higher forms of salvation in eternity by controlling access to special temple rites. While Hugh B. Brown was one leader who valued humour within an overall balance of life, the broad ambivalence of laughter is reflected in those who reckoned that the Mormon Prophet, Joseph Smith, was 'never known to laugh', despite the fact that he described himself as not only having a cheery temperament but also of having 'been guilty of levity'.[58] Certainly, as *The Teachings of Spencer W. Kimball* demonstrate, the issue of control underlies the LDS understanding of group membership. Kimball asked fellow believers, 'Do you laugh raucously?', and enquired as to whether they possessed any annoying mannerisms, encouraging them to 'eliminate' these 'one at a time until you are a very normal person'.[59] The explicit desire that a fellow LDS should be a 'very normal person' reflects the nature of a religious group that accepts a relatively uniform theology and reflects it in a relatively prescribed way and through a moderated emotional spectrum of which controlled laughter is one key index. Joseph Smith's successor, Brigham Young, wrote that he had 'seldom laughed aloud for twenty or thirty years without regretting it'. He encouraged fellow Saints not to 'give way to vain laughter'. His comment that he always 'blush(ed) for those who laugh aloud without meaning'[60] indicates the interplay of ideological meaning within behaviour and typifies the sociological notion of *habitus*. Even so, religious communities always contain individuals who, to some degree, may vary in one or two particulars as long as other features of their life truly reflect underlying group preferences. Brigham Young (1801–77), for example, was followed as Prophet by John Taylor (1809–87), who has been described as one capable of a 'hearty laugh that shook his entire body' but who, otherwise, was 'erect in posture, fastidious in dress', with 'calm and deliberate' speech.[61] The offsetting of a 'hearty laugh' with 'calm and deliberate speech', as well as 'fastidious dress'

[58] Hugh B. Brown (1965: 50); Roberts (1930: i. ch. 3: 37).
[59] Kimball (1982: 296).
[60] Widtsoe (1978: 241).
[61] Paul Thomas Smith (1992:1440).

renders acceptable an otherwise potentially problematic element. A similar example from the Prophet David O. MacKay (1873–1970) encouraged a general lightness of spirit and laughter among friends as long as accompanied by 'high and noble ideals'.[62] Such emotional offsetting reinforces the importance of emotional repertoires within religious groups and shows how historical traditions influence subsequent generations.

Laughter remains a significant aspect within Mormon life, as within all communities, precisely because of its power in public contexts. Though individuals may laugh in private, it is the public occurrence of laughter that is significant when it becomes a marker of group values. This is an important factor when considering the difference between, for example, the 'ritual' of entertainment and that of worship for Mormons. For example, Joseph Fielding Smith (1876–1972), the tenth LDS Prophet, was happy to say that the 'gospel permits laughter and merriment' but was equally keen that such an attitude should not be struck during 'solemn assembles'. His reason for this was that it would 'detract from the teachings and the influence of the Spirit of the Lord'.[63] In that very expression, 'influence of the Spirit', he captures the LDS commitment to the mood of an occasion deemed to reflect the spiritual condition of participants as they engage with the divine presence. Such a phrase will, of course, describe quite different expectations in other groups. While the preferred LDS 'influence' is of a calm, relatively quiet, and thoughtful attention to proceedings and to the person speaking at any one time, the preferred 'influence' at a Charismatic Christian meeting might well be exuberantly noisy, with many clusters of activity in a group, though at other times more silent moods may prevail. It is likely that a religious group will find some validation for its perspective in sacred texts as well as framing it in the established interpretations of the community.[64] The control of laughter has been widespread in Christian traditions, as recalled by the fourth President of the LDS Church, Wilford Woodruff (1807–98), whose memory of youthful years in Connecticut noted a Presbyterianism that forbad leisure activities from Saturday night until Monday morning. The fact that folk should neither 'laugh' nor 'smile' was something that, as he said, 'had [its] effect upon me'.[65] These Mormon cases reveal a high-grid and high-group

---

[62] See McKay (1953: 253).
[63] Joseph Fielding Smith Jr (1954–6: iii. 303).
[64] Book of Mormon ([1830] 1981: Alma 26: 23, and 3 Nephi 9: 1–9), described laughter in negative ways.
[65] Woodruff (1946: 181).

pattern of control and contrast markedly with a low-grid and low-group context, as might be exemplified by liberal Protestantism, where personal wishes, desires, and idiosyncrasies are more permissible. Protestantism does not organize life in phases so as to involve anything like a missionary phase, nor is behaviour involving dress, or speech, brought under such sharp control. Religious beliefs, too, exist on a much wider spectrum, and there is no necessity to hold a cognitive theory of emotions.

This brief excursus into Mormon laughter thus reveals the importance of the bio-cultural schooling of emotion within religious communities, underpinning corporate life, and affording immediate means by which individuals engage with their group's beliefs. Daily behaviour and its associated attitudes constitute the most basic opportunity both for corporate cohesion and for a distinctive identity to emerge. In general, laughter is a behaviour that has undergone several radically different kinds of control over the centuries and in different societies. In terms of emotions, laughter occupied an interesting place in Darwin's early study of human life. He noted Edward Spencer's 1863 treatment of laughter, which suggested that 'various muscles had been specially created for the sake of expression', allowing us to communicate with each other, though Darwin was not inclined to such special muscle creation. Indeed, he indicated that he had been 'inclined to believe in the principle of evolution from 1838', when he started his observations relating to expressions and emotion, and before reading Sir Charles Bell's work.[66] Darwin had, in a clearly empirical fashion, used a questionnaire sent across the world in 1867 to ask about emotional expressions: from the thirty-six responses received, he concluded that 'the same state of mind is expressed throughout the world with remarkable uniformity', which he took as demonstrating the similarity of 'the races of mankind'. More recent studies stress laughter as a natural behaviour readily available as a vehicle expressing a variety of values. Jauregui described laugher as a 'mechanism of censorship',[67] while Gilhus analysed the history of laughter, including the role of early Greek philosophers and the influence of early Christian theologians, who incorporated laughter into their theological critiques.[68] She constructed a valuable analysis of laughter in terms of its life-giving or regenerative powers and its destructive capabilities,

---

[66] Charles Bell (1864). Spencer ([1852]) 1891). Charles Darwin ([1872] 1998: 15). Darwin acknowledges Charles Bell's *Anatomy and Philosophy of Expression* as laying the foundation for emotions' study.

[67] Jauregui (1995: 164).   [68] Gilhus (1997: 61).

a study that was partly influenced by Mary Douglas but that we cannot pursue any further here. Another closely related field of considerable importance that also has to be absent from this study is that of 'sacred faces'. This domain involves a cluster of factors of perception of emotion, of alterity, and of reciprocity associated with the faces of deities, ancestors, saints, and the enlightened, as well as of holy figures, that reflect their attributes. Just like the depiction of laughter, of the smile, or of 'the remote and disdainful glance' in art, so, too, the study of the portrayal of sacred faces might well reveal a great deal of the human capacity for face recognition in relation to emotional interaction and expectation.[69]

CHILDREN'S SOCIALIZATION

Whether in terms of laughter's positive or negative functions, or of any other value for that matter, all social groups reproduce themselves by passing their clustered values and allied emotional repertoire to new generations. For their part, children are predisposed to acquire knowledge by imitation of others, as with language and the implicit values of their group. They are also often subjected to learning through more formal schooling. Some time ago, Sperber usefully summarized these differences in terms of 'symbolic' and 'encyclopaedic' forms of knowledge, with symbolic knowledge having a cumulative and transformative effect as new material integrates with previous data, changing it and being changed itself in the process, and encyclopaedic knowledge, explicitly learned in school contexts, tending to remain relatively self-contained.[70] In practice, of course, each form of knowledge may influence the other as children's developing experience of a group's emotional repertoire and ritual-symbolic activity engages with its ever-expanding knowledge of its society's world view. Rites of passage and intensification provide one avenue for the acquisition of values in alliance with the emotionally transformative capacity of ritual. Here Victor Turner's approach to ritual symbols is valuable, for his suggestion that any symbol may be regarded as having two poles, one being 'ideological' and the other 'sensory', parallels Sperber's distinction between encyclopaedic and symbolic forms of knowledge. Turner's ideological pole of a symbol refers to ideas or doctrines, and

---

[69] See Zaki (1999: 167–82) for an account of neurology and artistic appreciation in general.
[70] Sperber (1975).

his sensory pole refers to feelings embedded in the symbolic object, but the implication of polarity is that there are zones of interaction between the two. This idea echoes a long-standing debate in anthropology over the nature of 'totems', objects with which particular groups forge distinctive attachments. Some had thought, for example, that, if a group was forbidden to eat its totem species except once a year, then the function of totemism was to preserve the animal species. This suggested that rules of totemism were rooted in the fact that something was 'good to eat'. Lévi-Strauss, famously, disagreed with this and argued that totems provided a kind of analogy between, say, animal groupings in the world and human groupings. This prompted the aphorism that totems were not good to eat but 'good to think'. More valuable still for our study is Goldschmidt's extension of this critique by aphorism when he argues that totems are 'good to feel'.[71] The affinity between a group and its key symbols helps foster emotional responses and, in the process, intensifies their associated values.

The wine of the Jewish Passover or Christian Eucharist, the water of the Mormon equivalent rite, along with the *amrit* drunk at a Sikh initiation, all exemplify how formal ideological themes and their historical associations also have a physical impact on taste and on the act of receiving and drinking. The ritual context of events also helps frame the act of drinking and the evocation of an emotional repertoire. Similarly, the water used in Christian baptism carries theological doctrines at its ideological pole, while also conferring sensations as 'water', sensations that are likely to have their own prior feeling states and emotional connotations such as washing away dirt to produce cleanliness. In practice, of course, the ideological and sensory poles interact in complex ways, allowing the emotional repertoire to pervade the theology and vice versa.

Many theologians have understood these issues in their own terms. Pope Benedict, for example, emphasized the importance of 'the energies of existence' and not simply 'the intellect alone' when it comes to 'seeing God', stressing the traditional shorthand reference to the 'heart' as 'the organ for seeing God'. Still, he retained 'soul' language when speaking of the proper 'interplay of body and soul', allowing 'man's perceptive powers to play in concert'.[72] Four hundred years earlier, Archbishop Thomas Cranmer of the new Church of England used the phrase 'the stomach of the heart' when

---

[71] Goldschmidt (1990: 177).
[72] Ratzinger (2007: 92–3).

trying to explain the processes of faith by which a believer engaged with God through the Eucharistic elements of bread and wine.[73]

When analysing such religious traditions, it is interesting to see how they cope with the issue of formal teaching in relation to the implicit acquisition of experience and knowledge. Many mix children with adults in religious ritual, allowing them to develop a sense of what is going on as they will. Others establish boundaries of participation for some rites and require tests of formal knowledge or of experience before allowing admission. The more literate a group and the more education plays a role in establishing the status of members, the more likely it is that tests will exist, with numerous Christian groups insisting that children await the age of discretion, sometimes about 8 or sometimes in teenage years, before assuming formal membership, after paying due consideration to a logical weighing of 'truth' prior to commitment. Others baptize babies and regard them as genuine members of the group and its ritual-emotional life from the outset. The issues of emotion involved in this are complex, as a child learns either that it belongs unreservedly to a group or that it belongs in a qualified fashion that still awaits its own future decision once the age of responsibility is attained.

LEADERSHIP AND RITUAL PERFORMANCE

These matters are often managed hierarchically by leaders reckoned to embody the doctrine-directed emotions. In some societies, as with Indian Brahmins and Jewish Levites, ritual specialists belong to particular family lineages, while in other traditions, as with Catholicism, priestly status comes through ordination into an elite professional class. Such groups manage and control an emotional repertoire in relation to formal liturgies, all driven by doctrinal and ethical values. They also stress the idea of the 'formation' of priests, through selection for office, followed by periods of training and ending with official decisions over whether to invest particular individuals with the authority of the religious group.[74] Similarly, Buddhist traditions recruit monks to the Sangha, where the control of emotion becomes a major aspect of spiritual training associated not only with meditation and formal

---

[73] Cranmer (1907: 202).

[74] The ancient Babylonian Epic of Gilgamesh speaks of 'high priest and acolyte . . . incantation priest and ecstatic', all of whom end in the underworld 'house of dust' (Heidel [1946] 1963: 60–1).

learning but also with many aspects of daily life, deportment, and relationships with the laity.

One of the best examples of such bodily training as a means of explicitly expressing culturally identifiable emotions in public performance comes from the Indian dance traditions of Kerala, which relate to the Sanskrit *Natyasastra* texts. This tradition trains young boys for some six years or more: their bodies are trained in postures such that 'an illumination of sorts occurs: what is being written in the bodies of the dancers is read *from the inside* by each of them'.[75] Schechner, whose work as a theatre director clearly marked the appeal of this tradition, has provided some interesting parallels between these classical facial expressions of emotion and cases drawn from Ekman's psychological studies of facially expressed emotions.[76] For him to speak of performers reading a text 'from the inside' is to discuss the complex interplay of learned postures and inner awareness of associated emotions, as well as of the desire to express formerly experienced outcomes of performance.

Certainly, each religious tradition develops its own preferred style of ritual performance and may be explicitly stage managed to a great degree. While some traditions may even possess a 'master of ceremonies', others may be quite unaware of the implicit management underlying their own performance. This would be the case, for example, among many Pentecostal Christians, whose leadership criteria lie more in the capacity of pastors to manifest, evoke, and foster the distinctive 'gifts of the Spirit' in a congregation. Authenticity comes not, it would appear, from training but through sincerity of heart, which allows the Holy Spirit to operate upon people. In this tradition it is not unknown for a leader to establish himself—and it is usually a male role—by the very fact of going to a location and creating a congregation around himself: his capacity for leadership is demonstrated by his evangelistic creation of a group, though the skill of evangelism is not always that of a pastor able to maintain a congregation on a long-term basis. During Pentecostal preaching, the people may respond to the preacher and add their own supportive affirmations, which, in effect, sustain both him and his message. This expressive repertoire enjoins a style of emotion favoured within Pentecostal churches, where worship tends to be vibrant and communal, as individuals may speak in tongues, gain visions or messages from God, and generally act as though in direct contact with the divine 'other' through the

[75] Schechner ([1977] 1988: 273).
[76] Schechner ([1977] 1988: 266–70).

immediate presence of the Holy Spirit. This use of 'spirit' references offers a local model of reality and classification of the world that easily matches an expressive emotional repertoire, which to an outsider may appear noisy and chaotic and which, for example, differs markedly from the quiet and orderly Catholic Mass that fosters an inwardly directed reflection on the sacred mystery of the divine manifesting itself in the sacramental bread and wine. This is not to say that Pentecostal-like factors do not sometimes appear within Catholic or other major denominations of an 'orderly' type, especially after the later 1960s rise of the Charismatic movement, with its manifestation of spiritual gifts, though this has tended to be in separate meetings and not at the heart of the Mass.

Types of leadership

Much is written on varieties of religious leadership, and here we can only allude to some issues that involve ritual contexts. One that is directly relevant to ritual, emotion, and religious identity is that of Harvey Whitehouse's 'two-modes' theory, with its distinction between 'imagistic' and 'doctrinal' forms of religion.[77] We will expand on this approach in Chapter 9, but we introduce it here for its relevance to leadership, group membership, and forms of 'learning'. Whitehouse's imagistic mode is associated with learning experiences of a traumatic kind, as in some forms of painful initiation ceremony of young people, usually male. Affecting small groups of people, such events bond participants and provide memories of the 'flash-bulb' or flash-back kind in which images may come to mind on subsequent occasions but which have very little by way of explicitly rational meaningfulness associated with them. The sporadic occurrence of these events in relatively small-scale traditional societies differs markedly from the 'doctrinal' mode of ritual in which large numbers of individuals are systematically and frequently taught their religion without trauma or pain. This doctrinal mode is important for this chapter, for it involves a leadership of formally instructed individuals who share a body of knowledge. Though some may be leaders of a more charismatic kind, the actual content of their teaching is what is important. Charisma is subject to content. This mode of religion facilitates widespread evangelism by education through school-like methods. It drives

---

[77] Whitehouse (2004a).

some of the main world religions, as their doctrines are taught across the world by formally trained leaders, while, locally, religious gatherings take the form of rites of intensification in which doctrines are taught, explained in sermons, and sung in hymns. Historically speaking, Rudolph Otto's influential *Idea of the Holy* had also differentiated between teachings that can be handed down across generations and the 'numinous', which 'is incapable of being so handed down'. For Otto, who speaks much of emotions and religious feelings, this sense of the holy is a unique category that is irreducible to any other.[78] Though Otto focuses much on the 'mind', his wider discussion appreciates the bodily impact of experience, as in liturgy, even though he does not have any 'embodiment' terminology by which to express it.[79]

Wisdom and self-development

One outcome of ritual as the medium for embedding religious teaching within an emotional context is to encourage a cumulative effect that, potentially, engenders a wisdom in devotees. Wisdom, a theme to which we will return in the Chapter 11, is important as signalling the link between religious thinking and action, doctrine and ethics. It typifies those phenomena that do not appear in lists of emotions but that represent the merged outcome of an experience-generated understanding of life framed by some theological or ideological world view. Such a wisdom reflects what Stephen Parish stressed in his study of the Newar of Nepal as 'moral knowing' and the 'sacralization and ethicization' of consciousness. For him, 'emotions are judgements, but judgements embodied reflexively in affective experience': he wisely steered a course between those who overemphasize the 'feeling' aspect of emotions, on the one hand, and the 'cognitive and social judgements' aspects, on the other.[80] He also emphasized the important issue of 'moral knowing', of the 'sacralization and ethicization' of consciousness that is aided by ritual processes in which educational information can be pondered within symbolic contexts. Here the notion of 'moral knowing' is particularly important if set alongside the theme of *habitus*, understood as a distinctive way of being. Though much used by sociologists from Weber to Bourdieu and beyond, *habitus* is a concept perfectly adapted to include emotional dimensions of

---

[78] Otto ([1917] 1924: 62).   [79] Otto ([1917] 1924: 191–8).
[80] Parish (2004: 150–1).

identity framed by ritual and extended into ethical activity of daily life. The notion of *Homo religiosus*, though introduced by an anthropologist, is often employed by historians and phenomenologists of religion, to embrace the ritual and ethical dimensions of life as they help to forge a preferred pattern of identity and a hallmark of wisdom.[81] Wisdom comes to denote particular individuals who embody both the outlook of a tradition and its preferred emotions. These 'wise' ones are knowledgeable of the emotional syndrome of the tradition and adept in drawing appropriately from its repertoire. As exemplars they make doctrines live; they show their worth, so that others are attracted to them and encouraged to live in their culturally preferred style. The role of the guru in Indian traditions, like that of the 'holy' person or saint in other traditions, shows the dramatic importance of how sacred values 'become' a body. This is why it is enough simply to be in the presence of one's guru, a context where 'trust' is born and fostered. Respected teachers of many traditions fulfil a similar role. It follows that religious 'meaning' does not always reside in its conceptual 'message' but can be 'seen' in a person and experienced in devotional practices. This suggests that ritual, for example, is not necessarily like a language possessing a code to be cracked in order to find its meaning, but can also be a behavioural end in itself, even if anthropologists go on to analyse its 'meaning', a situation not unlike ordinary speech in which people simply talk while linguists analyse the structures that allow the speech event to take place.

SUMMARY

This chapter has, then, sought to show that the meaning inherent in practice, including ritual practice, helps generate and sustain an identity that is replete with emotion. It has argued for the emotional outcomes associated with the completion of events on the basis that, as human animals, we seem to gain some positive *sense of things* when a behaviour pattern is completed. One expression of such a feeling state probably underlies people's comments about feeling good because they have done 'the proper thing', or have observed custom, or even about how they are praised by others for having seen that

---

[81] See Marett (1933) for *Homo religiosus* as an inclusive term avoiding 'civilized' or 'uncivilized' connotations.

tradition is maintained.[82] This echoes Aquili and Laughlin's once amazing proposition that ritual afforded humanity one of its few means of solving 'ultimate problems and paradoxes of human existence'.[83] Aquili's extremely positive view reinforces the theme of ritual as a creative phenomenon that has run throughout this chapter. We have seen how ritual can be understood as helping to create a sense of self as individuals gain the opportunity to develop their identity as different life events are acknowledged by their communities. Emotions, too, are part of these processes of change and of a growing self-understanding of a person's place in society and the world at large. What is important to recognize is that most of life involves patterns of behaviour, flows of moods and peaks of emotion, with 'ritual' being notable only for its focused concentration on core social values and 'religion' for a sense of the ultimate validation of those values. The intensification of emotion in combination with core values enhances the self as a social being and frequently aligns the devotee with a transcendent 'other'. Many social rites are, then, affirming and often celebratory in emotional tone. In many religious traditions this is reflected in the idea of salvation and of the various afterlife destinies of the individual. We will return to this theme when considering 'peace' in Chapter 10. But ideas of salvation also speak of their negative partner-concepts of damnation, loss, or some other privation. For everything in human life is not positive; indeed, a great deal of it is experienced as negative, whether in terms of physical and material deprivation or in more psychological domains of mental distress. One of the major functions of what have come to be called 'religions' is to explain and contain the negative emotions that pervade numerous life contexts such as fear, anxiety, and distress, and the desire to survive against the perils of life. It is to do justice to this negativity in life that this study will go on to develop the notion of 'identity depletion' as a way of describing negative emotional experience within social contexts when people sense a relative loss of meaning and of hope in life, along with a reduced engagement with 'otherness' and an inadequate network of reciprocity. It is this potentially destructive dynamics that makes a person less of a person that we will now consider in the next chapter.

---

[82] Douglas J. Davies (2002: 112–23).
[83] Aquili and Laughlin (1979: 179).

3

Identity Depletion

Taking up the notion of 'identity depletion', this chapter moves from the positive effects of a group's emotional repertoire on a person's sense of religious identity to describing negative phenomena that foster fear, anxiety, and uncertainty. One reason for choosing the term 'identity depletion' to capture this state of affairs is to explore the negative aspects of meaning and hope, otherness and reciprocity—the core concepts of this study. Accordingly, identity depletion would include life circumstances where a sense of meaninglessness and hopelessness begin to pervade a person's life or even the life of a community, and where otherness becomes malevolent and reciprocity constricted.[1] In such contexts the commitment of an individual or a group to its survival may be challenged, as a sense of despair pervades life, with no energy left to seek further resources or even to seek help. Within an individual's life there remains no drive to achieve anything, motivation is lost, and, in some cases, a deep depression emerges. Psychologists are familiar with such forms of depression, and, in the terms of this study, we see the problem as one in which a person simply seems to want to withdraw from otherness and from any reciprocal relations that would demand ongoing response. Many images from different societies account for such a collapse of the self. A person may be said to curve in on himself, to lose the will to live, or to become withdrawn. The image of a person being at a low ebb offers an apt analogy, with its image of a scene in which the tide has gone out to reveal a barren shingle. The life force may be thought to have left him or some enemy may be thought to oppress him. Here the notion of vitality is valuable, for identity depletion accompanies a decrease in vitality. If we take 'vitality' to refer to a basic sense of force or dynamism, then we can see it as something that is processed in ways that energize a person's social identity. Identity depletion then expresses the bio-cultural aspect of humanity that we have

[1] See Turnbull (1972) for a community example in draught-stricken Ethiopia.

discussed in Chapter 1. One common experience of such identity depletion is often associated with bereavement and the loss of a partner who helped generate the self-identity of his or her spouse.[2] In a strong couple-companionate union, the death of one of them, so tellingly described as a 'loss', can easily be experienced and described as a shift into a meaningless life, albeit for a limited period. It is no accident that religious patterns of behaviour across the world have embraced death and the experience of grief, providing rites and rationale for surviving individuals, as the following chapter will show.

Such psychological and existential descriptions of loss can be paralleled with more sociological accounts of decline in a sense of identity of a person that various life events may instigate, such as loss of fortune, good health, or the standing of a person in his community. Indeed, this very idiom of reduced 'standing' itself indicates a lowering of position. Similarly, in cases covered by the idiom 'loss of face', we find a combination of this shift in social status and a corresponding change in psychological well-being. In Chapter 9 we will encounter a specific example of this in the idea of a 'crisis of presence', while in this chapter we will see how experiences of guilt may affect identity depletion. Yet another dimension involving identity depletion occurs if a person is exiled from his community or, for example, excommunicated from his religious community. In such a case the spatial sense of moving away from the 'centre' of social action to some peripheral position echoes our account of Mary Douglas's work in Chapter 2 and the image of a society as concentric circles extending from a social core. Here issues of geography may combine with architecture in that a person whose identity depletion is marked in social exclusion may be banished from a building or a territory. In many modern societies this pattern can also be symbolically inverted, in that criminals are, for example, banished from society to prison: their identity, in terms of social status and potentially in more psychodynamic ways, is also depleted. The religious idea of excommunication, for example, offers its own case of identity depletion, one that operates at several levels. It formally removes people from the ritual life of their church and, as such, removes them from the realm of ultimate salvation, just as it may remove them from the company of other believers and, therefore, from regular social support. This will, almost certainly, carry an influence for their psychological well-being while also affecting their capacity to access sacred sites of their tradition. The role of cursing can be dramatically

2 Parkes, Stevenson-Hinde, and Marris (1991: 2–3).

effective, even causing the death of the cursed individual, in communities believing in its power, as attested for Voodoo.[3] Indeed, Lévi-Strauss, when approaching the role of 'the sorcerer and his magic', cited Cannon's work as an example of 'psycho-physiological mechanisms' that can reduce a person to death if all social supports are removed through a community rejection of that individual. As he so powerfully expresses the issue, 'physical integrity cannot withstand the dissolution of the social personality'.[4]

That very notion of 'dissolution of the social personality' is precisely what is reflected, albeit in a reduced and modified form, in the idea of identity depletion, and it is this latter expression that I will take as my interpretative concept for embracing psychological and sociological factors of human integrity and its rupture. It indicates a destructive domain brought about sometimes by life circumstances and sometimes by intentional acts of individuals or a society against one or more of its members. As a caveat, it is worth noting that this kind of theoretical analysis may convey the false impression that reason holds some kind of control over emotion, while, as Kapferer firmly reminds us, in many circumstance experience may exceed the meaning available to 'contain and structure it', as he, rather like Cannon, demonstrated in cases of fear-inducing sorcery.[5] In the remainder of this chapter we explore a wide variety of contexts, emotions, and thinkers who give substance to such negative dynamics of human experience. While the varied disciplines invoked symbolize the extent of the problem inherent in creating and sustaining an integrated human identity against many forms of its potential depletion, we should always recall Kapferer's judgement that 'experience and the emotionality of experience is always more than the cognitive or language categories of its construction'.[6] It is to emphasize the totality of negative impacts on people, including emotional domains, that we choose to speak of identity depletion and not simply of a 'meaning deficit', which reinforces cognitive aspects of life. Still, 'meaning deficit' remains an extremely valuable term, as developed by James Fernandez to describe 'the impermanence and transitoriness of our individuality *vis-à-vis* our imagination of the possibilities of its perpetuity', all as part of his concern with 'revitalization theory'.[7]

---

[3] Keane (1908: 54) speaks of 'faith-dying' as the 'reverse process of our Christian Scientists' "faith-healing"' among Australian Aborigines.

[4] Cannon (1942); Lévi-Strauss (1963: 167–8). Cannon (1929) has also been used by Galanter (2005: 68–70) when discussing how groups have gained some knowledge of these processes and have used them 'as a tool for their ritualized management of behaviour'.

[5] Kapferer (1995: 139).   [6] Kapferer (1995: 148).   [7] Fernandez (1995: 22).

FLAWS, ILLUSIONS, AND EVIL

We begin with Erich Fromm's challenging psychoanalytically influenced volume *The Fear of Freedom*, with its stress upon 'the fact that ideas have an emotional matrix' being 'of the utmost importance' as 'the key to the understanding...the spirit of a culture'.[8] Fromm was writing during the Second World War, but his interest in how a society produced a 'character' within its people resembled the American 'culture and personality' approach to anthropology and psychology that endured into the 1960s and that fully acknowledged the importance of emotions.[9] His contemporary Ernst Bloch, from his magisterial philosophical approach, acknowledged identity's 'dark and indefinite' aspect that 'does not know its name'. He spoke, rather similarly, of 'canonical types', 'guiding images' that can take dramatically diverse moral forms that 'move ahead' of young people, inducing them to follow and be formed in the 'virtue' that time and place find appropriate. But, while that motivation may conduce to gaining a 'peace that is not only inner peace', under despotic leadership and fascism it may also generate a 'raging crowd' of 'extinguished individuals'.[10] When, in his qualified Marxism, Bloch spoke of 'the sought for Totum' as the utopian goal lying beyond fractured identity, he echoed the notions of both otherness and reciprocity that underlie this study.[11] For it would be through such distinctive forms of relationships that hope might be felt and a designated goal set; he even uses the term 'salvation' to describe it.[12]

Within all such plans of salvation, emotions play their vital role in human endeavour. Indeed, one of Bloch's contributions to the role of emotions in religion and identity is the fact that he takes cognitive and affective factors as a single whole. His guiding types, whatever ideals they advocate, are replete with emotions to be desired and emulated. As valuable are his accounts of the emotional bases of such aspects of life as solitude and its allied elements of,

---

[8] Fromm ([1942] 1960: 240).

[9] Note how Thompson (([1963] 1968: 393) praised Fromm for stressing the 'inner compulsion' of Nonconformist religion during the Industrial Revolution, and for taking this motivational argument further than Weber's Protestant Ethic scheme.

[10] Bloch ([1959] 1986: 930–1, 966 respectively). Such types include 'the warrior, the wise man, the gentleman, and especially the citoyen', the last being a Marxist ideal type of comrade.

[11] Bloch ([1959] 1986: 972). Here 'Totum' refers to the totality of things.

[12] Bloch ([1959] 1986: 969–73).

for example, 'the dreary Sunday', 'sexual restlessness', or 'homesickness',[13] or of the unfinished self of youth aware of its desire to become someone as the drive for a personal meaning is affected by the hope that it be so. Here, a sense of otherness and its hope-fired Totum lies in the goal to be achieved, just as the means of its attainment are dependent upon reciprocal relations with others.

For most societies, evidence suggests that people sense their identity or life circumstances are not what they would wish them, a fact reflected in their religions. At a mundane level, for example, the famed Victorian Protestant Charles Spurgeon addressed himself to emotional shifts in a minister's life and to their weariness: 'How often, on Lord's-day evenings, do we feel as if life were completely washed out of us!'[14] More philosophically, William James, concluded his *Varieties of Religious Experience* with a low-key focus on an 'uneasiness' about existence and 'its solution'.[15] Ages before James, Eastern traditions, including Hinduism, Buddhism, and Sikhism, agreed and located the source of this depletion in consciousness, while Middle Eastern and Western traditions of Judaism, Christianity, and Islam tended to locate it in time. The former ponder the theme of illusory *maya* and look to *moksha* or freedom from its bondage, while the latter speak of a divine creation, fall, and redemption.[16] Even these simplistic sketches highlight the human assessment of life's imperfections and allied emotions that tend to be focused in what have come to be called religions whose mythologies and theologies shape thought, and whose rituals seek to cope with evils, even desiring to transform them in processes of salvation. In terms of social evolution 'salvation' is an expression of the human drive to survive and flourish amid these constraints, some experienced as negative powers deeply rooted in natural disasters or social regimes, or configured by religious institutions as personifications of wickedness in devil figures. Although evil, as a general description of these negative aspects of life, is theorized in all traditions, its importance in this and subsequent chapters lies in the emotions that cluster around experience of frustration, pain, and suffering.

In terms of the previous chapter, the Jewish Passover ritual and the Christian Eucharist are examples of religious identity construction set against

---

[13] Bloch ([1959] 1986: 958).   [14] Spurgeon (1876: 170).

[15] James (1902).

[16] But note that Kelly (2006: 32) argues that Genesis 1–11, the Creation to the Tower of Babel, was relatively irrelevant to Jews compared with elements surrounding Noah and 'the giants'.

an emotional awareness of the hazards of existence.[17] The Passover starts with a captive people and ends with their deliverance, while the Eucharist becomes a thanksgiving rite grounded in Christ's sacrifice for humanity's sinfulness. The ongoing nature of these rites, with roots lying in the enduring form of sacrifice, demonstrates their continued importance to human experience. In the nineteenth century it was common for anthropologists to speak of some rituals as 'survivals' from a previous age in which their meaning was full and influential, whereas now it was but a shadow-like custom devoid of intrinsic power. But this was an unwise path, for rites are seldom practised unless they carry contemporary significance. Dale Martin, for example, argued that one reason why early Christianity became successful was because it offered the masses deliverance from 'the threat of harm from possibly malicious daimons'.[18] He suggests that, just as Greek intellectuals had labelled Christianity a kind of 'superstition' because of such beliefs, so, with time, Christian intellectuals turned the tables to deem worship of 'pagan' gods as superstition. What is evidentially true today, however, is that the Christian belief in the power of God, often through the name of Jesus, is a major force underlying Christian practice in many parts of the world, especially in numerous African contexts, where the power of Jesus and the Holy Spirit is regularly set against the power of Satan and evil spirits. One formal example may be found in the Church of the Lord, which originated in the African Aladura movement of the early twentieth century, whose innovative Christian liturgy includes the following versicles and responses.

PRIEST: From the attacks of wizards and witches.
PEOPLE: Good Lord deliver us.
PRIEST: Over those who employ spirits against us.
PEOPLE: Good Lord give us victory.[19]

In many Pentecostal and Charismatic forms of Christianity in Europe, the Americas, and South East Asia, similar control of evil spirits is practised. It is noteworthy, for example, that the novel *The Exorcist*, and the film made of it, quite seriously shook the emotions of many people who saw it: it made them

---

[17] Theological arguments that exist over whether the Last Supper, used as a model of the Eucharist, was a Passover meal or not are irrelevant to this chapter, which takes them as separate cultural rites.

[18] Martin (2004: 243).   [19] Tovey (2004: 82).

afraid.[20] At the heart of this story is the conflict between good and evil, as a Catholic exorcist is pitted against an evil spirit possessing a young girl who displays many of the classic Euro-American motifs of possession in levitation, vomiting, vile language, and insider knowledge, but the scene that shocked most was when the young girl's head turned itself through 360 degrees. Normal heads cannot do that, and the ability of cinema to replicate a novel before the viewers' eyes intensified the idea. Reflecting popular fascination, this book, first published in 1972, had sold more than twelve million copies by 1979. Some thirty years later, even some societies often described as secular still host groups interested in spirit worlds marketed by clairvoyants and spiritualist mediums. This is because there is much in life that is uncertain and many forces that constrain happiness and survival, with death remaining an experience in everyone's life, leaving a significant number wanting to know if their dead are 'all right' in their afterlife world.

Experiences of misfortune, disappointment, shame, and illness all reflect the many ways in which human identity is felt to be fractured or life circumstances problematic, with a major feature of religions then consisting in answering these concerns. While this is especially the case for death, to be considered in Chapter 4, it is worth noting here one paradigmatic scene of Buddhism's origin that describes the young man Guatama, who had previously led a privileged and protected life, encountering sickness, old age, and death in those he now meets. He sees that life is not perfect and is prompted to set out to discover how one might live in the face of such bitterness. The broad Buddhist notion of *Dukkha* covers a variety of these meanings of human pain and death that cause bitterness and disease in life and express both the specific and general 'suffering' that Gautama sought to engage. His pursuit involved many hardships, until he gained a unified understanding— combining intellectual and emotional awareness—that it is not until human craving for possessions, experience, and even for a fixed sense of identity has ceased that 'sweetness' may ensue. Expressing it in a different idiom: the heat of life's desire is cooled and the thirst for existence quenched.[21] All these terms of thirst, heat, or desire reflect feeling states while also expressing ideas philosophically. Buddhism has, more than any other tradition, explored many forms of meditative exercises to train the mind within its bodily

---

[20] Blatty ([1971] 1972).
[21] The Pali word *tanha* expresses such a thirst.

base to deal with the negative dynamics of desire, albeit with its various schools constructing extensive vocabularies for different stages of meditative development.

The wider traditions of India, out of which Buddhism developed, also constructed many bodily and mental practices, including the well-known Yoga, aimed at gaining an ultimate release of the self from its earthly resistances. This included the notion of a self-transmigrating from one bodily or material entity to another under the cosmic influence of *karma*, which operates in terms of a person's action during any one lifetime and highlights the importance of reciprocal processes in this moral scheme of things. One underlying concept of these traditions of Hinduism and Sikhism, for example, is that of the illusory deception of things—*maya*—which itself denotes an unsatisfactoriness of earthly existence and reflects a kind of dislocation of identity. In the new religious movement of the Falun Gong, originating in China in 1992 and reckoned to possess millions of adherents even by the mid-1990s before being banned by the government in 1999, it was even thought that one might inherit either karma or, its opposite in 'virtue'.[22] And such positive or negative energy was expected to influence one's good or bad health and welfare in this life.

This unsatisfactoriness of life takes many forms, as when Robert Turcan described ancient Roman religion and its transition into Christianity, arguing that 'the religion of ritualism, like the quest for new gods and unusual cults, implies a kind of unease'.[23] Part of such a quest is also likely to imply a shift in the dynamic 'tension between controls and releases' within a culture, as Rieff indicated might have been the case as Christianity made its presence felt amid Roman culture.[24] Then, with Jung's psychological view of the human self, we find him arguing for a deep influence of 'opposites' within experience, one that is often portrayed as external in origin in terms of demons or saviours but that, ultimately, needs to attain a level of conscious engagement before any resolution is possible.[25]

---

[22] Chang (2004: 5, 75).   [23] Turcan ([1998] 2000: 165).

[24] Rieff (1966: 200).

[25] Jung ([1953] 1968: 7). Cf. Mestrovic's comment (1992: 141): 'Jung's "mystical" psychology is still forbidden in postmodern Universities.' Though not a Jungian, I think that a pity.

FEAR, HATRED, AND EVILS

This uneasiness of self pressurizes meaning-making processes, including their moral significance, and comes to expression in forms of fear and anxiety prompted by dangerous physical and social environments. Humans have long encountered perils, not only from animals and natural catastrophes but also from enemy groups and their hostile deities, making forms of anxiety and fear beneficial in alerting people to hazards in the world around them and, thereby, aiding their survival.[26] As for one's own community, it is also far from being an entirely safe arena, evident in the widespread human experience of envy.[27] Notions such as that of the evil eye abound in relatively small-scale societies, where people's knowledge of each other's possessions and resources is extensive and where the sense of jealousy in someone is believed to be able to affect the one of whom they are jealous. The 'evil eye' is the jealous eye from which the ones envied need to protect themselves. This feeling of jealousy is interesting in terms of identity depletion because it indicates a negative value arising in a person through comparison with some other, better-placed, person, and underlies the desire to harm the other as a response.

Awareness of such potential dangers from other human beings underlies the development of rules and legal conventions both within groups and between them, aiming to control danger, alleviate fear, and reducing anxiety.[28] Laws against murder, for example, play a significant part in the rules of many societies, and, in the process, human nature has frequently been defined by human beings as possessing an evil or morally dubious undercurrent. A more problematic context emerges if a state, itself, induces 'fear, anxiety, and terror . . . as a means of social control', as was once argued for El Salvador.[29] In all such contexts the response of flight and escape becomes one appropriate reaction.

---

[26] Malthus ([1798] 1960: 205–8), whose work on populations influenced Darwin, identified 'necessity' of food, etc., as vital for survival and for energizing humans who otherwise would be lethargic.

[27] Neyrey (1998: 19), where 'envy of success' can become a cause of high status in the one known to be envied by others, as in certain biblical contexts.

[28] Exodus 20: 17. The last of Israel's Ten Commandments warns against 'coveting': such desire for what belongs to another is closely linked to jealousy and to the potential of malevolence against them.

[29] Jenkins and Valiente (1994: 166).

Technically speaking, it is wise to be alert to the possibility of emotions such as fear, anxiety, and terror being merged, since, as Fessler expresses it, 'emotions appear to blend like colours on an artist's pallet'[30]—an issue that is applicable, for example, where the fear of being shamed exists. Rue thinks that 'the fear profile is the best understood of all the emotions'.[31] He sees one result of research being that some people are simply more fearful than are others, citing Jerome Kagan's research to the effect that about '20% of infants inherit low stimulus thresholds to fear', with only about a third of these having 'their fearful temperament persist beyond childhood'.[32] What is obvious is that fear can be a highly advantageous emotion when creating a sense of the potential danger present in any environment. However, fear does not stand alone but is partnered by potential danger: fear is always fear *of* something, whether it is actually existing or imaginary. In terms of human and social evolution and of contemporary life in many parts of the world, fear plays its strongly positive role in aiding survival by avoiding potential hazards or being prepared to respond to them when they spring upon us. The well-known flight or fight response to encountering danger is an excellent example of this survival procedure. In this sense, then, fear can be seen to have a positive adaptive significance. But even in terms of this deeply engrained reaction we cannot ignore social contexts and the way particular communities themselves define different types of fear. Karen Lysaght, for example, showed how people in a Northern Ireland context of complex political-religious dangers and community approval and disapproval 'live with and manage fear in their daily lives' through such things as a 'complex mapping process' dividing 'space into safe and unsafe zones', an issue we will address in Chapter 10.[33]

As a profound emotion, fear should not be so deeply embedded in apparently biological aspects of life as to ignore the cognitive abilities that have created their own foci of fear. In coming to grips with both fear and danger, the human imagination has regularly depicted evil sources lying beyond human society in supernatural figures and powers, often believing them to behave malevolently towards people unless treated in appropriate ways through being given gifts or offered sacrifice. Figures such as Satan or the Devil within Judaism, Christianity, and Islam, as well as evil spirits, have all had different religious careers, seeing the devil sometimes as an adversary

---

[30] Fessler (1999: 91).   [31] Rue (2005: 84).
[32] Rue (2005: 110).   [33] Lysaght (2005: 127, 140).

acting under an ultimate and good deity and sometimes as a disobedient creature now acting on its own disposition. The figure of *Mara* in Buddhism typifies one such evil antagonist of humans, and especially of the Buddha in his progress towards enlightenment. Within Hinduism, aspects of negation and destruction, often allied with death, are associated with the goddess *Kali*, whose iconography shows her dancing, tongue rolling, blood drinking, and decorated with skulls, while sacrifices are made to her through the death of animals, and once also of humans. Yet her role is also caught up with positive aspects of the pantheon, especially with the male god Siva, allowing evil and good to be part of a cosmic interplay of forces. Within Bengali traditions, the conquest of evil is identified with the many-armed and weapon-wielding female deity *Durga*. During the annual *Durga-puja* celebrations of her triumph over evil, symbolized in the evil buffalo *Mahisa*, which she beheads, devotees create life-sized images of all concerned and offer worship (*puja*) through them, before processing them to a river so that their immersion may send them back to the lands of the deities. These ceremonies engender a diversity of associated emotions involving joy and loud celebration at the conquest of evil as well as a quieter acceptance of the 'departure' of the deities.

In terms of religious studies, it is important to treat the depiction of 'evil', whether in the buffalo-demon, the Devil, or evil spirits, as a social construct reflecting human emotions of fear amid life's uncertainties. Indeed, perhaps the risk-filled nature of human experience needs special emphasis for social elites living in the safest environments ever known, where disease and pain are much controlled and the perils of infant mortality and early death much reduced. Such safe environments of developed societies easily blind people to the pain-racked and hazard-filled and identity-depleting situations that still abound across the world. Though many are able to empathize with poverty and disease-ridden contexts, the very expression 'charity fatigue' marks a limit of mutual feeling. Religions have, of course, played a major part in explaining such situations of need. Some see sickness and death as punishment by God for evil deeds, with some versions of the Hindu notion of *karma* explaining a person's plight in terms of wickedness in a previous life. The idea of fate and the will of God also plays its role in human spirituality, including strands of Islamic thought. Yet others speak of divine love as a motivation for helping the needy, serving the sick, and seeking to alter political and economic situations to improve living conditions. From a social-scientific context, it is important to give full force to the human capacity for malevolence and destruction, especially since one tendency of human beings is to accept that evil has an existence of its own and to project it upon some Satanic or evil 'otherness'. This is an interesting example of the inevitable implication of social science with ethics, for, once it is accepted that 'evil' is a potential of human beings, questions of responsibility arise, in terms both of life experience and genetic constitution that make people what they are, and of how society should take responsibility for malevolence.

Apart from the fear of evil sources, one frequent reference to fear occurs in terms of fear of God.[34] The very phrase 'god-fearing' for religiously devoted people expresses this attitude towards an ultimate moral authority and is intended as a means to ensure good behaviour in this world. One of the roles of preaching involves the inculcation of a god-fearing respect and is, for example, well known within Islamic piety, whose preaching and storytelling core has been described as 'moral education', where exhortation was 'meant to be sobering' and where the afterlife was a major means of fostering 'righteous behaviour'. Rustomji analyses cases, such as that of the seventh-century Islamic convert Ka'b al-Ahbar, who is prompted by the caliph 'Umar to speak about the Day of Judgement and Hell.[35] She sees 'Umar as 'wanting to feel fear in order to reinforce his moral rectitude'. To 'evoke the terrible fear that 'Umar desired to experience' and to highlight his 'desire to experience the Fire vicariously' is to see something of the interplay between emotion and spirituality in this Islamic tradition. It could easily be replicated in other traditions, notably in medieval Christianity or the 'hell-fire' preaching of some later Protestantism. Such traditions draw a great deal of their power from this foundational emotion of fear by integrating it within a supernatural environment and with a scheme of rewards and punishments that, as we see in Chapter 7, is a basic feature of human social experience.[36]

It is one thing to feel a sense of guilt or distress for failing to achieve moral standards but quite another to cope with a sense of revulsion over atrocities perpetrated upon helpless victims. All societies possess their own range of unacceptable behaviours that prompt a strong emotional response against the apparent cause of evil, whether in the evil self or, as in some forms of witchcraft and spirit possession, in some malign force against which various forms of exorcism may be practised.[37]

---

[34] Famously, Proverbs 1: 7.   [35] Rustomji (2008: 102–3).

[36] Schweitzer ([1907] 1974: 67–76). Speaks of the 'numbness . . . numbness' generated by Christian preaching of eternal death as a prompt for belief in eternal life.

[37] Douglas (1970).

Secular perspectives also comment on the plight of human beings and their experience of suffering. In traditional Marxist thought, for example, the idea of alienation of individuals from their capacity to fulfil their own potential and status as individual members of society reflects a form of evil and identity fracture that is regarded as open to transformation through social revolution. Sigmund Freud's *Civilization and its Discontents* also argued that people needed to control and, in a sense, sacrifice aspects of their own selfish desire in order to benefit from the advantages offered by membership in their protecting society.[38] Devastating events such as the First World War of 1914–18 focus the mind on the potential fragility of civilization, as described by Stanley Baldwin, speaking at Edinburgh University in November 1925.

Civilization itself is but the ice formed in process of ages on the turbulent stream of unbridled human passions, and while this ice seemed to our fathers secure and permanent, it has rotted and cracked during the agony of the Great War, and in places the submerged torrent has broken through, leaving fragments in constant collision threatening by their attrition to diminish and ultimately disappear.[39]

This was after the First World War, which was said to end all wars, only to be followed by the world war of 1939–45 and many other, albeit more localized, wars since then. Despite the many calls for peace and the political agencies established to strive for it, the human animal continues to reveal its pugnacity and mutual hostility, as competition for status, wealth, and resources influences leaders and nations. Freud and others who may not share his psychological explanation of the origin of human self-concern are, nevertheless, wise prophets of humanity's emotional destructiveness. Whether or not time for biological–social evolution will help change this before humanity actually destroys itself remains for the future to tell. Certainly, there is much evidence to suggest that many who live in 'safe society', cushioned from violence, have too rosy a view of humanity's fractured identity.

---

[38] Freud (1930). Freud's theory of emotional ambivalence, of love–hate emotions expressed towards the same object, has been taken by some as 'the fundamental phenomenon of emotional life' used to explain phenomena such as cannibalism (Sanday 1986: 10–26, 49–50, engaging with Sagan 1974).

[39] Baldwin ([1925] 1939: 98).

PAIN, DISEASE, AND DEATH

Even if some do not encounter direct violence, human identity still finds resistance in pain, disease, and death. Pain is a difficult theme for emotions, religion, and identity, for it brings the biological basis of human sensation into close relation with each society's capacity to explain, reduce, ameliorate, or remove it. Pain varies in such a way that it is difficult even to use the same word for different degrees of its intensity. While its origin lies in anatomical structures that protect normally functioning bodies, accidents or disease may generate an unbearable intensity of pain. Our capacity for awareness of being in such pain then engenders the sense of suffering and a potential for feeling a sense of distress under the duress of cruelty. The ordinary life world of emotions is redundant, as new orders of feeling overwhelm a person. Such pain is hard to describe to someone who has not had such an experience and may be one reason why names for types of extreme pain have little by way of social currency, though people who have shared the same illness find it easy to acknowledge the other person's experience. Tellingly, such pain does not appear within the lists of emotions previously considered, but pain is, however, perfectly able to prompt fear, fear of not surviving, and even of disgust or anger at one's body for generating such a torment within itself and against itself. One religious response to such pain is to question the moral nature of any deity who may be ultimately responsible for the world. In Christian theology, this is the question of theodicy, of how a good God can be justified in the face of the kind of pain and torment that the deity's creatures endure.

Though pain is a fundamental aspect of human life, grounded as it is in our nervous system's response to harm done to it, many living in 'safe societies' may now go through life without ever having suffered such intense anguish caused by severe pain. They remind us of the notion of 'proprioception', a 'neurological concept' denoting the 'body's internal sense of itself', which is normally of a 'low level of awareness of sensation inside the body' but which is transformed if severe pain is felt.[40] Those who have experienced such pain and survived carry a mark upon them that is not easily removed. Here I refer to what we would often call physical pain, sensations triggered by a condition of illness or disease that disrupts the ordinary life of the body.

[40] Elkins (1996: 136–7).

Those who know such pain often sense a bond, a sense of shared life, making it authentic to say 'I know what it is like'. Those who have not experienced such a pain simply live in 'another world'.

As with 'physical pain', so, too, with the mental pain felt as anguish or distress by the bereaved, by those suffering injustice at the hands of others, and by individuals with various mental illnesses. Our self-awareness, itself part of the wonder of being human, can turn against us as we think about harms done to us and feel them again and again through memory, or of the harm we have done to others. Here the dynamics of emotions often has a dual capacity for positive and negative outcomes and for invoking moral and religious questions of blame. In philosophical theology Kierkegaard, above all others, devoted himself to exploring the nature of self-understanding and of the despair that may arise in the process of attaining such self-knowledge. For example, he devotes much time to developing a descriptive 'psychology' of 'the concept of anxiety' as a means of elaborating Christian ideas of sin. His early nineteenth-century terminology, which is essentially philosophical, describes 'Man as a synthesis of the psychical and the physical... united in a third... spirit'.[41] Within this dynamic interplay there emerges 'the sickness unto death', his description of 'despair' as a kind of negative obsession of the self seeking to understand the relationship it has with itself but finding only a negative outcome. For him there is an eternal demand made upon human beings that they 'become themselves', a task set them 'before God', or, in the terms of this book, of otherness. Kierkegaard is often described as the source of the philosophical perspective of existentialism; what he certainly does do is subject a wide variety of human experiences and emotions to detailed description. But his overarching commitment to Christian belief drives him to his concern with 'the seriousness of existence' and with the demand that a person should decide to become himself.[42] Decision lies at the heart of religious identity, so that, for him, 'the definition of faith' is that, 'by relating itself to its own self and by willing to be itself, the self is grounded transparently in the Power which constituted it'.[43] In quite different terms his perspective can be rendered as one that seeks identity fulfilment against the pull of identity depletion.

At a much more psychological but non-theological level we find Kleinman, for example, writing on 'Pain and Resistance', to pinpoint the

[41] Kierkegaard ([1844] 1980: 43).
[42] Kierkegaard ([1842] 1941: 261).
[43] Kierkegaard ([1842] 1941: 262).

importance of local contexts where individuals encounter 'suffering' defined as 'the result of processes of resistance (routinized or catastrophic) to the lived flow of experience'.[44] Our 'life plans and practical actions' meet opposition, they encounter resistance from misfortune, the death of those we love, serious illness, breakdown in relationships, or the simple fact that we lack the resources to achieve our goals. In all this Kleinman emphasizes locality and the individual's own experience of resistance, for, despite the universal nature of misfortune, pain is novel to an individual when felt for the first time, and the way that person is able to deal with it will depend upon many local factors. But how does a person make sense of life in relation to resistances? In his work on survivors of the Chinese Communist Cultural Revolution, he saw how bodily illnesses served as one response to overwhelming control, often an inadequate response but all that was available at the time. This issue of 'illness as an idiom of distress' has many applications. In other cases he speaks of the American fear of 'falling from grace' in the sense of losing out on 'economic advancement and social mobility', a kind of 'secularized soteriology'.[45] The point is always one of detail in seeing how individuals use the wider cultural resources to make their own way in the world against the resistances they encounter. Evans-Pritchard's account of witchcraft and magic among the Azande offers one classic example of how misfortune was interpreted as the outcome of magic and could be overcome by appropriate recourse to oracles whereas other cultures might deploy police or medical doctors.[46]

Terror

Following Kleinman's marking of 'this dark side of experience', we include here the theme of terror, along with pain, as part of this emotional darkness.[47] Consider a person who knows that a great danger is just about to overtake and destroy him; he feels helpless; he is running as fast as he can but he knows there is no escape; hopelessness sweeps his body as an incoming tide submerges a horse in quicksand. Then, turning to face his enemy, as the emotion of fear is surging to overwhelm him—he wakes up! Sweating, lying in bed, he

---

[44] Kleinman (1992: 169–97, 174).
[45] Kleinman (1992: 180).
[46] Evans-Pritchard (1937).
[47] Kleinman (1992: 174).

is not sure for some seconds whether he is safe in his own room or still in that dreamland nightmare. His relief is enormous. But imagine that same person waking up to find that, really, he is in the room where his terrorist captors hold him ransom, a gun to his head. There is no relief, no sense of escape. Such examples illustrate the power of fear that many experience in their own way and may even trigger an impact on us through our imagination. In itself the very notion of terror seems to take 'animal' fear into a new cultural domain of human anticipated dread that others may inflict upon me. Such intentional malevolence allied with actual or anticipated pain and death lies at the heart of terrorism, and, although one cultural sense of terrorism might describe it as 'senseless', it will possess a logic of its own for the terrorists, as Christopher Taylor demonstrated for the Rwandan genocide of 1994. There he reveals the Tutsi 'as sacrificial victims in what in many respects was a massive ritual of purification . . . intended to purge the nation of "obstructive beings" . . . imagined through a Rwandan ontology that situates the body politic in analogous relation to the individual human body'.[48]

Hope's absence

Any consideration of such terror and of pain involves ordering images and symbols within local cultural classifications, often with some reference to hope or hope's loss. Hope is a valuable concept for this study for, while it is not an 'emotion' in the sense of being on psychological lists of emotions, it is difficult to account for religious rites without some such concept of hope as an orientation to the future sustained by a complex of current emotions and moods embedded in narratives that tell of life's direction and prized values. This centrality of a vitality-grounded element that helps drive a sense of identity makes life all the more poignant when it is lost or much depleted. One such context, for example, is that of pain, for severe pain may not only prompt a hopelessness towards any positive sense of future possibilities but may also bring a foreboding of death. Here, then, identity depletion is valuable when bridging the physical pain of the body and the mental pain derived from self-awareness of inability to survive, or when suffering shame, guilt, or even betrayal. Shame and guilt we will consider here, retaining betrayal for Chapter 6 as the negative partner of love.

[48] Cf. Christopher Taylor (1999: 101).

Shame and guilt

Shame and guilt take us into a long-standing field of fractured human identity, though they do raise the problem of just what names to give to certain feelings as they arise in distinctive cultures. Aristotle's *Ethics*, for example, argued that it is incorrect 'to speak of shame as a virtue, for it is more like a feeling than a moral state'.[49] For him a virtue had to do with a state of character, whereas feelings lie beyond that cultivated condition. Accordingly he thought of shame as a feeling relating more to the young who 'live by feeling' and are in the process of developing a mature identity. It is a 'kind of fear of dishonour', similar to fear of danger, except that it is more likely to be visible as a blush rather than in the pallor of fear.

All societies have their own understanding of how ideal virtues relate to felt experiences, though it is often wise not to make overly sharp distinctions and to pay close attention to local contexts as exemplified in Obeyesekere's magisterial study of religious experience among some Sri Lankan ascetics. His detailed biographies included a case of spirit attacks upon a person where he interpreted 'the whole episode' as 'a symbolic representation of the feelings of guilt' of the 'patient' that forms a 'cultural idiom ... used to objectify personal drives and motives', despite the fact that 'there is no word for guilt and no associated vocabulary in the Sinhala language for it'. There is, however, 'a complicated, incredibly large, subtly graded vocabulary of shame'. Obeyesekere deals with this context by seeing shame as 'primarily a social emotion', while guilt he reserves for 'psychoanalytic theory'.[50] By contrast, Stephen Pattison disagreed with setting certain Eastern societies such as Japan as 'shame' focused against the USA or UK as 'guilt' focused.[51] This was partly because of his own experience of shame: 'I believe myself to have been a shame-bound person for most of my life, regarding myself as unworthy, valueless and defiled, with a deep desire to hide myself away from the "legitimate" negative judgement of others'.[52] This he felt was due to his own early commitment to the Christian Church, where the practice of confession, when introduced too early, could result in 'young people turning

[49] Aristotle (1963: 91).   [50] Obeyesekere (1981:79).
[51] Pattison (2000: 171). Cf. Paul Ekman (in Darwin ([1872] 1998: 391): 'I think that guilt and shame expressions do not differ from each other, and that they differ from sadness only in the attempt to hide the face.'.
[52] Pattison (2000: 7).

inwards upon themselves', generating a 'private hell' and a 'lifelong melancholy and pervasive shame'.[53] Other reasons for disliking such confession have also existed, as in Victorian England, where auricular confession was held in particular distaste by most Anglicans and is said to have 'aroused hostility . . . wherever it was found', in part because of the belief that it might 'excite sexual passion in women', something that could 'lead to infertility'.[54] In the quite different context of twentieth-century political life in the USA, we can see how 'confession' offers its own window not only into culture history and its religious valuation but also into the potential manipulation of people through false practice drawn from the deceit repertoire of human beings. Some might see this, for example, in the case of former US President Bill Clinton, and his 'testimony . . . enacted as a matter of sincerity, of plain style rather than rhetorical performance, of contrition rather than eloquence', when, at a national Prayer Breakfast at the White House in September 1998, he admitting his erstwhile hidden sexual encounters in the Lewinsky affair.[55]

This reveals the capacity of the human voice as a most powerful vehicle of and for expressing emotion and the ongoing expression of mood in contexts of actual or potential identity depletion or, indeed, of identity affirmation. Two examples show this through the particular vocal feature of 'choking'. In the one we hear of a man on death row asking his lawyer, someone who had become his friend, to 'spread some of his ashes' around a particularly significant spot after his execution and cremation, and we are not surprised that the request was made with 'his voice choking'.[56] This phenomenon of 'choking', often described as someone being 'overcome by emotion', is widely read as a sign of sincerity of emotion and frequently occurs when something of deepest personal significance is shared, as in our second example, that of testimony-giving among Mormons, when individuals speak about how their church has influenced their life. Their relatively quiet and restrained tone may well be interrupted by this emotional vocal stop, which symbolizes authenticity and is understood and appreciated by fellow believers. We will return in Chapter 9 to some further, positive, aspects of confession.

Here, then, we are in complex areas where memory, ongoing rites, and cultural preference produce their own situations. Some imagine, for example,

---

[53] Pattison (2000: 264).   [54] Bentley (1978: 33).

[55] Melling (1999: 107–8). This was an act set against the historical US background of Puritan simplicity and directness of speaking out about 'experiences—feelings of guilt, joy and sinfulness'.

[56] Sharp (2005: 155).

that changing attitudes to life and behaviour may shift our actual experience
of the past. That is an optimistic view. But, for example, let us imagine that
we once did something of which we were ashamed and guilty. Years later,
when recalling the event, we deal with it through our present-day feeling
system and, again, we feel ashamed and guilty. This scenario assumes that we
are still living in a social world operating on the same system of emotion in
relation to the particular acts of the past. But, what if we now live in a
different context in which our cognitive understanding has changed? Perhaps
our understanding of ourself has changed. And this may well have been
because of some new religious involvement or engagement. Now, when
that former event is recalled, I need not bring to it the shame–guilt element
of my present feeling system but may perhaps bring to it quite a different one,
perhaps of joy. So, for example, what I would once have experienced in a
negative way, having interpreted my behaviour as a sin, I now see as something for which I have been forgiven and 'saved'. My new idea of salvation
allows me to recontextualize the past. But that may not always be so easy, and
Pattison's study offers a telling account of the power of shame emotions in
people's lives, not least when induced or fostered by Christianity itself. He
speaks of the need for people to 'create a language for shame' and of how this
becomes integrated within 'wider social narratives' as one means of pursuing
personal integration, but he notes the opinion of many specialists that deep-
seated guilt and shame may never be fully resolved.[57]

This may help us understand the nature of religious testimonies and
conversion narratives as stories that restructure past events in the light of
succeeding life events and in the light of how we feel in the present moment.
Here, too, the role of religious ritual is important. Imagine a person giving
testimony within the context of a religious meeting that has already involved
hymns, prayers, and collective activity that prompts a sense of group security
and happiness of being involved. The scene has already activated positive
feeling states within the individual when he or she stands to recall that
memory from the past and bring it to life in the present feeling moment. If
strong concepts are at work within individuals, such as spiritual rebirth or
new-found membership in a new community deemed to be the community
of salvation, then it is likely that they will engage with their memory of the
past through a positive feeling state. Instead of recalling a sin and currently
wallowing in it through a present feeling state of guilt, they recall it as a

[57] Pattison (2000: 169).

person who now feels freed from it: their current experience of their 'memory' has changed from past 'experiences' of their memory. Many religious liturgies exist to create current feeling states, sharp emotions of the present moment, and to perpetuate them to some degree as ongoing moods of salvation. The Sikh tradition, for example, is strong on the role of pride and human self-bondedness (*haumai*) in preventing people from sensing the ultimate nature of deity and the bliss arising from it. Indeed, at its core lies the desired transformation from being self-yoked (*man-mukh*) to being yoked or united with the true Lord (*gur-mukh*).

Death

Another context of deep emotion that intertwines negative and positive elements is that of death, an event often fostering identity depletion. The fear of death, one of the 'inescapable existential questions of culture',[58] is, for example, broadly covered in Joanna Bourke's opening chapter of her cultural history of fear, where she dwells upon the fear of death and hell within Christianity as a means of encouraging good behaviour. Interestingly, she cites an 1878 article in *Popular Science Monthly* to the effect that hell beliefs were now obsolete. Shortly after, the *Catholic World* reminded the faithful that hell was 'not a theological opinion but revealed dogma'.[59] This issue of the decline of 'hell-beliefs' in the nineteenth century is an important one, not least in relation to their final demise in much of Europe, as many would suggest, in the wake of the First World War, when the thought of hundreds of thousands of young soldiers going to hell became socially unacceptable, not least at the time when the 'greater-love' motif began to rise in connection with the war dead. This image identified dead soldiers with the self-sacrificed Christ, repositioning the nature of war death as a form of sacrifice and, as Jon Davies argued, created a form of Euro-Christianity in the process.[60] Historical change and the nature of particular context are vital in these arguments, not least in terms of fear and the kinds of things that people fear at different times and places. Bourke, for example, cited various terrorist plots after New York's Twin Towers destruction to assert that 'by the twenty-first century danger did not strengthen but weakened the individual, who needed to enlist the help of a set of professionals to cope with the trials and tribulations of

---

[58] Daniel Bell ([1980] 1991: 353).
[59] Bourke (2006: 46).   [60] Jon Davies (1995).

life'.[61] An important aspect of fear in relation to death is to understand that it is neither universal nor indeed constant in any one society, since social status, gender, age, ideology, and state of health are all contributing factors.

War

One major social influence on emotions is that of war. William James (1842–1910), for example, once spoke at the Universal Peace Congress held in Boston in 1904, a time of relative optimism over the world's future development and progress. His broad concern reflects one of the major themes of this book—namely, 'man as a rational animal'.[62] He emphasized the way philosophers then preferred to deal with the rational dimension of existence while often ignoring 'the animal part' of humanity's being. And it was that 'animal part' that he pondered in Boston, most especially in terms of 'our permanent enemy . . . the rooted bellicosity of human nature'. For him, 'man, biologically considered, and whatever else he may be into the bargain, is the most formidable of all beasts of prey'. He felt that even 'a millennium of peace would not breed the fighting disposition out of our bone and marrow'. I quote James here, because he spoke prior to the two major world wars, and numerous other wars and battles in Korea, Iran–Iraq, and the Balkans, in numerous African and South American contexts, and in terrorist-political movements in Europe, Sri Lanka, and elsewhere. The twentieth century would become a period of almost immeasurable loss of life through active killing, initiated by peoples regarding themselves as highly civilized and with noble causes. But he spoke before all that, deeply alert to a certain ethic of military might, of a code of honour, and of self-regarding courage that forged strong character and saved societies from a softness devoid of valour. He was aware of the deep privilege of a very few who lived in an 'ease-economy' while most of humanity lived under a 'pain and fear economy'.[63] Yet, he hoped that reason, despite being like a sandbank amid raging tidal currents, might develop over time to become immovable and influential over war, allowing 'civic passion' and 'civic' honour to absorb ideals that otherwise would drive a militaristic ethic of duty and striving; his idea was a kind of 'army enlisted against *Nature*', of young men—specifically men—conscripted not into the

---

[61] Bourke (2006: 379–80).
[62] James ([1904] 1950: 240–1).
[63] James ([1904] 1950: 244).

army but into all sorts of arduous jobs, so that all, including the wealthy classes, should find a dignity in hard work and come to respect all through it.[64] For James, war was the only phenomenon that had hitherto served to integrate communities; this new 'human warfare against nature' in 'iron and coal mines', in 'freight trains and fishing fleets in December, dish-washing...road-building and tunnel-making...and the frames of sky-scrapers', would serve the same purpose but in a creative way.

TRUST, RESPECT, DIGNITY, AND FLOURISHING IDENTITY

Two world wars, a cold war, Middle Eastern wars, and events such as the Rwandan genocide have tested James's optimism that respect might follow a 'warfare against nature'. Such failure of optimism may be explained by those like Girard who see human nature as intrinsically grounded in violence that needs channelling in warfare or some substitute activity.[65] Marvin and Ingle, for their part, saw military life and soldier sacrifice as integral to maintaining the unity of the USA.[66] Whatever the theory, even as the twenty-first century moves into its second decade, not even the strong scientific heralding of impending ecological disasters associated with global warming seems to have motivated political leaderships to focus on worldwide human needs. The hunger and thirst of millions demonstrate a degree of lack of respect for the dignity of victims of inadequate provision, despite the protests and the valiant work of numerous charities, often religiously motivated. These themes of respect and dignity are vitally important, because they bring a distinctive moral colour to the notion of identity. Respect implies that a person is worth looking at and being drawn into some relationship maintaining a sense of dignity. Respect and dignity become verbal indicators of the emotional dynamics of identity, and a closer analysis of their use soon reveals their importance as markers of self-esteem. Here it is important to stress that these abstract nouns—'respect' and 'dignity'—are, essentially, markers of deep emotional feelings, and underlying both of them is the primary social emotion of trust.

---

[64] James ([1904] 1950: 247).

[65] Girard (1977); Hall with Schuyler (2000: 192–9), for example, explore fear in terms of 'cultural paranoia' as evident in self-destructive apocalyptic sects.

[66] Marvin and Ingle (1999).

'Trust' is a word that, in English, carries a wider spectrum of ordinary meaning than many others, a fact indicating its power to express a diversity of basic human interests that find a focus in processes of reciprocity and in attitudes towards otherness. We relate to others and engage in personal and social life with them because of a certain moral charge that we bring to those relationships—namely, trust. Sometimes this involves contexts of status and hierarchy and sometimes the status-less contexts of love. While it can, of course, be given explicit significance in some contexts, it is often the pervading force of the fabric of life that is left unspoken. Here, we draw attention to trust in its manifestations of respect and dignity.

'Respect', as an expression of how one person wished to be viewed by another, became a commonplace—even an imperative—in a certain kind of British street talk among some young people's groups.[67] Interestingly, it seemed to flourish among groups where even the way one person might 'look at' another could be perceived as a challenge. 'Respect' became a designation that sometimes went with aspects of violence or strength or style in dress. The emotional dynamics of such worlds is, as everywhere, extremely complex and would need a deep analysis in terms of child development and patterns of family nurture as a background for understanding the public life of groups, especially of gangs and gang culture, before the profounder aspects of a desired dignity could be assessed.

At approximately the same time as 'respect' expressed a desired attitude among certain youth groups in the decades around the turn of the twentieth and twenty-first centuries in Britain, an allied notion came to be associated with elderly groups—namely, 'dignity'. Dignity described ways in which the elderly should be viewed and treated, especially when they became infirm. It gained particular significance in terms of dying and death. To be treated with dignity carries with it a fear of its opposite, of being disregarded and, in that sense of 'seeing' or being 'looked at', of being ignored and viewed as a relatively worthless entity. Because respect and dignity share the characteristic of being abstract nouns entailing deep emotive roots, they serve a prime function as windows into the notion of identity, highlighting the role of emotion within the perception of social identity.

The desire for respect and identity carries with it the fear of actually encountering their opposites in disrespect and indignity, states that help denature identity by depleting it. Their association with age grades highlights

---

[67] Cf. Sennett (2003) for US comparison.

the nature of identity at quite crucial phases of life. For teenagers, identity involves the process of being shaped through contexts of family, friends, and potential enemies. To have 'respect' is to be acknowledged as being a person in one's own right, most especially in the kinds of societies we are largely assuming in this book while, of course, acknowledging that in some other societies respect may apply to the family or clan group as such, with individual wishes and preferences having to serve that end. Old age, too, involves shifts in social status and identity. Though some tradition-focused societies have cherished the old, according them a high status, this is widely perceived to be decreasingly the case in modern and postmodern social worlds in which the working life as a means of wealth generation comes to be a major source of identity outside any family group. The image of an old people's home has often attracted a negative image as a waiting room for death. This is understandable in societies where identity is grounded in the working life and occupation. Many speak of 'being' what they do, and this has become an increasingly widespread attitude among those who were not manual labourers, for whom retirement from increasingly arduous labour was much desired. The more professional, service-oriented, and people-involved occupations, however, with their status- and dignity-conferral capacities, offer a quite different scenario. One of the characteristic aspects of many kinds of professional life in contemporary societies involves the degree of control over life, time, and activities. What enhances a sense of identity is the sense of control people have over their own life and, to some degree, also of the control a person has over the lives of others. Contrariwise, it is the fear of the loss of such control, and the eventual loss of it, that affect the idea of respect and dignity. Because the final loss of control is, inevitably, the fact of death and, for many, the fear of incapacitating illness preceding death, it is not surprising that the theme of dignity has come to be allied with these events. Dignity in dying expresses the hope for ongoing control and for an identity that is rooted in the continuing respect of society in its wider and narrower contexts. It is here that a fear of fractured identity arises, and this is accentuated in secular contexts, where many individuals do not live in a world of trust in a God that envelops their immediate future as well as their ultimate destiny. In this context, ideas of euthanasia and doctor-assisted suicide have become, in the early twenty-first century, a major social, medical, and political issue, as we will see in Chapter 8.

Just how these issues will work out depends upon how the individual relates to the group, and this, itself, is a potential problem in any society. I am not assuming that either great freedom or limitation of choice necessarily enhances a person's quotient of life satisfaction, since freedom can lead some to lonely unhappiness, just as a fixed role in an intensely integrated group can provide contentment for others. What would seem widely desirable, however, is that human life is accorded a significance that allows an individual to contribute in a positive way to his social world, a viewpoint as basic to Marxist as to most religious thought. Just as Marxism would give individuals a wider sense of identity as members of a people's political party with its own philosophical theory of history and hope of social change through revolution, so Christianity asserts the status of a person incorporated into the Christian community and said to have become part of 'the body of Christ', itself an intriguing metaphor of identity.[68] Both schemes carry their own sense of participatory suffering for the emotional benefits of community, but suffering producing not identity depletion but potential fulfillment.

SUMMARY

In this chapter we have used the abstract notion of identity depletion to describe a very wide variety of feelings and contexts in which human beings sense themselves assailed in their desire for a meaningful life. It has also served as an umbrella term for the interests of thinkers from different disciplinary approaches to the human condition. As explained at the beginning of this chapter, the identity-depletion motif has enabled us to invert the core concepts of this study—especially meaning, hope, otherness, and reciprocity—so as to examine their negative dynamics. One valuable use of this term has been to reinforce the issue of the integration of biological and social aspects of human life highlighted in the Introduction through the biocultural approach to people stressed in Chapter 1. Identity depletion has described the experience of a reduction in or absence of the dynamic or energy-focused drive that people bring to their society's way of life. Just because we have spoken of a depletion should not, of course, suggest that we speak of an absence of feeling or of awareness of being a person in reduced circumstances but, rather, of feeling a contrast. It is important for this study to account for the variation of negative and positive feeling that comprises individual lives within their cultural contexts, most especially when religious

---

68 1 Corinthians 12: 26.

institutions and their symbols and rites help construct and manage those feelings. The value of gaining such an overview has always to be set alongside the loss of detail that ethnographic studies provide. But that is always the case in comparative studies within social science as well as in the humanities. It is with this comparative view and with the need to balance negative and positive dynamics of emotions in mind that we now turn to a chapter that does just that, taking as its focus the identity depletion evident in contexts of grief before considering the positive dynamics that intensifies identity through rites and persons that ensure the 'securing' and 'promoting' of life.[69]

---

[69] Hocart ([1935] 1973: 46, 47) offers a strong positive sense of the value of ritual.

4

Grief, Intensive Living, and Charisma

Continuing the idea of identity depletion as an overarching concept for approaching negative dynamics of emotions, the first part of this chapter explores the equally negative realm of grief, before switching sharply to consider dynamic aspects of identity enhancement through the concept of intensive living. Identity depletion and intensive living are, thus, taken as valuable theoretical concepts for interpreting negative and positive aspects of identity. Uniting them in a single chapter emphasizes the dynamic nature of human emotions as they arise within individuals but relate to wider society through formal patterns of behaviour expected by social institutions. This goal is reinforced by the inclusion in this chapter of the notion of charisma, which exemplifies one kind of link between individuals and institutions in the person of charismatic leaders who are an embodied intensification of certain values and associated emotions.

IDENTITY DEPLETION AND GRIEF

We begin with grief, for seldom are emotions more poignant and powerful than when surrounding death and seldom is religious activity more embraced than in funerary rites. The 'words against death' underlying religions' ritual response to death oppose its sharp challenge to human identity and to life's very rationale,[1] instantiating Aquili and Laughlin's assertion:

When ritual works (and it by no means works all the time), it powerfully relieves man's existential anxiety and, at its most powerful, relieves him of the fear of death and places him in harmony with the universe. It is no wonder that a behavioural phenomenon so powerful has persisted throughout the ages.[2]

---

[1] See Douglas J. Davies (1997a: 6–8; [1997] 2002: 1–23) for a theory of 'words against death'.
[2] Aquili and Laughlin (1979: 178).

Despite the fact that early twenty-first-century people in developed and 'safe societies' have much less experience of death than at any time in humanity's history, and may not be personally bereaved until their middle age, it is in death-associated emotions more than in other aspects of life that peoples share a commonality of emotion. The many 'corpses' of media detective autopsies bear little relation to the immediate stillness of the real dead. Fiction apart, this complex field of death-related emotions involves many different cultural lenses that often highlight the way social life and its historically developed mourning practices help shape the feelings of grief that come from the physically embodied lives that have been bound together in some way.

Though our appreciation of death contexts depends to a degree on our prior experience, our capacity to empathize with others remains potent, as exemplified in Susan Sharp's study of 'the effects of the death penalty on families of the accused', in her book *Hidden Victims.* She tells how her work changed her life and spelled out her difficulty in maintaining 'complete neutrality'.[3] Few descriptions of emotions surrounding identity depletion, or perhaps we ought even to say of identity fracture, are as incisive as hers, nor do they reveal the obvious yet often ignored fact of the emotional life of the scholar in relation to her 'subjects'. She depicts the interplay of descriptive accuracy and 'neutrality' with her inevitable engagement and emotional response to the complex and often tragic lives of condemned criminals on death row in the USA, of their families and friends, and of the murdered victims. Her raw description of fear, desperation, forgiveness, friendship, guilt, hope, horror, and stigma surface through the lives of numerous individuals. The stark fact of the state killing condemned killers, occasionally providing last-minute reprieve, or revoking such hope, triggers an almost inevitable sympathy. In her account of 'botched executions' she tells how two women watch their son and brother 'convulsed' and struggling for breath when the supposed fatal injections were given: they watch through a window; the sister wants to help but cannot; they are horrified. And here, for once, that word is filled with the meaning it so frequently lacks in everyday use. In an important chapter she explores theories of grief in these complex and tortu-ous circumstances to show how different grief is for ordinary bereaved people who gain support from others when compared with the relatives of death-row criminals. She notes how some were helped through personal faith, while

---

[3] Sharp (2005: 178).

others ceased to believe in God, and she outlines what she calls the BADD Cycle of bargaining, activity, disillusionment, and desperation, as part of a 'protracted grief process'.[4] In that study of extreme contexts, the powerful role of emotions, especially of fear, surfaces as a drive to survive engages with a need to explain overwhelming circumstance; with time, a mood of anxiety pervades life as some escape is sought.

In ordinary circumstances, the help others provide us, as social animals, offers a much-needed sense of security through family and kinship bonds as through friendship, business, and other alliances. The loss of any such support group can be problematic, while the loss through bereavement of some key supportive individual can become radically so, highlighting grief as a pivotal emotion whose frequent absence from lists of emotion ignores its most widespread human presence. The death of those to whom we have been attached in this life, who have helped create our own identities and given us a sense of hope in a meaningful world, can be hard enough in ordinary life, but the contexts of murder and capital punishment trigger much greater hardship, as all concerned face the horror of a fragmented world where social support fails and 'meaning' evaporates. Still, such dramatic examples cannot detract from the millions who experience much more 'ordinary' bereavement and for whom life becomes enormously hard, whether for shorter or longer periods of time. The death of a life partner, child, twin, or devoted parent can transform a colourful world to one of grey banality, aggravated by the need seemingly to continue as normal. The turmoil of a personal life and shaken identity grates alongside the controlled and managed emotion of wider society.

Such 'ordinary' losses often create their own form of otherness, as people begin to experience their dead as ancestors, in dreams, or sometimes as aspects of themselves. My own research, for example, revealed that approximately a third of the British public have some such awareness of their departed.[5] One response to death that seems oppositional to grief, though it may be related to 'sensing the dead', lies in what has been called 'intensive living'. This describes moments or periods when daily life or 'life' itself comes to be seen as precious and worthy of deep appreciation. As we argue below, this intensity is sometimes expressed in charismatic leaders who offer meaning

---

[4] Sharp (2005: 48, 163). She relates this to a balanced and critical appraisal of Elizabeth Kübler-Ross's well-known account of 'stages' of grief.

[5] Douglas J. Davies (1997b: 139); research taken from a large sample of 1,600 Britons, fully described in Davies and Shaw (1995).

and hope through this concentration of 'life' within them. Indeed, the notion of vitality offers a distinctive interpretation of this notion of charisma in religious or other forms of ideological leaders.[6] Vitality, as an awareness of being alive and of possessing an energy to achieve goals, underlies the idea of intensive living. Standing as one kind of opposite to vitality is Durkheim's notion of *anomie*, to which we will return below, a term that indicates a sense of a depleted self in withdrawal from social integration and the goals offered by social life. Indeed, one might argue that grief involves a kind of anomie, as a person experiences a decrease in vitality and a corresponding depletion in identity. At the more obvious pole to vitality is, inevitably, mortality, or the sense of approaching death. One telling literary example speaks of Don Fabrizio, a princely character, who had, 'for a dozen years or so', 'been feeling as if the vital fluid, the faculty of existing, life itself in fact and perhaps even the will to go on living, were ebbing out of him slowly but steadily, as grains of sand cluster and then line up one by one, unhurried, unceasing, before the narrow neck of an hourglass'.[7]

DEATH, EMOTION, AND RELIGION

Such emotions, hard to name experiences, and also memories surrounding death all remain central to much religious action and individual identity related to gods, ancestors, and the recently departed. One variant of vitality well known in the early anthropology of religion lies in E. B. Tylor's notion of animism. This described the perception of life forces in many kinds of objects and places that create their own sense of the otherness of the world with which people could engage in reciprocal relations; indeed he developed a theory of sacrifice to account for this.[8] For him, death was a major source for the origin of religion itself, as notions of spirits and souls interplayed with ideas of ancestors, gods, and God, with what this study describes as 'otherness'. A generation later, Robert Hertz valuably analysed death through 'double burials' where the 'wet' phase of decay removed the dead from their life status, with rites for their 'dry' remains imparting new ancestral identity to

---

[6] Godfrey Lienhardt (1961: 317) discussed the voluntary death and burial alive of the master of the fishing spear among the Dinka, as leading to 'a concentrated public experience of vitality'.

[7] Lampedusa ([1958] 2007: 183).

[8] Tylor ([1871] 1958: ii. 8, 10, 448).

the dead. His account of how 'the element of repulsion and disgust' was replaced by 'a feeling of reverent confidence' in the newly made ancestor shows how alert Hertz was to emotional issues as changes in the bereaved paralleled physical changes in the deceased.[9] Shortly after, Bronislaw Malinowski explored death-related emotions in his studies among the Trobriand Islanders, where he described 'the double-edged play of hope and fear' in the face of death, and pondered the mixed experiences of longing, fear, and disgust surrounding the dead. Indeed, he even spoke of death rites as serving some 'biological function of religion'.[10]

Gilgamesh and Darwin

Moving from ethnography to mythology, we find one of the oldest available human narratives of grief in the Babylonian epic of Gilgamesh. Written in cuneiform text on clay tablets, this tale of adventure turns into one of deep grief when Enkidu, princely Gilgamesh's bosom friend, dies, prompting an emotional state that remains recognizable to this day. He weeps, 'crying bitterly like unto a wailing woman', but one who weeps from the heart and not by convention. An evil has robbed him of his friend, who sleeps a strange sleep, whose eye does not open, and whose heart does not beat. Gilgamesh pulls out his own hair, vowing to let it grow long in mourning. He removes his fine clothes and goes a-wandering. In one of humanity's earliest written statements of emotion, he announces: 'I am afraid of death.'[11] Then, grief, sorrow's accomplice, enters his heart, as he roams the desert and sets off to discover the secret of eternal life. His fear of death is pinpointed as an emotion arising in one who was, in this myth, half-human and half-divine, for in these days even gods could 'perish through violence'.[12] Death was, however, pondered not so much as a final end but as a comfortless and hopeless shadow land from whose afterlife one might even return as a wraith.[13] Gilgamesh's search was successful; he was given a plant that would confer eternal life on earth, but, tragically, it is stolen by a serpent, when our hero stopped to bathe in a cooling pool of water. Gilgamesh now

---

[9] Hertz ([1905–6] 1960: 56–7).

[10] Malinowski ([1948] 1974: 51, 53).

[11] George (1999: 70). See also Alexander Heidel ([1946] 1963: 62–3).

[12] Heidel ([1946] 1963: 137).

[13] Heidel ([1946] 1963: 99). A Sumerian version tells of a hole punched in the underworld allowing 'the spirit of Enkindu' to issue 'forth from the underworld like a wind'.

weeps in this poignant mythical moment, 'his tears flowing over his cheeks'.[14] He has suffered a double loss, in which an echoing grief resonates with his original grief for Enkidu, an emotion now intensified by a final loss of hope for a fullness of life.[15] Gilgamesh, who had held onto the body of his dead friend even to the point when 'the worm fastened on him' and decay had begun, and who had been driven by the fear of death to search the world for some means of conquering it, finally returns home and comes to accept that he, too, will die.[16] As part of that acceptance, he looks at the great walls of his city and acknowledges that these will be his memorial. He will die, but he will be remembered. Such myths and narratives of great lives reveal the emotions of grief, reminding all that their own experiences of loss are not unique. In the New Testament, for example, Jesus weeps when confronted by the death of his friend Lazarus and the weeping of Lazarus's sister. He also weeps when approaching Jerusalem and anticipating its future disasters.[17] He does not weep, however, during his own experience of intense physical suffering. His weeping, being relational and not self-directed, also offers its own form of comfort, all long before the more formal 'theories of grief' began to be constructed by psychologists and others, especially from the later nineteenth century.

Aspects of Gilgamesh's response to loss, for example, are reflected in Charles Darwin's account of bereavement, in which grief is set between exciting and depressing emotional sensations, an early version of what we have described above in terms of vitality and identity depletion. Accordingly, a mother loses a child and becomes 'frantic with grief' and 'walks wildly about, tears her hair or clothes and wrings her hands' and 'blames herself'. All express the state of excitement, and Darwin explains part of her movement as being due to the 'relief experienced through muscular exertion'. This then explains the wringing of the hands as a person's 'tendency to energetic action' under difficult circumstances. Shifting the scene from the exciting–active mode to a depressed–passive mode, he speaks of how 'despair or deep sorrow takes the place of frantic grief', as the 'sufferer sits motionless, or gently rocks to and fro'. He speaks of the blood circulation as languid and as respiration almost forgotten, so that deep sighs follow. Muscles collapse and the eyes become dulled. He talks of how others encourage activity so as 'not to give

---

[14] Heidel ([1946] 1963: 92).
[15] See Douglas J. Davies (1997a: 172–3) for 'echoing grief'.
[16] Sanders ([1960] 1978: 103).
[17] Luke 19: 41; John 11: 35. Edited as a single verse, 'Jesus wept' was poignantly highlighted.

way to silent, motionless, grief'. Darwin's explanation of that kind of encouraging activity is that 'exertion stimulates the heart, and this reacts on the brain, and aids the mind to bear its heavy load'.[18] His observation of grief includes the description of eyelids drooping, the head 'hanging on a contracted chest; the lips, cheeks, and lower jaw all sunk downwards from their own weight. Hence all features are lengthened.' He then makes the cultural link with the expression that on hearing bad news a person's face is said 'to fall',[19] and even to be 'down in the mouth'.[20] He also describes something more like a paroxysm of grief, where an individual experiences something like choking as the *globus hystericus* rises in the throat, which he likens to 'sobbing of children'.[21] All this leads Darwin into one of his extended discussions of facial musculature and its part in creating particular expressions in particular contexts. This time his concern is with what he calls the 'grief muscles', whose contraction partly furrows the central section of the forehead and causes vertical lines and, as it were, a lump to rise between the eyes in a form of horseshoe. He sees it as a 'complex movement for the sole purpose of expressing grief; and yet it is a comparatively rare expression, and often overlooked'.[22] Darwin's interpretation of this action is debatable and debated; suffice it to say that these grief muscles or grief eyebrows, as they are also sometimes termed, have been observed by some even in the newborn in association with energetic crying.

Milton's emotions

Darwin's excellent descriptive observation of behavioural anatomy has been paralleled by the creative work of philosophers, authors, and poets, not least John Milton, whose personal life was, in one six-year period, plagued by loss of sight and the death of two wives and two children. His *Paradise Lost* portrays the biblical myth of Adam and Eve's sin and fall from divine grace into a self-conscious awareness of their new destiny in death. They anticipate having children born into 'this cursed world a woeful race' to be 'devoured by Death at last'. To avoid that, Eve suggests that they have no sex and both commit suicide, so as to bring no children into this world. She describes themselves as 'shivering under fears, that know no end but Death'. Eve is

[18] Darwin ([1872] 1998: 84–5, 176–7).   [19] Darwin ([1872] 1998: 177).
[20] Darwin ([1872] 1998: 191).   [21] Darwin ([1872] 1998: 177).
[22] Darwin ([1872] 1998: 187).

rendered speechless by 'vehement despair', her cheeks dyed pale, while Adam, having focused 'to better hopes his more attentive mind', will not accept her proposal; indeed he even sees in her despair 'something more sublime'. He thinks that God will not be cheated by suicide and will have some further fate for them. As the tale of God's decree to banish them from Paradise unfolds, so does a panoply of emotions. Adam, for example, being 'heart-strook with chilling gripe of sorrow stood'. Sight and smell are both evoked, and they even wonder how they will manage to breathe the air in the world beyond Paradise. The Archangel Michael, who is sent to banish them from Eden, tells Eve not to 'set her heart' on what is not to be hers but to be grateful that at least she will not be lonely but will have the company of Adam.[23] Milton explores the paradoxes of death as an end and yet an end that cannot be achieved with ease. The pair need to live knowing they will die, experiencing cross tides of emotion; they are not far from the same realization that came to Gilgamesh.

However, for most of human history, the fact of death came to be countered by religious belief in an afterlife much more positive than a shadow land of wraiths. Even so, increasing minorities now accept that death is the end of individual life. even though they may interpret death's decay as part of a natural cycle of life.[24] Still, whatever the creed, periods surrounding death frequently intensify emotional experience and prompt involvement with ritual specialists, as issues of identity come sharply into play, as parents become ancestors, heaven-dwellers, or memories; their offspring become orphans and may assume new identity as household heads, while spouses become widowed. Social circles of the bereaved acknowledge their changed circumstances and provide rituals of reciprocity and engagement with 'otherness' of fundamental kinds. In the next chapter, for example, we consider widow cremation in India as one classic example of identity bonding of a high-status husband and his wife.

OTHERNESS, RECIPROCITY, AND GRIEF

Here our key motifs of otherness and reciprocity resurface, as the sense of loss reflects prior dependence and the meaning made of life through mutual

---

[23] John Milton, *Paradise Lost*, bks X and XI.
[24] Davies and Shaw (1995: 92–3). Some 32% of a sample of 754 members of the Church of England reckoned that 'death was the end', compared with 14% of a sample of 271 Catholics.

interdependence of spouses, children, and kinsfolk. Life partners help forge adult identities through the fundamental reciprocity of marriage, with its innumerable engagements of intimate and wider social life. Individuals become a concrete focus of otherness for their partners in relationships created and developed through many reciprocal acts involving time, money, or care, before the emotions surrounding death help transform the deceased into a different kind of otherness, one with whom or with which the living may still have some engagement as a dead parent, partner, child, friend, or even celebrity. The deceased now occupies a place in memory, which is, itself, part of the ongoing consciousness of the relative or fan. As such, they may simply 'come to mind', as their memory is triggered by some object, event, or sensory prompt in smell, photograph, or music. Funeral ritual and events following death help channel these emotional changes of relationship to the otherness of others and reveal the value of reciprocity theory for understanding emotion and memory.

The passage of time is also significant as anniversaries of death, weddings, birthdays, and the like trigger emotions and foster moods, often reinforced by the material culture of objects that belonged to the dead, including their graves and memorial sites.[25] Though the literal otherness of a partner is increasingly experienced through its location in memory, the nearness of the dead can become almost tangible in contexts where the embedded memory of the dead is activated and the bereaved 'realize' the transformed relationship with all its emotions of loss, sadness, regret, and love. Here Margaret Gibson speaks of 'spectral histories' to describe how some people come to see others in their own actions or demeanour: 'that other person is already part of our self'.[26] But, of course, for religious traditions that motivate afterlife beliefs, other emotions of hope for the dead in their new existence may be found, often prompted by post-mortem funeral rites occurring months or even years after death. Such hopes may be tinged with fear and with a desire to provide for the comfort of the dead through ongoing rites, but attitudes change in these areas. Today, for example, the death of a much-longed-for child or devoted life partner is often described as 'tragic', eliciting much grief, while the death of aged relatives can prompt 'a feeling of relief rather than sorrow', especially if they suffered illness.[27]

---

[25] See Hallam and Hockey (2001) for a fine text on material culture and death.
[26] Gibson (2008: 135) speaks of 'spectral histories'.
[27] Liveris (1999: 254).

The psychological notion of grief and its complementary sociological domain of mourning thus highlight emotion in social contexts as do few other aspects of human life. Though this chapter will not detail grief theories, it is important to emphasize their import for emotion and identity, given that bereavement alters the ongoing status, roles, and psychological dynamics of survivors, with most theories identifying a cluster of emotions typically including a sense of shock, numbness, and potential disbelief. As intimated above in relation to anomie, these theories frequently describe how life may seem to lose its meaning as a sense of hopelessness arises and the bereaved person may withdraw from ordinary life to a listless searching for the 'lost' person. Over time some accommodation occurs and ordinary life is re-engaged, albeit with a new narrative memory of its past. This 'recovery' may also involve a sense of intensive living as vitality is restored.

Different theories will, however, always interpret emotions of grief, depending upon their distinctive views of human identity. Sigmund Freud's psychoanalytic view, for example, is one of emotional attachment, loss, detachment, and reattachment. His 'grief-work' is grounded in a theory of identity operating on notions of psychological energy, not unlike our account of vitality, though an idea not to be equated with it in terms of its psychological origin. A person invests much energy, that of the libido, in attachment to a relative, and it is the break in that attachment that results in emotions of loss, as the survivor's identity is assailed and he or she needs to disinvest in the dead person and find some other focus for attaching the psychological energy. Another version of attachment theory, developed by John Bowlby, under the influence of evolutionary ideas, stresses the need we have for others in order that we may survive as a group. The benefit offered by attachment for survival purposes carries the inevitable cost of emotional distress when bereavement occurs. The emotional reciprocity implied here is that grief is the price paid for love.

Acknowledging the power of relationships and of memory in human life has fostered a view of grief described in terms of the 'continuing bonds' many experience with their dead. Instead of advocating a process of detachment, it encourages a realignment and re-appreciation of the bonds between the living and the dead in an ongoing narrative of existence. This allows for the impact of memories within a person's sense of identity and is consonant with many ethnographic accounts of grief, though it is wise to see this approach as one model among the others if we are to get a rounded view of human grief in social context. Loss and ongoing attachment can be two different moments within the dynamics of grief.

What becomes questionable in this context is the popular notion of 'closure'. This psychological idea concerns a person's 'need for unambiguous answers' and may be perfectly apt in some life contexts but not in terms of emotion, identity, and grief.[28] When Brian Whittle and Jean Ritchie, investigative journalists who wrote an account of the 1999 Harold Shipman case, spoke of this medical doctor's conviction for serial murder of many of his patients, they spoke of a 'sense of closure' for the 'families of the victims included in the court case'.[29] This highlights contexts in which public and social factors are deeply involved in loss and grief, especially where 'closure' refers to the completion of judicial processes relating to a death. This suggests that it may be unwise to apply 'closure' too readily to personal aspects of life, especially if credence is given to the continuing bonds motif of bereavement. Nevertheless, in terms of our key concepts, 'closure' relates to meaning, hope, otherness, and reciprocity. It signifies some resolution of 'unfinished business', a phrase bearing its own family likeness to 'closure', and suggesting an unintelligible matrix of emotions and social expectations. Still, many issues remain outstanding over theories of grief, not least whether grief should be viewed as some kind of illness or as a normal if deeply troublesome aspect of life that all can expect. Within developed societies, there is also the question of the power that professional medical or counselling services may attract to themselves in dealing with bereaved people.[30]

A case of memory

One example, from Thomas Maschio, will illustrate several such theoretical features. He documented the Rauto of Melanesia in the way they coped with death, especially through the use of mourning songs to help make sense of personal and community loss. These reflected a 'range of situations or scenarios in which particular emotions are typically experienced'. Maschio achieves a considerable goal in identifying the subtle theoretical difference between the feelings evoked by songs and the way 'songs create a metaemotion for and a metathought about the character of death and loss'.[31] This process of creating meta-level emotion and thought is valuable for our concern with bio-cultural aspects of emotion and how it impacts upon

[28] Fiske (2004: 88, 164), drawing on Webster and Kruglanski (1994).
[29] Whittle and Ritchie (2005: 350).
[30] Craib (1998: 164–7) argues against professional 'formulae for living' or for grief stages.
[31] Maschio (1994: 191–3).

identity. As in many ethnographies, Maschio unearths a dominant motif that, at one and the same time, names and expresses a feeling—namely, 'the emotion of makai'. *Makai* betokens 'a feeling of plenitude' or of 'full sadness'. It is a kind of nostalgia likely to occur during periods of personal insight and growth involving 'a series of emotions and moments in which the person finds an aspect of his or her identity'.[32] *Makai*, as a 'feeling of emotional fullness', is described as arising, for example, when a bereaved person sees someone else dancing in the mask that belonged to a deceased kinsman. This seems to prompt a cluster of factors that induce *makai*. These are likely to involve the memory of past dancing and of the one who dances no longer even though the dance still goes on. There is also a sense that the departed person can also watch this dancing of the living and feel a sense of personal loss. Here we have a dynamic sense of empathy grounded in memory and coupled with an appreciation of what the departed spirit may be feeling to yield an overall kind of 'dialogue with the lost person'.[33] There is an echo here of an argument within rabbinic Judaism that the living ought to refrain even from the ordinary aspects of life fulfilment, including loud sociability and sexual behaviour, in the presence of a corpse, lest its spirit, which is still nearby, might be provoked by its inability to enjoy these things when now separated from its body.[34] What is dramatically evident in both cases is the deep contextual nature of emotional engagement with the deceased, which provides a depth and meaning for empathy that differs so markedly, for example, from the de-contextualized 'empty empathy' created by film and media reports of suffering in places far removed from the viewer.[35]

Such ethnographic material is useful in prompting reflection in individuals from different societies. It might, for example, ask how grief may help people grow as individuals? Medical approaches to grief, for example, can easily think of it as an illness from which some cure may be expected. This is especially easy in societies where relatively few people are bereaved when they are young and where they experience few such losses over a lifetime. Many modern 'safe' societies protect and insulate people from extremes as far as survival is concerned; they engender an underlying and relatively easy sense of trust. It may be, of course, that other forms of loss are encountered that challenge the dependence of individuals upon others, as in some cases of

[32] Maschio (1994: 27–8).   [33] Maschio (1994: 72–3).
[34] Kraemer (2000: 21).   [35] Kaplan (2005: 93–100).

divorce, when children or young people have to deal with disrupted parental relationships and learn how to come to terms with a changing identity of their own. Nevertheless, the separation of death typically involves new kinds of experiences, for which appropriate resources are required. It may well be that societies that place a high value on individualism also require an individual resource at the time of grief. But attitudes differ greatly on this subject, as does, perhaps, the variation in resource that persons have to bring to their own time of loss. One response in 'safe' societies lies in the expert systems of professionals, whether medical doctors or grief counselling and support agencies. These, in their own ways, furnish their own account of 'meta-emotion', of the way to survive the immediate present and, if possible, to flourish in the future. They maintain their own structures of trust amongst people.

GRIEF, TEARS, AND DURKHEIM

One sociologically important account of emotions in relation to death and bereavement occurs in Durkheim's work on death and weeping within funerary rites. This account exemplifies the cultural aspect of weeping and control of funerary behaviour with a relatively strong downplaying of biological factors and 'psychological' explanations.[36] This reflects Durkheim's stress on the social component of human beings in which 'human nature is the result of a sort of recasting of the animal nature' involving 'losses and gains'. Indeed, he wonders just 'how many instincts have we not lost?' For Durkheim, society is the environment to which humans become adapted; he sees 'society' finding it 'necessary that we should see things from a certain angle and feel them in a certain way'.[37] This involves his powerful theoretical argument that the very categories by which we think come from society.[38] Here, then, Durkheim is valuable precisely for his concern with emotions and the fact that he is concerned with how they are formed, despite his theoretical concern that sociology should avoid 'psychological' theories and utilize only sociological ones.[39]

---

[36] Durkheim ([1912] 1976).

[37] Durkheim ([1912] 1976: 66).

[38] In the 'Introduction' to *The Elementary Forms*, he deals with 'religious sociology and the theory of knowledge', arguing that the basic categories of thought by which we organize our ideas and classify the world are socially derived.

[39] See Lukes (1973: 16–22), and Moscovici (1993), for this sociology–psychology divide.

As for mourning, two strands of thought run through his theory, with the dominant one focusing on social forces and the other on the individual. Most critics stress the former, to the entire disadvantage of the latter. Gary Ebersole, for example, absolutely underlines the view that Durkheim was entirely unconcerned with individuals: 'refusing to accept that these actors feel any personal emotions'.[40] This is somewhat misguided, because the individual can be found, for example, when Durkheim speaks of bereaved relatives who 'bring their own personal sorrow to the assembly'.[41] Still, Durkheim's argument is that personal feelings must be subordinated to the requirements of the wider group and, in that group context, 'the only forces which are really active . . . are the emotions aroused in the group by the death of one of its members'.[42] Here we note his emphasis on the arousal of emotions by the group. The participants themselves are unaware, he reckons, of the 'psychical mechanism' (he means psychological) underlying their negative feelings and desire to mortify themselves in their grief. What they come up with as their own explanation of how they feel is that there is a soul of the dead that now demands painful responses from the living. His starting point is the moral unity of a corporate group.[43] 'A family which allows one of its members to die without being wept for shows by that very fact that it lacks moral unity and cohesion; it abdicates; it renounces its existence.' It is group cohesion and the part played by individuals in this cohesion that largely but not completely occupies Durkheim's thought. This leads him to argue: 'The foundation of mourning is the impression of a loss which the group feels when it loses one of its members.' This loss arouses emotions in the group, emotions that are felt as negative and that come to be focused on the 'soul' of the deceased, which, at this time, is accorded a negative value. This fear of the dead is, really, a fear of the negative feelings aroused by the group at the loss of a member. This brings him to his assertion that 'men do not weep for the dead because they fear them; they fear them because they weep for them'. While this fear passes with time Durkheim was concerned to show that the dead remain significant for the living during mourning. He takes the experience of grief to be aligned with a belief in the continuing identity of the dead. Mourners feel that their grief is or must be related to some ongoing aspect of the deceased, and here Durkheim is slightly hesitant but obviously wants

---

[40] Ebersole (2004: 204–6).   [41] Durkheim ([1912] 1976: 399).
[42] Durkheim ([1912] 1976: 401).   [43] Lukes ([1973] 1975:524–9).

to assert that 'the idea of immortality' is born of this assumption.[44] Durkheim's concern lay not with personal loss but with society's loss. That is why he explicitly disagrees with Jevons, asserting that 'mourning is not the spontaneous expression of individual emotions'.[45] But, while loss is given as the main reason for funerary responses, Durkheim adds another factor, that of regret, suggesting that 'mourning itself, when once established, aroused the idea of and taste for posthumous regrets', for mourning represents the corporate action in which 'human sentiments are intensified' and the community integrated at a time of potential disruption.[46] It involves the creation of 'a state of effervescence'. In highlighting this social dimension and the idea of intensification of emotion, it is worth reiterating Durkheim's express recognition that relatives, who are affected the most directly, bring their own personal sorrow to the assembly.

Durkheim's theory of ritual, expressed here in the idiom of effervescence, will serve well as a pivotal point in this chapter, as we turn from negative to positive dynamics of identity; from a discussion of identity depletion to identity enhancement through a development of the notion of intensive living. Just as there is much in Durkheim's thought that can easily be expressed in terms of identity depletion—whether in his sense that the individual seems to lose the social charge within life at large, or in his discussion of suicide where a person seems to become disengaged with social life, both embraced by his notion of *anomie*—so there is much in his work that deals with an intensification of identity, most especially through ritual activity.[47] Indeed, his theory of ritual argues the case that social values as symbolized in totemic objects become the focal point of collective behaviour, which strengthens and transforms those who participate in them, an idea developed from Robertson Smith and to be discussed in Chapter 7.

INTENSIVE LIVING, IDENTITY, AND SURVIVAL

Here, then, we turn to widespread human experiences of intensity, where life is affirmed and identity enhanced, as depicted in literature of many kinds and typified in that most popular writer Paulo Coelho's description of one of his

---

[44] Durkheim ([1912] 1976: 402).
[45] Durkheim ([1912] 1976: 397), citing Jevons (1896: 46).
[46] Durkheim ([1912] 1976: 398–400).
[47] Mestrovic (1992: 119–21).

heroes, who 'lived every one of his days intensely since he had left home so long ago'.[48] In line with our present focus on death, this notion of human sentiments being intensified can, properly, be associated with the 'performance' of grief and of other sentiments, as developed both by Chapple and Coon in their notion of rites of intensification described in Chapter 2 and, more recently, by myself.[49] There is a strong potential affinity between rites of intensification and the notion of 'intensive living' if developed in relation both to the sense of hope and to the notion of vitality.

We may formally identify the provenance of 'intensive living' with Glaser and Strauss's conceptualization of one of three types of 'fighting behaviour' that may be found in those who are dying, the other two being visiting 'alternative' doctors or participating in experiments. These are understandable responses of individuals who have a sense of their impending death and who strive for a continued experience of life and of avenues that seem to promise its prolongation. While 'living life to the full' or 'increasing the patient's fullness of life before he dies' are intelligible responses in the context of a more explicitly acknowledged mortality, there is much more that can be said in terms of a non-impending death awareness of life.[50] As a classic example we draw from Albert Schweitzer, one of the most distinguished thinkers and humanitarians who, born in 1875 and dying in 1965, straddled the most crucial historical period of world fortune, disaster, and theological reappraisal since the sixteenth-century Reformation.

Theological intensity

Schweitzer's work in biblical studies, philosophy, and music were magisterial, and his life turn from European fame to the building and running of a hospital in Africa after committing himself to medical training at the age of 30 were once universally known and, indeed, acknowledged in his Nobel Peace Prize for 1952. In the face of the suffering he encountered in Africa and the fact of the First World War, when he was interned as a German prisoner of war for a short period, he seriously questioned the ethical direction taken by Christian civilization. Perhaps there were few minds of the twentieth century, and fewer lives committed to the service of mankind, that were as

---

[48] Coelho ([1988] 1995: 114). Allusively, in Huxley ([1925] 1951:174), 'positive living'.

[49] Chapple and Coon (1947); Douglas J. Davies (2002: 139).

[50] Glaser and Strauss (1965: 131).

pregnant with potential resource for solution or as pained in their production as was Schweitzer. The facts of his case are more apt than any fictional account or intellectual reappraisal could be, for it was on a canoe journey up river in French Equatorial Africa, and at sunset as they passed through a herd of hippopotami, that the means of apprehending the meaning of life dawned on him. It came in the phrase 'Reverence for Life'.[51] In his native German that phrase—*ehrfurcht vor dem leben*—also carries the sense of awe as well as of respect, an obviously emotional component that resonates with Schweitzer's account to provide a valuable example of emotional contexts and the framing of identity.

Schweitzer described how he had lived 'for months on end . . . in a continual state of mental excitement'. Even while carrying out his medical duties, he focused his thought on linking ethics and world- and life-affirmation: images of impenetrable thickets and unmovable iron doors reflected his emotional state; he directly speaks of being 'already exhausted and disheartened'. Then, when taking a long journey up the Ogowe river to visit a sick patient, he sat covering 'sheet after sheet . . . with disconnected sentences'. And then, at that sunset moment among the hippopotami 'there flashed upon my mind, unforeseen and unsought, the phrase "Reverence for Life"'. Now he speaks of the thicket opening into a path and the iron door yielding. For Schweitzer this was, above all, an intellectual venture, albeit one he deeply desired amid the emotional commitment of his life's work in Africa: he needed an ethics 'founded in thought'. His exploration of this theme is extremely valuable for this study, for he wants to get beneath the phrase itself to its more fundamental dynamics, which is, at the same time, both philosophically stated and yet an account of emotional elements. His excavation of the 'reverence for life' motif took him to its logical foundations in much the same way as the seventeenth-century René Descartes had sought some idea that could stand against any further doubt, finding it in his famous statement 'cogito ergo sum', 'I think therefore I am'. Interestingly, Schweitzer described Descartes's formula not only as an 'empty, artificial act of thinking', but also as 'the stupidest primary assumption in all philosophy'.[52] This damning judgement lies in Schweitzer's view that one simply cannot think without thinking *of* something, and for him 'the most immediate act of consciousness is the assertion: "I am life which wills to live, in the midst of life which wills to live".

---

51 Schweitzer ([1931] 1933: 186). By 1948 this book was already in its seventh impression.
52 Schweitzer ([1931] 1933: 186. [1936] 1962: 183, respectively).

At this very point emotions make their presence felt, as he describes 'an ardent desire' within the will-to-live to experience the 'mysterious exaltation' of 'pleasure', but fully aware that there is also a 'fear of destruction' inherent in life, a fear aligned with 'that mysterious depreciation of the will-to-live which we call pain'.[53] In Schweitzer this pain–pleasure complex of emotions has its centre of gravity in the will to live that drives a reverence for life. This leads him to describe life as ethical only when 'life, as such, is sacred to him' and when he experiences 'the feeling of responsibility in an ever-widening sphere for all that lives'. This brings him to a summary statement that 'the ethic of Reverence for Life, therefore, comprehends within itself everything that can be described as love, devotion, and sympathy whether in suffering, joy, or effort'.[54]

This particular social sense can easily be ignored when emotions are treated as feeling states of the individual, even though emotions such as fear frequently occur within a social environment. The 'feeling of responsibility', if understood as a felt experience, inescapably attests to the social nature of individuals. It affords a very good example of the bio-social nature of human identity as a complex interplay of an intellectual analysis of life and the world resulting in an attitude of commitment to both. Here Albert Schweitzer makes a radical contribution to the idea of intensive living, one generated by extensive life experience, not least, of the extreme suffering of those he encountered in his African medical centre. While different from Glaser and Strauss's account of intensive living as an existential response of those knowing themselves to be dying, it complements it; their intensive living and his will-to-live share an existential dynamism in an awareness of the value of life and of commitment to living it. They certainly do not exhaust the possibilities of methods of engagement, which can be seen to range from 'the Emersonian gesture of approaching the world through a kind of mourning for it',[55] through to Gadamer's view of 'real experience' as consisting in 'man' becoming 'aware of his finiteness', where 'genuine experience is experience of one's own historicity'.[56] Beyond these, again, lies the entire subject of solitude whether understood in terms of negative emotions of destructive loneliness or in terms of positive emotions allied with creativity.[57]

[53] Schweitzer ([1931] 1933: 186).   [54] Schweitzer ([1931] 1933: 188).

[55] Das (1997: 67), citing Cavell (1995).

[56] Gadamer ([1960] 1989: 357). Gadamer makes no reference to Schweitzer.

[57] Lake ([1980] 1983: 29): 'loneliness is an illness that attacks the ability of people to communicate'; and Storr ([1988] 1997: 88): discussion of 'aesthetic enjoyment' as the enjoyment of oneself in or through some other object.

Literary insights

Less philosophically, there are many other forms of insight generation or, simply, of gaining some personal understanding of life and our place in it. The influential literary figure George Bernard Shaw, for example, a contemporary of Schweitzer, spoke of his own disbelief in being told as a child that the family dog and parrot were not 'creatures like myself, but were brutal whilst I was reasonable'. Not only did he disbelieve it but 'intellectually formed the opinion that the distinction was false' and, when told later about Darwin's views, announced that he had 'found out all that' for himself when 'ten years old'. Shaw's similarity with Schweitzer lay in his identification of this 'sense of kinship of all forms of life', as not only 'a conceivable theory, but an inspiring one'.[58] Shaw's sense of inspiration and Schweitzer's reference to 'the feeling of responsibility' is particularly important for the study of emotions and religious identity, because it alludes to a sense of awareness of self in the world and in society and of an anticipation of social action. To sense an affinity is to gain a perspective that amounts to an ongoing motivational basis in life as part of a person's social identity and commitment to community life.

Sometimes a society needs a jolt to create an awareness of its own ways and to appreciate or change them. One literary example may suffice in Samuel Butler, who, a generation before Schweitzer and Shaw, published, in the same year as Darwin's *Emotions*, a kind of social-science fiction—*Erewhon*—whose prophetic sense advocated a balance between 'instinct' and 'reason'. It remains remarkable in the light of today's genetic discoveries, not least in wondering how the 'germ' material of living things can produce in one case a rose and in another an elephant.[59] He was interested in how humans related to natural evolution, on the one hand, and the rise of machines, on the other, and this involved the issue of consciousness and emotions. In terms of emotions, for example, he reckoned that the reason 'we find it difficult to sympathize with the emotions of potatoes and oysters is because they make no noise on being boiled or opened', and because humans link noise and pain.[60] This relates to his chapters on the rights of vegetables and of animals, all in relation to the difference between humans and machines in the light of the theory of evolution. Butler's satire was, in effect, a fictional anthropology,

---

[58] Shaw (1967: 111).   [59] Butler ([1872] 1939: 203).
[60] Butler ([1872] 1939: 193).

describing *Erewhon* ('nowhere'), and its customs all expressing values that sharply contradicted those of his Victorian industrialized society. This contrast, and his prophetic accuracy, is nowhere clearer than over death, for in his imaginary society people created monuments of themselves while alive, and at death had their bodies cremated and ashes placed at any site of personal choice, when 'no one is permitted to refuse this hospitality to the dead', leading people to choose 'some garden or orchard which they have known and been fond of when they were young'. All this was twelve years before the first formal cremation in Britain and a century before ashes did sometimes come to be disposed of in this way. He then describes 'superstitious' people as believing 'that those whose ashes are scattered over any land become its jealous guardians from that time forward', and that 'they shall become identified with this or that locality where they have once been happy'.[61] In this he gets close to today's situation, in which some individuals do use emotional language to describe places where they would like their ashes to be placed or in relation to the innovatory practice of woodland or ecological burial.

Philosophical insights

Though many will find such literary excursions valuable for stimulating insight on life and death, some others gain a great deal from a more technically philosophical approach, as, for example, in Ernst Bloch. One valuable direction of his work takes us back to the notion of 'otherness', and to seeing how its intimate embeddedness within a contemporary quality of experience may reshape our sense of identity. This comes from his discussion of how people orient themselves to thoughts of death, something he approaches through the rather difficult expressions of 'the Now which is this That', and of 'the Novum'.[62] After sketching the afterlife schemes of the world religions, Bloch approaches death by means of the 'utopian aura in man', itself a kind of 'joy and astonishment', a 'revelation of gained life-content, core content'. Such an awareness involves an 'astonishing turn-about' that avoids the general gloom of death and is due to an encounter with 'self-intensification' and 'self-realization'.[63] More correctly we ought to speak of this as a possibility of something that 'would involve' such an

---

[61] Butler ([1872] 1939: 112–13).
[62] Ernst Bloch ([1959] 1986: 1178–82); *novum*, from Latin for 'new'.
[63] Ernst Bloch ([1959] 1986: 1180).

awareness, because Bloch's philosophical conviction, grounded in his attitude to history, to social development, and to human desires for utopias, always points to a future condition and not to the present. But it is possible to take a different and existential approach to argue its possibility within some individual lives, as in Schweitzer's case, that 'wherever existing comes near to its core, permanence begins, not petrified but containing Novum without transitoriness, without corruptibility'.[64] Bloch writes in his secular existentialism in a way reminiscent of theological writing about the last things: for the *eschaton* is awaited, whether by a social revolution conducing to insight of life as it is, or by a divine disclosure of ultimacy. From this we could see the significance of otherness as stimulating an intensification of life through an appropriate sense of death's transformation of others into corpses. That transformation involves an unusual reconfiguration of reciprocal relationships, of meaning, and of hope in a reappraisal of identity. I have discussed elsewhere the human animal's self-conscious awareness needed to adapt to the fact of death, interpreting funeral rites across the world as 'words against death', a response that does not leave death as an unexplained destruction of identity.[65]

Charisma

One of the primary ways by which such an outlook of hope arises and a vitality-driven 'intensification of life' achieved is through reciprocal relations with powerful leaders possessed of a magnetic personality that attracts and inspires a following. Here the notions of charisma and emotion are directly linked. Though this idea is often associated with the sociologist Max Weber, it is also possible to find religious devotees identifying this powerful leadership characteristic within their own groups.[66] One nineteenth-century Mormon, John Hyde, for example, provides an early, non-sociological, account of what would later be identified as 'charisma' when describing how a great leader is able completely to 'centre in oneself a thousand interests and the deep affections of a thousand hearts' coupled with 'a magnetism that attracts and infatuates, that makes men feel its weight and yet love its presence'.[67] A similar description of William Clowes, born in

---

[64] Ernst Bloch ([1959] 1986: 1182). [65] Douglas J. Davies (1997a: 1–8).
[66] Weber ([1922] 1965). [67] Hyde (1857: 154, 170).

1780 and an influential early leader in the Primitive Methodist movement in England, portrays one who was

a magnificent animal, splendidly proportioned, harmoniously developed, of muscle and sinew, force and fire all compact. To all this were added the attributes of an impressive personality—a massive brow, bold piercing eyes, and a voice of great compassion and sweetness, and a marvellous gift of personal magnetism.[68]

The sense of confidence and excitement that such a charismatic leader may engender is especially powerful in groups where large-scale meetings are possible and where the individual leader may not be openly accessible to all. But it is not simply within religious contexts or even in groups that this personal impact is felt. Indeed, it also has its effect in personal interactions, where it can sow the seeds of a much wider social reputation. Artist Pablo Picasso, for example, was described by the Catalan writer and poet Jaume Sabartés as one who confused him 'with his fixed stare'. He describes leaving Picasso's studio thus: 'I stepped in front of him to say goodbye, I was ready to bow, stunned by the magical power that emanated from his whole being, the marvellous power of a magus, offering gifts so rich in surprises and hope.'[69] Almost as a hallmark of these first-hand accounts is the reference to the eyes, which obviously help direct the interaction and sense of authority between individuals, as the leader and led forge a relationship. Indeed, the idiom of 'staring' or 'bulging' eyes has widespread currency in popular images of 'cult-like' religious leaders. Tellingly, Charles Darwin often focused on the nature of eyes and of how they appeared to others in his study of emotions.[70] Alan Bryman, who has listed numerous other cases where the eyes of leaders have been pinpointed as influential forces on followers, also includes discussions of other factors such as 'oratory . . . energy, confidence and endurance', as well as 'a special ability to feel intuitively what people want'. Nevertheless, his ultimate preference is not for 'something that resides in the individual leader' but for a 'particular kind of social relationship between leaders and their followers' that entails 'reciprocal interdependence'.[71] Bryman's account is interesting, for, while his method is clearly sociological and largely avoids psychological theories, his attention still focuses on matters of power and hope that inevitably entail emotion. The charismatic leader offers promise of

---

[68] Ritson (1909: 37).   [69] Huffington (1988: 44).
[70] Darwin ([1872] 1998: 38, 221, 278–9, 319–21).
[71] Bryman (1992: 44, 47, 50, 51).

aligning his followers with some kind of power promising a hope for a better future, most especially at times of crisis and distress.

Ultimately, charisma needs both sociological and psychological consideration precisely because it draws from the deep social vein of trust. Against that dual background it becomes obvious that, while charisma may become an end in itself if a person deploys it to develop self-status, it is frequently part of a process by which some ultimate theological or political message is conveyed as a new direction of trust for the future. In its complexity, charisma is an embodiment of a sense of power that validates a message felt as welcomed news to the follower, and, as such, the charismatic leader may serve well as a means of relating people to the forces they conceive of supernatural agents of ancestors, spirits, and gods. Those agents are believed to be able to protect the living, and their capacity to do so is reinforced by the dynamic nature of the charismatic leader. This desire for protective safety at times of crisis or, indeed, in the wider uncertainties of life fosters the view, typically expressed by Sigmund Freud, that God is a projection of a human wish to be protected by a father-figure not subject to all the failings and the ultimate failure through death of every human father.[72] A Heavenly Father, by contrast, will never fail the weak human being. Such beliefs, and the attitude of faith that sustains them, raise issues beyond present concerns, especially the question of whether 'faith' involves some kind of emotion, compound of emotions, or some ongoing mood.[73] This is a difficult issue, which has not been addressed in this study because of the complexity presented by each religious tradition. Robert Solomon, for example, in his advocacy of a 'naturalistic spirituality' as a 'passionate life' embedded in 'love, reverence and trust', decided to leave 'faith' aside because of its ambiguous nature within theology—viewed sometimes as a 'species of rationality', as in Kant, and sometimes as one of 'irrationality', as in Kierkegaard—and because it is 'too exclusively wedded to a small number of religious traditions'. If pressed, however, he thought of 'faith' as 'a kind of reverence and a variety of trust (as well as a variant of love)'. His preferred description of the passions of a naturalistic spirituality lay in 'reverence, trust, and love': these 'are the very essence of spirituality'.[74]

[72] Freud ([1927] 1973).
[73] Cf. Needham (1972) for discussion of whether 'belief' involves special 'feelings'.
[74] Solomon (2002: 29).

THEOLOGICAL DEPENDENCE ON OTHERNESS

We will touch again on 'faith definition' in our concluding chapter, but our immediate concern remains with the idea of desired security, which returns us to our earlier theme of otherness as a focus for dependence, not in the psychological terms of Freud but in the philosophical theology of F. D. E. Schleiermacher (1768–1832).[75] His piety-infused upbringing among the Moravians along with his own life experiences of bereavement and loss of love conduce to that 'sense of absolute dependence' for which his work is often discussed. Though it is hard not to treat Schleiermacher's thought without considering the numerous philosophical, theological, and devotional influences upon him, we limit our portrayal to key features that have a bearing upon this study's motifs of otherness and reciprocity underlying social and religious identity. His much-debated 'feeling of dependence' is accounted for as an expression of 'the double constitution of self-conscious-ness', or of the 'two-fold consciousness within us'. Here, self-consciousness comprises 'two elements', one that is 'self-caused' and one that is 'non-self-caused'.[76] He characterizes the two elements as those of 'receptivity' and 'activity', with the latter being spontaneous in nature: he speaks of their relationship in terms of 'the Reciprocity between the subject and the corre-sponding Other'. Schleiermacher's particular theological emphasis upon the topic of 'feeling' in his interpretation of faith acknowledged that 'the capacity of people for emotion is very various' and changes at different times.[77] Many other theologians and spiritual writers of earlier epochs of Christianity have, inevit-ably, also dealt with emotional themes, always influenced by the devotional emotion of their church communities. Notable among these is, for example, the fourth-century monk, ascetic, and teacher Evagrius Ponticus, whose psycho-logical-like accounts of the spiritual life include notions such as *apatheia,* describing spiritual awareness and development in mastering human passions.

Another influential figure was the German Thomas à Kempis, whose *Imitation of Christ* of the later fifteenth century offers one prime example of the Christian spirituality of devotion to Christ as one sensed and known in

---

[75] See, e.g., Sykes (1971) and Mariña (2008: 457–73) for, respectively, a short introduction and an application to emotions.

[76] Schleiermacher ([1821–2] 1928: 12–14): *Sichselbstsetzen* and *Sichselbstnichtsogesestzthaben.*

[77] Schleiermacher (1830: 487).

and through this earthly life. Thomas can speak 'of familiar friendship with Jesus' in terms of Jesus being present and of speaking 'inwardly to us'. He speaks of 'the grace' that surrounds moments of blissful feeling, 'that good and sweet affection which thou sometimes feelest is the effect of grace', when a person is 'suddenly rapt on high'.[78] He is, however, all too aware that such moments of perceived closeness and intimacy pass rapidly, leaving devotees back in a worldly frame of mind. A great deal of Thomas's self-reflection takes the form of an inner conversation with Christ, and in this he resembles St Augustine of the late fourth and early fifth centuries, whose *Confessions* typify this style of talking with God. Dependence and security come to be grounded in this inner sense of divine presence. Though not using the same type of language of devotional love, Schleiermacher is also party to a relationship of dependence standing as its own theological scheme of human relationship to the world and to its ultimate source in God. To compare Schleiermacher and Durkheim is, then, to highlight a dramatically different explanation of otherness, and to underline the complexity facing anyone wishing to cope with the diversity of human thought on its own nature and place in the world.

SUMMARY

This chapter has, then, brought together a variety of views on negative and positive dimensions of emotions typified by the notions of identity depletion and intensive living and has related these dimensions to the ideas of vitality and *anomie*, especially in the field of grief. More than this, we have extended this account of the dynamics of identity, vitality, and *anomie* to embrace the concept of charisma. Though it may have seemed odd to include a discussion of charisma within a chapter focused on grief, this was quite intentional, to allow us to see how a sense of vitality can be perceived in certain persons who are responded to in such a way that they become religious leaders. And, in sensing that vitality, especially in problematic contexts and times of confusion or social *anomie*, devotees discover through their faith a sense of intensive living and a new purpose in their sense of identity. Indeed, this alliance of charismatic leadership with intensive living has allowed us to make a further contribution to the idea of identity depletion and its transformation,

---

[78] Thomas à Kempis (n.d.: 118).

previously discussed in Chapter 3. It will also be of real value when we come to discuss issues of conversion and spirit power in Chapter 9.

Throughout this chapter's account of the complexity of emotions, their media of expression, and their management, much has been said about 'people' or 'humanity' in general, as is frequently done in many studies of emotion. But this ignores one major factor, that of sex differences between men and women. With that in mind, the time has now come to focus more directly on sexual distinctions, given that they lie at the heart of all social life and are of inestimable influence on individuals and their life course. Most certainly, the parts played by men and women, and the cultural perceptions of differences between these sexes, have deeply influenced the rise and development of religious traditions and the way they, in turn, have portrayed and managed human emotions within the framework of personal identity. The distinction is also important as far as attitudes towards death are concerned, at least within a British context, and these we will carry forward into the next chapter.

5

Gender, Identity, and Purity

As indicated in the previous chapter, when it comes to the interplay of identity, emotions, and religion, the issue of gender stands above others as far as the practical outworking of those concepts is concerned. This we now explore in some detail, since sex differences often affect a man's or a woman's capacity to engage in religious behaviour or hold religious office, with formal priesthoods almost always being restricted to men in traditional societies. Such differences have also been of major importance for the way particular societies have described their repertoire of emotions and managed those feelings among men and women. And, although in the previous and in succeeding chapters we speak rather generally of emotions in terms of 'people' at large, it is important in this chapter to highlight the fact that societies and religious traditions often classify and manage emotions along male–female lines and with firm expectations of their mutual relationships. We will, as an example, consider how male–female differences are expressed in attitudes towards death and afterlife in the empirical context of Great Britain at the beginning of the twenty-first century.

The male–female distinction is, perhaps, to be expected, given that the physical differences that become increasingly apparent as infants develop into older boys and girls and then into men and women offer an immediate basis for organizing symbolic ideas and for associating particular kinds of emotion with each sex. The division of labour, and all that is associated with that in the allocation and use of power in the practical domains of economic, domestic, and kinship life, has also been largely influenced by male–female status differences. Indeed, this factor of power, its possession and mode of use, has been of major importance in the developed societies of the second half of the twentieth century and the beginning of the twenty-first century, as issues of gender equality have become of central ethical concern. Since religions have usually regarded themselves as the guardians of ethical codes and, in practice though not necessarily self-consciously, have also validated and often managed the emotional preferences of male–female living, it is vital to devote a chapter to this area of human life. Also, in terms of the history of religions, it is also important to gain some sense of the way the deities and the realm of the other have often not been left untouched by this divide, as male and female deities or ancestors take their place in heavenly or afterlife worlds.[1] In symbolic terms, it is also worth thinking about the nature of the persons set aside to serve those deities.

SEXUAL PREFERENCE

In strictly human terms, gender identity has often affected the early survival of infants, with boy babies often being valued more than girls, with some traditional societies practising female and male infanticide for a variety of reasons from the availability of food to an active preference for males as hunters.[2] Similarly, many leadership roles, including priesthood, have also been reserved for men and sanctioned by religious authorities within world religions. Such preferences have been a major factor in the self-conscious action of numerous modern societies to establish equality of opportunity, occupation, and legal inheritance from the later twentieth century. Social change often influences the status and opportunities of men and women, as became evident in the later twentieth century over the question of the ordination of women to the priesthood within the Lutheran and Anglican traditions, and of the firm resistance to the idea within Catholic and Ortho-dox domains. Similar issues have occurred over the status of being a rabbi within different traditions of Judaism, while Islam has also had some voices raised over the possibility of women playing a larger public role in religious worship than has traditionally been the case. Religious activities, then, pre-sent a significant factor in ritualizing the identity of devotees, in managing their associated emotions and moods, and in creating strong attitudes to-wards prime social values and their symbolic expression in ritual: and these are the concerns of this chapter.

---

[1] Cf. Mestrovic (1992: 28) for a creative sociological analysis of feminine and masculine voices in the narratives spun from and counter to the Enlightenment, especially in Durkheim.

[2] Reynolds and Tanner ([1983] 1995: 79–97).

Sex, religious status, and performance

Few topics were more hotly and apologetically disputed in the closing decades of the twentieth century in Western societies than that of sex in relation to religion and identity. Sexual politics, the use of male and female identity as a basis for arguing issues of status, power, and significance, became widespread as part of the social concern with civil and human rights and included questions of emotional similarities and differences. These debates reflect the widespread fact that most religious ideologies, and the cultural bases with which they are almost always embedded, make their own clear classifications of the differences between male and female, often having some sense of these as divinely sanctioned. Such traditional schemes have their own way of ongoing maintenance and avoidance of change. One of the best known of these scenarios, one that drives church organization in more Catholic forms of Christianity, argues that Jesus was a man and chose men for his inner circle of disciples, who, in turn, became the first apostles of the new religion and the core of the Christian priesthood. These topics are all questionable in historical-critical terms, as feminist and other forms of theology have shown. The fact that the rite of the Mass is celebrated with a male priest symbolizing Christ offered another kind of argument against the ordination of women, and to this we will return to consider what other, less obvious and perhaps less self-conscious, factors may also be at work in maintaining this position. But, first, we remain with the fact that many myths of origin of human identity dwell on the obvious fact that human beings exist as male and female and the equally persistent theme of how the male–female relationship operates to create some form of mutuality or unity.

Sex, myth, and leadership

The Hebrew creation myths of Genesis, later also adopted by Christians, offer two accounts of creation. The first describes God creating man 'in his own image' as 'male and female'—an account that, if taken literally, would indicate that God was 'male and female'.[3] The identity of the created pair is closely aligned with the creativity of God, and they are given the command- ment to be fruitful and to multiply on the earth. The second myth describes

---

[3] Genesis 1: 27.

God as making a man from the moist earth and breathing into him the breath of life. When this Adam, or earth-born, figure is already set up as a gardener in a fruitful paradise, God states that it is not good for man to be alone and causes a deep sleep to overcome Adam, during which God takes one of Adam's ribs and makes from it Eve, the first woman. The rationale of this myth seems to be that a man and a woman should be bound together and leave their parental homes so to do.[4] If read together, these myths can be taken to speak of gender differences as the basis for creative mastery of the world garden and for mutual support within it. Other ways of reading them are also possible. Some have seen a strong male bias or androcentric attitude in them. Erin White, for example, takes Paul Ricœur's well-known approach to the Genesis stories as setting up Adam as both sinner in relation to God and victim in relation to Eve and, thereby providing a 'flattering view of Adam' as capable of both freedom and innocence.[5] White sees the original myth as androcentric, with Ricoeur reinforcing that primary outlook. By sharp contrast, the approach taken to these myths in Mormonism, for example, which could be defined as theologically androcentric, neither makes Adam a sinner in any ultimately devastating sense nor does it make him a victim of Eve. Following the Christian idea of the Fall as an ultimately fortunate event, Mormons speak of Adam's 'fall' as the beginning of the process of humanity's progression into joy.

Many other Christian traditions took these myths as the basis for parts of their doctrine and as justification for male priority over the female in religious leadership.[6] To generalize, it seems that, in priesthood hierarchies involving public ritual performance, it is the male who is accorded primacy, while, within domestic rites, women also often have ritual duties. In Catholic Christianity, the male priesthood also came to adhere to celibacy, partly as a means of ensuring that church property could be retained within a central institution and not be inherited by children. But this essentially male core of church organization also developed a particular devotion to Mary, the mother of Jesus, that found no place within Protestantism, where marriage became normative for all, including church leaders. In both Catholic and Orthodox forms of Christian spirituality Mary is accorded a distinctive status, with Catholic dogma extending not only to the widespread belief in her virginity at the time of Jesus's birth, his conception being due to the influence of the Holy Spirit and not Joseph, her human partner, but also to

---

[4] Genesis 2: 18, 21–5.   [5] White (1995: 80).   [6] 1 Corinthians 11: 3–12.

the idea, known as the Immaculate Conception, that she was kept free from the effect of the contagion of the original sin that affected all other humans, even from her conception. This was formally stated as Catholic doctrine by Pope Pius IX in 1854. One consequence of this doctrine, as of attitudes and practices preceding its formal statement, was the convention that special devotion could be paid to her on a level higher than that to the saints at large but less than that to God.[7] The presence of statues and icons of Mary has played a significant part in people's devotion, echoing her underlying role as Jesus's mother. While Western, Catholic, Christianity came to speak of Mary as the 'Mother of God', Eastern Orthodoxy spoke of her as *Theotokos*, the one who bore or gave birth to God. These images have been able to support a wide range of emotions and ongoing moods of devotion among the faithful, often related to the cultural experience of natural parents or at least of their idealized images. For many women, especially mothers, the figure of a young woman called by God to a special task and to the pain and suffering of caring for a son who would, himself, suffer and be killed, is obvious but none the less potent. In Luke's Gospel, shortly after Jesus's birth, when he was blessed by an elderly and devout Jew, Simeon, Mary was told that a sword would one day pierce her heart because of what would befall her son.[8] The whole account of her life, framing his life, death, and resurrection, has given to millions, especially but not only to women, an affinity of suffering and care. Hirschon described how traditional Greek Orthodox women 'feel the immediate bond of a shared experience with the *Panayia* (All Holy One), as she is often called, and in the everyday difficulties of life they most often appeal to her. The attributes of ideal womanhood, self-sacrifice, love and devotion to the family are patterned on this archetypal figure.'[9] From a slightly different perspective, an additional doctrine, that of the Assumption of the Blessed Virgin Mary, reinforced this spiritual liaison with Mary in an otherness of profound consequence. Though formally promulgated by Rome only in 1950, this doctrine, with its roots in the fourth to sixth centuries, described her as being taken into heaven when she died. The effect of this view was that Mary was someone with whom one's prayers were not fruitless and whose sympathy, as of a mother, was readily available.

As already intimated, in symbolic terms, Mary is often regarded as a kind of second Eve in an analogous way to Jesus being the 'second Adam'. Just as

---

[7] *Dulia* to saints, *hyperdulia* to the Blessed Virgin Mary, and *latria* to God (Cross 1997: 513).
[8] Luke 2: 35.   [9] Hirschon (1978: 68).

he is the sinless and obedient one who reversed the sinful disobedience of Adam, so Mary, his mother, incarnates the obedience to the divine will. In this way they furnish a theological core for hope in a world of sinful despair. The image of Mary has, itself, been periodically intensified by reports of her appearing to faithful believers, as to Bernadette Soubirous at Lourdes in 1858, since when many have made pilgrimages to the grotto and chapels built around it as a place, as some believe, of miraculous healing. This context exemplifies the attitude of hope that is grounded in traditions of faith and extends to physical healings as well as to inner spiritual consolation and the strengthening of faith. Many other parts of the Catholic world have their own version of Marian appearance and devotion.

Protestant groups have seldom favoured such attitudes to Mary, largely as part of their protest against Catholicism, but this has not prevented various attempts at wishing to establish a female aspect of deity. Within Mormonism, for example, there has long been a popular sense of there being a 'mother in heaven' as partner to the heavenly father, who is, himself, endued with a physical body and the attributes of sexuality. Eliza Snow, one of the plural wives of the founding Mormon prophet, Joseph Smith, wrote a much-loved hymn that pursued this theme and in which she asks, 'In the heavens are parents single?', and affirmatively replies: 'No, the thought makes reason stare! Truth is reason, truth eternal, Tells me I've a mother there.'[10] This mother–God motif complements both the Mormon emphasis on family ideals and also its sense that physical bodies, albeit glorified ones, exist in heaven. This sexual complementarity in heaven validates and reinforces the Mormon ideal of a strong division of religious identity on earth.

From quite a different Protestant quarter emerged Lois Roden, who rose to a leadership position within the Branch Davidian apocalyptic sect of the Seventh Day Adventist tradition, which had previously been led by her husband Ben and which would become infamous under the subsequent leadership of David Koresh. He was instrumental in the devastating conflict in 1993 between this group and American Federal Authorities after its move to Waco, Texas, where many died. Lois emerged as a strong leader in the 1980s and claimed to have seen a vision of what first appeared to be a 'silver angel' but which she came to realize was 'not actually an angel at all, but a representation of God the Holy Spirit. The message she had been give . . . was that the Holy Spirit was female.'[11] It was an idea that, apparently and

---

[10] Douglas J. Davies (2000: 148–9).   [11] Newport (2006: 158).

understandably, caused about a half of that group's current membership to leave. In a play on the English spelling of the Hebrew word *shekinah* used as an indirect reference to the divine dwelling or presence, she began publishing a magazine that emphasized the first three letters, to highlight 'she'. The femininity of the Holy Spirit was a key feature of its purpose, and her reading of the Genesis account that God created humanity in his own image but as 'male and female' was a sure basis for knowing that there was a feminine basis in God. Moreover, since Eve was made from Adam's rib, while he was made simply from dust, Eve was a superior creature.[12] It seems that Lois Roden had a strong feminist drive in her theological innovation that was associated with her self-identity as an emergent female prophet in a traditional male-focused group.

In many mainstream Protestant groups, as also in Reform Judaism, there has been an influential interpretation of biblical texts set within their past and present cultural contexts in such a way as to validate and encourage women in leadership roles hitherto restricted to men. The acceptance of the ordination of women within some of the Protestant Free Churches and in the Lutheran and Anglican traditions in the closing decades of the twentieth century and the early years of the twenty-first has brought with it major changes, but often not without rearguard action by some who object to women taking on such management of religious groups. In these debates religion shows its strong conservative dynamics and its commitment to a division of identity and labour over sexuality and its expression in social gender: to invoke the divine will in revelation or tradition is to furnish powerful validation of the status quo. But, more than that, long-standing academic traditions of theology have also tended to assume a male perspective, even when the perspective is assumed to be simply 'academic'. The complex way in which early Christian thought was influenced by its own cultural day to produce a genre that then assumed a normative nature for the succeeding two millennia is difficult to unravel.[13]

BIO-CULTURAL SEX

The threefold theme of emotion, identity, and religion is seldom more powerfully encountered than in the biological fact that women are mothers

[12] Newport (2006: 162–3). [13] Børresen (1995: 245–55).

and that procreation involves them in deep emotional dynamics. No less intimately involved in motherhood are the dual topics of meaning and hope, on the one hand, and otherness and reciprocity, on the other. In other words, the seven topics that undergird this study take firm shape in the issue of motherhood. Every culture and historical period frames these issues after their own fashion. Hank Glassman's study of medieval Japanese ideas of pregnancy, neonatal death, and the role of ghosts of mothers and of dead babies, turns around his hypothesis that, in 'medieval Japanese Buddhism, the salvation of women increasingly came to be understood as the salvation of mothers'.[14]

The ambiguous power of holy women is, in symbolic terms, very complex and draws from identities grounded in virginity, motherhood, and the devoted wife as well as from a kind of reversal of their potential as sources of ritual impurity. Menstruation, for example, is widely circumscribed in many traditional societies as a period when women ought not to engage in ritual activity, in formal gatherings for worship or, more domestically, even in cooking.[15] The rationale for this is also complex but cannot be separated from the fact that menstrual blood is, essentially, the negative outcome whose positive pathway is that of birth and social reproduction. Women stand at the core of society's survival, and their reproductive capacity is much guarded in traditional societies and where issues of kinship alliance and the preservation of property are concerned. Religious rules or conventional practices frequently frame this creative capacity, which lies at the heart of a society's reciprocal relationships.[16] But the expression of these issues varies from society to society, as their dominant ideology deploys them to good effect.

One study of a traditional Turkish Islamic context, for example, tells how menstruation came to women 'because of Hawa's (Eve's) act of disobedience against Allah' in paradise: along with it came other forms of 'dirtiness', including excrement. Moreover, as Carol Delaney argues, both menstrual blood and semen are in this cultural context 'powerful and potentially polluting substances'.[17] 'Menstruation condenses the conceptual cluster having to do with corporeality, time, and decay—unlike seed, which carries meanings of creativity, spirituality, and the eternal.'[18] She provides a symbolic

---

[14] Glassman (2008: 175).   [15] Buckley and Gottlieb (1988).
[16] Lévi-Strauss (1949) argued that 'exchange' of women constituted society's core activity.
[17] Delaney (1988: 80).   [18] Delaney (1988: 88).

analysis of the way girls and boys are largely free agents until the time they approach puberty, when the girls now have their hair covered and the boys are circumcised to uncover their penis, an operation that demonstrates their courage and focuses upon the penis as, itself, a sign of manly identity. But she also argues that this prevents semen from being held under a foreskin, a substance deemed strongly impure, just as menstrual blood is impure. Men must also conduct a rite of ritual cleansing if they have a nocturnal emission of semen. Sexual intercourse also requires such an act, but it is thought to leave the woman with an ongoing defilement more enduring than that of the man. Sex is forbidden during menstruation, in accord with the Quranic injunction that menstruation is an illness and that women should be left alone at such times.[19] Delaney explores the theological basis of identity in terms of the belief that, because Eve was taken from Adam's rib, men have the power of procreation, and this is evident when they impregnate a woman, whose womb is the medium for the growth of his seed. In this, 'procreation teaches the lesson of Creation' and involves the notion that 'women are subordinate to and dependent upon men, implying that they should be *muslim*, or obedient, to the will of their husbands as the world is to Allah'. 'Men give life, women give birth.'[20]

It is just such symbolic complexity that underlies theological interpretations of human identity in its male–female division and affects many other realms of life, including behaviour at places of worship, as we will see in Chapter 10. Anticipating that, it is important to highlight the division between the sexes that has played an extensive role in religious life and identity, often with a clear overlap between the way men and women are classified in ordinary social life being carried over into religious worship. Corrigan's analysis of some nineteenth-century American religion, for example, argued that the very practice of vocal prayer carried a sense that prayer was 'manly in its boldness and womanly in its trust that emotion was fundamental to prayer'.[21] Then, in traditional Jewish and Islamic worship, we have men separated from women, with an insistence on male leadership in many religious roles. Though Sikhism gave a high place to its womenfolk, there remains a tradition of men and women sitting apart in *Gurdwara* devotions. As with ancient Judaism, the Roman Catholic and Orthodox Churches have insisted on restricting their priesthoods to male occupants,

---

[19] Delaney (1988: 83), quoting Qur'an 2: 222.   [20] Delaney (1988: 86).
[21] Corrigan (2002: 207).

even though, at an apparently higher level of religious value, the status of a saint is accorded to appropriate Christian women.

However, behind all such specific roles and statuses in any tradition, we should never ignore ordinary individuals and their sexuality within a tradition's attempted management of emotion and identity. Within an extensive study of young adults in the USA, for example, Christian Smith has argued that attitudes towards sexual activity before marriage plays an important part in the impact of 'cognitive-emotional dissonance' upon a person's religious identity and degree of commitment towards religious institutions. Where a tradition advocates sexual abstinence before marriage and where individuals decide to be abstinent, then they experience less dissonance and are likely to be reinforced in their religious identity. By contrast, a certain 'discomfort' and 'move away from religion' tends to accompany those who become sexually active at that youthful life stage.[22]

GENDER AND RITUAL

While a great deal of formal management of such emotions and behaviour has been traditionally conducted by men in most of the established world religions, it is noteworthy that this began to change from the later twentieth century, in both Jewish and Christian groups. The call for the ordination of women within Anglicanism, for example, came about, albeit with a degree of resentment from Catholic and Orthodox traditions, in which a male hierarchy occupies a dogmatic position. One of the wider social realms of ritual and religion in which women have come to play an increasingly significant role is that of funeral directing. While women had often washed and dressed the dead, in many cultures it often fell to the men to bury or cremate the prepared corpses. The later twentieth century witnessed the beginning of change here in some societies, as female funeral directors entered the male scene, to the degree that in Australia, for example, some 'all-women funeral firms' were created, which seem to have an appeal to 'older women' as they plan funeral rites.[23] The White Ladies company in Australia, for example, developed a niche-market identity with their all-female service, including collecting and preparing bodies, meeting bereaved families, carrying coffins,

[22] Smith with Snell (2009: 240).
[23] Liveris (1999: 255).

and doing all that male funeral directors would have done in the past. In clear symbolic expression of the shift, they wore white clothes with red hats, gloves, and shoes instead of the traditional male black or grey.

In Sydney there was some evidence that this White Ladies programme, which was, initially, thought to be especially relevant when dealing with the deaths of babies, also came to have an appeal to some gay members of society.[24] It is especially interesting that some homosexual men would choose a service delivered entirely by women, itself a potential protest against Australian machismo values. This very theme of homo- and heterosexuality has caused a considerable degree of tension within several mainstream religious groups and pinpoints crucial issues over identity and emotion for some.[25] Within an American context, where issues of sexual identity are set between the compelling dynamics of conservative Christian traditions, on the one hand, and civil rights, on the other, one Protestant minister who had left her congregation, divorced, and adopted identity as a lesbian could speak of being 'rich with loss ... inseparably intertwined with a nascent freedom and joy'. In her struggle 'to find patterns of language and genre' that might cope with her transforming identity, she exemplifies just how forms of experience can, themselves, shift under radically changing circumstances. Finding no easy categories by which to label such experiences, this minister adopts the form of a poem that, reflexively, says: 'To come to voice this way is to risk death.'[26]

As already intimated, one reason for the traditionally sharp male–female divide that underlies the need for that poem probably lies in sexuality, not least allied with menstruation. Many societies have circumscribed the activities of women while they are menstruating, sometimes restricting their cooking activities, for example. Ideas of ritual impurity are often used to explain this attitude and merit some consideration, because this is far from a simple idea. Nevertheless, perhaps the simplest way of thinking about ritual purity is to combine the idea of a person being fully competent for engaging in ordinary social life with the idea of core social values and their protection. We argued in Chapter 2 that ritual purity is one way of thinking about behaviour related to core social values or to the persons, objects, and places embodying or enshrining them. One of the most important of all social values is the reproduction of the population, and here a woman's capacity to

---

[24] Information from 'White Ladies', personal communication.
[25] See Cline (1995: 308–11) on problems for bereaved lesbian women.
[26] Hutchins (2002: 231, 244).

bear children is of the greatest importance. Menstruation is, in one obvious way, the prime symbol of female maturity and capacity to reproduce, but, as with many symbols, a strong positive meaning also often carries with it the potential for a strong negative element. The more something is prized, the more care is needed in relation to it. In this connection, blood frequently carries a powerful force, as is also evident in some male rites of initiation, where scarification or circumcision are involved.[27]

CIRCUMCISION

One key rite that cannot be ignored in terms of embodiment, identity, and gender is that of circumcision. Best and longest documented is the case of Judaism, in which male circumcision is interpreted theologically as a sign of covenant between the people of Israel and their God, and is conducted on a baby's eighth day. One perspective on this Jewish practice argues that it is a survival or transformation of a pre-existing custom of child sacrifice in Israel.[28] In directly scriptural terms, however, the rite is reckoned to have been instituted as a divine command to the 90-year-old Abram, who was childless by his wife, Sarai, now post-menopausal, but who had already fathered Ishmael by his wife's servant Hagar.[29] God's promise that Sarai would bear children and that these would become a large nation causes both husband and wife to laugh in disbelief.[30] In due course Isaac was born to them and, in turn, was circumcised on his eighth day.[31] Numerous other societies also practise circumcision, but not all remove the entire foreskin; often only a portion is removed. Some fundamentalist Christians in the USA also adhere to circumcision for its biblical overtones. The interesting feature of the situation in the USA is that male circumcision became normative well beyond Jewish populations, with approximately a third circumcised in the USA by 1910, moving to a rate peaking 'at around 1980 at about 85 percent or possibly higher; by 1990 it had declined to about 60 percent'.[32] Reasons for this development from the later nineteenth century were largely medical

---

[27] Glick (2005).
[28] Levenson (1993).
[29] Genesis 16: 1–16; 17: 1–27.
[30] Genesis 17: 17; 18: 12, respectively.
[31] Genesis 21: 4.
[32] Glick (2005: 178, 213–14).

and emphasized cleanliness, avoidance of disease, or the control of masturbation; it was made easier when many births occurred in hospital. In Great Britain, it seems that upper- and some middle-class children in the nineteenth century were circumcised on the understanding that if they went to administer their Empire in hot climates their new status would be more healthy. Few of these non-religious reasons are sustainable today, when there is a considerable move to avoid the practice under recognition both of the importance of foreskin for sexual pleasure and of the pain experienced by small babies as opposed to the traditional wisdom that ignored the actual pain responses of babies at circumcision without anaesthetic, arguing that they felt little or no pain during circumcision. At quite a different level, much more could be said of discussions surrounding circumcision in relation to fears of castration, as developed quite extensively within Sigmund Freud's mythical-psychological reflections of the Oedipus Complex, but this would take us too far afield.[33]

Interestingly, it is in the strong sacramental system of Catholic Christianity, whose prime symbols lie in the bread and wine that become the symbolic body and blood of Christ through the ritual of the Mass, that the activity of women in the place of worship has been most extensively controlled. Indeed, until 1992 women were not allowed into the sacred space of the sanctuary that surrounded the altar. Reasons for this are complex and take us from theological–rational arguments into the more complex domains of emotional attitudes and sensitivities, always remembering that Catholic priests are celibate males.[34] The idea of a menstruating woman being able to celebrate the Mass would, as likely as not, introduce a series of competing symbolic idioms that are not prompted by a male priesthood. Both the woman's menstrual blood and Christ's symbolic blood in the sacramental language of the Mass are associated with the capacity for life-giving: one gives ordinary and the other eternal life. These very ideas would, for many, be forbidden territory as far as popular debate is concerned, yet they can hardly be ignored.

Gender, pagan modernity, and power

One domain in which menstrual blood has gained a symbolic position of some importance is that of modern Paganism. Susan Greenwood, for example, describes the importance of menstrual blood as 'the symbol of

---

[33] Freud ([1964] 1977: 117–21).
[34] Except for married priests from other traditions who are received into the Catholic priesthood.

femaleness par excellence' and cites references to and symbols of it and of menstruation in numerous contexts, not least as 'women's innate route to their shamanic deeper magical selves'. This turns what was 'for long the subject of taboo' into a 'powerful symbol of female magical identity', allowing women to reconnect with their innate power.[35]

Greenwood's work draws attention to the way 'feminist witchcraft ideology is grounded on the connection between politics and spirituality', especially 'as a form of resistance to mainstream patriarchal culture'.[36] The force of emotions and emotional expression is important throughout her study as a vehicle by which these women affirm themselves, seek to heal themselves of varied ills, and establish unity, with the life force of the earth denoted as Mother or as a feminine entity. The place of ritual symbolism is extremely significant, either when women perform private rites or, more especially, when they engage in collective action. One Halloween rite she describes as taking place in a derelict garden of a south London house set up the points of the compass and involved a sweat lodge, into the darkness of which the women crawled before 'huddling together "like piglets in the womb of the Mother"' to sweat out their 'anger and negativity' as they 'howled and screamed out' their feelings. They made 'babyish noises to symbolize (their) rebirth' as they crawled out and were 'hosed down with icy water before being dried by the heat of the fire'. Further rites followed that included pondering the year that was gone and what was desired for the self in the year that was to come. Each was then to shout her name, perhaps her 'magical name', before being admitted into the collective circle and hugged by the others.

Greenwood's study allows easy access to the complex theme of power in relation to gender and does so both implicitly and explicitly. There is the obvious theme of some women feeling relatively disenfranchised in an essentially male-driven society and now feeling able to take control of their own sense of identity. But there is also the sense of power deriving from magical resources of the self, the earth, or the cosmos at large. These powers merge and are symbolically manipulated in a great variety of ways. In the process a great deal of mystery is combined with esoteric knowledge. And it is not only women who may feel themselves empowered by these rites and the mythical world into which they enter and reform a sense of their identity. She

---

[35] Greenwood (2000: 130); cf. Steiner ([1956] 1967) for analysis of the concept of taboo and ritual purity.
[36] Greenwood (2000: 128).

also tells how men may equally come to 'feel special' and cites the case of one man whose engagement with magic enabled him to lose 'feelings of humiliation' that surrounded his ordinary family life and occupation.[37]

GENDERED GODS

India has often taken the issue of gender into its pantheon and often did so while giving voice to a repertoire of emotions. For example, in traditional nineteenth-century Punjab, Sikhs worshipped *Sitala Devi*, one local manifestation of *Devi*, also known as Kali. As a goddess of diseases prompted by her wrath, especially smallpox, she could also serve to cure the sick if her anger could be assuaged. These divine emotional states were described through idioms of heat and cold set within a wide social classification of such things as the 'hot' days of Sunday, Tuesday, and Saturday dedicated to the sun and the 'cool' days of Monday, Wednesday, Thursday, and Friday related to the moon. It was said that 'only by keeping Sitala cool could everyone be protected' from sickness.[38]

Joel Gereboff's summary on studies of emotion in Judaism and in Hebrew biblical texts stresses the importance of gender for future studies, especially in the light of how some 'emotion'-linked words such as love, joy, and grief are set more in the context of social performance of activities rather than any clear description of 'inner' feeling states. Though the role of covenants and obligation to relate to the divine in an appropriate way may have driven these ancient texts, it is easy for later commentators, especially if they come to this material with the Christian eyes of a particular tradition, to emphasize the inner feelings of faith over formal performance.[39] This raises the interesting question of whether a gender distinction is lost in the process.

Another problematic aspect of gender, identity, and emotion in religion depends upon the very basic categories by which male and female persons tend to be classified and understood. This is a very complex field and depends to a great degree upon local culture. There is little to be gained, for example, by perpetuating images that almost amount to caricatures, as when 'masculine consciousness' is said to consist in 'analysing, selecting and separating'

---

[37] Greenwood (2000: 134).
[38] Oberoi (1997: 164–5).
[39] Gereboff (2008: 100).

and constructing abstract theologies, whereas a feminine consciousness, as in 'contextual theology', concentrates on 'the experience of the whole and on the interconnectedness of everything happening'.[40] Such stereotypes themselves lose the richness of contrary cases through their own abstraction of 'types' of person.[41] As significant is the fact of the 'complexity of the individual personality, involving cross-sex and cross-gender identifications'.[42] It is, for example, extremely difficult for some Christian groups to handle the occurrence of individuals who are, biologically, neither simply male nor simply female—a problem engendered by any overly literal reading of Genesis (1: 27) and its creation of male and female as distinct persons. The complementary creation myth of Genesis (2: 22–3), however, speaks of women being made from a rib of the man, potentially suggestive of some deeply shared characteristics.

POWER

As we have seen in most preceding chapters, the theme of power lies at the heart of all social life and, by extension, of religious life, where it becomes implicated with ideas of supernatural power to influence status and identity. The significance of differential access to power or of being influenced by people with power is nowhere more directly obvious than in terms of males and females. One of the main arguments of feminist thought concerns the way men control access to power and limit it as far as women are concerned. This led some anthropologists, for example, to interpret kinds of spirit possession among women in terms of a deprivation theory. Being deprived access to the power to achieve the status they desire, they experience spirit possession as a means of attracting the attention of the more powerful men and gaining some goods from them. A similar argument can be mounted for relatively marginalized males who also become possessed. The work of Ioan Lewis on Zar spirit possession among some Muslim women is typical of this approach.[43] Others have seen how 'power' may be interpreted differently by

---

[40] Edwards (1995: 185).

[41] Jordanova (1980: 64) aptly criticizes the 'nature/culture' dichotomy, when paralleled with 'male/female' polarity, as bearing 'little relationship to the messiness and pragmatic complexity of lived experience of the majority of the population'.

[42] Craib (1998: 96).

[43] Lewis (1971).

men and women in Christian Pentecostal conversion narratives, where, for example, the power of the Holy Spirit—often deemed a male entity in that tradition—seemed to involve a 'subtext of eroticism largely absent from male narratives'.[44] On a larger canvas, Max Weber, the foremost among sociologists of religion and one often identified with the rational aspects of religious activity, made incisive comment on the interplay of eroticism and religious control of life but with relatively little concern over its gendered nature. For him, sexuality at large and eroticism in particular are associated with 'a gradual turning away from the naive naturalism of sex' under the power of the 'rationalization and intellectualism of culture'.[45] The absence of a gendered perspective in his work is most apparent when he deals with 'the brotherly ethic of salvation religion' and its 'profound tension with the greatest irrational force of life: sexual love'. Still, there is much in Weber on emotions in terms of descriptions of 'sensations' associated with distinct forms of religious identity, but always with reference to the power wielded by religious traditions.

In the different context of Britain, Matthew Wood has also developed an understanding of power, status, and identity in his detailed analysis of groups that entertain various forms of 'possession' and would often be defined as New Age but that he insistently and properly describes in terms of non-formative spirituality. Wood notes the 'prominent role of women in the network' of groups he studied in the UK Midlands.[46] He specifically avoids, indeed sees as inadequate, the kind of approach of Heelas and Woodhead, which views women as 'turning to spirituality to express themselves free from constricted social roles', to argue that these women, and some men too, are best seen as 'professionalized working-class' individuals who experience a 'status ambiguity' of a problematic kind in that they 'remain significantly unfulfilled in terms of salaries, and occupational autonomy and advancement'. Wood sees their non-formative pattern of religious involvement as 'aspirational' between different authorities and not solely as dependent upon any one. For him 'formative' means being subject to a single source of authority and being shaped by it: 'non-formative' refers to an existence situated between different authorities and, to a degree, with each of them being somewhat relativized by the others.[47]

---

[44] Chesnut (1997: 95).
[45] Weber ([1915] 1991: 344).
[46] Wood (2007: 170).
[47] Wood (2007: 159).

Moving from issues of experience of 'power' to those of belief, I draw from my own research focused on issues of life, death, and afterlife to show the dramatic differences between British women and men. One study, grounded in interviews with nearly 500 people in Great Britain in the 1990s, revealed that, while some 60 per cent of women reckoned to believe in life after death, only some 38 per cent of men did so. In terms of active disbelief, only 17 per cent of women said they did not accept an afterlife, compared with 37 per cent of the men.[48] An even larger, but contemporary, study conducted in England and Scotland revealed a similar profile amongst some 1,600 people interviewed in their own homes. This project adds further details, so that, of all who thought the 'soul passes on' at death, 63 per cent were female and 37 per cent were male, while—inversely—of those who thought that 'life ends' at death with nothing afterwards, 39 per cent were female and 61 per cent were male. When it came to the possibility of 'coming back as something or someone else', a phrase selected for use instead of reincarnation, there was a similar 63 per cent agreement from women, with a 37 per cent agreement from men. In all of this, the sense of continuity was much stronger among women than men. In terms of interpretation, it seems as though the identity of the majority of the women included a dimension that extended beyond death when compared with the men. This was reinforced in questions relating to 'sensing the presence of the dead', for, although only approximately 35 per cent of the total sample had such experiences, it was the women who did so approximately twice as much as did the men.[49] While such results might not apply to other societies, it is interesting that such highly significant differences seem to exist between British women and men. Just how these differences influence identity is hard to say. From one perspective they could be interpreted as a commitment to continuity among the women compared with the men, in that one might interpret afterlife beliefs as a reflection of this-worldly identity and of the value placed upon the continuity of inter-personal relationships. In the light of such evidence, it is perfectly under-standable that it is women more than men who tend to visit Spiritualist Churches after bereavement to gain some sense of contact with their dead or to know that all is well with them in the spirit world.

In many ways such information raises more questions than it answers, but it does highlight the need to explore female and male sexes in relation to

---

[48] Douglas J. Davies (1996: 22); Rural Church Project Study conducted in England.
[49] Douglas J. Davies (1997b: 138–9).

beliefs and experience rather than assume some uniformity of outlook. Just what such research on afterlife beliefs might reveal, for example, in a largely Islamic society remains to be seen. For, there, men participate in frequent ritual acts that refer to the otherness of deity, which might well conduce to attitudes of a post-mortal existence when compared with the relative infrequency of male participation in public rites in Great Britain's traditional Christian culture.

These pragmatic perspectives serve well as complements to the kind of questions that more formal theology raises, as, for example, with St Augustine's pondering over whether gender differences would exist in the resurrection of the dead. His starting point was a biblical text that speaks of believers coming to a fullness of knowledge of the Son of God, to being a perfected, completed 'man',[50] which some took to mean that only men would exist in heaven and therefore that women would be resurrected as men. Augustine's view, by contrast, was that, once the capacity for lust and its provocation is removed, as it most surely will be in heaven, then woman's sexuality, which is perfectly 'natural', will have its proper place, albeit one free from childbearing. He then takes it upon himself to liken Adam to Eve on the basis of Christ to the Church. The analogy lies between the deep sleep of Adam, associated with God taking a rib and making it into Eve, and the 'sleep' of death of Christ on the cross, and in the blood and water that came from his side, which are the basis for the Eucharist and baptism—basic forms of the Church.[51]

RITUAL PURITY–IMPURITY

Augustine's symbolic reflections serve well as a basis for the final section of this chapter, which sketches the complex concept of ritual purity as the social–moral status required of people when engaged with the core symbols of their society—a status that has, more often than not, been accorded to men rather than to women. As a general term, ritual purity is widely used to discuss the state a person or object should be in before he or it can act in contexts involving sacred symbols, while ritual impurity covers conditions preventing such ritual action. Examples could be drawn from most major

---

[50] Ephesians 4: 13, *eis andra teleio.*
[51] Augustine, *City of God,* bk XXII, ch. XVII.

religious traditions. Ancient Judaism, for example, prevented women who were menstruating or men with seminal discharges from engaging in various forms of worship and social life.[52]

In conservative forms of Judaism, ideas of ritual impurity continue, and women visit a ritual bath (*mikveh*) after their period of uncleanness. This also applies after giving birth. Attitudes to these acts have changed dramatically in Reformed Jewish groups. As for early Christianity, it too seems to have viewed women as relatively unfit for formal leadership and teaching roles in its first churches, even though the menstruation factor seems to be absent in the formal scriptural texts.[53] Even today, however, in some more conservative traditions of Greek Orthodox Christianity, mothers instruct their daughters on limits to their domestic and ecclesial involvement when menstruating, even if there is no formal theological basis for such constraint. Major Christian traditions certainly prevented women's ordination until some of the Protestant denominations underwent major shifts of opinion in the later nineteenth and twentieth centuries.

Beyond Christianity, Hinduism's caste system has been deeply grounded in purity behaviour, both between the sexes within a group and also between caste groups, as all seek to develop or retain their social status, a desire especially evident during periods of social change, though far less common in villages relatively unaffected by social change.[54] One dramatically clear expression of gender division and complementarity in Indian ritual terms is probably that of *sati*, the death and cremation of a widow on the funeral pyre of her husband. This practice brings together in a dramatic way the elements of religion, identity, and emotion in the most direct form of embodiment. It also highlights the theme of ritual purity in quite direct ways that exemplify both impurity and purity. Impurity is evident in that a menstruating woman could not be immolated. By sharp contrast, there was a popular belief that a woman dedicated to her husband and to the goals of this rite would light the funeral pyre herself; normally it would be lit by the eldest son or some other appropriate male. This idea was then taken one symbolic step further in the belief that a really dedicated women would be in a state of such ritual purity—*sat*—that she would possess the power to self-ignite through that very power and then, indirectly as it were, the pyre would ignite. The role of popular belief in relation to such events is evident in Fisch's experience of the

---

[52] Leviticus 12: 1–8; 15: 1–32.
[53] 1 Timothy 2: 11–15.
[54] Nandy (1989: 158).

few, yet significant, cases of *sati* in the twentieth century. The rites that were further back in time possessed the greater number of witnesses, even though 'in most cases it was known that a clearly identifiable person had carried out the task'.[55] This is an interesting example of how ideal forms of action, events, or individuals become increasingly idealized as time passes, and within religious traditions such events become increasingly invested with a sense of sacred power. One result of this in terms of material culture is the creation of temple sites where notable sati has occurred—places that attract infertile couples as potential sources of vitality in terms of fecundity.[56]

For much of this activity it is impossible to distinguish between 'religious' and caste or social identity at large. Contexts of food, drink, and marriage have been prime foci for such behaviour. The ancient Zoroastrian religion, not least in its modern Parsi identity in India, Britain, and America, has also pursued notions of purity in connection with its prayer and funerary rites. Issues of purity are related to identity as in-born Parsis, with problematic questions arising over non-Parsi wedding partners and the children of such unions. Here purity has a great deal to do with the boundary-marking of the traditional community; further issues of purity and impurity are associated with menstruation. One objection to one Parsi event in a Hong Kong context dealt with objections to having a priest's wife living on sacred premises, because its wooden floor, being 'a porous substance', could be more easily polluted during her menstrual period than would concrete or marble.[57] This instructive example depicts impurity almost as an exuded substance that contaminates sacred space. This reflects widespread Indian ideas that metal objects 'transmit' impurity much less easily than earthenware. Death is often another context in which impurity is incurred, by contact with a corpse. The traditional priest or *cohen* of Judaism, for example, was not allowed contact with corpses, in the belief that this would render him unfit for immediate religious duties.

The significance of the idea of ritual purity for identity in religion lies in the way prescribed and proscribed behaviours involve strong emotional responses. There is a scale of intensity of response here, from one of strong satisfaction if prescribed rules are observed through to outright revulsion if

---

[55] Fisch ([2005] 2006: 253, 270, 271) cites 1,153 burnings in Benares, and 5,119 in Calcutta between 1815 and 1828 ([2005] 2006: 476).

[56] Anand (1989: 164); Chakrabarti (1974: 221) discusses Sanskrit texts on human sacrifice in India.

[57] Hinnells (2005: 181).

they are contravened. This is quite understandable if a community's emotional repertoire has been attuned to specific ways of engaging with the prime symbols of their culture; to find them abused is to sense one's own identity as under attack. Some, for example, would feel a strong negative sensation, probably of anger, to see their national flag burned by opponents, or even more so by dissident compatriots. Similarly, devotees find a sense of disgust if their founder, leader, or prophet is ridiculed. Here we can recall Mary Douglas's approach to society that possesses prime symbols at its core and that requires behaviour to be controlled when engaging with them. In her terms, and in this she follows Durkheim, those things that symbolize the core of society are sacred and demand an appropriate status or condition in those persons or things involved with them.[58] It is also from that social core that individual identity ultimately derives, making a bridge between personal identity and ritual purity. So, to reiterate the point, to engage with the core sacred symbols, one must be in an appropriate state, and that state is one of ritual purity. The role of emotions in marking out states of purity and impurity is quite significant, because it brings a dynamic power to bear upon what might, otherwise, be seen as abstract rules and regulations. The very fact that members of a society can 'feel sick' if their prime symbols are attacked is an index of the power of society underlying individual identity. By contrast, intense engagement with core symbols of cultural worth can give a powerful sense of enhancement and value to individual members of a community. Park's account of the recent innovation of Bible-copying among ordinary Korean Christians affords a prime example where Christian commitment to the Bible, and an enduring Confucian cultural ethic of self-development in calligraphy, combine in activity that has proved dramatically popular among many people, but especially among older women. Here a personal sense of identity is one way of speaking of the integration of personal meaning within community identity. When Rappaport called such symbolic foci the 'ultimate sacred postulates' of a society, he was emphasizing the emotional power that key social values can carry within themselves.[59]

Whether or not such values can be associated with gender-like attributes is a theme of some interest, although we can only allude to it here. Mestrovic, for example, argues that Durkheim, as one of the most influential sociologists of religion, employed a 'feminine conceptualization of religion' involving a

---

[58] Douglas (1966).   [59] Rappaport (1999).

'mystic sympathy amongst humans' associated with and leading to social integration.[60] Taking this argument in a very particular direction, he argues that the idea of 'civil religion' in the USA, an idea closely associated with Robert Bellah that describes a kind of general American cultural image of shared religion and national interest, entirely reversed Durkheim's conception of religion as 'fundamentally feminine' to focus on 'God the Father' as the 'centerpiece of American civil religion', with an emphasis on 'rewards and punishments' and with a strong voice raised in support of war. This he associates more with a Protestant cultural base.[61] Though this approach assumes that certain emotional attributes are characteristic of men and women as defined within a particular society and not, necessarily, as universal characteristics, it still raises powerful questions about the emphasis of a particular tradition, or about the centre of gravity of its emotion-influenced values. One analogous issue that could be explored in a similar way is posed by the very phrase 'Mother Church', frequently used within Christianity for the Catholic Church. The dynamic interplay between such an idealization, often with additional references to the Virgin Mary as the mother of Christ and, indeed, in more Orthodox traditions as the Mother of God, and the role of the male priesthood, typified by the title 'father' for priests, could be analysed at considerable length. Indeed, one fruitful avenue of research on emotions and religious identity could follow the ways in which different religious traditions depict the quality and nature of relationships between the devotee and their formal religious 'bodies' or institutions.

SUMMARY

In this chapter, then, we have seen that the male–female divide entails many consequences, not only for family life, economics, and social organization, but also for identity, religious behaviour, and some attitudes to death. Gender differences also furnish clearly nuanced axes when the nature of the embodiment of social values is discussed with men and women in societies with different religious duties and expectations allied with their complementary identities. We have also seen how gender has offered humanity two rather obvious 'natural symbols' around which emotions can be identified and

[60] Mestrovic (1992: 100–1), a significant, creative reappraisal of Durkheim's work.
[61] Cf. Marvin and Ingle (1999) for an analysis of American religion and war.

managed in relation to the core values of the group, even to the point of including the deities as engendered entities.

The next three chapters consider some of these core values and the emotions associated with them, always seeking a degree of close integration of value and emotion. Still, it will not always be possible to describe each value or emotion in terms of how each society associates it with males or females. Although many religious traditions do frequently align particular values and emotions with either males or females, it is only through detailed ethnographic studies that such fine-tuned cultural practice is accessible. On the whole, that will be possible only for some very specific cases amid our more general account of, for example, love, joy, mercy, and humility in Chapter 6; of merit, grace, and pardon in Chapter 7; and of despair and hope in Chapter 8. However, in a distinctive contribution of this study, we will be able to highlight the way in which values and emotions find an intimate association in what is described in Chapter 6 as the 'humility response' and in Chapter 8 as 'moral-somatic' relationships.

6

Love, Mercy, Humility, and Betrayal

This chapter and its two successors recharge our concern with the value-laden and nuanced emotions that move people and that are intensified through their religious significance, often typified in paradigmatic scenes. To speak, as we did in the previous chapter, of males and females is to create an impression of being interested only in general categories of people or in 'society', but this study does not wish to ignore the individual level of life, the daily and periodic activities that bring meaning to life and engender hope in each of us. It is at this level, too, that meaning is made through reciprocal relationships, and it is with that in mind that the next three chapters focus on emotions and feelings that, in pragmatic reality, touch the lives of individuals. Feelings of love and betrayal, for example, are obvious enough in many worlds, embodied in well-known literary and scriptural characters. These we address in this chapter, as also the less obvious phenomena of humility and mercy, which really pinpoint the importance of a bio-cultural approach to emotion and identity, for in these experiences too the nuanced influence of social ideals becomes all too relevant.

HUMAN CAREER

One valuable reminder of the individual who feels these nuanced emotions comes from Walter Goldschmidt's theoretical emphasis upon what he calls the 'human career', upon the 'paradigm' of the 'individual as a motivated actor' who seeks to satisfy not simply 'the physical appetites, but also the satisfaction of needs of another order: the social self'. He speaks of the symbolic self, emerging through evolution and generating a person 'laden with feeling', who is not 'emotionally neutral to his own self'.[1] Within this

---

[1] Goldschmidt (1990: 2–5).

'human career', individuals are ever negotiating their feelings in relation to the requirements and demands of their social world, and this 'lifetime pursuit of satisfactions, both physical and social', focuses on what Goldschmidt identifies as 'prestige'. Indeed, this sense of prestige as 'the recognition of individual merit' is a 'quality that a person has' or has conferred upon him by others and is 'the very soul of the social order'. What is more, it can rise or fall within the human career; it is something that he even describes as a 'mystic substance'.[2] Goldschmidt's interest in this perspective was driven by his sense of the importance of 'the role of emotions', which he thought, even writing in 1990, had 'received markedly little attention'.[3] In this study we accept his view that the 'pursuit of career is an emotion laden process' and that there are key 'explanatory systems' and 'ritual acts . . . designed to order the sentiments and arrange the feelings' of people.[4] Indeed, our goal is to explore such processes, systems, and ritual acts in terms of both their positive and their negative influence on people's religious 'career'. Accordingly, we devote this chapter to our first cluster of emotion-embedded concepts including love, a sense of flourishing, and happiness, acknowledging that local cultural influences inevitably mark these aspects of life. So, too, with the notion of humility, which, in this chapter, is developed into the notion of 'the humility response', an idea that helps explain the bond between an individual and society under particular circumstances and that is allied with meritorious behaviour. Then we move to a brief account of mercy as an attitude that shares a certain family resemblance with the humility response, except that, while the humility response places a person as an object before society, mercy also offers the possibility of seeing a person as a subject showing mercy to another. Finally, ever mindful of the interplay of negative as well as positive flows of emotion in human life, the chapter ends with a discussion of betrayal, a behaviour pattern that inverts and contradicts, love, humility, and mercy.

All these qualities of human beings reveal an immense canvas of human life, one that challenges any simple description let alone explanation. Indeed, it is probably best to approach them in terms of a search for an 'understanding' or insight that acknowledges the role of empathy in human life. One such entry point that fully comprehends these issues is available in the classic but often ignored approach of Gerardus van der Leeuw (1890–1910), whose

---

[2] Goldschmidt (1990: 31–32).
[3] Goldschmidt (1990: 21).
[4] Goldschmidt (1990: 174). He avoids any definition of 'religion' as such.

classic phenomenological study, *Religion in Essence and Manifestation*, includes the key themes of alterity and reciprocity that underlie this present study. His motivation was to provide an overall classification of world religions organized through patterns of 'power' driving feeling states and related to a '*highly exceptional* and *extremely impressive "Other"'*: the outcome described religions of struggle, repose, unrest, strain, infinity and asceticism, nothingness and compassion, will and obedience, majesty and humility, and love.[5]

Though much could be said on each of these, it is to his section 63 that we draw attention for its assertion that 'the most important type of profoundly emotional utterance is *praise*. Whoever is deeply moved emotionally, praises: he cannot possible avoid doing so; for in praise there lies self-forgetfulness.' He speaks of a person turning away from self and towards an other, whether ancestor or God, with the outcome being either the voiced sound of worship or a silence produced from a 'deep emotional agitation'.[6] Interestingly, in terms of our concern with reciprocity, he aligns praise with sacrifice in a concurrent 'stream of gifts'. But, while observing Mauss's theory of reciprocity in its threefold requirement of giving, receiving, and giving again, he engages only with its inalienable 'fourth obligation' when emphasizing 'the cycle of power' inherent in the 'stream of gifts (that is, of power)' that ensures that 'the stream of life should continue to flow'.[7] At the core of his work, 'power' engages with experience, whether positively or negatively: in positive terms, 'salvation' becomes 'power experienced as good'.[8] Despite criticism of his broad generalizations,[9] van der Leeuw still offers a valuable perspective on moods of salvation, even for ethnographies written after his death.

Though it would be feasible, albeit overly restrictive, to engage with van der Leeuw's presentation of 'power' for all the emotions explored in the following chapters, it has been important to mark his grasp of the emotional dynamics inherent within the study of religious identity. Having said that, this chapter will now take up the themes of love, humility, mercy, and betrayal, all selected for their role within religious traditions and their capacity to influence individual identity by fostering or frustrating life's

---

[5] Van der Leeuw ([1933] 1967: 23, 597–645; emphasis in original). Cf. Wood (2005: 41–77) for a valuable contemporary and empirical analysis of 'power, self, and practice'.

[6] Van Der Leeuw ([1933] 1967: 430, 432).

[7] Van der Leeuw ([1933] 1967: 357, 354).

[8] Van der Leeuw ([1933] 1967:102).

[9] Baal and Beek (1985: 204–5).

meaning and hope. In theoretical terms these phenomena help focus our argument on issues of otherness and reciprocity, whether in the form of deities and worship or in the form of positive and negative relationships with other people.

LOVE

Expressions of love flow within many religious traditions, yet few words are more susceptible of differences in meaning. Whether in human life or in the divine relations modelled on them, love can denote a respectfully fearful obedience to deity conceived as a superior overlord or a mystical devotion mirroring the passionate warmth of aroused lovers. Sometimes love resembles parental tenderness, the longing for the well-being of a child, and sometimes it marks filial piety or the fond friendship of equals. On occasion, love may speak of intense moments of emotion or of enduring moods of fond memory and current affection. Yet other human models for love-like relations with supernatural beings include alliances and covenant relationships. These experiences, in their positive modes, and through reciprocal relationships, afford meaning to personal life and bring hope to a strengthened sense of identity. But, because negative forces also play their part in life, this chapter will not ignore love's shadow side of identity depletion in betrayal. Only in the partnering of these realities will the significance and mutual linking of each be fully appreciated.

Traditional expressions

Religious traditions have often become the stage on which love motifs have found social expression beyond the domestic arena. In that more public world of myth, doctrine, ritual, and ceremony, the ideals of love, commitment, and devotion are advocated and assume their own form of appeal. In Chapter 2 we have already seen something of this spectrum in the strong feelings between the mutual heroes Gilgamesh and Enkidu in the Babylonian myth on mortality. A similar scene lies in the biblical account of David, who is said to have loved Jonathan as he loved his own soul.[10] In John's Gospel,

---

[10] 1 Samuel 20: 17.

love is given primacy of place as the characteristic attribute of the Christian community of Jesus's disciples.[11]

In the *Bhagavad Gita*, a text described by the notable scholar of Indian religion, R. C. Zaehner, as the most significant text in the whole history of religion, we encounter a theophany in which the deity Krishna appears to Arjuna and reveals himself in his many forms.[12] Astonished, Arjuna experiences the dread of holy terror, his hair standing on end as the deity's terrific mode is seen engulfing all things in a symbolic mouth that devours the cosmos. Arjuna, recovering himself, yet with 'trembling heart', prostrates his body, 'bending low', and asks his adored Lord to bestow grace, 'as father bears with son, as friend with friend, as lover with beloved'.[13] The deity tells Arjuna that the revelation he has seen has been granted him by the divine grace, for it cannot be achieved through scriptural knowledge, sacrifice, study, or austerity, for, as Krishna says as he assumes a form to accommodate to his earthly hearer,

> Only by undivided love
> can I in reality be seen
> in such a guise as you perceived
> and both be known and entered in.
>
> So work for me, intent on me,
> and free from ties, have love for me...[14]

This form of devotional mysticism creates a distinctive identity in which the self embraces the otherness of deity and also feels itself embraced in a reciprocity of inalienable love. To reach that experience is far from easy, for, as we saw in Chapter 3, pride is a major barrier, with Sikhism as one major tradition emphasizing this poisoning of identity. In text after text the Sikh Gurus tell that no amount of spiritual discipline, austerity, pilgrimage, or learning can guarantee or engender the experience of knowing the Lord, yet they know it is possible for the divine one to cast a creative glance and make the union possible. It is always 'through the grace of the Guru' such spiritual union takes place.

> The Lord is the Spouse who on His couch
> Enjoyeth the love of the Righteous.[15]

---

[11] John 15: 9–17.
[12] Zaehner (1970: 117).
[13] *Bhagavad Gita* (11: 14, 44); Parrinder (1974: 63, 67).
[14] *Bhagavad Gita* (11: 54–5); Parrinder (1974: 69).
[15] *The Sacred Writings of the Sikhs* (1960: 67).

The guru figure in Sikh thought, as in many other Indian traditions, provides a focus for love and devotion. Even in the mainstream of Sikh life, where the historical gurus are reckoned to have been replaced by a combination of the community and the sacred texts, there remains a strong personification of this focus of commitment and piety, for love requires a language of personal relationships.

Such devotional mysticism is widespread. Christianity's St Thomas à Kempis, already mentioned in Chapter 3, is in the same emotional frame in the sixteenth century when speaking 'of the sweetness of God's love': 'when thou art present, all things do yield delight ... quietness of heart, and much peace, and pleasant joy.'[16] It is, certainly, impossible to do justice to such streams flowing through most religious traditions without encountering love as a means of describing that most significant other. Given the many analogies between human and divine loves, this is one area that proves how unwise it is to draw any sharp divide between 'religion' and wider life. Darwin, for example, spoke directly about 'the emotion of love', but acknowledged that what he most appropriately called the 'tender feelings' were 'difficult to analyse' but remained important for integrating 'affection, joy and especially sympathy'.[17] Indeed, love is a complex concept to approach in relation to the idea of emotion, for it seldom appears in lists of emotion. One interesting example of this complexity lies in Harold Dearden, who also highlighted 'the tender emotion' as one end of a spectrum of emotions that included fear and anger. For him each emotion was an expression of an 'instinct', itself 'an inborn tendency towards a certain kind of behaviour', albeit an inherent tendency much 'modified' by 'experience and environment'.[18] For him the 'tender emotion' was embedded as the 'almost universal tendency of adult animals to care for their young, to protect the weak and helpless and, ultimately, to produce the practice of law and justice'. As a medical practitioner embedded within Victorian–Edwardian attitudes a generation after Darwin, he believed that it was this tender emotion that had had such 'far-reaching and beneficent influence on society as a whole'. Even so, he located love as part of this nurturing instinct expressed as emotion in a chapter on 'the sex instinct'. Love is a form of 'self-forgetfulness'; it is 'the highest and most spiritual expression of the primitive emotion of "lust"'. His

---

[16] Thomas à Kempis (n.d.: 175).

[17] Charles Darwin ([1872] 1998: 214). By 1929 (pp. 96–103), Harold Dearden (1925: 101–3) could list 'the tender emotion' along with fear and anger as 'the principal emotions'.

[18] Dearden (1925: 101–3).

was, admittedly, a popular book intended for well-meaning people seeking their own moral betterment. As his summary aphorism reads: 'Lust is the grub, and Love the gorgeous butterfly.'[19]

As for Darwin, with his deep fondness for his own children, he would almost certainly warm to one illustration of this parental capacity expressed in Boris Becker's description of the occasion of his son's birth with its overwhelming sense of 'unconditional love' as the greatest event of his own life.[20] This is not an uncommon experience, but its significance for Becker lies in his prestige as an outstanding twentieth-century tennis champion. Champions can, of course, be easily overwhelmed by their victory over opponents, but, in the context of birth, the very image of contest is reversed in the radical interlinking of mother, child, and father: otherness becomes complex and, in this case, deeply fulfilling. In historical-cultural terms it is interesting that Darwin, and most men of many ages and cultures, but unlike Becker and others in some contemporary societies, would never have been at the birth of their children.

As for 'love', Darwin, whose work on facial expression and muscular movement was extensive, explicitly and significantly noted that this emotion 'can hardly be said to have any peculiar means of expression', something he finds understandable, since it 'has not habitually led to any special line of action'. Paul Ekman's editorial commentary on Darwin agreed that 'there is no distinctive facial expression for love' but disagrees over the reason for this, arguing that 'love is not an emotion'. His basis for saying this is because 'emotions are brief and episodic, lasting seconds or minutes', whereas 'love is an affective commitment, in which many emotions are felt'.[21] James Elkins, speaking both personally and as an art historian, similarly speaks of not being able to imagine clearly his wife's face 'as a picture' when she is not there.[22] This is intelligible, since people change moment by moment, and close contact with others depends more upon interpreting those changes and engaging, reciprocally, with them rather than developing one single image as the standard expression of others. Perhaps we should also note that this human capacity for reciprocal commitment can also extend to the non-human world of animals and plants. Darwin, for example, responded to a letter from his friend the Revd John Brodie Innes by saying that dogs 'are wonderful animals and deserve to be loved with all one's heart, even when they do steal mutton chops'.[23]

---

[19] Dearden (1925: 253).
[20] Televised interview by Piers Morgan, UK, ITV 1, 17 Oct. 2009.
[21] Darwin ([1872] 1998: 83, 212).
[22] Elkins (1996: 162).
[23] Clark (1984: 75).

Flourishing

Despite its apparent ordinariness, this telling sentiment indicates a form of human flourishing that transcends utilitarianism, for pets hint at the kind of meaning that animal companionship may bring to a person. A dog, for example, is not necessary for life but still enhances it, especially for those living alone or for childless couples, and such enhancement seems to be a distinctive feature of human societies, which, once basic needs of survival are met, creatively engage with phenomena that foster flourishing. This significant dimension of religion and identity is easily overlooked when discussing the kind of meaning that religious activities often confer. Music, singing, dancing, or ritual movement, as well as the creative arts of painting, sculpture, building, and decoration, seem to allow human creativity arenas for action.[24] Time produces elaborate myths and complex doctrines, sacred texts are copied and illustrated, and musical forms allow human experiences to live in and through them.

For some the drive for meaning does not find it easy to stop. It is one thing to arrive at some philosophical expression of world explanation; it is quite another not to play with that explanation in numerous ways. Some theories of religion and identity, for example, that of Sigmund Freud, tend to stress the negative needs of humanity, or speak of a deprivation that begs satisfaction. Indeed, the sociologist and psychologist Erich Fromm criticized Freud's approach to people precisely because it was grounded in a 'psychology of want' that ignored 'phenomena of abundance, like love or tenderness'.[25] Yet, it is just such an abundance that is frequently sought and often provided to offset 'want' in the religious cultures of the world and their salvation-achieving goal. The idiom of love and of mystical union, as well as many myths and doctrines of creation, all contribute to the religiously fashioned sense of flourishing abundance, even if the potential shadow side is never entirely absent.

Bodily abundance, happiness

One example of such abundance, albeit coupled with the potential for loss, occurs in Nerina Rustomji's valuable exploration of Islamic experiences of heaven and hell in her volume the *Garden and the Fire*, a title indicating these

---

[24] Otto ([1917] 1924: 181) compares artistic and musical creativity with religious revelation.
[25] Fromm ([1942] 1960: 250).

opposing contexts of joy and sorrow.[26] Though not a study of emotions, her work offers fine access to a wide experiential spectrum of sensation, showing how Islamic ideas of the afterlife awaiting the faithful in their resurrected lives in the paradise garden or in the igneous place of suffering focus on the emotional experiences of the body. In the Garden it will be perfect, freed from all earthly hindrances, being of a perfect age and with perfect beauty. Indeed, beauty will increase week by week and be noticed. Faces will beam within the everlasting banquet that comprises this eternity, where no sense of jealousy or hurt will exist. Kinsfolk will abide together, and even sexual capacities will exceed those of earth, with all married to enjoy them. This future state is, inevitably perhaps, contrasted with earthly conditions. Rustomji interestingly adds information on the senses of sight, smell, and touch. In terms of smell, important place is given to perfumes coming from trees, rivers, and fountains as well as from people themselves. Some of these smells that will suffuse the atmosphere were, she suggests, known only as rare commodities in the actual life of Muslims. In the case of both camphor and musk and, perhaps, ginger, their perfume 'was known only by name', making the promised access to the Garden a promise of 'a luxury good never smelled during a believer's lifetime'. By contrast, she describes the way in which sound and the sense of hearing play a minor role both the Garden and the Fire, citing only one tradition in which the voices of the *houris* or female companions in heaven 'are sonorous'. As Rustomji says, 'even if the Garden and the Fire are full of life, they are remarkably silent realms'.[27] By contrast, the early Christian apocalyptic vision of heaven, portrayed as a city and not as a garden, albeit a city from whose divine throne room flowed a 'river of the water of life' embraced by the 'tree of life', was a vision filled with sound. The mystical 'four living creatures', the 'twenty four elders', as well as 'every living creature in heaven and on earth and under the earth' pronounce words of glory to God.[28]

In terms of the emotions of smells, Rustomji's material deals with the anticipation of smells that are now known only in terms of the substances that produce them and not in terms of the smells as such. She shows how the power of known emotions triggered in this life by smells could be used as a motivating force for fostering an ethical life that would lead to a paradise flooded by intoxicating scents. In other words, our present knowledge of

---

[26] Rustomji (2009: 83–4).
[27] Rustomji (2009: 70–1).
[28] Revelation 4: 6, 10; 5: 13.

wonderful scents can be used as a motivation for living in ways that will grant us even more exotic joys in an afterlife.

The very idea of bliss within religions bespeaks the place of feeling and of the high value placed upon the positive sensations of an exalted state, albeit one that passes. Thomas à Kempis, again, makes this clear when describing to neophytes that 'the good and sweet affection' they may sometimes feel is, truly, 'a sort of foretaste' of their 'heavenly home', and, while it is granted by grace, so that they feel themselves 'rapt on high', it is experienced as coming and going.[29] This transience of feeling would seem to indicate an emotional compound in which excitement and hope cohere within an attitude of devotion. Devotion, however, may continue as an enduring attitude, while exalted sensations come and go; it is also indicative of the relational nature of piety. Thomas's cautionary advice on the intermittent nature of elevated feelings highlights just how important the management of emotion and mood has been within religious traditions, especially those fostered within the relatively closed world of monastic communities. From a different Christian theological perspective, Bonhoeffer warns against seeing the body as a means to an end, even a heavenly afterlife, and reflects on the body as 'an end in itself' and on the inherent 'nature of joy' that is 'spoilt by any thought of purpose'.[30]

The psychological theme of attachment and loss, previously discussed in Chapter 3 in the context of bereavement and grief, is also valuable when considering aspects of religious management of emotional engagement with the divine. One obvious application is the sense of loss that sometimes accompanies or follows a deep sense of attachment to deity. One feature of many kinds of piety involves the sense of an intimate relationship with a deity. The love of many ordinary devotees to Krishna, Jesus, and some other divine figures, for example, can be experienced in ways that resemble emotional bonds with another human being. This can also be seen in the more specialist theological writings of some mystics, which explain the variations in the feelings surrounding their relationship with deity—as with St John of the Cross (1542–91) in the sixteenth century and his description of various 'nights' through which the 'soul' passes as it moves from attachment to the senses to a different kind of attachment to the knowledge of God. Part of this

[29] Thomas à Kempis (n.d.: 118).
[30] Bonhoeffer ([1949] 1955: 113).

process of change describes the mental pain of the devotee moving from familiar realms into domains of lesser certainty that demand new forms of trust. Phrases such as 'the dark night of the soul' are used to express the nature of the interplay of 'abundance' or spiritual blessing, on the one hand, and of a deprivation or self-sacrifice aligned with a sensed absence of the divine, on the other. This language resembles the terminology of attachment and loss associated with bereavement and grief, indicating something of the congruence between parent–child and deity–devotee relationships. Indeed, there is even some evidence to suggest that the pattern of attachment of child to parent as described by psychologists is correlated with the nature of reported relationships with God.[31]

As for happiness, many traditions set out an agenda for the life of feelings and the cultivation of an ethical way of life. Gereboff, for example, summarizes emotions in Judaism showing how some studies focus not on 'happiness as a subjective feeling manifested in a given moment or for a short period of time' but on 'an objective state of affairs', as life is lived in an orderly and well-regulated fashion.[32] This polarity between inner state and social convention lies at the core of most emotions research, precisely because the bond between individual and society is the key issue in all social and human sciences. The question of how best to live the 'good life' resonates across all social worlds and has often become something of a prerogative of religious institutions that direct which feelings should be cultivated and which controlled or eliminated. Nevertheless, just what might conduce to 'happiness' remains complex. Jung, for example, argued that, while there is 'nobody who does not long for it', there is no 'single objective criterion which would prove beyond all doubt that this condition necessarily exists'. He curtly adds that, 'as so often with the most important things, we have to make do with a subjective judgement'.[33] This applies to many aspects of experience in religious identity, since the awareness that motivates religious lives often involves commitments, certainties, and doubts hard to express but inescapable in their capacity to sustain faith.

---

[31] Parkes (2006: 185), citing Kirkpatrick and Shaver (1990), who saw 'secure' people as more likely to be evangelicals and the 'insecure' as seeing 'God as distant'.
[32] Gereboff (2008: 98).
[33] Jung ([1953] 1968: 148).

HUMILITY

This attachment to society along with its potential for developing individual identity carries a powerful reminder of Chapter 4's theological discussion of the feeling of absolute dependence in Schleiermacher's nineteenth-century theology. Though that perspective offers one fruitful route for dwelling on the next issue we wish to explore, that of humility, we take a different direction here, following classical scholar Walter Burkert's account of religious rituals of submission rooted in acts and postures evident in social and political life, especially that of the ancient Near East. Just as the social inferior pays homage to the superior in bowing or prostration, by making himself 'low' in relation to the high, so do devotees do homage before their gods. Burkert locates such deference in our animal origins, exemplified in higher primate behaviour. Daniel Fessler, too, invokes animal ancestry when analysing human shame in relation to its partnering notion of pride. He considers the 'logic, feeling and display' factor of emotions, and also sees shame and pride as evolutionary expressions of a sense of inferiority and superiority evident in primate behaviour. For him, pride relates to a dominant status that brings a greater capacity to reproduce oneself. This would encourage individuals to strive for dominance and therefore would foster the emotion of pride. Accordingly, shame and pride underlie the emergence of a 'system of social control premised on conformity to cultural understandings', which has the advantage of allowing 'for enormous increases in both social and cultural complexity'.[34] Indeed, it is hard to overemphasize the importance of shame as a social control factor, whether within a person's private relation to a deity, or in some group context of family, profession, gang, or club.[35] Although caution is necessary when making these animal–human comparisons and when exploring their cultural and theological symbolic contexts, their essential body-based significance of creatures alert to status hierarchy should never be overlooked. There is little doubt that physical posture possesses an affinity with particular forms of sensation, and, if these are framed by theological notions of divine power and human weakness, or of a deity's holiness and a human's sin, then posture bespeaks the belief to the individual as well as publicly announcing the condition of things. The very

---

[34] Fessler (1999: 90, 102).
[35] Pattison (2000: 171).

fact that humility as a word is derived from Latin *humilitas*—lowness or insignificance—and ultimately from *humus*—the earth or soil itself—is indicative of the spatial effect in the perception of power. Ultimately, humility has to do with power understood in terms of social worth; it becomes especially obvious when pondering the nature of humiliation as degrading a person's dignity and causing him a sense of shame.

Even to speak of 'degradation' invokes the Latin *gradus* or step, involving the notion of physical height, with someone being 'taken down' a step or two. Humiliation is a widespread experience, whether in its weak form of a social 'put down' when someone is 'belittled' in the presence of others, through occasions of 'loss of face' in significant contexts of mutual status, to events of abject suffering in the privacy of victim with torturer. As social animals that value status and are all too alert to the nature of pain, humans have not been slow to combine these in creating humiliation and inflicting pain on many. Even in apparently developed and economically wealthy 'safe societies', the fact of bullying is far from rare and has gained widespread recognition as some schoolchildren, with their mass ownership of cell phones and personal computers and access to the Web, engage in 'cyberbullying' victims, some of whom have even committed suicide.[36] Here the very growth of electronic personal communication has influenced the possibilities for enhancing and destroying personal identity. The enormous growth of Facebook as an electronic medium for self-presentation has, for example, both fostered and frustrated many in their human desire to know and be known socially, an issue to which we return in Chapter 10. At the international level, too, pride of status holds a vital place, as Isaiah Berlin deftly displayed in his analysis of the eighteenth-century European identities involving 'a sense of collective humiliation, later to turn into indignation and hostility, that sprang from wounded pride'.[37] He tells of East Prussia's 'semi-feudal and deeply trad-itionalist' self-focused world view being 'deeply wounded' by modernization tendencies, not least as pressed by the French, and of its rejection of things that one 'cannot achieve oneself'. This, says Berlin, is a 'response of the humiliated' that fostered nationalism and the 'will to live one's own regional life'.[38] When such a sense of freedom combines with a religious tradition to

---

[36] Bird (2009: 9) describes suicide after 'cyberbullying' and, paradoxically, the comfort received by the bereaved girl's parents from supportive comments 'on various social networking sites'.

[37] Berlin (1997: 563).

[38] Berlin (1997: 567–8); he notes Hegel's *Bei-sich-selbst-seyn* utopian-like ideal of freedom to be oneself untrammelled by imposed constraints.

create an identity believed to be legitimated by ultimate truth, powerful social forces ensue that can explode in hostility, whether in medieval or in modern crusades, between some Christians and some Muslims or between different sects within the same tradition, as with the Irish 'troubles' between contemporary Catholics and Protestants. All reveal the competition for status and the hatred of being degraded by others.

Humility response

But there is quite another, and extremely positive, form of status differential evident in what I have elsewhere tentatively described as the 'humility response', a behaviour in which a group praises a worthy individual for service to the community and that person responds with a sense of being humbled and filled with a sense of gratitude for this applause. There appears to be no pride or arrogance in this 'humility response', a reaction perfectly explicable through Durkheim's notion of society as a moral community dependent upon collaboration for its survival and upon that sense of well-being flowing from being accepted by others and from contributing to their expectations. This mutuality shows the profound integration of reciprocity with otherness in generating a meaningful and hope-fostering life. Occasionally, however, the community highlights and makes explicit these normally implicit expectations and recognitions. The fact that individuals accorded special recognition often respond with deferential gratitude reveals the very social nature of human life. One of the most unexpected examples came in October 2009, when American President Obama was awarded the Nobel Peace Prize and, in a response framed by genuine unexpected surprise, spoke of feeling 'deeply humbled' by the act. A British example occurred when the head of the British Army, General Sir Richard Dannatt, retired from his leadership position in August 2009 and addressed those he had commanded: 'It has been a tremendous honour and privilege and a deeply humbling experience to lead you all for the past few years.'[39] The fact that this individual had demonstrated much bravery in his soldiering for some twenty-five years or more previous to this, for which he had been awarded the Military Cross, and had later been knighted, provides an interesting background to his later sense of gratitude and humility, revealing, in its own way, his commitment to the army as its own social world. This response

---

[39] *Daily Mirror*, 29 Aug. 2009, p. 23.

to the privilege of having been granted powerful responsibilities indicates something of a society possessing notions of 'service' and the checks and balances that create a mature democracy. Where leaders dominate rather than reciprocate power relations, a sense of self may replace any sense of otherness, as, perhaps, with Joseph Stalin. Though rising to rule the Communist Party in the former USSR, Stalin began his education by training for the Russian Orthodox priesthood before leaving his seminary for a political path to power. He died in 1953. One of his biographers described him quite simply as 'a killer', possessing a 'vast desire to dominate, punish and butcher', and as being in his politics 'exceptionally suspicious, vengeful and sadistic'.[40] One classic religious example of the interplay of humility and pride underlies the role of Satan in Jewish and various subsequent Christian scriptures.[41] This reaches one clear formulation in the beliefs of Mormons, who speak of Satan as having once been Lucifer, a morally sound agent in the heavenly kingdom of God, but who became rebellious when his offer of a plan of salvation for humanity, one that would have brought him great honour, was rejected by the Heavenly Father in favour of the plan offered by Jesus. It was Lucifer's piqued pride that then became transformed into envy and rebellion.[42]

MERCY

These negative attributes, with all their capacity to engender the equally negative emotion of fear, stand in sharp contrast to the property of mercy and its capacity for creative human responsive experience, especially if we see mercy prompting some kind of response akin to that of humility as a response to social approval. What I suggest, here, is that the praise that prompts the humility response may resemble the attitude of mercy that prompts a response of gratitude. In terms of social organization and relationships, mercy belongs to contexts of hierarchy and differential power; it is something shown by a superior to an inferior as indicated by one mid-eighteenth-century theologian who encouraged the rich to have 'emotions of benevolence and compassion' upon fellow creatures suffering distress.[43] But, unlike the humility response, mercy is not grounded in the approved behaviour of the

---

[40] Service (2004: 12, 10).
[41] Kelly (2006).
[42] Douglas J. Davies (2010).
[43] Foster (1752: 254).

recipients but, on the contrary, is accorded them despite their failure or inadequacy. Mercy shows the largesse of a deity, dignitary, or society to a failed member, just as it accords praise to an obedient member. What is interesting, however, is that the response to mercy can resemble the response to praise, one involving a form of transformative gratitude, a kind of creative humility. When mercy involves divine and human figures, the same kind of dynamics can be invoked and has, for example, played a major role in many religious traditions. Christian and Sikh forms of spirituality reveal this, and it is no accident that mercy, along with compassion, stand as foundational concepts within Islam. For Islam's characterization of the attributes of deity also emerges from a hierarchical order but brings with it a sense of the potentially radical nearness of Allah to each individual. To preface intentional statements in speech with an assertion that one speaks in the name of this deity who is compassionate and merciful is to highlight the relational nature of faith and of religious duty. The context in which mercy may be shown and received is one in which the legal ground rules of reciprocity, as embedded in law, are fully acknowledged but transcended for a particular purpose in a particular case. William Shakespeare famously addressed the topic in *The Merchant of Venice* when Portia describes the 'quality of mercy' as doubly beneficial: 'it blesseth him that gives and him that takes.' In so doing it is evocative of Mauss's 'fourth obligation' within reciprocity theory, to which we return in the following chapter. Here, however, we observe how the issue of hierarchy frames the scene, for what is very clear in Shakespeare's understanding is that mercy is 'mightiest in the mightiest'; he sees it as 'enthroned in the hearts of kings' and as being 'an attribute to God himself'. At that point he argues that earthly power is most like the divine 'when mercy seasons justice'.[44] There is a great deal of Christian theology informing this judgement, for mercy has played a considerable part in the framing of its doctrines of salvation, from extensive Jewish roots developing throughout New Testament texts.[45] A generation after Shakespeare, William Law would affirm that 'Christian Redemption is God's Mercy to all Mankind'.[46] Through all this language there emerges an experiential sense of gratitude, with St Paul, for example, seeing the 'mercies of God' as evoking a proper response in the transformation of the human mind and in humility of life.[47]

---

[44] Shakespeare, *The Merchant of Venice*, Act IV, sc. i.
[45] e.g., Numbers 14: 18; Psalm 89: 1; Hosea 6: 6; Luke 1: 50–8; 1 Timothy 1: 2.
[46] Law ([1728] 1893: 179–80).
[47] Romans 12: 1–3.

BETRAYAL

There now remains one emotion-touched and mood-based relationship to consider that takes us away from a self-sacrificial response to mercy and that brings a negative shadow across the broad canopy of love. It is that of love's and mercy's negation in betrayal, that distinctive capacity of a human being to hurt another. Here we encounter identity depletion in which negative dynamics pervades life's meaningfulness and reduces hope. While potentially extending from physical harm to mental punishment, betrayal marks the spot where a person's sense of self is forced to acknowledge that a relationship with another has been unfairly ruptured by that other person. This touches the deep current of reciprocity in human life and of the moral values of mutual fairness embedded within it. Parents and children, siblings, friends, neighbours, and workmates, all have their codes of co-responsibility operating on a basis of anticipated behaviour of fairness on which survival, flourishing, and identity depend. And it is when this mutual expectation and satisfaction is fractured that betrayal strikes at the moral core of justice and absolutely contradicts moral expectation. In colloquial English, the expression 'feeling gutted' dramatically expresses the emotional sensation that can accompany the knowledge of betrayal, with its hint of having the core of one's body removed. There is no fixed rule as to how individuals will respond to betrayal, but for many their view of the offender will be marked for ever, as a sense of bitterness enters their memory of a relationship terminated against their will.

This kind of experience explains why sacred texts alluding to betrayal can gain so much power. They speak *of* the human condition *to* the human condition. Within Christianity the case of Judas has provided the personification of this inhuman action in a classic paradigmatic scene where he, one of Jesus's twelve disciples, leads soldiers to arrest Jesus in a place where he had gone to pray. In John's Gospel this story is told with poignant symbolism, for Jesus, who knows what is to befall him, shares the fact of impending betrayal with one of his closest disciples by giving some bread to Judas while they all dine together. Judas is then said to have left the house and, in this Gospel, which plays so much on the motifs of light and darkness as symbols of good and evil, the text adds, 'it was night'.[48] When the soldiers and police come to arrest Jesus, guided by Judas, they come carrying lanterns and torches with their weapons. Now, in this dark place Judas

---

[48] John 13: 30.

stands in the background: he remains in the dark. In Mark's Gospel, in a more direct narrative undirected by grand themes of light and dark symbols of good and evil purpose, those who come to arrest Jesus, once more guided by Judas, carry swords and clubs but no lanterns and torches, and Judas plays no background role as part of the darkness to which, theologically speaking, he belongs. Instead, as key player he meets Jesus, addressing him as teacher or Rabbi, and gives him a kiss of greeting, turning the mark of positive relationship into the symbol of betrayal.[49] Matthew's Gospel has Jesus use the word 'friend' immediately after Judas greets him and kisses him as Rabbi; here there are no lanterns or lamps, but a focus on harmful weapons.[50] Luke's Gospel seems to combine aspects of a strict narrative with both theological and human motifs. Jesus seems to pre-empt Judas by asking if he is to betray him with a kiss? Again swords and weapons play their part, as someone's ear is cut off and, although there are no lanterns, the text has Jesus speak of the event as 'your hour, and the power of darkness'.[51] To have such texts within a religious tradition is to furnish individuals with at least one means of relating their own pain of abandonment and betrayal to central images of their faith.

Such accounts, whether in their more directly narrative, heavily theological, dramatic, or artistic forms, have played a powerful role in furnishing a paradigmatic scene of betrayal within Christian-influenced culture across history and across the world. In some churches this topic of Christ's betrayal is recalled in the rite of the Eucharist, as it is in Paul's biblical description of the Christian fellowship meal that took place 'on the night when he was betrayed'.[52] This most theological of cases magnifies the issue of betrayal by setting it within a text stressing the love and mutuality of friends, including that of Jesus, who is identified as a divine son of a heavenly father. In the developed theology of later Christianity he is identified as divine. This makes the issue of betrayal all the more profound, as human beings betray their God.

SUMMARY

In this chapter, then, we have seen something of how the human career has its power, vitality, or 'mystic substance' enhanced through acts of love and

---

[49] Mark 14: 45.
[50] Matthew 26: 49–50.
[51] Luke 22: 53.
[52] 1 Corinthians 11: 23.

mercy and shows its deep social embeddedness if it is ever fortunate enough to experience the humility response. Similarly, we have seen how that sense of self-identity can be severely depleted, as through acts of betrayal. Continuing with the theme of this study, we can see how the dynamics of these emotions is often schematized and managed through the social processes and institutions characterized as religious. Their textual narratives and liturgical performances provide some powerful opportunities for the emotional dynamics of Christian spirituality to foster identity. We will now develop these creative religious engagements further, as we turn in the next chapter to the domains of merit, grace, and pardon.

7

Merit, Grace, and Pardon

To the previous chapter's themes of love, joy, humility, and mercy we now add those of merit, grace, and pardon, as we continue to develop a spectrum of emotions and emotion-related concepts that contribute to a profile of religious identity. These particular socially constructed concepts—merit, grace, and pardon—constitute a fundamentally significant group in relation to the prestige and identity of individuals and, by extension, also of their religious identity. This is because they describe different expressions of, or responses to, reciprocity, itself the fundamental process of human life. These core values, lodged within the lives of devotees, become pervaded with feelings often held with the deepest affection. Of the three, merit is especially interesting, because it is the most widely shared concept in world religions, certainly more common than that of a deity. In this chapter we will deal with merit as a kind of salvation capital, a commodity capable of affecting a person's destiny.[1]

To understand merit as such a valued outcome of reciprocal relations is also to see its double potential: its positive form conduces to salvation but its negative form reveals destructive forces. In many traditions these are discussed in terms of one's status in the afterlife, whether one of pleasurable reward or one of suffering punishment. In terms of the other concepts discussed in this chapter, we will see that the negative capital can be offset both by pardon and by grace, terms often endued with distinctive religious significance of salvation of some kind. In terms of a person's developing religious career, we will, then, see how identity is enhanced through the positive social forces intensified through grace and pardon, forces generated through the many reciprocal forms of relationships that help create a

---

[1] 'Capital' in the sense of an accumulated benefit has become extended from its economic root to describe 'social capital', 'cultural capital', 'religious capital', and 'spiritual capital'; see Davies and Guest (2007: 3–8). But cf. Fine (2010) in criticism of the wide use of the capital and social capital model to interpret many phenomena inappropriately.

meaningful social world, all pervaded by a sense of hope.[2] And it is the *sense* of hope, as of 'grace' and 'pardon', that makes these issues so fundamental for any study of religious identity, for they are 'felt' strongly by devotees and do not remain simply as theological notions. So, our starting point is with people's reciprocal relationships both among themselves and also in relationships to key others of their religious world, be they ancestors, spirits, or deities. Such reciprocity is fundamental for understanding the dynamics of religion, because it underlies the notion of merit as a kind of moral 'commodity', which is gained by engaging with or practising the core values of a society and which, as 'salvation capital', is frequently believed to be invested with a supernatural value that affects one's ultimate identity, whether pre-mortal or post-mortem.

GENERATING MERIT

At the daily level, societies survive and flourish to the extent that their members sustain core values, with groups offering rewards in the form of social status or prestige for supportive behaviour, just as they express disapproval of bad behaviour through punishment or deprivation of status. What we often call religious traditions mark out those behaviours that focus on core values, often reckoning them to be divinely revealed commandments or codes overseen by ever-watchful ancestors. What is more, the 'merit' accruing from obedience is believed to result in salvation, just as the de-merit or sin that results from breaking laws may be seen as the ground for future punishment. But, here, salvation is a difficult word, because it carries different meanings in the major religious traditions, whether in Buddhism's forms of consciousness and enlightenment, in Islam's submission to God leading to admission to the eternal Paradise, or in Christianity's faith with its promise of heaven.[3] Then, in many traditional and local traditions, salvation may take the form of good health, many descendants, and fruitful harvests, all as a result of ancestors blessing their care-giving and attentive descendants. But, whatever the system, 'salvation' finds its root in merit. Merit is the stuff of salvation. As salvation capital, it is a moral commodity resulting from people being social-

---

[2] Crucially identified by Stanner (1960a: 124) in what he called the 'natural triad' of person–object–person.

[3] See Douglas J. Davies (1984a) for an approach to salvation through the sociology of knowledge.

moral and self-conscious animals, not least with a sense of destiny, often in an afterlife.[4] In secular contexts, too, the power of moral codes and social judgements remains strong, affecting social status and desired identities, often through the operation of legal systems.

Reciprocity, then, is as important for the comparative study of religion as are ideas of deity, and clustering about it are cognate ideas of temptation, which generate situations demanding pardon that effects a positive solution to the negative forces of fractured identity described in previous chapters. This theoretical perspective allows us to appreciate just how reciprocity theory provides the means of interpreting the important idea of grace. As with salvation, grace is always qualified by specific theological doctrines, and, because it has frequently been the cause of major disputes within and between Eastern and Western religions, it raises the question as to whether it can be defined in non-theological terms. This chapter argues that it can be so understood through the basic motifs of meaning and hope along with otherness and reciprocity. The discussion of the humility response in the previous chapter has already gone some way in preparing for what might be called a sociology of grace, a venture that demands some account of contemporary theories of reciprocity, as also of psychological issues of self-abnegation, self-security, and sociological factors of community cohesion through the maintenance of social rules. These concerns reflect Weber's Protestant Ethic thesis and its interest in the formation of human identity in terms of emotions aligned with the social approval of behaviour.[5] As this discussion of grace realigns issues of merit, it will also begin to indicate one possible emotional reframing of altruism.

Though this is beyond the scope of this study, it is also worth noting here, parenthetically, that some psychologists think it likely that human evolution favoured the selection of genes related to reciprocal behaviour patterns that enhance human interaction.[6] Whether that is the case or not, it is obvious that exchanges of gifts, time, place, and persons, with their obvious religious forms of dedication, blessing, sacrifice, and praise, constitute the domain of religious values and the triggering and fostering of emotions and moods. Reciprocity and affectivity are partners in humanity's generation of identity, with ideas of deity having, in their turn, developed upon a similar model: the

---

[4] See Obeyesekere (1968) and Tambiah (1968) for classic accounts of merit-making in Buddhism.

[5] Weber ([1904–5] 1976).   [6] Rolls (2005: 446).

ancestors and the gods enjoy gifts given in sincerity, just as they abhor the insincere offering.[7]

Merit, fear, and hope

Be that as it may, in merit we see how moral codes relate to emotional factors of identity, fully alert to the attrition of moral values in the complexities of daily interaction as well as in more dramatic events of social disruption. For the moral system tends towards homeostasis, with societies having created processes of reparation through the invocation of various forms of merit, grace, pardon, and punishment. Merit helps create a rationale that helps assuage uncertainty, fear, and the cumulative sense of unfairness, while also fostering hope for the future, despite the fact of experience that many transgress the moral laws.

In all this, merit, as the salvation-capital outcome of moral reciprocal processes, becomes the prime candidate for a universal concept underlying all religious and cultural activity focused on prime values, whether in mono-theism, polytheism, or secularism. As Walter Burkert affirmed: 'In religious dealings, gift exchange is simply ubiquitous . . . another universal of religious history as of anthropology.'[8] He documents the role of gifts and gifts to the gods for the world of classical antiquity, suggesting that reciprocity has its roots in human commensality. Furthermore, he wonders whether 'the prin-ciple of reciprocity' might have become 'fixed in men's minds as a widely successful strategy for dealing with reality' by creating a 'mechanism of optimism' within an otherwise chaotic world through relatively closed circles of people, 'which indicate stability'. The moods of fear and hope inherent in his approach express his underlying commitment to a biological view of social life as homeostatic, with reciprocity helping to maintain its 'transient stability'.

Just how people assess, quantify, and commodify aspects of exchange is a complex issue, as the case of the renowned Victorian Evangelical hymn-writer Frances Ridley Havergal shows. She approached 'time' in this commodified way and exemplified the idea of the Protestant work ethic in the process: 'For more and more do I feel what valuable capital Time is, capital which must

---

[7] Godfrey Lienhardt (1970: 284) describes the Anuak idea of *gwith*, a kind of blessing or curse that is at its strongest when spoken by a dying man, as that is when a person is revealed as he really is.
[8] Burkert (1998: 134).

not be put out at merely *any* interest, but as far as possible at the best and highest.'[9] Life and work become precious commodities whose experiential base was to be fostered in terms of sensing the presence of God and living in ways that transform 'otherness' into a relationship of intimacy. This kind of spirituality is deeply committed both to the idea of merit and to its inversion or transcending. As in Havergal, there is a profound sense in the importance of activity and of using God-given 'gifts' to the best effect, much as Max Weber documented in his foundational study of Protestant orientation to the world, yet many Christian hymns and Sikh scriptures, for example, speak of the ultimate uselessness of human endeavour and of the essential need for divine grace that supersedes it.

GRACE AND VIRTUAL RELATIONSHIPS

This indicates that there is something in 'grace' that conceives of a human being, not in terms of moral merchandise but as another domain of relationship in which reciprocity is transcended, in which otherness comes to be understood more in terms of mutuality and even of love. Part of the rationale of this form of spirituality is that, in the Christian case, the individual does not seek to achieve his own 'merit' but comes to rejoice in the merits possessed by Jesus Christ and which he is believed to share with the beloved believer. Not that this insight is always present in popular Christianity, where the simple market economy of cause and effect in work and pay often prevails. Ideally, however, two factors interact with each other, and each involves a motivational base in experience.

First, the commitment to merit as something achieved through endeavour remains but is focused on the person of Jesus. He is the one who fully observed divine commandments and did so at great emotional cost to himself—hence the almost excessive Christian preoccupation with Christ's passion, suffering, and death. He is interpreted in terms of ancient Jewish motifs of sacrifice, and becomes the sacrificially slaughtered Lamb of God. He experiences physical pain and status degradation: he is whipped, mockingly dressed as a noble, and crucified. In terms of the economics of salvation, he earns all possible merit through his obedience and suffering. The narrative motif of his 'passion' in the Garden of Gethsemane pinpoints both his

---

[9] Havergal (1880: 11).

suffering, symbolized in the 'sweating' of what looked like blood, and his uttering of the words of submission that it must be the divine father's will and not his own that must be done.[10] Through this obedient suffering Jesus is believed to have become the source of merit for all. It is very likely that the affinity many find with this image of Jesus is grounded in their own suffering, albeit a suffering not necessarily aimed at holy obedience to divine law. Empathy with the pain of others is a deep-seated human capacity and is likely to be one reason for the success of this form of Christian iconography in particular social contexts. We return to it in the next chapter in relation to Mormon religiosity.

The second factor involved in 'grace perception' relates to human experiences of love or in longing for love, in the sense of a driving emotional attachment to a much-desired figure. This may find its origin in the parent–child bond of dependency or of romantic love between partners.[11] In what is, essentially, a love–grace union, devotees long for the partner and sense a deep emotional attachment to him or her. In the process, merit is not forgotten; indeed, the social nature of human beings is hard to ignore in any context, but is now achieved in and through this union. The nature of the reciprocal relation between lover and beloved belongs to the inalienable processes of exchange: the benefits of the lover's merit are achieved almost unintentionally. Grace not only comes to describe the way the devotee thinks of the deity but feels the presence of that otherness. The beloved sees the lover as graceful: what the one has comes to the other as unearned; issues of merit fade away beneath the glow of mutual love.

While there are, doubtless, some people incapable of such a style of bonded spirituality, there are millions of devotees in many religious traditions whose world is inhabited by a divine presence conceived of as a person, as one to whom and with whom a relationship is forged. While to non-believers such a presence may simply reflect an overactive creativity resulting in an imaginary friend, albeit a divine one, to the believer this relationship can be as powerful as the 'real' encounters with other human beings. It is precisely such conceptions that foster prayer, devotional singing, and the offering of gifts of love. There are innumerable patterns of piety in which devotees are encouraged to imagine themselves as part of the drama of the life of their deity. Susan Karant-Nunn, for example, has detailed such acts of piety in early

---

[10] John 22: 42–4.
[11] Jankowiak (1995).

modern Germany as in von Cochem's descriptive narrative of Christ's suffering *The Great Myrrh-Garden of the Bitter Passion*, in which 'the worshiper should envision every detail as though present'.[12] It is but a short step from such emotion-inducing imaginative relationships to those evoked in songs like the African-American spiritual 'Were you there when they crucified my Lord', which evokes the crucifixion of Jesus and includes the emotional sentiment that 'sometimes it causes me to tremble, tremble, tremble: were you there when they crucified my Lord'. While such spirituals are seen as having helped 'African-descended people construct a sense of selfhood', they certainly did so with the powerful help of evoked emotions and a sense of relation with the divine Saviour.[13] The emotion-laden nature of divine bonds, especially when established in childhood, can ensure their extreme durability throughout life, especially since many ritual processes intensify them periodically. Moreover, the human capacity for interior dialogue easily facilitates a sense of relation with the other.

Merit and ethics

In its many formulations, then, merit plays a fundamental role in religious and ethical life, always crediting to this single term 'merit' its local significance, whether in terms of love–grace unions, in release or enlightenment motifs, or in the benefits gained from ancestors or the natural world. Because this concept is crucial for this study, we will now outline some of the theoretical background of reciprocity theory and then consider selected key manifestations and associated emotional repertoires of merit in the notions of salvation, temptation, pardon, eternal life, sacrifice, and the humility response. The topic of temptation will demand an emphasis all of its own, not only because it relates to strong emotional dynamics but also because of its frequent identification with sexuality rather than, for example, with 'lust' for power, money, or property. Temptation is also important because it constitutes part of the process in and through which key religious leaders such as Jesus and the Buddha are reckoned to have become meritorious agents.

---

[12] Karant-Nunn (2010: 172).
[13] Peters (1996: 682–4) classifies nine types of Spiritual, most of which identify emotions—e.g. the first embracing 'sorrow, alienation, desolation'.

Trust, reciprocity, and intuition

Society's survival and flourishing depends to a very large degree on trust between its members, a concept closely allied to hope, as explained in Chapter 1. Yet, trust would appear to be less an emotion that periodically bursts upon us than a more sustained mood supporting ongoing life values. In some societies it will be embedded in notions of family, clan, or age mates with whom one has undergone some form of initiation or learning experience; in others it underpins the professional standing of a person within say a medical, legal, educational, scientific, or religious institution. Sometimes family- and non-family-based statuses will overlap. Trust exemplifies the interplay of this study's motifs of otherness and reciprocity in generating a meaningful and hopeful basis of life through relationships of self with others. It assumes a certain mutual quality of perception and even of affect: we hold a certain feeling for those with whom we are happy to engage in a variety of exchanges. Within a market economy, as Marcel Mauss—the key figure in the development of reciprocity—argued, money becomes an important medium of exchange, as one person buys and another sells some commodity. Money comes to be the medium of trust that underlies the moment of exchange. The only real fear that could undermine this trust is one of counterfeit money or that the vendor is knowingly cheating the purchaser over the quality of goods. Modern market economies seek to overcome these potential difficulties through forms of insurance or guarantee, itself a legal version of trust. When the world financial system came close to total collapse early in 2009, much emphasis was given to the loss of trust in banks and market systems. Indeed, the deep loss of confidence in financial experts was surrounded by references to trust and to fear in a period in which money as the symbol of social trust and even of the stability of entire societies came under the deepest of threats. Bankers and companies that had long been trademark signs of respectability were destroyed within a matter of weeks, which reflected the way trust, as one of the most intangible of mood-based attitudes, exerts a foundational influence in the most developed of societies. Something similar underlay a loss of trust in the religious capital of parts of the Catholic Church in the later 1990s and early twenty-first century over the topic of child sex abuse and involved some US dioceses in paying millions of dollars in recompense to those so abused. This was a classic case of an institution that is normally grounded in trust being found wanting; we will return to this in the next chapter.

MAUSS, GIFTS, AND AFFECT

Marcel Mauss was deeply aware of the problems of depersonalization that followed the shift from direct forms of exchange between people in traditional societies to the impersonal use of money in market economies.[14] When the conventions underpinning this impersonal symbol break down, it is not surprising that a sense of fear spreads far and wide, since money has become the most widespread medium of social trust in modern life, and saving and investment often symbolize a hope for people's future. Money now helps establish many individuals' sense of identity through jobs and professions, making the near collapse of money markets with its consequent loss of jobs and fear for long-term funding in retirement deeply problematic. While trust is, then, among the most intangible of social moods, it is also among the most powerful. Mauss's theoretical contribution to our understanding of exchange between people and people and between people and their deities is important not only within the history of social thought but also because of its association with emotions and identity: it is also germane, because of more recent theories of cognitive science. The latter complements the former in a mutually reinforcing fashion that will be stressed below, but, first, we must clarify two aspects of Mauss's theory of gifts—namely, the 'threefold obligation' and 'the fourth obligation'. The 'threefold obligation' pertains to his best-known idea: that gifts are given with the recipient feeling an obligation to return a gift at some future date. Here he spoke of some 'force' in a 'gift' that presses a person to accept it and, later, to reciprocate with some appropriate return 'gift'. Here the notion of 'gift' can mean anything from an object to some action or expression of interest and support, all within a threefold process of obligation.

This process largely involves alienable gifts, objects, or services that are easily and obviously transferable.[15] His 'fourth obligation', however, involves inalienable gifts, characterized as phenomena linking persons with their

---

[14] Mauss ([1925] 1966).

[15] Though even here purchases can result in some recognition of relation between people—say merchant and regular customer—that surpasses mere market value (Certeau, Giard, and Mayal ([1994] 1998: 96–7).

origins, or engaging individuals with their core values, especially those enshrined, for example, in land, ancestors, or deities. Just as with Aristotle's fourth-century BCE observation that 'there is something about gifts that makes them akin to votive offerings', we soon find that inalienable gifts involves some emotional charge.[16] Their power cannot be understood apart from this emotion they engender; their emotional charge is integral to their significance. Within families or between individuals, for example, we often speak of what are, essentially, inalienable objects as having 'sentimental' value, a term that expresses a depth of personal meaning pervaded by a fond memory or charged with emotional significance. It is precisely this kind of symbolic object that is beyond price; it can neither be bought nor sold but is, rather, a mark of intimate relationship and often passes from generation to generation. It is this process of reciprocity embedded within the fourth obligation that undergirds many aspects of identity formation associated with religious institutions, their texts, interpretations, rituals, and leadership. It also evokes a certain form of otherness embedded in those intimacies.

SALVATION AND MERIT

One obvious application of merit is to the sixteenth-century Protestant Reformation, and the role and idiom of monetary exchange in relation to salvation that came to a head in the phenomenon of papal indulgences. The fact that these authoritative documents could be purchased and were reckoned to speed up the process of salvation in the afterlife played a significant part in Martin Luther's theological opposition to Catholic authority in relation to salvation. He favoured a more direct and less mediated access to Christ's merit, as the doctrine of the priesthood of all believers came to enshrine in Reformation theology. The psychologist Erich Fromm interpreted indulgences as 'a particularly good illustration of the influence of growing capitalism'. He identified the Pope as 'a monopolist owning an immense moral capital and using it for his own financial advantage and for his "customers'" moral advantage'.[17] But he also saw in Luther's and Calvin's Protestant religious outlook, especially in Calvin's, a 'despotic God, who wants

---

[16] Aristotle (1963: 76).
[17] Fromm ([1942] 1960: 61).

unrestricted power over men and their submission and humiliation', albeit without the mediation of priestly authority. Fromm took this attitude to be 'the projection of the middle class's own hostility and envy'.[18] For good or ill he interpreted conscience as a 'slave driver put into man by himself'.[19] As for the 'new aristocracy of money', they gained a new sense of 'freedom' and 'a new feeling of mastery and individual initiative'. Fromm took the very culture of the Renaissance to be grounded in this 'new sense of human dignity, will and mastery', though he reckoned there was also a measure of despair and scepticism built into it.[20] For him this was especially true of the working classes, where 'feelings of insignificance and resentment' grew and for which 'Protestantism was the answer to the human needs of the frightened, uprooted, and isolated individual who had to orientate and to relate himself to a new world'. Fromm sees 'social process' as moulding the character structure of a class.[21] One of his insights pivots around power and the *'lust for power which is not rooted in strength but in weakness. It is the expression of the inability of the individual self to stand alone and live.'*[22]

When it comes to grace, Fromm held an instructive approach through the 'phenomena of abundance, like-love or tenderness', which he believes are absent in Freud's scheme, which is, essentially, 'a psychology of want'.[23] We mentioned in Chapter 2 how the anthropologist Hocart identified one function of ritual, especially in its celebratory mode, as being to secure and promote life. And it is this security that emerges here, one that allows the power of human sociability to engage with the sheer fact of numbers to give a sense of the durability and potential of human life: the very idea of celebration implies an abundance. Hocart also emphasized the very 'quest for life' that he believed to underlie some ritual activity.[24] Unlike play in children that may be preparatory for work in adult life, the 'quest for life' may have an immediacy of effect about it rather than any intended teleological scope. The quest for life is an end in and of itself. Having said that, the ritual celebrations

---

[18] Fromm ([1942] 1960: 82).   [19] Fromm ([1942] 1960: 84).

[20] There is a sense in which the fourteenth–sixteenth-century cultural Renaissance and its stress on the individual was closely linked with similar themes, religiously conceived, in the sixteenth-century Reformation.

[21] Fromm ([1942] 1960: 86, 87).

[22] Fromm ([1942] 1960: 139).

[23] Fromm ([1942] 1960: 250).

[24] Hocart (1933: 137), similar to Charles Taylor's 'fullness' motif (2007: 5–12).

that are an end in and of themselves, possessing a 'terminal' quality that need not extend beyond the moment, can still convey a sense that positive times lie ahead. The sense of abundance engendered by such rites reveals a creative aspect of humanity that acknowledges the possibility, indeed the likelihood, that this experience will be repeated and leads us to understand that things expressing abundance are often called a 'blessing'; they belong to the inalienable aspect of exchange relationships and often elicit gratitude and praise. We find a similar notion, that of 'plenitude' or 'superabundance', taken up by Thomas Maschio from the work of Maurice Leenhardt,[25] a contemporary of Fromm. Maschio, in his study of a Melanesian society, found the 'sense of plenitude' valuable when interpreting, among other things, the nature of funerary rites and the way acts of memory or memorialization could evoke in the living a sense of how former generations had contributed to the identity of the living, who, in turn, were now fostering yet new generations. Echoing Leenhardt's, Maschio's work is valuable for its analysis of the 'aesthetics of ritual performance' in which emotions enter into the sense of self generated within ritual contexts and the mythical worlds framing them.[26]

OTHERNESS, RECIPROCITY, AND WHOLENESS

One significant aspect of the emotional dynamics of grace is Jung's significant description of 'the feeling of grace' that 'always characterizes' the experience of a person catching 'a fleeting glimpse of his wholeness'.[27] Jung is important for his psychological emphasis upon 'feeling' in that theological discussions of grace easily fall prey to philosophical and legalistic schemes that avoid the sensory domain. Within Christianity, for example, theologians often classify grace into different types and assert their own church's right to administer the 'means of grace' in the sacraments because of the authority of their various priesthoods and ministries. Whether grace came through such church organization or more directly through a person's individual Bible-led and Holy Spirit-inspired knowledge of God was a major factor in the European Protestant Reformation of the early sixteenth century. This movement influenced the world's religious map in one of the first processes of

---

[25] Leenhardt ([1947] 1979: 169).
[26] Maschio (1994: 204, 41).
[27] Jung ([1953] 1968: 7).

globalization, especially in the Protestant rise of missionary societies in the late eighteenth and early nineteenth centuries. Seldom has the role of emotional experience been more influential in the history of the world than when experience has transformed or radically redirected the life course of individuals like Martin Luther at the Reformation, Paul in the first, Augustine in the late fourth and fifth, Muhammad in the fifth and sixth, and Guru Nanak in the fifteenth and sixteenth centuries, along with the Buddha in the fifth and fourth centuries before the Common Era.

Along with these, thousands of individual followers have had their lives transformed by experiences of change. Jung's psychology of religion is but one approach that pinpoints 'the tension of opposites' within religion that often underlies such conversion processes and moves individual development towards some degree of personal maturity or wisdom. More historically, some see the evangelical conversions of the eighteenth and nineteenth centuries as important for providing more detailed and explicit narrative templates for individual change than are found, for example, in the front-line Reformers such as Luther or Calvin. Certainly, the later evangelical folk often reveal a negative self-appraisal before the moral laws of God in feelings of 'dread, sorrow, mental agitation, and much weeping', prior to all doubt 'vanishing', with all sadness and unrest of heart 'being taken away at once', as one account of early modern English Evangelicalism put it before contrasting this transformation with 'the pathological autonomy of the secular individualist self that has often been taken as the normative development of the Enlightenment'.[28] This should not be too surprising, since evangelical conversion has its deep negative self-judgement rooted in a social code, albeit expressed as a divine commandment, and, when the sense of release from sin comes, it is within the religious community that it is framed, expressed, and appreciated. Such conversion involves a passage through nihilism grounded in the sense of otherness perceived as God and rooted in a reciprocity of exchange—command and obedience—albeit sensed as failure. This is precisely why the transcending experience of failure's sadness becomes a rejoicing in grace, for within this Christian schema grace belongs to the inalienable cluster of relations and experience with divine otherness, which is now shared and sung about within the community of the redeemed.

[28] Hindmarsh (2005: 58, 348).

Cognitive systems and reciprocity

There can, of course, be no guarantee that all will attain wisdom or even gain a glimpse of wholeness such that a sense of grace ensues, but the possibility of such developments is made possible, as indicated earlier in Boyer's summarizing work on cognitive science, through numerous mental-processing systems deployed when people engage, for example, with 'ancestors, gods or spirits'.[29] He speaks of various 'systems', with the 'intuitive-psychology system' giving us a sense of dealing with 'intentional agents', which our 'Person-File system' further specifies as 'distinct individuals'. Then, he cites both an 'exchange system' and a 'moral system' as actual partners involved in reciprocal events. These various systems are assumed to have developed within us over the course of human evolution, with each of them dealing with aspects of human awareness and intuitions about the world in a practical and applied way and not as processes dedicated to handling abstract questions. In other words, the mental processing of apparent causes and effects amid which we find ourselves occurs without our consciously analysing them. 'None of these systems is designed to handle such abstract questions' as to whether the ancestors, gods, or spirit exist. We simply find ourselves having an intuition that they do. We find ourselves acting as though there are agents we cannot see, that they have some interest in our moral actions, and that we can engage in a give and take with them. In this approach, the language of 'intuition' and of human mental processing assumes that such processing delivers intuitions to us, regardless of our critical philosophical examination of the ideas they seem to connote. That is to say, we simply sense that there are supernatural agents, that our moral behaviour is somehow monitored, and that our gift exchanges make sense: this is why the otherness and reciprocity idioms of this study are integrated necessities. Boyer draws from various psychological studies to argue that these various systems, which operate as he often likes to say 'in the basement' and without our being aware of their action, come together or interplay with each other to produce more than the sum of their parts. For him, to speak of 'religion' is not to speak of some very different and specific religious 'sense' or 'experience' but is to think of a pattern of interacting systems giving a sense of things. More particularly, it is to think of these systems as giving a sense of things in

---

[29] Boyer (2001: 361).

particular contexts: 'most religious thoughts are about particular situations, particular people, particular feelings.'[30] This is why we devote a later chapter to sacred place, worship, and music.

What Boyer takes from cognitive psychology and evolutionary biology in terms of how different inference systems interplay can be related to Mauss's work in terms of Boyer's 'exchange system' and Mauss's threefold scheme of exchange of alienable gifts, while the further combination of Boyer's 'moral system' embraces Mauss's 'fourth obligation'. To this we could add the role of the 'Personal-File system' responsible for identifying ancestors, gods, or spirits as definite agents. Then, we need to observe that the manner in which our overall 'intuitive-psychology system' confers a sense of 'intentional agents' in any particular group or religious tradition will depend upon its history. And this will also apply to the emotion terms and expressions that have developed to describe the intuitional basis of awareness. Any extensive study of these issues would need to observe how the rise of priesthoods or elite guilds that handle sacred narratives, theologies, and rituals set about systematizing ideas that are seldom systematic in the ritual and ethical practice of people.

Structures of pardon

Another valuable application of Mauss's approach to reciprocity concerns the phenomenon of pardon by which formal forgiveness for an illegal act changes the guilty recipient's status. Pardon thus assumes a jural system in which someone possesses the authoritative power to release an offender from an existing conviction. Then, just as an earthly ruler may pardon a criminal, so a deity can be viewed in a similar fashion. Within Christian theology, for example, divine commandments have been equated with laws and their contravention with sin. In the process of divine law-breaking, God is said to be offended, with sin being an affront to his honour. Accordingly, forgiveness of sin makes sense in terms of pardon, when the authoritative source acts in benign goodwill towards offenders and pardons them.[31]

The nature of the reciprocal element may vary according to tradition and context. Solomon Schimmel, for example, stressed the way in which Jewish

---

[30] Boyer (2001: 365).

[31] See Page and Brash (1891: 81) for the Wesleyan Methodist idea of 'holiness' being possible only after 'pardon is obtained'.

tradition approached pardon in terms of the obligation a person has towards 'a repentant sinner', while Christianity tended to highlight it as a divine gift to humanity.[32] One aspect of the relationships underlying such schemes concerns the question of sincerity as a quality of intention, for, as far as associated ritual may be concerned, there is always the issue of how verbal formulae of pardon may or may not involve, evoke, or trigger particular emotions. When, for example, Schimmel explored the theme of repentance from his Jewish perspective, he speaks of how the annual Jewish Ten Days of Repentance involve practices 'designed to arouse one emotionally so that the repentance will not be hollow, a ritualistic formula devoid of spiritual-psychological substance'.[33] This touches the theme of sincerity with its cultural assumption that formal words may 'only be words' and not carry some conviction that reaches into some inner depths of an individual. Here cultural assumptions can be problematic when trying to evaluate the nature of religious rite or other ceremony, as when someone swears on the Bible or other sacred text in a law court and people might wonder whether the truth will be told or not. Indeed, the very rite of swearing on the Bible within a historically Christian culture, as in Britain, seeks to bond sincerity with social expression, ever mindful that someone may commit perjury.

Another sociological perspective on pardon comes from anthropologist Robert Herz as garnered by Mauss after Herz's untimely death. Here 'pardon is a mystical operation, achieved by way of rites, which destroys sin, appeases the collectivity of the gods and, at the same time, restores the good state of the sinner'.[34] In sociological terms, the 'mystical' element seems to describe the force inherent in ritual activity that reverses the negative social evaluation of one who has transgressed commandments. These are sociological terms that also represent some kind of emotional awareness of a state of guilt. Mauss, himself, considered the removal of guilt, either through payment or through pardon, and linked the former with 'simpler' and the latter with 'higher' religions. For him, as Parkin saw, 'the absence of pardon' was 'the fundamental characteristic of paganism'.[35] While such judgements belong to an outmoded evolutionist style of thinking, they still highlight distinctions between forms of reparation that restore social disorder in particular forms of social organization. If we were to interpret these distinctions through

---

[32] Schimmel (2002: 46), reflecting upon Worthington's 'Pyramid of Forgiveness'.
[33] Schimmel (2002: 177).
[34] Parkin (1996: 135).   [35] Parkin (1996: 138).

Mauss's own gift theory, we might link the 'payment' type with his first-order reciprocal obligation of an offender to give and the offended to receive a gift, as, for example, with a money payment, while the 'pardon' element might better pertain to the fourth obligation of inalienable gifts, where a superior agent passes to the inferior something of profound significance that simply cannot be purchased.

DEATH, SACRIFICE, AND DESTINY

In most non-pardon situations it is easier to think of merit as a commodity gained by observing moral laws and fulfilling social obligations or lost by non-observance or by committing acts that attract negative merit. One frequent property of merit is that it has long been related to beliefs in the identity of the dead in an afterlife. As one of the oldest religious ideas, it relates to human ideas of justice and judgement, operated either by a supernatural judge after the model of human courts of law, as in later Judaism, Christianity, and Islam, or else as some impersonal cosmic process, as in Hinduism, Buddhism and Sikhism. In many traditional societies where afterlife ideas take the form of ancestor beliefs but without elaborate notions of luxurious heavens or punishing hells, merit systems often work by seeing the ancestors as judges of human behaviour, rewarding or punishing their living descendants as appropriate to their behaviour. It now remains to sketch merit's more explicit role in a variety of religious traditions.

Karma, death, and destiny

Merit is essential within the karma concepts of Eastern religious traditions as a moral application of the idea of reciprocity to human identity to determine a person's destiny after bodily death. Karma forms a cluster of concepts with law, commandment, obedience, disobedience, sin, and a judgement operating as a principle of the way things are rather than on the model of a law court with personal judges. This impersonal form of principles in the karma complex of Hinduism, Buddhism, and Sikhism differs from the judge and court format of Judaism, Christianity, and Islam, where the righteousness of a deity comes to underlie commandments for living and where disobedience takes the form of sin against deity.

As one case study of the role of merit karma in religious destiny, we take developments within contemporary Japan, especially in terms of death ritual, which is performed for the majority of Japanese by Buddhist priests. Indeed, Japanese Buddhism has come to be so closely identified with death that some Buddhists feel it has not engaged enough in wider social issues and life concerns, or even that it has compromised some fundamental Buddhist ideas about the ultimate non-existence of a 'soul'.[36] In several traditions rites are performed to ensure merit transfer to the deceased, and this is but one form of merit transfer operating in many Buddhist cultural contexts to offset the negative merit accrued over the lifetime of ordinary people who are unable to sustain the Buddhist precepts, including celibacy.[37] One avenue of merit acquisition, which can be economically costly, involves the status of a deceased lay person being changed to that of a priest-monk by post-mortem ordination.[38] The dead is given a new name and, as part of the status change, receives a lineage chart showing a link to the Buddha himself. This can even be written in 'ink made from the abbot's blood', and placed in the coffin in which the deceased now passes into the afterlife.[39]

In Pure-Land traditions yet other rites emphasize the compassion of Amida Buddha, who comes to greet the dying and conduct them into that Pure-Land of the afterlife. This case offers a good example of the encounter and paradox of merit versus compassion or, in nearly analogous terms, of merit versus grace, or commandment versus love, in the Christian context. As we have already seen, this form of spirituality, wherever it appears, tends to stress the interpersonal nature of reciprocity and the personal nature of otherness through which the believer finds meaning and hope. It involves a sensed quality of relation unlike the impersonal operation of a quasi-judicial or even of a mechanical operation of a mathematical principle of bad and good karma.

MEANING, HOPE, AND WHOLENESS: SACRIFICE

One arena in which positive and negative aspects of moral credit have most frequently intersected within many religious traditions is that of sacrifice, and

---

36 Tanabe (2008: 325–48).
37 Walter (2008: 268–9).
38 Covell (2008: 293–324).
39 Williams (2008: 217).

it is here that Mauss's gift theory and Boyer's exchange and moral systems assumptions cohere to advantage. In Chapter 2 we mentioned William Robertson Smith (1846–94) as a profound influence on Durkheim; the reason for that lay in the idea that ritual helped integrate society. Though Robertson Smith was a believing Christian, his evolution-inspired reading of ancient Semitic religion created an image of a society whose sense of group unity was posited upon belief in totemic ancestors. Durkheim saw in this a powerful means of reading society as a community integrated through ritual, but, because he did not believe in deities or supernatural powers, he interpreted a group's perception of 'powers' as an awareness of the force created by the group itself. It was 'society' that the community experienced and not god (s): or, to phrase it in a fairly traditional expression of Durkheim studies, God is Society and Society is God.

Robertson Smith was, himself, a theologian and Professor of Hebrew influenced by evolutionary thought, including the work of his fellow Scot J. F. McLennan. He was familiar with life in the Middle East, where his travels had led him to meet the great Victorian traveller Sir Richard Burton. As Robertson Smith pondered ancient Jewish religion, especially thinking about the nature of sacrificial ritual, he came to argue that it had undergone processes of evolution. Here he shared a sense of excitement with other late nineteenth-century thinkers for whom Darwin's theory of evolution had brought a new and focused impetus to earlier and more philosophical-historical ideas of change and progress. When dealing with how communities developed, Robertson Smith explicitly spoke of 'communities formed by the survival of the fittest' that led to a 'self-confidence and elasticity . . . engendered by success in the struggle for life'. For him religion existed not 'for the saving of souls but for the preservation and welfare of society'.[40] What came to be called Robertson Smith's communion theory of sacrifice was the idea that, as a kinship-related group came together to share in animal sacrifice, they not only felt a strong bond linking the living, but also felt as though their ancestors were also present.[41] This integrated group was now stronger as a result of this sense of total communion or community. The symbol of blood was 'the primitive symbol of kinship', with religion being the 'elation of all members of a community to a power that has the good of the community at heart'.[42]

[40] Smith (1889: 260, 29).
[41] Smith (1889: 265): 'Sacrificial meal . . . cements the bond.'
[42] Smith (1889: 44, 55).

Though Robertson Smith deals with experience without using the language of emotion, we cannot ignore the place of emotional experience in his work as also in Durkheim's.

Depletion again

This sense of integration achieved through group cohesion constitutes an appropriate context in which a sense of unity may arise that is congenial to emotions of grace, mirroring Jung's description of grace as a person catching 'a fleeting glimpse of his wholeness'.[43] Quite a contrary dynamic of human experience lies in what we explored in Chapter 3 as identity depletion where life circumstances create experiences opposite to those gained in contexts of grace, as, for example, in the context of betrayal depicted in the previous chapter's conclusion. Now, once more, we end a chapter with a similar negativity enshrined in its own local cultural construct, that of defamation.

'There is something pleasing to many in the sight of a great man dragged down; it gives a comforting belief in the justice of fate, if not of law.'[44] So wrote Margaret Irwin in her biography of Sir Walter Raleigh, a great Elizabethan Englishman finally beheaded after malicious politicking. She describes the tip of that iceberg of human emotion enshrined in the German term *Schadenfreude*, which captures the pleasure some get in seeing harm come to another. This valuable insight highlights no simple emotion but a complexity of perspectives that come into play within human beings as we have a sense of our own status in relation to others and are happy to see them defamed. The status hierarchy evident in many higher primates here takes on its human form of pleasure at the downfall of others.

The self-awareness that names certain feelings is a remarkable thing made more remarkable by the emotions that help construct the process of our life in ways of which we are not aware. This means that the relationship between an individual's feelings and the capacity of others to empathize with them or to understand them will always remain a problem. To draw a distinction between empathy and understanding is valuable here, for, while it is relatively easy for one person to get a feeling of what another person experiences in the rough brushstrokes of, say, joy at some good news, or relief in news that some potential disaster has not occurred, or in the sadness accompanying news of a

---

[43] Jung ([1953] 1968: 7).
[44] Irwin ([1960] 1962: 174).

dead relative, it is quite another to be able to understand the finer details lying behind that experience within the life history of another. But, as just indicated, we should not assume that empathy necessarily tends to a positive attitude, but accept that some emotional responses to the plight of others can be 'sweet'. Just because 'revenge is sweet' when intentionally perpetrated does not mean that a sweetness may arise when simply hearing of the downfall of another. The history of a person's experiences, prior disasters, triumphs, moral victories, and gloating pleasures all colour immediate emotional responses in ways other persons simply cannot access. The mass of humanity now living in cities cannot be aware of the complex emotional lives of those passed daily in the street or even met at work. This is one reason why religious groups are important in urban life, providing space and time for sharing experiences, for evaluating them in moral terms and, often, for fostering positive goals despite the negativities of life—negativities to which we turn in the following chapter. Such small-scale communities show the importance of contexts in which individuals may experience shared emotion in ways that are intelligible to others and conduce to a sense of meaning in life.

SUMMARY

Such a sensed awareness of shared meaning brings to an individual an enhanced sense of well-being. Indeed, we have seen in this chapter how the fact of reciprocity and the notion of merit for those fully participating in social obligations easily lead to what is often identified as religious behaviours and ideas, not least that of merit as salvation capital. In fact this natural spectrum shows just how difficult it is to separate 'religious' activities from the apparently secular forms of ordinary reciprocal exchange and the attributing of status and prestige to people in everyday life. We have seen how the choice of these key topics of merit, pardon, and grace has allowed us to see 'religious' motifs emerging from the widespread fact of reciprocity. Similarly, we have seen how the theme of identity and emotion moves quite naturally from the apparently mundane into the heartland of religious classification of ultimate values and the management of experiences conducive to salvation.

This chapter has shown the value of selecting reciprocity as one of the foundational ideas underlying this study without which it would be impossible to understand the nature of merit and grace and, consequently, of concepts without which most studies of religious identity and experience would be greatly lacking. Now that we have established the significance of reciprocity, it is time to highlight another of this study's foundational ideas, that of hope, and to show its significance for understanding emotion and identity. Once more we will see how a key concept interplays with other ideas that frequently align themselves with religion—namely, suffering and despair. Just as this chapter has shown how emotional experiences frame and pervade social values, the next chapter will take such bonding further by developing the idea of moral-somatic relationships. The importance of the present chapter as a lead into this new idea lies in the understanding we have gained into how moral power or merit is generated through obedience to social rules. For, in the idea of moral-somatic relationships, we will see the potential for both positive and negative outcomes of behaviour that may seriously affect an individual's or a group's sense of well-being; hence the next chapter's interest in both hope and despair.

8

Moral-Somatics, Hope, Despair, and Suffering

From the immediately previous chapters on how social values engage with emotions to influence religious identity, the two ideas of the humility response and of social merit's transformation into salvation capital stand out as directly relevant to a further concept that will be developed in this chapter, that of moral-somatic processes. This concept will reinforce our study's concern with embodiment—that interface of social values and emotional experience—that generates identity and continuously negotiates it through a variety of life's contexts. The idea of moral-somatic processes highlights the way human bodies respond to social values and the actions of other people. In so doing it incorporates the experiences of hope and despair that are not only endemic to daily living but are also elevated to serve a religious function in many traditions, not least in the context of suffering, which stands as a major issue in many religious traditions. While acknowledging the fact that in complex societies religion is often differentiated from other aspects of social life, we reiterate the fact that religion is a difficult entity to define and to separate out from many other aspects of human activity at the level of an individual's life. This is especially the case when issues of suffering and contexts of despair and hope are concerned. Many aspects of life dealing with those features seem to attract the notion of religion and be dealt with in patterns of behaviour, often deeply symbolic, and managed by ritual specialists. In terms of previous chapters, then, this one will explore how core values and their emotions become embodied and operate through what we will call moral-somatic processes.

MORAL-SOMATIC PROCESSES

In theoretical terms, to speak of moral-somatic relationships is to develop Durkheim's *Homo duplex* notion within the realm of embodiment theory.[1] Modelled on the familiar idea of psycho-somatic factors, these moral-somatic phenomena concern the way an individual's feeling state is influenced by social context. Here, 'moral' follows Durkheim's notion of society as a moral community, since, for Durkheim, 'sociology is a sociology of morality' not in the sense of 'moral rules for the prescription of living but in the sense of describing, analysing and explaining the moral rules' by which different populations live.[2] Society is a world of reciprocal relations between people whose collaborative endeavour creates a moral community of which each individual is a part and yet is sensed as being 'beyond' the individual. This expresses the Durkheimian paradox that 'otherness' is nothing less than 'society' itself. For our purposes, it would be better to say that otherness marks the relation between the individual and society. Society is sensed as beyond the individual, is experienced by the individual when acting communally, and is a primary resource for the individual when alone. Emotion, then, lies at the very heart of Durkheim's description of ritual action, as it generates a sense of transcendence over people's ordinary life and conveys a sense of something greater and beyond themselves. He was happy to say that what they experienced and understood to be divine was in fact social. This is a good example of a case where the analyst offers quite a different explanation than the people having the experience.[3] Whether in Durkheim or in today's cognitive psychologists, this question of experience and interpretation of experience remains a crucial factor in the overall understanding of life and religion precisely because it involves our personal experiences and how we explain them to ourselves and how we even come to understand ourselves through them.

Theologians often criticize Durkheim for turning society into God, or reducing God to nothing but society, and, from a theological standpoint, that is understandable. But it is equally possible to take Durkheim on his own

[1] As indicated in Douglas J. Davies (2000). The *Homo duplex* theme of a person's double nature asserts the intimate alliance of somatic, bodily life, with social or moral life.

[2] Parkin (1996: 140).

[3] Often described as the difference between the 'emic' nature of local explanation and the 'etic' nature of the analyst's interpretation.

terms and to see him accord to society the same kind of enormity that religious believers accord to God, at least as far as human experience is concerned. Just as theologians often use the phrase 'to take seriously' when emphasizing some idea or practice, so we might say that Durkheim takes society seriously: it is the foundation for human life, conferring language and a whole way of seeing or classifying the world.[4] Society is great in much the same way that some believers speak of God as being great: each taken as a core concept for interpreting life. This is potentially problematic for any discussion between different parties, because it is characteristic of groups to compete over similar concepts.

Still, sociologically speaking, to highlight moral-somatic processes is to mark the complex interplay between membership in a social network with its core values and the physical processes of bodily life activated by both memories and future goals. Consider the apparently simple case of a blush: this may be prompted even in private when a person remembers a situation in which embarrassment first caused blushing in a social context where some social value was broken and a sense of shame caused the neural-chemical processes of the body to redden a person's facial area. Memory recreates the scene and the person responds accordingly. This is perfectly understandable for a social animal with years of evolutionary adaptation behind and within it. Blushing highlights the way self-consciousness opens the boundaries of self to others. However, it lies entirely beyond the competence of this study to consider just how the biological and neural aspects of life produce these effects. Our task lies in exploring the more middle-range issues of social experience as such.

One such middle-range arena is the socially important realm of the administration of justice and power in society and, in particular, cases where a sense of injustice at the social level influences the bodily level of well-being. In popular terms, injustice makes us sick, just as justice that is done and seen to be done brings a degree of comfort to victims. At the personal level it also applies to the betrayals that sometimes beset people in ordinary life. In such social and personal worlds of relationships, this moral-somatic idea highlights the bio-cultural dimension of feeling and thought introduced in Chapter 1. It could be seen, for example, in the previous chapter's reference to religious institutions, which exist to be trusted and to

---

[4] This is the importance of the 'Sociological Theory of Knowledge' that prefaces his *Elementary Forms*.

engage with the truth, being found to have some leaders who betray that trust. Some Catholic Dioceses in the USA, as in cases in Ireland, for example, have been found to have some priests who sexually abused children and young people. Once this gained public knowledge and scrutiny, it led not only to much financial recompense but also to the expression of the mental and physical harm done to the victims, their families, friends, and others. The act of betrayal of trust by people existing to be trusted touches the depths of the moral-social bond. The fact that religious groups speak about truth and often reckon that their scriptures or some other revelation undergird moral codes magnifies the deceit if their representatives contravene these truthful codes. Another well-known example of social justice and its impact on individuals can be seen in the restorative justice procedures of South Africa's post-apartheid reconciliation processes, in which individuals and families that had been wronged as victims by others were brought together to express their respective feelings and thoughts on what had been done to them and on what they had done, whether as victim or criminal oppressor. Such inter-action has also occurred, to a limited degree, in some other societies where victims meet those convicted of offence against them. The emotional en-gagement that becomes possible is all the greater because of the meeting of persons in a sustaining social space. In one slightly indirect and more ritually symbolic sense, this encounter resembles the contexts of pardon in the previous chapter, where the co-presence of deity and devotee allows the former, who is reckoned to have been offended by the sins of the latter, to pardon the latter.

The degrees of engagement of an individual with his society, and the corresponding levels of emotional support received from it, vary a great deal. It can even help define whether a society values the discrete individual more than a group-focused member or not. This can be illuminated through Durkheim's 1897 study of suicide, which expressed his view that sociology is a discipline focused on the identifiable phenomenon of 'society', a distinctive world of its own that can and should be studied in its own terms and not, for example, in terms of psychology or any other discipline.[5] Despite that formal stricture, there is, as we have already seen, a great deal in Durkheim about human sentiment and emotion, albeit presented in more sociological terms. In *Suicide*, for example, his prime concern was with the degree of embeddednes

---

[5] For an excellent account of Durkheim, see Lukes (1973). Also Moscovici (1993) for a critique of any formal separation of sociology from psychology.

of an individual within society, whether the individual–social bonds are strong or weak. On that basis he described three types of suicide: egoistic, where the self had only weak bonds with society and a person no longer saw a point in living; altruistic, where there was a strong bond with society, and where 'honour' might demand suicide; and anomic, where persons might deem themselves beyond its rule-based control. This notion of anomie—of the breakdown of social rules and their influence over society's members—offers an interesting avenue into the place of emotional life, whether socially involved or introverted.[6] Similarly, the fact of suicide among human beings, contrary to any animal equivalent, also offers insight into 'the relationship between the physical being and the symbolic self'.[7]

Conceptually speaking, anomie—as a state of meaninglessness inducing hopelessness—is the direct opposite of the notion of intensive living described in Chapter 4. As such, religions will oppose anomie precisely because it is the embodiment of those states and a denial of the power of religion to confer meaning and hope. It is also—within the psychological world of the self—rather like the state of chaos out of which, on a cosmic scale, the deity fashioned a world order. Since religions, very largely, have emerged as a human behaviour pattern fostering life and creating order, it is understandable that they should outlaw suicide except in so far as martyrdom, self-sacrifice, or fasting have all been prized at times as behaviours sustaining prime values of the faith and its cultural vehicles. In today's changing worlds, especially in secularizing contexts, the role of engendering hope and meaning falls to other social processes than religion. In many respects politicians seek to manage such secular societies, albeit in alliances with religious groups or charities that are often influenced by people of personal religious conviction. It remains to be seen just how successful modern nation states will be in ensuring hope in a complex and often fearful world. The certainty of fixed enemies during the hot and cold wars of the twentieth century helped politicians in their provision of a hopeful future for their citizens. But events such as the near financial collapse of world economic markets in 2008–9 revealed how potentially shallow is the state and international corporation basis of twenty-first-century life. Fear was often directly expressed during this

---

[6] See Durkheim ([1902] 1984) for accounts of family life and professional groups as alternative focus of orientation of people. See also Lukes (1973: 5–7, 265).

[7] Cf. Goldschmidt (1990: 82). Goldschmidt sees suicide as an index of the power of 'the recent invention of culture to induce a human being to engage in an act that defies the force of three billion years of biological evolution'.

period as the complex symbolic nature of money was shown to be less dependable than popularly thought. What is more, many developed societies are now entering an era in which the demise of traditional religious codes of conduct and bases of hope raises the question of how to source moral and hopeful worlds for mass populations apart from the influence of traditional religious values.

HOPE

One key aspect of meaning within human life is hope, and, though it is hard to define, we have taken hope as a fundamental property of social identity in this study.[8] Whilst it is easy to accept that hope represents 'an anticipated sense of continued availability, endurance and persistence of an activity which will provide meaning over time', it is vital not to ignore its experiential timbre.[9] This is reflected, for example, in the first of Default's and Martocchio's six dimensions of hope, which they list as affective (dealing with emotions and feeling of hope); cognitive (having to do with imagination, interpretation, and judgement); behavioural (relating to decisions to act to ameliorate possibilities); affiliative (an optimism generated through relations with others or with God); temporal (embedded in experiences of past, present, and future); and contextual (in the form of 'circumstances that activate or test hope').[10] All these can also be seen as echoes of the idea of intensive living explored in Chapter 4. From his more literary and cultural-critical perspective, George Steiner says of hope that 'there is no word less deconstructible', and he uses it to describe 'Sunday' as a day whose lineaments, even for non-believers, 'carry the name of hope'.[11] And, although 'hope' is the concluding motif of one of Steiner's most important works, *Real Presences*, it is also allied with 'the condition of trust', and that is significant, for trust underlies the practice of reciprocity through which we engage with others.[12] That link of trust that unites 'hope' with 'others' is fundamental to this chapter and will also figure strongly in Chapter 9, where we elaborate the

---

[8] See Miller (2008: 276–89) for a general description. It is intriguing that Leeuw ([1933] 1967), one of the greatest descriptive phenomenologists of religion, did not engage with the topic of hope.
[9] Barton (1977: 34).   [10] Default and Martocchio (1985: 381–8).
[11] George Steiner (1989: 232).   [12] George Steiner (1989: 211).

theme of 'otherness'. Hope is one aspect of human self-consciousness in which planning for the future takes a positive emotional direction. Moments of hope and periods of despair set society its greatest challenge—of fostering the first and coping with the second. The success of social groups, large or small, depends upon their capacity to sustain hope against despair, and this is where religion often serves its primary purpose.[13] Despite the many difficulties of defining 'religion', we have emphasized the merits of Geertz's cultural definition, which gave clear importance to 'powerful, pervasive and long-lasting moods and motivations' that are experienced as 'uniquely realistic', an emphasis on mood and motivation that affects hope and despair as experiences that, each in their own way, engage with fear.[14]

Hope offers a transcending of fear. It acknowledges the hardships and difficulties of life but does not remain bound by them. It brings a new time perspective to people, showing that tomorrow will be better than today. Within the Jewish–Christian–Islamic worlds, and in ideological movements emerging from them, including Marxism, much is invested in anticipating a future state of affairs. God's kingdom will come in some way or a socialist revolution will create a new world order of freedom from want, pain, hardship, and oppression. Hope becomes partnered with ideas of time and the future goal of perfection inspires the present moment of hope. Earliest Christianity developed the Jewish hope in the establishment of God's Kingdom through the work of the divinely anointed one or Messiah. Jesus was the focus for this movement that identified him with the Messiah and believed that he somehow conquered death by being resurrected and would soon come again on the clouds of heaven to establish God's perfect reign on earth.[15] One problem faced by first- and second-generation Christians was that Jesus did not come as expected, and the hope that believers would be caught up in the air to meet him was questioned, especially as Christians began to die, and it seemed that this hopeful expectation was in danger of being crushed. This prompted early leaders to rethink their ideas, as they stressed a post-death time of 'sleeping'[16] and a future resurrection of all rather than a rising of people passing directly from this life into the air to meet the coming Christ without having died at all.[17] In this way Christianity embedded

---

[13] Thompson ([1963] 1968: 427) speaks of 'an oscillation between periods of hope and despair' in the British Methodist history of conversion.

[14] Geertz ([1966] 1973: 1–46).   [15] Mark 13: 26.

[16] 1 Thessalonians 4: 13.   [17] 1 Corinthians 15: 23–58.

the opportunity for hope within the very context of death. With time, this hope of Christ's second coming led to ideas of heaven as a place to which the dead might finally be admitted. Further ideas of a divine judgement after death also developed the idea of hell as a 'place' of eternal punishment for sinners and of purgatory as a place of transformative cleansing of sin-stained believers prior to gaining admittance to heaven itself. The attention paid to purgatory and hell in medieval Christianity included much art depicting future suffering that must have played on many individuals' sense of fear about their destiny. In an intriguing way, then, Christian hope became intertwined with fear in a complex religious ritual process involving prayers said for the dead at the Mass and the practice of gaining indulgences through pilgrimages or even through monetary purchase that allowed a degree of freedom from purgatory.[18] One of the driving forces within the Christian Reformation of the sixteenth century involved opposition to this practice of indulgences.

One of the theological responses to combining hope and fear in the afterlife was John Calvin's scheme of double predestination, which developed biblical ideas of divine election to argue that God had, from all eternity, chosen two groups of people, one to be damned and one to be saved. The human problem was that no one knew who was in each group. Human nature being what it is, this created a sense of uncertainty over one's destiny, with the result that people sought it by an indirect route. Living faithful lives, they invoked another Christian idea—namely, that God blessed his chosen ones and caused them to flourish. So, when their disciplined lives engendered success outcomes in life, they could, indirectly as it were, gain a sense that they were among God's elect. As we have seen earlier in this study, Max Weber termed this 'The Protestant Ethic', describing the controlled lives of Protestant merchants, bankers, and others that resulted in an economic and social success running parallel with a personal desire for a certain type of Christian identity in relation to salvation.[19] In the later twentieth century, one stream of Evangelicalism, far removed from the formal Calvinist style of Reformed Christianity, advocated what has been called the 'Prosperity Gospel', which developed in a most explicit fashion the idea that God blesses his people and wants them to gain earthly benefits such as financial success.

---

[18] Indulgences represent a form of pardon grounded in a hierarchy of power and a treasury of merit.

[19] See Weber ([1904–5] 1976).

Preaching especially to relatively poor people, it tapped into the emotion of hope in a very direct way. One other, and quite different, development of a long-standing theological motif that involved the interplay of hope and fear within Christian identity occurred in the USA in the later decades of the twentieth century, when some Evangelical Protestants began to focus on the rapture, the idea encountered above in the earliest Christian belief that Christ would soon come again and believers would be caught up in the air, or 'raptured', to meet him. Many millions of American Christians adopted this perspective, encouraged by the *Left Behind* novels of Tim Lahaye that described how true Christians would be removed from the earth by divine miracle, with sinners being 'left behind' to endure the 'great tribulation' to be brought by the devil.[20] These books had sold over fifty million copies by the start of the twenty-first century. Some have seen the appeal of this rapture idea as part of the 'terror rhetoric' that has its own tradition within American Protestantism. One allied US phenomenon that stimulates fear is that of the 'hell-house' performances in which people experience dramatic scenes of angels and demons trying to capture human souls in a battle of good and evil. Brian Jackson described this as a kind of terror brought especially on young people within a religious context and aimed at conversion. Drawing from cultural historian Ethan Blue, he emphasized the fact that a broad sense of dread brought on by the terrorist attack upon New York's Twin Towers probably intensified the 'cultural politics of Christian fear' triggered by traditional Christian motifs.[21] Whether in the twelfth or the twenty-first century, the powerful emotion of fear remains a ready resource for acting in a dynamic tension with hope under ever-changing cultural circumstances to generate religious identity. Beyond such Christianity, what might be called the esoteric fiction of Dan Brown, also read by millions, simulated a sense of anxiety in a battle between good and evil over protecting some mystical truth that the anti-hero wished to access for personal gain and for anti-social purposes. This came to a focused climax when his labyrinthine novel *The Lost Symbol* revealed that mystic truth in its single-word conclusion: 'hope'. After the evil figure Mal'akh has been killed, the epic's hero and expert 'symbologist' Robert Langdon stands in Washington DC touched by the warmth of the rising sun and 'he felt a powerful upwelling deep within

---

[20] LaHaye and Jenkins (2001). See also DeMar (2001) for a critique of this approach.
[21] Jackson (2007: 52).

himself. It was an emotion he had never felt this profoundly in his entire life. *Hope.*'[22]

Yet, this triumphant sense of embodiment came only after considerable mental anguish in his heroic battle with Mal'akh, reflecting the long-standing human conflict with forces described as evil and often associated with Hell as its vile matrix. In many West European contexts, such a popular belief in Hell took a major change of direction in the life of many Christian denominations after the world wars. So many hundreds of thousands of people suffered and died in painful and devastating contexts that artistic images of an afterworld of punishment seemed entirely redundant. Moreover, the language used of fallen soldiers was frequently drawn from biblical texts of love and self-sacrifice. Far from the dead being seen as going to hell or purgatorial cleansing, they were described as having 'laid down their lives for their friends' or for their country.[23] Hope, in these contexts, came to pervade the hope of their survival in another world, as the popularity of Spiritualism and the desire to contact the deceased at this time indicated. From a different cultural world's approach to negative and positive life experience, Stanner's classic work on the Murinbata of Australia described how male initiation involved a shared experience of 'refuge and rottenness', which he designated a 'covenant of duality' that was neither rooted in nostalgia for any past age nor optimistic awaiting a new age: life experience is described, portrayed, or revealed to initiates as a 'perennial good-with suffering'.[24] This kind of existential realism involves a focus on the present, on how life is actually experienced, and on how individuals need others in the process of survival.

In general terms, religion fosters hope and opposes despair while yet engaging with it. Such hope and despair frame fear, itself a primary emotional core of human existence, and emphasize the fact that the drive for meaning that typifies human beings is not simply a rational-philosophical activity but is also strongly experiential. Hope and despair move in opposite directions away from what we might consider as a central core of daily meaningfulness of life sustained by a balance of optimistic and pessimistic factors. Even some theologians find it too easy simply to take hope as an inescapable feature of the human condition, a stance that makes '"religion" (and theology as its intellectual arm) . . . something used to sustain and articulate human hopefulness'.

---

[22] Dan Brown (2009: 509; emphasis in original).
[23] See especially John 15: 13, with its 'greater love' of laying down one's life for one's friends.
[24] Stanner (1959–60: 44, 45, 58, 70).

Rachel Muers, for example, rather like Stanner, pursues these issues by preferring to focus on life situations and not on hope in general; she speaks of hope as something 'learned through its practice in engagement with particular situations'.[25] The Classicist Robert Turcan's account of ancient Roman behaviour towards the deities argued that, 'for the Romans, religion was not a belief, a feeling, or, *a fortiori* a mystique: it was purely utilitarian practice' conducted by those who 'lived in obsessive fear of hazards, the occult powers that threatened or hampered human actions' in daily survival or 'the war that must be waged against its neighbours to safeguard present or future harvests'.[26] The 'self-interested realism' emerging from this involved ritual action, largely individual and domestic but sometimes involving the state, related to particular needs and grounded in a knowledge of which gods were best invoked for which needs. In certain calamities it was even wise not to be too specific lest a mistaken identity further aggravate the situation, as in the case of earthquakes. Here the theme of ritual reciprocity is extensive and context dependent. With changing circumstances, it is the case, he argues, that 'religions wear out'. If they fail to answer 'the innermost or doubt-filled questionings of their own believers', they may keep going under the force of habit until some new force, or new religion, makes them redundant.[27]

Such experiential learning can be interpreted through the sociology of knowledge and its concern with plausibility generating processes embedded in family, leisure, and the many activities of daily living. These processes bring emotional charges to ideas and, thereby, transform them into values. Indeed, to see this transformation of 'ideas' into emotion-charged values is a useful means of approaching the difficult concept of salvation in religions. Some time ago I proposed a definition of salvation capable of application to a wide variety of religious traditions, viewing it as a 'state of sufficiency of durable plausibility existing for an individual or group, under given ideological and social structural conditions, such that no alternative is sought'.[28] Whatever its inadequacies, including its overly cognitive nature, this definition is open to embracing the complexity of emotion and mood pervading 'plausibility'.

At its most basic, hope thus involves a creative optimism of survival, whether focused on the immediate present or on some anticipated future of

[25] Muers (2004: 121).
[26] Turcan ([1998] 2000: 2) also argued that there 'was really no such thing as Roman religion'.
[27] Turcan ([1998] 2000: 155).   [28] Douglas J. Davies (1984a: 33).

the world or afterlife. It prompts people to respond to present hardship in a way that does not accept an inevitably negative outcome. While the human species would hardly have survived without some sense of hope, we should not assume that it is a guaranteed possession, for people may lose hope. Those experiments with primates that led to what has been called 'learned helplessness', whose characteristics have also been identified among humans during appropriate contexts, especially of grief, are lesson enough.[29] It is precisely to militate against such negativity that many ritual situations are created at times of hope depletion and serve as processes of and for cultural intensification, when ideas are charged with emotion to generate values that motivate ongoing cultural moods.

Food, hope, and dying

At its most pragmatic level, hope as a mood of survival is often symbolized in and through food, the quintessential symbol of survival. It is perfectly understandable that some basic emotions are intimately aligned with basic human biological needs for drink, food, shelter, and company, and these become transparent in contexts of poverty. Paul Farmer's account of human suffering embedded in poverty in Haiti's central plateau, for example, stresses the fact that mere statistics and demography do not suffice as the basic for describing this aspect of life, but that 'the gritty details of biography' serve better to convey the reality to those who have no experience of it.[30] So he gives brief biographical narratives of selected individuals to show 'how tenuous the peasantry's hold on survival is', with a constant 'fight for food and water'.[31] From quite a different perspective, Christopher Justice raised the challenging issue of appetite and food in relation to death, working from his anthropological studies of a hospice-like context at Varanasi, where some Hindus come to die. He observed how, prior to cremation in that most holy of cities, many stopped eating as part of their preparation for making a 'good death'. He contrasted this with American notions of the vital importance of 'feeding the dying'. Since an appetite for food is integral to human experience and cultural practice, it is deeply significant for human emotional life. In terms of despair and hope, this is especially interesting, since, in India for

---

[29] Stroebe and Stroebe (1987: 69).
[30] All before the January 2010 earthquake in Haiti, with its impact on the island.
[31] Farmer (1997: 262–3).

example, the practice of fasting has long been associated with religious exercises as one means of managing religious experiences. The role of fasting within a social repertoire of behaviour has also allowed it to become a vehicle of protest, in Indian terms 'a fast unto death' to achieve some social or political goal. Justice wondered whether fasting was a natural response to impending death, as in some other animals, and, if it was, whether a clinical insistence on 'feeding' those close to death might be a medical intervention that hindered a 'natural death', even if it satisfied the living that they were doing their best for the dying.[32]

Blessing

At the ritual level of life, hope is deeply enshrined in acts of blessing, which encourage positive feelings of flourishing and an overcoming of negative forces. Blessing can best be interpreted through Mauss's 'fourth obligation' in that to receive a blessing is to become aware both of the importance of designated others within society and of the inalienable nature of their goodwill towards us. True, blessing cannot be bought, as typified in the biblical example of Isaac being tricked by his son Jacob into blessing him rather than Esau, his elder brother. It is a narrative replete with emotions surrounding mortality, deceit, desire, anger, and hatred.[33] The power of blessing within kinship descent groups shares in the category of mystical rather than jural forms of activity, though it may complement legal features.[34] To want the 'blessing' of a parent or superior on some life venture or undertaking is to desire the support of others and invokes something of the force that comes from the otherness of society, which enhances hopefulness. The kind of blessing that comes with marriage rites in many societies is aligned with the hope of reproductive fertility, an idea that unites life's pragmatic necessities with the knowledge that many misfortunes may befall us, a knowledge that, perhaps, can be obviated by blessing. Blessing has roots in the notion of survival itself, and in the expression of the desire that another person flourish. As we have indicated, its full significance lies in the contrast with its partner concept of the curse. Blessing and curse furnish the grammar of verbal and behavioural discourse of the moral community that is human

---

[32] Justice (1997: 236–7).
[33] Genesis 27: 1–46.
[34] Needham (1980: 71).

society and reflect the emotional field of hope and fear. The act of blessing is intended to cause the recipient to flourish and betokens a positive relationship between the giver and the receiver, one that enables the 'power' possessed by society, embodied in the one giving the blessing, to be passed on. To bless is to express the positive goodwill of the community; one might even speak of it as a form of secular grace. Certainly, blessing has been adopted as a major element in many religious traditions. It often accompanies moments of status change, especially when the recipient is to undertake some venture or enter into a new stage of life that will also foster his community's welfare.[35] Blessings regularly express the generational transitions associated with birth, marriage, and death rites, frequently managed by religion.

In a fundamental sense, blessings express the power of society and, in theological terms, of God. If, for the sake of argument, we distinguish between the 'natural' groupings of human societies and the 'artificial' societies constructed by churches or other forms of discrete social organizations, we can, all the more clearly, see the function of blessing. Churches, quintessentially, comprise institutions of moral power, creating opportunities for its expression and furnishing the foundation for wider meaning-making aspects of life in doctrinal, ethical, or philosophical terms. A religion with a doctrine but no means of blessing would be nothing more than a kind of philosophical seminar, and seminars do not bless. By contrast, it is no accident that most religious groups end their formal activities with some form of blessing, just as they often begin them with an invocation of a spiritual force to frame its more rational endeavours.

Compassion and tolerance

Two further attitude-driven perspectives that complement blessing in the field of positive social feelings are those of compassion and tolerance. Compassion is especially important because of its emphasis within Buddhism, which has paid extensive attention to it as a means of contextualizing life's ills while engaging with a path that leads to enlightenment. Many treatises describe states of conscious awareness that constitute 'compassion' and, along with it, the attitude of loving kindness.[36] The philosophy framing this perspective argues that, contrary to ordinary life experience, the sense of

---

[35] Blessing in relation to rites of passage is a topic worthy of future detailed research.
[36] Following P. Harvey (2000: 103–9).

possessing a permanent self is misleading. Ultimately, there is no self, and what humans experience is a desire to be a centre of selfhood, with life taking the form of a craving for permanence and an attachment to things that would help achieve such a goal, even though such desires only yield bitterness. By contrast, the Buddhist path towards enlightenment that leads away from such cravings finds a powerful affinity with an attitude of loving kindness towards people still embroiled in those misguided perceptions. Such loving kindness involves the capacity for a degree of distanced self-knowledge and freedom from encumbering attitudes binding us to those people.

The cultivation of emotions driving these attitudes reflects the somewhat different notion of tolerance, itself often regarded as a mark of civilization. Indeed, the very concept of 'civilization' may, itself, be interpreted in terms of tolerance as a shared 'urbane' attitude among those who disagree over many things. One historian of religion described what he saw as 'the noblest achievement of the Western world' as lying in 'the conduct of controversy without acrimony, of strife without bitterness, of criticism without loss of respect'.[37] Tolerance is one key mode of emotional control, one that acknowledges the likelihood of people being annoyed by the opposing views of others and that sets out to moderate any negative response. It is an attitude demanding careful development and needing to be aware of other human tendencies to give offence and, indeed, to be offended. Tolerance is allied with a person being prepared to engage with views quite different from their own, something that can become problematic in terms of religious beliefs and practices. Some religious people, however, are so convinced of and committed to the truthfulness of their own beliefs that they could hardly find it possible to tolerate opposing beliefs that they may associate with ideas of evil or moral wrong. In other words, the very concept of religion can be antipathetic to tolerance, just as a common human drive for prestigious identity is antipathetic to the Buddhist notion of 'no-self'.

DESPAIR

So, in compassion and tolerance we have concepts entailing deep emotions that stand at the cusp of religious possibilities that easily slip into the opposite attitudes of hatred and intolerance. Just what keeps these perspectives apart is

[37] Bainton ([1951] 1958: 259).

not easily ascertained, but one factor concerns the difference between the way we approach a person as opposed to a creed. It is easier to have compassion for another human being than it is for a system of belief.

At heart these issues express a person's sense of safety within his own perspective and his anxiety and fear lest the system that sustains his own sense of identity be questioned. As intimated in Chapter 2, the way abstract formulations of 'truth' in the form of creeds and doctrines relate to the emotional dynamics of religious group life can involve devotees being prepared to fight to the death for what is, essentially, a defence of their identity, but which is expressed as a defence of doctrinal truth. To lose that fight would, potentially, be to lose that form of identity that composes salvation itself. Emotions of fear, including the unspoken fear of loss of meaning, identity, and hope in life, as well as fear of loss of institutional power, run high within such controversies, which, in due course, develop histories all of their own and can entrench hostilities for centuries as in some conservative Catholic–Protestant divides. John Foxe, for example, who produced his *Book of Martyrs* on the European continent in 1563 having fled from England during the Catholic Queen Mary's reign, gives account after account of the emotional terror and pain suffered by good Protestants at the hand of wicked Catholics. It is difficult not to read his accounts without thinking of torture as itself a kind of ritual, reminiscent of the early Christian martyrs in Roman arenas, endured for the sake of the Protestant reading of the Bible and grasp of doctrinal truth. One account runs thus:

During this extremity of anguish, while the tender frame is tearing, as it were, in pieces, while at every pore it feels the sharpest pangs of death, and the agonized soul is just ready to burst forth and quit its wretched mansion, the ministers of the inquisition have the obduracy to look on without emotion, and calmly advise the poor distracted creature to confess his imputed guilt.[38]

Such religious strife emphasizes the deep levels of emotion underlying religious doctrines and personal identity and reflects both the strong reciprocal bonds among the faithful and the sense of otherness that provides the ultimate validation of belief. This is not to assume that all share the same level of commitment to beliefs, but religious leaders, prophets, and reformers arise precisely because they elicit commitment from a receptive public.

---

[38] Foxe ([1563] n.d.: 63). My copy of this undated and popular version had once been given as a Sunday School prize for good attendance to one James Buxton of Leigh in 1910.

The maintenance of high-level commitment is achieved in many ways, especially through rites of intensification, not least because religious groups are well aware of the capacity of individuals to lapse and succumb to states such as that of 'sloth'. Indeed, the very desire of leaders to encourage religious dedication has, as in the case of Buddhism above, generated a keen observation of mental and bodily states. The Christian monk Evagrius Ponticus of the fourth century, for example, explored the types of mood that accompanied the experiences of those seeking to develop their spiritual lives. This involved using a variety of terms in increasingly technical ways, as with the Greek notion of *Apatheia*. To modern ears of English speakers, this has strong links with the notions of apathy and pathos, the former referring to a certain absence of any motivating emotion and the latter to a sense of pity for someone. In derivation these take us back to the Greek *pathos*, referring to something that may befall us, some suffering or misfortune.[39] However, in its more technical theological sense it came to describe a reduction of disturbing feelings and a 'serenity that makes spiritual love possible'.[40] The way to such a state of serenity was not easy, and one of the hindrances to it lay in *accidie*, understood as the experience of restlessness and unease in a person, a condition that might easily befall monks in the routine life of a monastery and detract them from their focused attention on prayer, study, or physical work. *Accidie* offers an interesting example of a term developed to describe experiences within a particular life context, especially one that brought a great deal of theological–cultural attention to bear on the ordinariness of everyday life. Today many people, not least students and scholars, experience a very similar condition, but without having a technical term readily available to frame their feelings and thereby help them cope. People often comment on finding it difficult to concentrate or lacking motivation when studying. In a secular age this would not be interpreted as a kind of temptation and a hindrance to spiritual progress, even if it was identified as hindering focused work. In religious contexts, where control of the body in all its ways becomes an important concern for one's spiritual development, it is perfectly understandable that detailed classifications of mental moods would emerge alongside ritual and ethical means of expressing them. Joachim Wach, in his sympathetic account of the much ignored religious leader and contemporary of Martin Luther, Caspar Schwenckfeld, for example, describes how this

---

[39] Liddell and Scott (1855).
[40] Cross (1997: 81).

mystic whose life was pervaded by meditative prayer advocated the simple 'lifting up of our eyes and the folding of our hands' in circumstance of 'great bodily weakness', when other forms of prayer were unachievable.[41]

Suffering and salvation

By such means religion frequently intensifies emotion as a physical experience through ritual practices that bring theological significance to experience, as Chapter 6 showed for the positive emotional world of joy. But it also applies to negative experiences, as when doctrine brings meaning to pain and suffering, often offering hope of a positive future outcome. In exploring this theme, we can also extend Chapter 3's concern with suffering as an encounter with a certain 'resistance' or obstacle that prevents life flowing in a desired direction. A person who encounters the 'resistance' of sickness, bereavement, or random misfortune and lacks any explanation for it is more likely to experience a sense of hopelessness and despair prompted by a feeling of lack of control over life's circumstances than someone able to invoke some explanation. This is precisely the point at which religious influences are often at their strongest, offering some means of explanation through engaging with the negative force of resistances. It seems that human beings prefer some idea of what may underlie their misfortune than suffering in passive ignorance. Here, the idea of salvation re-emerges in the overcoming of such 'resistances', for, while 'salvation' can be viewed as an abstract doctrine relating to ultimate human destiny, it is often manifested at local and individual levels of life in various forms of deliverance, from illness, misfortune, or distress through prayer or healing ritual.

Spirits and power in healing and cursing

One widespread form of healing, with its own ritual accoutrements and forms of emotional management, is found in shamanic practice. This much-debated notion of shamanism describes individuals who employ some form of trance and musical accompaniment to enter into a state through which they contact spirit powers to help heal members of their community. Having often survived some personal suffering, described in terms of a symbolic death and rebirth, shamans deal in the serious issues of

---

[41] Wach (1951: 148).

suffering, life, and death and have been found in many traditional, small-scale, societies. From later decades of the twentieth century, however, some Western groups adopted the phenomenon as part of new ritual practices aligned with the development of well-being. Such a selective borrowing and decontextualizing of shamanism risks robbing a ritual intervention of its natural community base, with all its accompanying emotional expectations and support.

Another form of spirit intervention concerns the exorcist whose work is grounded in the belief that evil forces, conceived of as spirits, exist and may influence or even possess an individual's body and sense of self, and in the allied assumption that certain persons have the power to ward off such influence or to drive out the possessing spirits. One major reason for the extensive growth of Christianity, especially in Africa and parts of South America, lies in the evil spirit and the Holy Spirit beliefs of Pentecostal and Charismatic forms of that faith. Local religious leaders can gain considerable status from being able to exorcize evil spirits by the name of Jesus and through the power of the Holy Spirit. Millions share in this form of activity and afford a considerable degree of emotional excitement and group partici-pation in the process. While considerable doubt exists over the efficacy of any healing of physical ills at such services, there can be little doubt over the sense of empowerment people may feel. Singing, utterances of praise, speaking in tongues, and other behaviours may occur in this sensed arena of conflict between good and evil. Indeed the motif of 'spiritual warfare', grounded both in a sense of fear and in the hope of its conquest, is often associated with this kind of activity. The pastor may place his hands on a person's head or chest and command the evil to leave, often shouting commands to this effect; a great deal of energy is involved and released, and this is not a time of restraint. Bodies engage with bodies, as, in typical forms of Charismatic rites, the exorcist works to the point where a person falls backwards into the arms of helpers. Being 'slain in the spirit' of divine power overcomes that of the devil in a physical and visibly dramatic form. Evil forces that have created 'resist-ances' to a person's life journey are not left with the last word. A degree of hope over fear is conferred in and through the exorcist in contexts of considerable excitement. Contrariwise, a great degree of fear can be aroused through beliefs and practices aligned with the cursing of people or by invoking evil powers, especially when accompanied by a group ostracizing the cursed individual. Various arguments have been made over these deeply negative experiences and how they may even lead to the death of the victim.[42]

A different and positive form of hope, though also related to spirits, is associated with ritual contact with the dead, achieved through spirit mediums. Widely known through the Spiritualist movement that arose in mid-nineteenth century in the USA, this phenomenon is also a worldwide aspect of humanity. Grounded in the belief that people possess some form of soul or life force that leaves their body a lifeless corpse at death, this view argues the possibility of contacting that departed spirit. Séances of many forms seek to do just that, offering some comfort to the bereaved, whose anxiety over the state of the dead can be reduced. Such anxiety and excitement, together with the anticipation of contacting the dead, combine within the social context of a supportive group, and, if only for a moment, clients may gain a sense of contact with their dead at an early point in their bereavement.

Stigmatics

Whereas suffering frequently engages people through bereavement, there are circumstances in which a person engages in a pattern of emotional life that brings its own distinctive religious suffering. One rare but historically identifiable example is found in those relatively few individuals within the Catholic tradition described as stigmatics, who possess marks on their bodies believed to resemble the marks carried by Jesus after his passion and crucifixion. This may involve open wounds reflecting the wounds made on Christ's feet, hands, side, head, shoulders, and back before and when he was crucified. This phenomenon involves a complex emotional process in which human feelings combine with theological ideas within devotional practices and framed by a particular historical framework to result in physical manifestations.

This clearest of all examples of a bio-moral form of embodiment emerged in the thirteenth century in the figure of St Francis of Assissi, whose devotion to Christ, especially in his crucified image, led to his reception of visible stigmata in September 1224. He is widely acknowledged as the first historical case of this phenomenon, with perhaps only between 300 or 400 recognized by the Catholic Church since then. This instructive example of the interplay of emotion and religious identity reveals the complex situation in which

---

[42] Young ([1996] 1997: 245–60).

biblical texts telling of Christ's suffering and death on a cross led, practically a millennium later, to the art form of dramatic crucifixes, formal artistic representations, often near lifesize, of the dying or dead Jesus. These often depict blood flowing from Christ's wounds. Francis, engaged in devotion to Christ, is said to have been given the stigmata from Christ himself. Indeed, the way he was referred to by church leaders closely identified him with Christ: he becomes another Christ or *alter Christus*, and is seen to continue some of Christ's ongoing work in the world. The later Franciscan Order was keen in patronizing art that represented these events and, simultaneously, reinforced the significance of their Order. The thirteenth century was also a period of extensive theological reflection on the nature of the Mass and, in particular, of the doctrine of transubstantiation, which brought the 'real presence' of Christ through his body and blood within the very substance of the bread and wine of the rite. 'Thus mystics of the thirteenth and fourteenth centuries described seeing the crucified body of Christ at the elevation of the Host; in their visions, Christ displayed his wounds to them as he offered them communion.'[43]

One modern stigmatic, Padre Pio, is said to have received his visible stigmata from a particular crucifix on 20 September 1918.[44] He has a considerable following among contemporary Catholics, who regard his life as exemplifying the miraculous and supernatural dimensions of their religion. Not only did some close to him say that, 'in Padre Pio the supernatural blended with the natural to such an extent that one could no longer distinguish where the natural ended and the supernatural took over', but described those supernatural features in terms of miraculous healings, bilocation, and a fragrance associated with his wounds. His close friend and doctor Dr Andrea Cardone attests to having had a conversation with Padre Pio early on the morning of 23 September 23 1968, several hours after the priest had, in fact, died.[45] These and many similar accounts are described by fellow believers as a kind of divine revelation and encouragement to the faithful. Another physician described the complete disappearance of the stigmata immediately after Padre Pio's death, something interpreted by the Archbishop of Naples, Cardinal Ursi, as being a 'sign of the resurrection'.

---

[43] Derbes (1996: 18).
[44] Freze (1989: 245).
[45] Ingoldsby (1978: 88–90).

This case reveals a complex interplay of the emotional world of one man with that of thousands of others who see in him a practical example of the theological beliefs associated with Christ. One might even speak of the 'career' of the phenomenon of stigmata, in that it originates in the narrative accounts of Jesus's death, passes into artistic representations of them, which, in turn, become objects of deep devotion reinforced by the rich symbolic universe of Catholicism, including the ongoing ritual of the Mass focused on the sacrificial death of Jesus. Such complex symbolism and its capacity to stimulate emotions of devotion among the faithful came to sharp focus on those occasions when Padre Pio celebrated Mass. For in that rite we have a priest who, as in every Mass, stands as a symbolic figure of Christ offering the sacrifice of himself for the sins of the world, but a priest who is believed to bear in his body the actual marks of crucifixion. The mirroring and interplay of such embodied symbols with their theological reference points would be hard to better.

Christ's passion: his agony in Gethsemane

The generating core of the stigmatic's devotion lies in the suffering of Jesus, especially that of his 'passion'.[46] This focused on the last days of his life, ending in the crucifixion, which emphasized the period's redemptive nature. Christ's sufferings reveal divine love and self-sacrifice in the process of winning the forgiveness of sin for the faithful. It is hard to overemphasize this centrality of Christ's suffering, pain, and agony within Christianity, much of which is symbolized in references to his blood, which carries a double symbolic message of suffering and death, on the one hand, and of life and deliverance, on the other: death to him, life for the believer. All this became enshrined in the central ritual of the Eucharist, in which the priest takes bread and wine and prays that, by God's divine operation, they may become the body and blood of Christ, to be taken by the believer as the means of salvation.

This bread and wine ritual serves as a classic example of a complex paradigmatic scene in which the scriptural account of Jesus having a Last Supper with his disciples, in which reference is made to the bread and the wine as his body and blood, comes to be framed by theological interpretations of his subsequent crucifixion as an act of sacrifice mirroring traditional

---

[46] From Latin *passio*, suffering.

Jewish animal sacrifice that made atonement for sin. The emphasis upon the agony suffered by Jesus is especially instructive, since 'agony' in English usage denotes both intense physical pain and mental distress. Its etymology, both in Latin and in Greek *agon*, indicates a contest, suggesting the interplay of a desire to understand the basis of physical torment. Here, most especially, suffering is far from pointless: in terms of emotions, 'agony' provides a very clear example of a bio-cultural process, one that brings formal meaning into the realm of intense physical pain.

By writing much on this suffering, Christian theologians show its centrality to their faith and its appeal to millions of people, an appeal grounded in the fact that most people suffer in life at some time, some even to the point of agony. Philosophically, too, it has also been argued that it is such pain that offers the possibility of a '*creative appropriation* of its hidden gift of possibilities' in opposition to nihilism.[47] But, certainly, the attraction of a religion depends to a significant degree on its ability to marshal emotions, to focus human feeling, give it meaning, and add value to it. The Protestant theologian John Calvin (1509–64), for example, proposed that Jesus's death was not a simple death of body as a sacrificial agent providing a ransom for sin, but that it involved 'another, greater and more excellent ransom, since he suffered in his soul the dreadful torments of a person condemned and irretrievably lost'.[48] He argues that, because Christ suffered in both his body and his soul, he was able to redeem both the bodies and the souls of believers. Here it is easy to see Calvin exemplifying the theme of embodiment, as he describes Christ's agony in the Garden of Gethsemane as a bitterness of soul that resulted in drops of blood dropping from his face as though it were sweat.

Four hundred years later, in the quite different tradition of emergent Mormonism in the early and mid-nineteenth century, this garden episode would be taken up afresh as a focus for Christ's atonement. While not ignoring his crucifixion as the completion of the task of atonement, Mormons stressed the way in which Jesus suffered as he took the sins and evils of the world into his own mental and physical life. So immense was the stress of that engagement with evil that his body sweated blood. It is as though the blood of atonement flows from the one who battles with evil in a real agony, always remembering that 'agony' has its derivation in 'contest'. Here he

[47] Levin (1985: 83; emphasis in original).
[48] Calvin, *Institutes of the Christian Religion*, bk II, chs XVI, X.

contests with evil, not least with the evil-one, Satan, who ever lingers on the margin of a Mormon understanding of the world and of human destiny. Images of Christ tend only to gain currency if they hold an attraction for the emotional lives of believers, in this case the theme of Christ's obedience to God in facing the terrors or crucifixion mirrors the Mormon commitment to obedience to divine commandments and the covenants they undertake in special temple rituals. The religious-ethical challenge of life to face all hardships with firm resolve is here typified to its final degree in Jesus. Seeing Jesus under pressure to do the right thing in the face of evil is to see oneself in the same situation. The prompt is to activity, and Mormons, in their early migrations into their great Salt Lake Valley home in what would become the State of Utah in the USA, were above all else activists under pressure from hostile neighbours and even a hostile US government. It is possible that the image of Christ, inactive and dead upon the cross, did not have the same emotional appeal to Mormons as it did to other Christians whose tradition of faith and ritual developed along different lines.

For the great majority of Christian theologians, this episode of Christ sweating blood in the Garden of Gethsemane, as he ponders the death that awaits him and prays that, if possible, he may be delivered from it, is overtaken by the subsequent event of the crucifixion. The cross not the garden becomes the prime site for sacrificial atonement, and the piety of the faithful focuses largely on it. One reason for this lies in the complex interplay of emotions of guilt, grief, and hope that allows individuals to bring their own sense of need for forgiveness to the ritual focus of the sacrifice for sin. Combined with this is a sense of grief gained in their own life experience and which can be identified with the dying Jesus. The symbolic attraction of crucifixion lies not simply in the negative factors of guilt awaiting forgiveness or the outworking of grief, but in the positive emotion of hope, for the crucifixion, especially in the Eucharistic rite, is framed by the complementary belief in Christ's resurrection.

Resurrection

The idea of resurrection is remarkable because it contradicts the basic human experience that dead bodies rot: it sets a hope of life against the experience of death. Historically, its emergence within Jewish thought a century or so before the time of Jesus was probably due to a belief that God would not let just people, especially martyrs, die in vain. By bringing them from the dead and giving them life in due course, God would vindicate their personal sacrifice. While, in Jesus's day the Pharisees held to this belief, his disciples believed that this general principle had now been realized in Jesus as God's appointed one. Belief in the resurrection became focused in Jesus as part of a wider belief that God was dynamically at work and would soon transform the existing world-order in a dramatic fashion. Christ would return to earth on the clouds of heaven and God's rule would be established in a new heaven and new earth, with Christian believers being given new 'spiritual bodies'. This did not come about, but, far from destroying belief in Christ's resurrection, it shifted the focus to some future event, when all would be resurrected in a day of judgement leading into a new heavenly existence or, in Islam, into Paradise. The remarkable feature of the idea of the resurrection, then, is that it took the fact of death and used it as a means of hope for new life in the future. The resurrection became a prime symbol of hope.

This is significant as far as human emotions and religious identity are concerned, for, while humankind has often believed in some form of spirit-based life force that leaves the body at death, resurrection belief takes the very symbol of death as the basis for future life. The emotion of grief occasioned by bereavement comes to be taken into funeral narratives of burial that are framed by belief in a divine act of recreation at some future date. Such an overarching belief is worked out in different ways in traditional Jewish, Christian, and Islamic thought and prompts different emotional patterns in each. One important dimension of the transition from death into the afterlife involves some form of divine judgement upon life lived on earth. This is a direct expression of reciprocity theory applied to rewards and punishment for ethical behaviour, and is similar in effect, though different in terms of process, from the effects of *karma* on the transmigrating soul in Indian-derived traditions of destiny. The experiential base of these processes is likely to be varied but would seem to include degrees of anxiety over the moral accounting of one's life in relation to its reward or punishment.

The very idea of having a 'good death' has played its own role in traditional societies as far as this is concerned, while in contemporary secular contexts a 'good death' applies as much to the surviving relatives as to the deceased, with 'resurrection' being interpreted accordingly as a renewed interest in life on their part. Clive Seale has explored a variety of what he calls resurrective practices, especially in the narratives created by people that help explain bereavement and the meaning of the lives of the dying and dead in relation to the living.[49] These seek for a meaningful explanation of death and for contexts in which meaningfulness may be energized so as to produce hope over despair.

SUMMARY

This discussion of death has shown hope and despair as powerful undercurrents of human lives and spiritual careers and has disclosed something of how religions stand as prime managers of the strong negative and positive potential inherent within them. This chapter has, in particular, advanced the idea of moral-somatic relationships as a prime concept for integrating the moral and emotional natures of both social and individual life. This idea, above all that we have discussed so far in this study, has demonstrated the nature of embodiment as the basis for human identity and has also provided the basis for interpreting the widespread concept of merit, whether understood in its ordinary sense or in its transformed value as salvation capital. This continuum between the ordinariness of life with its core values and allied emotions, on the one hand, and the extraordinariness that emerges when these are intensified, on the other, reveals both the relative arbitrariness of the notion of 'religion' and the value of retaining that word for the intensified forms of ordinary experience that frame the destiny of identity. To reiterate the point: it is precisely in connection with processes of intensification that the value of a 'religious' designation of behaviour becomes theoretically valuable. The next chapter will develop this very notion of intensification, as we construct, from the familiar notions of revelation, conversion, and spirit power, the more innovative notion of superplausibility.

[49] Seale (1998: 202–4).

9

Revelation, Conversion, and Spirit Power

The previous chapter discussed core values and emotions within the moral-somatic processes of life underlying the ongoing negotiation of a person's embodied identity, including the transformation of merit into salvation capital. This chapter continues this account of the dynamics of religious identity by exploring the vitalizing 'power' that possesses the capacity to transform social values into personally appropriated beliefs. One of its sources lies in the ritual behaviour of groups and another in the creative spontaneity of individuals. This complementarity reflects the historian of religion Wilfred Cantwell Smith's strong preference for abandoning the word 'religion' to speak, instead, of the cumulative tradition of a group and the faith of its individual members.[1]

Taking what has already been said about 'hope', this chapter will explore ways in which the emotional intensification of experiences drives explanations of life through the phenomena of revelation, conversion, and spirit power. This will highlight the individual within the group, showing how the capacity for creative experience engenders the sense of being an 'object' before a powerful 'other'. It will also exemplify how classic cases of revealed texts exhibit the experience of being 'written through' by another power whether in the Bible, the Koran, or the Book of Mormon, and of being 'spoken through' as in prophetic figures or in glossolalia. The process of developing an identity is then explored through forms of religious conversion, including the much-ignored idea of 'crisis of presence', taking up, again, the notion sketched in Chapter 1 of the transformation of the human drive for meaning into a sense of salvation. This transformative process of superplausibility incorporates the previous chapter's suggestion of how ordinary forms of merit become transformed into salvation capital. One implicit consequence

---

[1] Wilfred Cantwell Smith (1963).

of that discussion is to question the idea of any sharp divide between the world of 'salvation religions' and other religious or cultural traditions that often involve a shift in self identity.

WORDS, POWER, AND REVELATION

The power of words that evokes emotion and cultivates ongoing moods is intensified for people when it combines with belief in the supernatural source of scriptures. Words make humanity by creating and naming relationships, while writing and the subsequent reading, chanting, singing, and the study of texts further intensify word power and help to create civilizations. Literacy facilitates the sedimentation of knowledge and the acquisition of wisdom understood as the reflective appropriation of human experience from tradition and from an individual life. Moreover, particular texts serve as identity cores and boundary-markers of groups, while also influencing their preferred emotional styles. It is, for example, difficult to think of Judaism apart from the Torah, Christianity from the Bible, Islam from the Koran, Sikhism from the *Guru Granth*, or Hinduism from its Vedas or *Bhagavad Gita*. Within pre-literate societies too, myths and epic narratives focused on the power of words in fostering tradition. Through such written or oral traditions, transient 'revelatory' experiences could become established as the 'revelation' of sacred texts. And in all of these contexts the emotional load vested in sacred texts and their vocal production is of importance.

TYPES OF KNOWLEDGE ACQUISITION

Prophets

Words require speakers, and among the prime category of sacred speakers are prophets who typically express a sense of being addressed by a divine source.[2] This is where both otherness and reciprocity become important as analytical concepts, for prophets both sense a 'call' from a divine Other and find their vocation in having to transmit its message to those for whom the prophet now becomes an 'other' divine voice. In the previous chapter we noted the

---

[2] See Grabbe (1995) for a detailed account of types of 'religious specialists' in ancient Israel.

slightly analogous figure of the shaman as one who enters into a trance to engage with supernatural spirit powers. In their bridging state, shamans speak words of power and significance to those for whom they are working. Sometimes their speech shifts from its everyday style to a spirit language bearing messages from the dead or information sought by the living. The immediacy of this communication is strongly interpersonal, and often occurs within a distinctive ritual setting involving music, sounds, smells, or subdued lighting. Millions engage in a great variety of spirit communication through people variously known as shamans or indeed as Spiritualist mediums. Even one ancient Sumerian version of the Epic of Gilgamesh tells how a hole is punched in the underworld allowing the 'spirit of Enkidu', Gilgamesh's much lamented friend, to issue 'forth from the underworld like a wind'.[3] The excitement involved in using such services today increases the expectation of contact with a world normally beyond reach, and, especially at times of personal crisis, sickness, and bereavement, some make use of intermediaries whose very existence indicates a reality that ordinary life ignores or even denies—namely, the spirit world. Though unusual to speak of this domain as one of 'revelation', this does seem an appropriate way of dealing with people gaining information from another world through shamans or mediums. When the 'communication' takes the form of an act of healing, the verbal element is often strong in its force but weak in informational terms. So, too, in Spiritualist messages to grieving relatives when what is said affirms a general state of well-being of the dead or of comfort to the living.

A similar immediacy of message embedded within a strong interpersonal context occurs in Christian Charismatic or Pentecostal worship, when someone is believed to be given a message from God for the group or for some individual within it. The Holy Spirit is thought to be the cause of such 'words of power'. One particular form of communication is that of glossolalia or speaking in tongues, which has influenced many millions in today's world and is fostered both by a series of new Christian denominational organizations, especially various Pentecostal churches, and by 'Charismatic' groups within long established churches.[4] When people find others or find

---

   [3] Heidel ([1946] 1963: 99).

   [4] Hovenden (2002) regards it as a unique Christian innovation; Samarin (1972) as potentially universal human paralinguistic ability; Cartledge (2006) as a useful summary of research and differing evaluations.

themselves producing what sounds like a language but with 'words' quite unknown to them, they are strongly inclined to accept it as a 'gift' from God. Indeed the idea of spiritual gifts is the main way in which glossolalia is often described. Theoretically it is an instructive phenomenon for issues of emotion and identity when approached in terms of social organization and embodiment theory.[5] Csordas, for example, pressed the notion of embodiment as a paradigm for social analysis, arguing that 'the sacred becomes concrete in embodied experience'.[6] Complementing the phenomenon of glossolalia is the activity of 'interpreting tongues', when someone explains the message in a scenario of double spiritual significance, with the linguistically strange gift being partnered by a clear verbal message from God. The intense emotional tone of excitement and expectation followed by release and relief at such events reinforces the idea of the divine presence and influences the sense of identity of the devotees. While others would note the use of tongues in calm, reflective, personal contexts devoid of that intensity, the interplay of public and private contexts is likely to be influential. Still, to many Christians, this phenomenon remains enigmatic, aware as they are of its potential for being 'either sincere or phoney'.[7] Yet, where present, it cannot be ignored as a major factor in identity definition, as the very existence of the term Charismatic Movement demonstrates.

Many studies reveal such processes of identity construction and reconstruction under different guises, as in Susan Greenwood's on 'magical identity' among contemporary Pagans in Britain. She pinpoints the 'intense emotional interaction' of individuals with some 'otherworld' encountered through ritual practices deemed to be 'magical techniques'.[8] These cases of prophets, shamans, spirit mediums, tongues-speakers, and denominational leaders highlight the dynamic of divine immediacy and of the power of language to foster excitement and a sense of being in close relationship with spirit power. Paul Friedrich has argued much the same point for the 'poet-prophet' whose verse 'instantiates the creation and transmission into marked language of understanding, insights, and vision that many regard as mysterious and crucial'.[9] In the next category of religious functionaries, a different profile emerges.

---

[5] Douglas J. Davies (1976; 1984b).   [6] Csordas ([1990] 2002: 77).
[7] Johnson (1998: 109).   [8] Greenwood (2000: 120–1).
[9] Friedrich (1997: 1193–4).

The scholar-priests

These emotionally intense prophetic-Charismatic cases need to be appreciated in relation to the more passive and restrained band on the emotional spectrum represented by scribes and scholar-priests who create a tradition's sacred texts and whose mood is engendered through reading, study, and commentary. In the Christian Charismatic context, for example, it is the biblical text of the Acts of the Apostles that tells of a moment in earliest Christian times when the disciples of Jesus themselves spoke in tongues, an act reckoned to be caused by the power of the Holy Spirit.[10] This event, identified with the Jewish Day of Pentecost, is often described by Christians as the birth of their church. It became part of the canon of Christian scriptures and, along with other scriptures, was accorded the status of divine revelation.[11] The Jewish tradition of revelation, rooted in the belief that God had given the Law to Moses on Mount Sinai and had written them with his own finger on tablets of stone, fostered the idea of divine revelation in connection with a material object.[12] The role of sacred texts in Judaism became of profound importance as scrolls used in worship and as texts for private study, with later Christian writings being identified in a similar fashion. The written text, first copied for centuries by hand and then printed at the time of the Reformation, assumed enormous significance for Christianity and, later, for Islam in its Koran, making it no accident that Jews, Christians, and Muslims are often described as people of the book.

The emergence of such texts as 'revelation' bears heavily upon the emotional spectrum of religion and of religious identity precisely because of the need for varieties of education in learning to read and interpret the texts, to copy and preserve them, and, not least, to explain and teach them to others. The pattern of devoted and disciplined scriptural reading and meditation has arisen in every major literary religious tradition, with the nature of learning and meditation being such that 'insight' into familiar texts can occur throughout a lifetime of study. Insight, in turn, becomes its own form of 'revelation', as, for example, in the Protestant theological commitment to the idea of the internal testimony of the Holy Spirit that allows individuals to come to new understanding of biblical texts. Words, themselves, lie at the

[10] Acts 2: 1–20.
[11] See Ehrman (2003) for early Christian texts not included in the canon.
[12] Exodus 31: 18.

heart of texts and foster emotion in extremely complex ways, not least when set to music in chants or hymns, as Chapter 10 shows. As such, words echo within people's private lives and also provide an emotional sense of connectedness with others and with the divine. Among the many forms of revelation that could be explored here as prompts and frames for emotion, we explore a small cluster, all taken from Christian contexts but with some parallels in some other religious traditions—namely, confession and absolution, conversion, testimony, and blessings.

Confession–absolution

Confession takes words into the domain of guilt as individuals tell their sins to a priest in a form of self-disclosure. Such a 'revelation', and here we understand the word in a distinctive and almost secular sense, is potentially dangerous, because it gives the other a power that could be used against the penitent to prompt the emotion of shame. For just such reasons, much ecclesiastical emphasis is laid on the secret nature 'of the confessional'. This verbal disclosure of sins is met with priestly words of advice, admonition, and absolution, to encourage repentance and a sense of forgiveness and inner peace. Here secret words are the immediate and prime tools for coping with emotions of guilt, forgiveness, stress, and release. This context highlights one aspect of what George Steiner called the 'life force' at 'the centre and mystery of language', an idea that is extremely helpful as far as emotional life is concerned within religion.[13] His invocation of 'vitality, of life-presence', is something activated in absolution, for to speak of vitality is to identify a form of perceived emotion involving an awareness of energy for and interest in living. Here religion's capacity to restore hope as a deep emotional resource becomes powerfully significant and potentially life saving in regaining a sense of 'life presence', an expression catching a sense of being alive or feeling alive. While this positivity echoes the 'hope' considered in the previous chapter, it should not ignore the negative potential of a sense of personal sin, wickedness, and harm done to others that shames a person before God and can be a dispiriting aspect of confession inviting despair, as indicated in Chapter 3.

Confession need not be private nor, indeed, religious in any strict sense, as the case of the Alcoholics Anonymous movement makes clear. It involves a person admitting to a group that he or she has moral failings and is an

---

[13] George Steiner ([1968] 1972: 104).

alcoholic, and gaining some support from that group in response. Galanter describes how this format was developed by the group's founder Bill Wilson from the group-confessional practice of the 1930s Oxford Group of Evangelical Christians.[14] Wilson had, himself, come into a conversion-style experience when his 'despair was transformed into transcendence', for, after crying out to God to show himself, he tells how his room was filled 'with a great white light' as he was caught up 'in an ecstasy which there are no words to describe'.

CONVERSION AND TESTIMONY

One experience often associated with such a conversion event is that of forgiveness and a consequent sense of feeling really alive, an intriguing phenomenon that illuminates the very subject of this study—emotion, identity, and religion. 'Conversion' carries different connotations within different groups. Sometimes it refers to the formal and almost legal sense of changing membership from one religious tradition to another branch, but at other times it also bears the additional psychological weight of emotions experienced when people undergo changes of life orientation, whether shifting group membership or not.

In terms of conversion, one clear theological expression of the interplay of psychological aspects with a theological commentary upon them occurs in Schleiermacher's early nineteenth-century study *The Christian Faith*. His work, often cited for its emphasis upon 'absolute dependence' upon deity, preceded William James's psychological studies of conversion by seventy years and provides its own description of conversions, which involve different emphases upon 'the pain of repentance and the joy of conscious fellowship with Christ'. There is a cluster of concepts surrounding Schleiermacher's approach to conversion. He regards conversion as necessary for all people, whether born within the Christian Church or not, and includes the notions of sorrow, suffering, despair, agonizing crisis, and unalloyed blessing.[15] Of especial interest is his focused acknowledgement of the problems involved in relating the sense of passivity to activity within a convert. He describes how,

---

[14] Galanter (2005: 174). He mistakenly speaks of the Oxford Movement and not the Oxford Group. The former was the nineteenth-century High Church movement arising in Oxford associated with John Keble and others, while the Oxford Group was prompted by Frank Buchman.

[15] Schleiermacher (1830: 488).

'in the consciousness of the person in the grip of conversion, every sense of human intermediation vanishes, and Christ is realized as immediately present'.[16] His argument sometimes seems to be hindered by the belief that the grand totality of conversion lies in God's initiative, which poses the long-standing theological quandary of what people may contribute to their conversion. For him, this lies in a 'desire for fellowship with God', which can lead to 'the feeling of need for redemption'—which is, itself, grounded in a 'dissatisfaction with the common state of sinfulness'; accordingly, conversion results in 'the evocation of (this) spontaneous activity in union with Christ'.[17]

For Schleiermacher, these experiences and feelings generate a new and 'real personality in a new world', and a 'higher form of life'.[18] Conversion in this context involves a sense of the self undergoing a change, as typified in Protestant Christianity's language of rebirth. Indeed, the Evangelical form of Protestantism has frequently taken 'spiritual rebirth', itself grounded in New Testament texts, as a hallmark of authenticity, with the image of the 'born-again Christian' becoming a well-known idiom for someone whose attitudes are likely to be strongly integrated within a new sense of self.[19]

Hugh Bourne, born in 1772 and one of the founders of Primitive Methodism, exemplifies this approach.[20] He was much concerned about his own spiritual condition and, when reading a work by a previous Methodist, John Fletcher of Madely, found himself converted.

I believed in my heart, grace descended, and Jesus Christ manifested himself to me. My sins were taken away from that instant, and I was filled with joy and peace in believing. I never knew or thought any one could in this world have such a foretaste of heaven. In an instant I felt I loved God with all my heart, mind, soul, and strength; and I felt a love to all mankind, and a desire that all, whether friends or enemies, might be saved. I heard an inward voice saying: 'Thy iniquity is forgiven and thy sin covered.' Life, light, liberty flowed in upon my soul, and such rapturous joy that I could scarcely tell whether in the body or not.[21]

Here we have an echo of conversion experiences alluded to in Chapter 7. From a theological perspective, it is believed that God, through the power

---

[16] Schleiermacher (1830: 492).
[17] Schleiermacher (1830: 495). Cf. Schleiermacher (1885: 405) for responsive love that had been asleep.
[18] Schleiermacher (1830: 486, 493).
[19] John 3: 1–8.
[20] A revitalization of Methodism, but separate from mainstream Methodism from 1811 until 1932.
[21] Ritson (1909:15).

and in the 'person' of the Holy Spirit, has a direct effect upon individuals, allowing them not only to gain a sense of their own sin and need of forgiveness but also to see how the sacrificial death of Jesus on their behalf can now allow a change to occur in which the forgiveness of their sins can be accompanied by a newness of life. The sense of relief in forgiveness of sin is spoken of as followed by a joy and sense of freedom that goes with a new feeling of purpose to existence. The social references show a desire that others might come to a similar experience, while, in this case, many expressions reveal prior familiarity with biblical or other religious texts. As another example, the Protestant hymn-writer Frances Ridley Havergal spoke of being 'brought into intensified views of everything', from sin to an 'uninteruptedness of watchfulness' of a 'happy sort'.[22] Her case is interesting, for, autobiographically, she wrote of having no special religious feelings until she was 6 years old. Not even being taken to see a dead child lying in its flower-strewn coffin evoked more than a curiosity that a child should lie so cold and still. But one particular sermon on the theme of sinners falling into the hands of the living God was remembered all her days, making a 'terrible impression' on her. 'No one ever knew it, but this sermon haunted me, and day and night it crossed me.' She remained afraid of God for some time, her mother's death deeply saddened her, and a long-standing sense of not being a Christian and of the vanity of life pervaded her consciousness. This passed into years of religious believing, but always with a longing for some deeper sense of divine presence, until on 'Advent Sunday December 2nd 1873', when she was 37 years old, she had an experience that she likened to a 'flash of electric light'—then a novelty—such that what she had seen she could not 'unsee'. This involved a sense of a full surrender to God and a 'cleansing' from sin. Her reference to being brought 'into intensified views of everything' is worth underlining.[23] In the same evangelical tradition a century later, albeit from the intense political intrigue of the US Watergate affair involving President Nixon's resignation, one of his advisers, Charles Colson, when converted in prison, spoke of 'the real mountaintop experience. Above me and around me the world was filled with joy and love and beauty.'[24]

Many such transformations were documented by William James in his *Varieties of Religious Experience*, where he differentiated between such

---

[22] Havergal (1880: 130). The influence of such texts can be extensive. This 1880 edition had already sold 222,000 copies.

[23] Havergal (1890: 126–30).   [24] Colson (1976: 370).

twice-born individuals, described in terms of religion of the sick soul, and the 'once-born' type of the religion of healthy mindedness.[25] A different psychological perspective was taken more recently by Batson and Ventis, who accounted for religious conversion as a kind of discovery procedure in which those involved might be challenged by some life situation, be presented with alternative potential solutions, or experience some resulting confusion, before finding themselves with a resolution of their problem.[26] In terms of emotion, the answer to their quandary simply 'comes to them', rather as in the case of Albert Schweitzer and the 'discovery' of 'reverence for life' discussed in Chapter 4. Batson and Ventis portray a psychological process of problem-seeking and ensuing solution-finding, much as scientists might be faced by some apparently intractable intellectual problem, which leads to uncertainty and confusion before the solution suddenly pops up. Experientially, the answer to their problem seems to 'come to them'. An analogous, though probably longer, process is involved in the anthropological experience of fieldwork, which can be its own form of conversion and testimony, evident, for example, in Lévi-Strauss's conviction that only individuals who have 'passed the test' of fieldwork should be able 'to decide' whether others have achieved a similar insight: indeed, he speaks of 'that inner revolution that will really make him into a new man'.[27] Here the acquisition of insight into how others live and organize their world is seen to impact upon anthropologists and the way their self-understanding changes in the process. While the cases of scientific and social-scientific discovery are, obviously enough, accepted as a discovery proedure, the religious domain of conversion interprets new understanding as the outcome of the Holy Spirit's power.[28] St Augustine's account of his own conversion exemplifies this process, as he moves from being 'sick at heart and in torment', experiencing 'fear and shame' while, he had nevertheless 'begun to move towards the resolution', even when 'a mighty storm arose' in him. Then, while 'weeping in the most bitter sorrow' of his heart, he hears a child's voice in a sing-song repeating: 'Take and read, take and read.' He immediately reads a passage that tells him to 'put on the Lord Jesus Christ and make not provision for the flesh'.[29]

---

[25] James (1902).   [26] Batson and Ventis (1982: 71).

[27] Lévi-Strauss (1963: 373).

[28] Sometimes an affinity between personal inclinations and a natural acceptance of formal ideas encountered later occurs, as with George Bernard Shaw and evolutionary ideas (1967: 110–11).

[29] Romans 13: 13.

Then, 'in that instant, with the very ending of the sentence, it was as though a light of utter confidence shone in all my heart, and the darkness of uncertainty vanished away'.[30]

For the Evangelical convert, such an emotion-rooted experience has the characteristic of a personal revelation, with the groups that emphasize the necessity of new-birth style conversion also stressing the nature of the Bible as a revealed document. The emotional sense of revelation as 'coming to us' in conversion naturally complements and reinforces the theological idea of the Bible as divinely inspired. This is where the theme of identity is doubly affected, through personal experience and group affirmation of the source of truth. The Evangelical experience confers a sense of identity in which an explanation of life's emotional dynamics coheres with an explanation of the world itself. More than that, it also offers a clear affirmation of an eternal destiny through the idea of the resurrection of the dead. This, too, continues the idea of transformation in a cognitive-affective affinity with that of conversion, for, if someone possesses a deep personal experience of change during the course of his life, it is coherent for him to think of death as involving yet another deeply significant change. What is more, the very language of death and of life pervades conversion discourse in terms of death to an old life and birth into a new life, which makes it relatively easy to extend these idioms into the themes of actual death followed by an actual, new, and transformed heavenly life.[31]

Crisis of presence

This is the case in Nicole Toulis's study of Jamaican women immigrants to Britain and their conversion within a Pentecostal Church context, where 'holiness' stands as a root paradigm or, more suggestively, still as a 'heart-word', with believers speaking not only of the need for a clean heart, cleansed by the blood sacrifice of Jesus, but also of a subsequent baptism of the Holy Spirit. Toulis demonstrates quite persuasively that conversion in this group is 'gradual and chronic... characterized by intense periodic spiritual moments which are necessary for perpetuating and maintaining conversion'. Indeed, she notes that 'the gains made by conversion are not necessarily permanent and can easily be lost'.[32] Accordingly, church events serve to intensify and

---

[30] Augustine ([413–426] 1945b: 139–42).
[31] John 3: 1–36.
[32] Toulis (1997: 125, 133–4).

develop previous experiences, with members utilizing the biblical notion of having to 'die daily', with the implication of an ongoing newness of life.

She follows George Sanders's theoretical development of Ernesto DeMartino's notion of 'crisis of presence', and goes on to differentiate between the individual person and the social self, the former emphasizing personal autonomy and the latter social networking.[33] 'Presence' is described as

a sense of self where persons are conscious of their own autonomy and instrumentality, where they can perceive themselves to be authors of their own intentions, actions and definitions of self. A crisis of presence thus arises when a person is no longer in such control but senses themselves as 'subject to the will of others'.[34]

In such circumstances, conversion to a new religious outlook offers a powerful opportunity, not simply for regaining a sense of 'presence' and of being master of one's own life and circumstances, but also for obtaining a new level of identity. It is precisely here that an emotional arena provided by doctrines of sin, the devil, repentance, and new birth through the Holy Spirit offers an opportunity for a new identity through religious belonging. One of Toulis's narrative accounts of conversion is quite typical, with her informant speaking of a night when she had been confronted by a demon but was so 'anointed' by the Holy Spirit that she drove the demon—who appeared as a white man with big teeth, a moustache, and an orange suit—out of her house: this enabled her to confront her errant son with his wrongdoings. This was followed by a good night's sleep and, on awakening the next morning, to a good feeling, 'as if I was coming from heaven' to a big place of 'green pastures' and with 'sweet melodious music'.[35] In many of Toulis's conversion reports, the place of experience predominates. People see brightness or light, are light-footed or feel sick; many varied descriptions occur that emphasize the emotional dynamics pervading the intellectual shifts in views that come about. But, whatever the diverse emotions may be, they are expected to lead to a new pattern of life of holiness espoused and ongoingly reinforced by the Pentecostal churches. This case demonstrates a clear relationship between emotion, identity, and religion, both within devotees' experience and in its sociological interpretation. It offers one concrete example of Ian Craib's 'paradoxical ideology'—namely, 'as individuals become increasingly powerless, we

---

[33] Toulis (1997: 126). She follows George R. Sanders (1995), who developed the notion of 'crisis of presence' from Ernesto DeMartino.
[34] Toulis (1997: 127).　　[35] Toulis (1997: 129–30).

develop an ideology of self-control and self-creation, as if we really could control ourselves and our lives'.[36]

Still, within Toulis's Protestant context, such events hold an important place in an individual's life story as well as furnishing a public role as a testimony of the power of God that is already an embedded theological view of the church. Though the date and context of conversion is often a prized item of information, it is also possible for some to have an extended period involving a variety of different experiences of good and evil before the final breakthrough occurs. In other churches, quite different dynamics are found. In the Church of Jesus Christ of Latter-Day Saints, Mormons hold a Testimony service once a month at which individuals voluntarily speak of events in their lives in and through which they have experienced God's influence, often involving the kind actions of other church members. This church has very largely avoided 'born-again' language, preferring to place a sharp emphasis upon the importance of entry into the church or of experiences within the church itself. The Church, believed to have been restored to earth by God through Joseph Smith, its founding prophet, takes precedence over the individual as the prime object of divine action. To be in the church is more important that to have been converted as an individual outside it or in any other church. Still, the role of testimony remains as the means of asserting the importance of the emotional changes experienced as a member.

The power of words to capture and express emotion and to indicate the influence of a divine presence cannot be overemphasized in these various cases. What is more, the social context of key actors is profoundly important for how they present and handle knowledge. This is significant today for example, for the way science and religion are understood in relation to each other, especially over the aims of religious revelation and scientific discovery. On the one hand, Philip Rieff argues that 'the language of science is not revelatory but analytic' precisely because the scientist can never 'claim that his own terms have a prophetic function', since that work is 'non-moral', but, on the other hand, when professional scientists occasionally speak of discovery in terms of the beauty of a solution and of its 'dawning' on them, their accounts resemble the testimonies of religious believers, even if they do not fully embrace the otherness and sense of personal encounter of the religious

---

[36] Craib (1998: 107).

devotee.[37] So, too, with some other problems and solutions, as one sociologist spoke of 'eureka moments': 'It's the brain that does it, not you. That's why it feels so strange. It's something that happens to you, not something that you do.'.[38]

Blessing

It is precisely this dynamic sense of reception or personal encounter that characterizes much religious affirmation and, as the previous chapter indicated, takes shape in blessing, when the power of words is experienced as an enhancement of the self. A good example is found in the Mormon Patriarchal blessing, which combines the power of prophetic words with the more literary aspect of texts while evoking strong emotional experiences. These blessings may be given by someone's father or by a formally appointed regional church Patriarch, whose task is to lay hands on the head of the recipient and to speak words of blessing on him by direct influence of the Holy Spirit; what is said is written down and a record kept by the individual and by the church. This act is highly personal and the message kept as a relative secret, in that a person would tend not to speak of it to many beyond a very close circle of intimates, if at all. This 'sacred-secrecy' echoes the secrecy of the temple rites undergone by Mormons, a secrecy that non-Mormons often criticize as some form of invidious silence.[39] In both Patriarchal blessings and the formulae of temple rites, however, what we see in their associated secrecy is something that guards a central mystery of language, a factor of profoundest significance in Mormonism as a tradition founded on newly revealed words, in this case the Book of Mormon and the further revelations believed to have been given by God to Joseph Smith as founding prophet. Something similar obtains in Islam, whose prophet Muhammad is also believed to have gained divine words by a similar route.

Tones and texting

Such 'mystery in language', as described by George Steiner, is a valuable commodity and should weigh heavily on those tempted to say all 'in the

[37] Rieff (1966: 201).
[38] Collins (2010: 44).
[39] Douglas J. Davies (2000: 80–2, 180–1).

market place of words': he commends the 'taboos and speech-zones reserved for occasions of special intimacy and seriousness', which help to vitalize existence. Words retained for intimacy are, he says, 'near the deep springs of language', with such 'verbal reticence' linking us with 'antique energies and sources of wonder'.[40] Far from being just a clever critic of postmodern theorists who display competence in wordplay to convey the favoured emotional tone of irony playing upon cultural rootlessness, Steiner is perfectly correct in seeing the 'dim places of feeling' as sustained by not exposing our lives and thoughts 'wastefully'.[41] 'Much that is best in man', he says, has been grounded in 'the miracle of speech', and, for the purposes of this chapter, it is when such speech takes the form of revelation and blessing that it becomes so miraculous in enhancing human vitality. Such vocal and textual emotion is profoundly important at a time when electronic communication engages millions in spending much time message-exchanging, engendering the notion of 'texting' in the process. Indeed, this new medium brings the nature of reciprocity, otherness, and emotion to bear heavily on issues of identity, where new generations 'text' each other and are frequently checking to see if they have received return messages. Such interaction affords a clear example of balanced reciprocity operating at very high speed. Not to receive a return and to experience paucity of communication when desiring it is problematic for some and affects their sense of inclusion–exclusion in friendship networks. Emotion pervades this new world of electronic togetherness, not only in the positive sense of a creative use of keyboard symbols to express emotion, as in the 'happy-face' sign, but also in messaging as a medium for bullying and aggression, not least among children. It remains questionable, however, just how texting reciprocity might embrace Mauss's fourth obligation of 'giving to the gods', an expression that might, in this context, be rendered as expressing or giving deepest commitments, or exchanging blessings.

What texting cannot achieve is the vocal tonality and embodied emotions of demeanour that, in most aspects of life and especially in the religious world, speak volumes in terms of the identity claimed by and accorded to a devotee. In terms of the Mormon world alluded to above, this becomes dramatically apparent at the monthly Fast and Testimony meetings where tone of voice deeply reflects the spiritual status of the speaker.[42] Its calm and

---

[40] George Steiner ([1968] 1972: 104).

[41] George Steiner ([1968] 1972: 97). Writing in the 1960s, he criticized the 'current triviality and megalomania' of those given to the 'criticism of criticism'.

[42] Douglas J. Davies (2000: 128–30).

measured tonality, combining with the possibility of brief emotional 'chok-ing', all betoken a genuine purpose in life and, therefore, of identity within a community of sincerity. And much the same could be said for many religious traditions and contexts, where many kinds of gestures enhance vocal tone.[43] Within the Society of Friends, this is taken into an even more complex area in which the nature and quality of silence in group meetings, with all that also means for stillness and bodily posture, is part of assessing the spiritual tone of the group.[44] The liturgies of the Greek Orthodox Church, by contrast, easily entertain people coming and going as may be necessary, all combined as part of the 'work' of worship.

From quite a different social world, Joel Robbins describes spirit power in what he calls the ritual of redemption among the Urapmin of Papua New Guinea, a newly evangelized tribal people with a distinctive form of Protest-ant Evangelical Pentecostal-like religion. In 'the Spirit disko', a gathering separate from main church services, individuals show erratically forceful behaviour as the Holy Spirit is believed to engage with a person's sins. Those under the Spirit's influence smash into others, may do damage to the church building itself, and pull those helping them one way and another. Robbins analyses this behaviour within its cultural context of interpersonal obligation and highlights the place of wilfulness and its need of social control, as this society begins to experience the impact of Christian missionary influence. The mood of salvation takes indigenous notions of aggression and the need to compel others to comply with one's will and exhausts them through the Spirit disko, whose success demonstrates the approval of the Holy Spirit, at least for some of those present. This behaviour of one possessed by the Holy Spirit seems to show two facets. On the one hand, they display the 'worst fantasies of how people would behave' if left to their own wilful desire, for 'the possessed person is, in some sense, an image of the will incarnate and unfettered'. But, then, once the Holy Spirit has achieved its task, those who had been 'heavy' through their sins now become 'light', with 'the final disposition of the possessed, lying limp on the church floor', being for the Urapmin 'a paradigmatic image of the person beyond the experience of sinful wilfulness. It is the very picture of a yielding, lawful way of being.' Robbins's use of the notion of paradigmatic scene here reflects its use throughout our present study as a means of capturing the combined emotional

---

[43] Tyson, Peacock, and Patterson (1988: 4).
[44] Dandelion (1996: 15–16, 238).

and ideological perspective of a group. He summarizes the event that generates this paradigmatic scene as one in which 'the Spirit disko . . . appears to heighten desire and allow for the expression of wilfulness at the same time that it transcends them'.[45]

OTHERNESS

These contexts of spirit power, along with those of blessing and confessing and the work of priests and prophets, all express forms of emotion-engendering and mood-sustaining relationships that conduce to otherness, a running theme of this study and vital for understanding human identity. While E. B. Tylor's well-known minimal definition of religion as belief in supernatural beings is easily glossed as antiquated anthropology and has certainly been bettered by his successors, it remains of value for pinpointing otherness as a factor of human experience developed in religious contexts.[46] Otherness is a characteristic attribute of human awareness, grounded in the fact that we are always aware 'of something', a point that prompted Albert Schweitzer's damning critique of Descartes's philosophical aphorism 'I think therefore I am' as 'the stupidest primary assumption in all philosophy'.[47] His objection lies in the conviction that thought always had an object: we always think *of* something. Schweitzer did not wish to take thinking back a step into a state of self-validating cogitation. Be that as it may, the fact is that we have evolved as conscious and self-conscious animals seeking to make sense of and to survive within physical and social environments that, together, furnish an 'otherness-environment'. If we wished to invoke Tylor again we might update his enduring concept of animism to remind us of the psychological processes that seem attuned to perceive potentially active forces in the world around us. For Tylor otherness was evident in 'primitive culture', whether in its 'supernatural' or its 'natural' domains.[48]

Within the sociological tradition, Durkheim's conception of the deities as an epiphenomenon of society developed the sense of otherness in terms of experience of self-transcendence in the corporate context of ritual. Within that tradition, however, Csordas opposed the way Durkheim established 'the

---

[45] Robbins (2004: 286–7).

[46] And far more direct than McCauley and Lawson's 'CPS' or 'culturally postulated superhuman' agents (2002: 8).

[47] Schweitzer ([1936] 1962: 183).   [48] Tylor ([1871] 1958).

social as a category sui generis' that allowed him to identify God with and as 'society', making the 'sacred' one with society and, thereby 'mystifying society making it 'worship itself'. Csordas considered Durkheim to have 'mistakenly...abolished the sacred as a category sui generis for anthropological theory'. He sees others as perpetuating this reductionist move of locating essential factors in the social realm, specifically identifying Geertz's definition of religion because it embedded a 'system of symbols' within the realm of social relationships. One reason why this is problematic for him is that the Geertz focus on religion as something that 'acts to establish long standing moods and motivations' has, then, to be understood within social and cultural concerns, while Csordas thinks that such a social realm is not the domain within which to understand their prime nature. For him 'the theoretical power to get at these moods and motivations may be found amongst the phenomenologists and historians of religion such as Otto, van der Leeuw and Eliade'.[49]

While it is understandable that Csordas wishes not to locate the domain of the sacred within social forces, it remains unclear as to where it belongs. To invoke Otto, van der Leeuw, and Eliade is no great help, since it is far from clear how each of those three would agree on how best to locate the sacred. For Otto, primarily a theologian, its source is within the divine, and van der Leeuw is similar in perspective though more difficult to assess on this issue. Eliade, too, is far from clear as to the source of the sacred, though in general terms would seem to locate it as a relational outcome of human awareness of the world. Within modern theology itself, as Fergus Kerr has made clear, 'the longings that human beings naturally seem to have for some sort of transcendence of finitude' is a fundamental issue.[50]

Csordas's own affirmation is that 'the sacred is operationalized by the criterion of the "other"', a criterion that becomes 'characteristic of human consciousness', with 'the sacred' being a 'modality of human experience'. Though Csordas would probably also discount the finality of explanation offered, because its ultimate origin is not in the divine as such, it is precisely here that Boyer's cognitive studies may be invoked as a means of indicating how, in neurological terms, this sense of otherness arises. While a theologian might wish, on the basis of faith and personal experience, to insist on God as the source of otherness, it seems to me that religious studies is better equipped

---

[49] Csordas ([1990] 2002: 82–3).
[50] Kerr (1997: 164).

to furnish in-depth accounts of otherness as reported by religious traditions than to give ultimate explanations of them on the basis of confessional belief. Phenomenology is better when acting in its descriptive than in an explanatory mode. The theological criticism of the cognitive-science approach as being, itself, ultimate and 'confessional' in working on a personal non-theistic judgement is fair and must simply be accepted. Unless one then wishes to espouse one theistic tradition over others, which I do not wish to do, it is wiser to remain with the 'ultimacy' of social-scientific and humanities-resourced explanations of the human sense of otherness. Theologians may, then, if they wish, take such findings of otherness and frame them in their own dogmatic terms, but that lies beyond the scope or intention of this study.

Remaining within the human arena, we locate the awareness of otherness within intuition, following Boyer's evolutionary biological approach to human schemes of thought and feeling that implicate 'domains of reality for which we have very specific intuitions that are not delivered by conscious, deliberate processes'.[51] We alluded to this approach in Chapter 4, when considering death, but now we can work from those assumptions on mental processes that involve intuitions but not explicit knowledge to see that some 'concepts are often vague and their interpretation idiosyncratic'. Accordingly, it is not too great an extrapolation to ponder the issue of otherness as just such an intuitive complex of the individual set in a complexly stimulating environment. Boyer's invocation of the Intuitive-Psychology system and the Animacy system would, together, suggest a way in which people could have a general sense of the otherness of their world. To this might be added more concrete information from the Person-File system that would contain source material on what fellow members of society have said or intimated about their sense of otherness. Though Boyer tends to place formal religious institutional material to one side, it is important to include it, precisely because the explicit statements about an awareness of otherness that has become focused and explicit in religious myths, texts, and rites would be evoked by a Person-File system.

When alluding to prophets, Boyer speaks of their followers, saying that 'it takes people with a prior disposition for concepts of invisible supernatural agents to make sense of such pronouncement'.[52] The impact of 'prior dispositions' can be considerable and may, for example, be evident in the

---

[51] Boyer (2001: 250–1).
[52] Boyer (2001: 357).

kind of philosophical understanding of India's eighth-century philosopher Sankara, who spoke of a need for a 'sense of discrimination of things that are permanent and things that are impermanent' (*nityanityavastu-viveka*) in a devotee.[53] At a more popular level, the historian of religion Kees Bolle rehearsed the anthropologist Paul Radin's distinction between two types of people present in all societies, those with a 'temperament' given to practical action and those 'given to contemplation'.[54] That individuals or traditions set upon philosophical reflection and meditative considerations should develop their own classification of feeling states related to modes of thinking is not surprising. Nor is it odd that those modes should be framed by religious conceptions and explained as forms of spirituality. Christian monastic traditions, for example, those associated with Mount Athos in Greece, can speak of different kinds of pleasure associated with the body and with the soul, with the latter embracing the very 'pleasures of knowledge and contemplation' that can be so influential as even to be described as 'a kind of lust, a spiritual kind of pleasure'.[55] That is feasible because of the existence of God as the divine other who may be contemplated and in relation to whom the pious may live in devotional and ethical reciprocity.

The significance of otherness, then, can be taken in different ways, whether as a preliminary argument leading into theological ultimacy or, for example, in a more literary-philosophical mode evident in that sense of presence described in his own way by George Steiner. Indeed, it is Steiner's *Real Presences* that identifies the status of otherness on a grand scale and with a sense of diverse ubiquity. 'Why there should be the other and our relations to that otherness, be they theological, moral, social, erotic, be they those of intimate participation or irreconcilable difference, is a mystery both harsh and consoling.'[56]

Steiner speaks of the 'inviolate enigma of the otherness in things and in animate presences', acknowledging the *'terra incognita* of our own selves', and affirming that we are 'strangers to ourselves, errant at the gates of our own psyche'. Yet, at the same time, we find a 'rendezvous with intelligibility'.[57] This particular strangeness coupled with an awareness of meaning becomes an intuition of Boyer's psychological perspective on the hiddenness of mental

---

[53] Bolle ([1968] 1993: 142).
[54] Bolle ([1968] 1993: 146), citing Radin ([1927] 1957: ch. XIII).
[55] Gothóni (1987: 78).
[56] George Steiner (1989: 137).
[57] George Steiner (1989: 139).

processes underlying conscious awareness. Steiner speaks of this *alterity* as the 'agonistic-collaborative presence of agencies beyond the governance or conceptual grasp of the craftsman'.[58] For him, the issue of alterity is, ultimately, that of the existence of God. Without that ultimate alterity all works of proximate creativity lack their rationale. In the terms of this study, the absence of otherness negates the sense of reciprocity, for creativity is, ultimately, a reciprocal activity. Such an intuition may even be prompted within the context of ritual to highlight the very idea of worship in which 'vitality' and 'life-presence', notions Steiner also sustains as distinguishing 'serious thought and feeling from the trivial', play a major role, often through the very sense of engagement with the otherness of the supernatural world.[59] Here we encounter what we might call 'low focus revelation', a term we develop from David Galanter's idea of 'low focus thought' which refers to a 'relaxed state' when thought is open to the play of analogy and metaphor as opposed to 'high focus thought' that is abstract and analytical. Edgewater cites this argument to emphasize the idea that emotion plays a higher role in the low- than in the high-focused form of thought.[60] Galanter argued that an emotion may be evoked by particular memories and that the brain works in such a way that different memories may evoke the same emotion and that through a process of 'affect linking'. This suggests that if a particular 'emotional code' is activated it may trigger a variety of past and differing events and offers a valuable approach as to how different aspects of information gained, scriptures heard, hymns sung, or thoughts pondered during worship may come to share an emotional frame redolent of Steiner's 'vitality' and life force.

THE MODES OF RELIGIOUS KNOWING

Against this background of otherness we now consider Harvey Whitehouse's double-focused theory of religion, which has already been sketched in Chapter 2 and which carries direct consequences for issues of emotion and religious identity. Whitehouse developed his approach from the 1990s by aligning types of memory with types of context in which related types of 'learning' occur. This led to discussions of the nature of religious groups

---

[58] George Steiner (1989: 211).
[59] George Steiner (1989: 141).
[60] Edgewater (1999: 170). Edgewater cites Galanter's perspective on this idea.

and their capacity for expansion that exemplify the management of emotion both in individual and in group identity. This integration of psychological and sociological factors highlights the interplay of 'medium' and 'message' in the respective 'two modes' of religion.[61]

Semantic–doctrinal: episodic–imagistic modes

Whitehouse, then, distinguishes between 'semantic' and 'episodic' types of memory that generate doctrinal and imagistic modes of religion. These 'two modes' of religion are grounded in 'two distinct mechanisms of long-term memory'.[62] This view assumes that new ideas are constantly occurring but with only some gaining acceptance within a religious culture. The 'cognitive mechanisms' involved in the underlying forms of mental processing comprise two types of memories—namely, semantic and episodic. The semantic or doctrinal form is typified by formal teaching and learning resulting in an acquisition of canonical-like information. This social competence in learned knowledge is gained from school or college education and is widespread in many societies, and its semantic–doctrinal form of knowing contrasts with contexts in which episodic memory impacts upon an individual's life by the force of particular events that create the distinctive emotional capacity for flashbulb memories. Such episodic memories return as pictures of an event, as reflected in Whitehouse's use of the expression 'imagistic' mode of religion aligned with this kind of memory recall. The image of some past event floods the mind and prompts powerful emotional responses. Here the two modes embrace the contexts and forms of organization of events that foster them: the psychological issues of memory interact with the social organization of groups. The two-modes theory then becomes as much a theory of social organization and forms of knowledge as of emotions and ongoing moods.

Whitehouse is alert to similar schemes recognized by previous scholars as, for example, by Dan Sperber's distinction between encyclopaedic and symbolic knowledge. The former, formally learned, sets knowledge within distinctive categories, while the latter, being more 'acquired' than 'learned', tends to integrate materials rather than isolate them.[63] He argued that human brains naturally integrate and deploy these forms of knowing as

---

[61] See Laidlaw (2004: 1–9) for a basic summary.
[62] Laidlaw (2004: 1); see also Whitehouse (2000).
[63] Sperber (1975: 88).

required, with it only being for purposes of analysis that they are differentiated. Various criticisms of Whitehouse's work tend to note the interplay of
imagistic and doctrinal modes of religion within a single society or religious
group. Indeed, it may be that at different times in its history a group may lean
more in one mode than in another or have members whose experience is
more of one form than of another. One significant theoretical predecessor is
W. E. H. Stanner, whose work on the Murinbata in Australia subtly analysed
forms of male ritual in which the initiates' personality could 'almost be seen
to change before one's eyes', as some form of 'indelible impression' was made
upon people, so much so that he suggested that 'there might be neural or
cortical changes' taking place in them.[64]

Semantic memory: doctrinal mode

Whitehouse describes the formal learning of set pieces of information from
authorized teachers as the 'doctrinal' form of religion, one often grounded in
a religious orthodoxy. It is ongoing and cumulative in effect. Resembling
Sperber's encyclopaedic form of knowledge, it results in 'more sober, organized, and verbal' forms of organization. People learn such doctrine and sense
themselves as part of a very large number of people who have learned the
same material. A 'widespread but impersonal solidarity results' in which
religious leaders as teachers maintain orthodoxy as part of a centralized
authority structure organized to reach many people. This organization
often involves a strong form of 'deference' and, as Bloch indicates, is often
experienced as 'a good feeling', as we 'allow ourselves to depend on others'.
This is especially gratifying in times of trouble, when 'there is not much else
we can do'.[65] This doctrinal mode of religion, with its deferential attitudes
firmly embedded in an extensive organization, is, then, capable of widespread
extension through evangelism, a phenomenon that can also be interpreted in
terms of superplausibility as we do below.

   The prime point at this stage is to appreciate not only that this knowledge
is exportable but, and this is to elaborate a point beyond Whitehead, that
it lies within the ongoing capacity of individuals to integrate and develop it
within their personal life circumstances, not least in contexts of worship. It is
not uncommon for theologically instructed individuals to appropriate and
reappropriate formal beliefs in deeply personal ways after years of group

----

[64] Stanner (1959–60a: 125–6).
[65] Maurice Bloch (2004: 77).

membership. Indeed, this capacity for reflexive conversion and ongoing insight generation is considerable and fostered by the pools of potential orientation to life inherent in a tradition's texts, commentaries, biographies, hagiographies, and diverse ritual and iconographic forms.[66] These resources may lie fallow until particular life circumstances allow an affinity with them to spring to life. Emotional factors of changed circumstance or of individual psychological orientation play a significant role in such processes of appreciation and appropriation. Within Christianity, for example, biblical texts describing the Holy Spirit's power to animate Christian believers and to bestow 'gifts' of speaking in tongues or gaining visions and the like were reappropriated in the 1830s by the new Catholic Apostolic Church, which practised glossolalia alongside very formal rites derived from Catholic and Orthodox Christianities and very unlike early twentieth-century Protestant Pentecostalism. Glossolalia was also adopted from the 1960s in Charismatic groups within numerous Christian denominations. Each of these reflects periods of theological acceptance and ritual intensification of biblical texts, especially those narratives of the paradigmatic scenes of the Day of Pentecost rehearsed in the Acts of the Apostles.[67] The emotional impact and influence of these forms of spirituality in constructing distinctive religious identities were enormous, and different social and cultural circumstances surrounded their emergence. Their theoretical import lies in the fact that the seminal texts on which they based a Charismatic identity had existed for centuries until the insight of particular leaders, an available following, and suitable social context turned latent capacity into appropriated reality. Some, like David Aberbach, would also stress the 'traumatized inner world' of the charismatic leader and its interplay with some 'external social and political crisis' as integral to a charismatic leader-led movement.[68]

The complexity of experience allowing learned texts to become enacted scripts in a Pentecostal drama militates against too sharp a divide between modes of religiosity, a point reinforced by a certain Protestant Evangelicalism, which was deeply suspicious of 'book learning', as of education in general, and which preferred the authenticity of immediate experience of divine power. These groups have often stressed the emotion of guilt and catharsis of forgiveness through the doctrinal teaching that Jesus was God's

---

[66] See Douglas J. Davies (1984a: 124, 135) for the pool of potential orientations.

[67] Acts 2: 1–21.

[68] Aberbach (1996: 104).

sacrifice for sin with preaching and textual images expressed in hymns prompting emotion and sustaining moods of piety associated with the experience of 'salvation'. Later nineteenth- and some twentieth-century images of Jesus as the sacrificed lamb of God dying in the place of otherwise condemned sinners were common. One hymn spoke of the newly converted believer being 'washed in the blood of the lamb', and asked others if they were so washed. Another hymn, taking its lead from John Bunyan's *Pilgrim's Progress*, spoke of sin as a heavy burden that now rolled away. The convert sang 'rolled away, rolled away, when the burden of my heart rolled away'. These powerful soteriological motifs were deeply embodied and emotionally expressed; dirty bodies were 'washed' and heavy loads shed. These contexts are reminiscent of Robert Hertz's work on sin and expiation and of the 'fear and guilt' embedded in the self-knowledge of being a sinner before 'an almighty god capable of punishing and forgiving'.[69] With ordinary life providing so many opportunities for wronging, it is not surprising that societies should have periods of moral cleansing. If populations are also undergoing rapid social change and social dislocation at the same time, the possibility of larger-scale revivalism grounded in self-acknowledged sin becomes both feasible and functional, as in the Methodist revivals in Great Britain or some periods of 'awakening' in the USA.

Imagistic memory: episodic mode

But it is to much smaller-scale societies and preliterate or relatively preliterate contexts that Whitehouse addressed his other mode of religiosity grounded in its own style of memory. Here people have not learned 'a script' or set liturgical form, nor even a set of formal behavioural practices: they have experienced 'an event', one that has become built into memory. Instead of a teacher dispensing formal knowledge, we have neophytes set in the 'learning' context of initiation rites in which no leader offers teaching on the meaning of what is going on. The 'meaning' of the experiences has to dawn on individuals as they ponder what happened to them. Indeed, this aspect of personal experience and making it explicit is important to Whitehouse, who thinks that Maurice Bloch, for example, had rather overlooked it in his analysis of the notion of rebounding conquest to which we return below. For Whitehouse, pain lies at the heart of these ritual events, and pain in relation to trauma is a complex issue. Young, for example, discusses the

---

[69] Parkin (1996: 128).

nature of traumatic memory and the way individuals with a strong post-traumatic condition may seek out a context resembling that which caused their condition in the first place precisely because it helps generate the chemical substances called endorphins within the body that help a person cope with extremely difficult circumstances. These natural opiates seem able to create a kind of dependency or addiction within a person, which leads Young to suggest that a person can become addicted not only to the effects of the substance but also to the 'memories that release these chemicals'.[70] Memory, especially 'flashbulb memory', which plays a vital role in White-house's theories, deals with the recall or the impinging of intense past experiences upon present life. We are most familiar with these from people having undergone trauma in catastrophes, warfare, or disaster situations. He describes ritual initiation contexts, which he believes generated similar ex-perience: things happened to them without any explanation of a theoretical kind. They were thrown into the deep end of experience in their ritual initiation. Later they would be responsible for initiating others, but not, necessarily or even probably, with any extensive explanation of what goes on. People were left with their own experience to make of it what they might. The concrete fact was that something had happened to them, usually as a group, and that helped bind them together because of the experiences as such.

Pain firmly marks the place of emotion in this imagistic mode and is much in evidence, for example, in Whitehouse's account of rites of terror, the initiation programme among some traditional Melanesian groups.[71] He speaks of the solidarity gained among initiates as 'lasting but also (as) difficult to generalize or extend'.[72] Indeed, the key feature of this imagistic type is rooted in 'mortal terror and physical pain'.[73] James Laidlaw describes similar rites of 'intense and traumatic' initiation for women when becoming ascetics in the Jain tradition, whose sporadic rites traditionally included the pulling out of the head-hair. These ascetics go bald, never wash, and sweep the road before them as they walk; they eat and drink with care so as not to harm any creature. He speaks of their initiation as an event that will 'certainly give rise to episodic memories, if not to "flashbulb" memories'. The rites help produce 'a very tightly bound small group of religious agents'.[74]

[70] Young ([1996] 1997: 257–8).
[71] Whitehouse (2004b: 132–48).
[72] Whitehouse (2004b: 144).
[73] Laidlaw (2004: 95).
[74] Laidlaw (2004: 102).

The symbolism of such ritual proceedings is important for anthropological accounts of these events, which is why, for example, Whitehouse argues with Bloch over the symbolic association between boys and 'pigs' in certain Melanesian initiation rites. Just what kind of 'pigs' are these boys who await initiation? Not pigs in general, and certainly not domestic pigs, but wild pigs. Here he argues that initiates come in some way to grasp that at one minute they are being treated like wild pigs, when they seem to be hunted by their initiators and treated as enemies, and then, in a switch of attitude, they are nurtured and cared for, a situation that will confuse them. Though he is not sure that anyone has got to the bottom of what these experiences mean to the individuals, he repeatedly speaks of 'the revelatory character of ritual'.[75] And this constitutes an important element within his work and, by extension, for religious studies in general: just what is 'revelation'? Here his imagistic and doctrinal classification is of interest, for what kind of knowledge is 'revelation', and what emotions are processed through it? He argues that from the New Guinea material at least the initiations 'confound everyday understandings ... and emphasize the multivocal and multivalent character of revelation'.[76] Indeed he sees the whole process as being 'resistant to expression in language'. He tries to make some sense of it by comparing these painful rites, where body parts such as the penis or arms may be cut or burned, as analogous to the experience of victims of terrorism and the way they may view their captors if and when violence gives way to some form of comfort. More than that, he also speaks of the dawning realization of the novice that he has actually overcome the ordeal.

Whitehouse dwells on the psychology of flashbulb memories in the life of initiates and their 'vivid recollections of inspirational, calamitous, or otherwise emotionally arousing events'. He notes that they do not discuss them, but that 'enlightening memories' may turn over in their minds for years as they ponder on their significance. He speaks of the 'unexpected nature of revelation'.[77] The ideas that were 'conveyed non-verbally to a great degree' may take years to make sense and may never gain any formal doctrinal expression in the small groups of those who shared such binding emotional events.[78] They possess little opportunity for organization of ideas in any doctrinal sense, and simply make whatever sense they can of what has

---

[75] Whitehouse (2004b: 138).
[76] Whitehouse (2004b: 140).
[77] Whitehouse (200b4: 142).
[78] Laidlaw (2004: 4).

happened to them: 'experience is emergent, not pre-formed. It changes. It goes on and on. The ethnographer must be cautious about creating an end that is artificial'.[79] Certainly, leadership in any structured sense is rare, and these groups are not organized for expansion, they are local in origin and intent, and they tend to occur in localized and small-scale societies, and, for the large part of history, in preliterate groups.

Mixed modes and images

As already indicated, these modes of memory and emotion may be co-present in some traditions, as Laidlaw noted for Jainism, whose ascetic renouncers are more imagistic while 'lay' Jains are characteristically more 'doctrinal'. More-over, the renouncers occasionally reinstate severe austerities in what he describes as 'often downright scary behaviour', which contributes to their 'ambiguous prestige'. He links this with the 'revelator' powers associated with fasting.

Given Whitehead's psychologically specific use of 'image' and 'imagistic' phenomena, it is worth differentiating it from the widespread role of literal images within religions lest Whitehouse's scheme fosters too strict a view of image within religious experience. Many traditions may be iconographically image-full without being psychologically imagistic in their emotional impact upon people. But that is not to ignore some very specific contexts where literal images may play a part in traumatic-like forms of spirituality. We have, for example, in Chapter 8 sketched the experience of stigmata within Catholic piety, which offers a most dramatic example of the way in which the material image of Christ's crucifixion produced physical pain and symbolic wounds in a small but notable company of devotees.

Whitehouse's approach to the doctrinal mode of religion, however, easily leads us to assume that its content is largely abstract and propositional. By speaking of semantic memory, it is easy to think of this mode as composed entirely of lists of doctrine and pages of sacred texts, but this would be to ignore the fact that doctrinal religion frequently employs visual images as part of its teaching and worship. This reinforces the importance of distinguishing between 'image' as a memory scene, derived from an experience in and of itself (in the imagistic mode), and an 'image', whether pictorial or metaphor-ical, derived from an explicit teaching situation.

---

[79] Good et al. (1992: 190).

A good example of pictorial images in general can be found within Mormonism, itself a religious tradition of complex constituency. In today's world it has a strong doctrinal component in which official truths are taught and learned. But it also had historical periods within the nineteenth century, when groups of the Latter-day Saints experienced suffering and opposition in events giving occasion for shared privation and a bonding that took them beyond that of simple doctrinal teaching. Moreover, the experience of missionary work has, for a minority, also presented opportunity for shared hardship that serves as a memory resource for later spiritual reflection. To all of this can be added the distinctive environment of temple ritual in whose sacred-secret ceremonies devotees enter covenantal promises with God and participate in a ritualized cosmic drama of salvation. For some this experience is relatively traumatic, with both positive and negative consequences, its being so totally unlike the very conventional congregational weekly meetings at the local church building. Outside the temple, too, Mormonism presents several paradigmatic scenes that enshrine key values and beliefs in a narrative story form that is easy to remember—namely, the pre-mortal Plan of Salvation, Christ's Gethsemane experience, and the First Vision of Joseph Smith. What is more, these images tend to become integrated as a set that dominates LDS thought and can interplay with the emotional experiences acquired in the temple rites. Not that these are the only narrative episodes with power in Mormonism, but their very existence makes it easier for others to be deployed. Sometimes the popularity of such narrative forms makes it possible for the more mythical kinds to interplay with historically based stories. Mormon stories of handcart migrants or of God sending seagulls to devour crickets that were devastating an early harvest in the Salt Lake Valley can easily interplay with Joseph's first vision of encounter with divine figures or of Jesus in Gethsemane. Clearly, then, a doctrinal mode of religion rooted in semantic memory, which often employs images in its teaching, can also possess some aspects of episodic memory.

Superplausibility

Such paradigmatic scenes are widely used in religions as commentaries upon life, exhorting while judging and adding significant dimensions to the every-day life world. Here, however, care is needed to do justice to different qualities of knowledge along with their potential consequences. If, for example, we adopt the language of the sociology of knowledge, we can describe everyday experiences in terms of plausibility theory.[80] Children are socialized into the life of their society, its system of symbols, and its core values, and its culture becomes plausible to them, much as Geertz's definition of religion suggests. The religious life of a society has often been part of that social learning resulting in experience of plausibility. But 'religious' institutions often speak of some kind of discontinuity between the ordinariness of things and some other domain. While many may be encouraged to engage with that discontinuity, it is often achieved by or restricted to a select few. If we speak of this in terms of superplausibility, there is much to be gained by recognizing the drive to knowledge that underlies daily life by allowing for its intensification: it also allows for an understanding of daily emotions and moods and of the possibility of their ritual intensification with its associated sense of power. In this grammar of discourse, superplausibility is a way of accounting for ideas of salvation, especially when the doctrines and ideas aligned with it judge everyday meaning and offer a replacement for it. Something of this higher-order engagement is germinally present in Rudolph Otto's discussion of Schleiermacher and the idea of 'a sheer overplus' of intuition and feelings, and also in his own evolutionary or developmental view of 'the loftier *a priori* cognitions' that are '"awakened" through the instrumentality of other more highly endowed natures', especially in prophets.[81]

Then, in the Indian-sourced traditions of Hinduism, Buddhism, and Sikhism, for example, we find notions of an illusion pervading everyday world meaning and an advocacy of deeper insight-finding in freedom from illusion, or enlightenment of everyday darkened thinking. Or they offer a new kind of love relation with the divine. The Jewish–Christian–Islamic traditions also begin with a judgement upon the world as we find it and then provide a scheme of salvation in counteraction to its idolatry and false gods. Yet, with time, these traditions all become part of that everyday life world and then we find them generating new subgroups that seek to revitalize the faith and intensify its emotional grasp upon core values and relations with the divine.

Stanner's work documented this brilliantly for the Australian Murinbata, arguing that 'each of the rites of passage initiated a male into a world transcending that in which he had been hitherto'. While circumcision made a man from a boy, it was the subsequent *Punj* rites that made 'a man

---

[80] Douglas J. Davies (1984a: 19–77).
[81] Otto ([1917] 1924: 151, 181).

into a man of mystical understanding'. Indeed, 'at each step' an individual 'discovered and had unfolded to him a life transcending the former limited reality', in what was an 'ontology of life'.[82] Much as in Whitehouse's episodic mode, these men seemed not to talk about those 'symbolic accompaniments of ceremonies' that 'became loved not for their recondite impact but for their own sake'. While there was but little 'abstract and explicit teaching and what there was seems obvious and banal', the venture involved a 'sacrosanctity, the higher degree of sacredness'.[83] Here, 'sacrosanctity' marks in emotional knowing what I also wish to confer in my own notion of superplausibility. Thomas Malthus, in his famed eighteenth-century essay on human populations, morality, and survival, which, typically, spoke of 'impressions' and 'passions' rather than emotions, indicated something of this transformation when arguing that 'the being that has seen moral evil and has felt disapprobation and disgust at it is essentially different from the being that has seen only good'.[84]

Much that resembles Stanner also appears in Bloch's later notion of rebounding conquest, also deployed when analysing initiation rites in which the nature of ordinary life in boys becomes transformed as they are made into men.[85] His language is one of conquest and deploys motifs of violence, of the hunt, and of prey. We alluded above to the idiom of 'pigs'; the boys are 'pigs' and are in a symbolic sense hunted out, captured, killed, and transformed into something else. Then they become men, who now hunt real pigs—wild pigs, as Whitehouse has it. Such rites provide opportunity for new experiences and for emotional creativity. As Bloch also indicated, the dynamics of 'rebounding conquest' have wide application, not least in religious conversion, when, in a Christian case of an individual like Saul of Tarsus, the 'old-nature' of the everyday life world is transformed into the 'new nature' of a Christian believer. Once converted, Saul—now involved in a name change to Paul—sets out to convert other Jews to his newfound insight regarding Jesus as the Christ and the new Christian community as constituting the 'body' of Christ. Conversion processes thus reveal processes of superplausibility. In Christianity this means that Christians need the Jewish scriptures and their theological assumptions in order to argue that these have now been superseded. Theoretically speaking, Christianity is to

---

[82] Stanner (1960b: 275, 245).
[83] Stanner (1960a: 126, 110).
[84] Malthus ([1798] 1960: 210).
[85] Maurice Bloch (1992).

Judaism as superplausibility is to plausibility. But religious processes are seldom static, so that, for example, a Christian sect such as Mormonism repeats this process in which Christianity becomes the plausible universe and Mormonism its superplausible transformation and replacement. Still, a cautionary note at this juncture should remind us that in many world contexts the many options of involvement in different churches generate tremendous complexity for analysis, as, for example, in the plethora of established and new groups in Latin America, where new identities are both sought and offered, as, for example, between traditional Catholic, Protestant Pentecostal, the innovative Condomblé set between forms of African traditions and Catholicism, and other longer indigenous traditions.[86]

SUMMARY

This last reference typifies the transformative processes of superplausibility achieved through creative changes prompted by human imagination and symbolic manipulation both of the world of ideas and of their allied emotional experiences of power. By utilizing a variety of theoretical approaches, this chapter has, then, shown something of the complexity of values and emotions as they impact upon the religious careers of believers. It has emphasized the sense of power that the use of words and different forms of language have upon people, thus ensuring that we do not take for granted the role of language, either within the corporate context or, as argued in Chapter 7, within the individual. We have, however, also noted Whitehouse's work on traumatic forms of experience generation unaligned with anything like extensive verbal commentary and ongoing verbal interpretation. While rare, in that most religious traditions are committed neither to traumatic forms of initiation nor to subsequent silence, it is the case that people in many societies have experiences that are highly influential upon their life but that are seldom shared with others.[87] Still, in all of this, we have also drawn attention to the broad theme of alterity, to the presence of some otherness as one of the key concepts of this study. In so doing this chapter has argued for a kind of transcendence of quotidian realities in various forms of insight, conversion, or revelation. This experiential sphere may, itself, help validate

[86] Rostas and Droogers (1993) exemplify this for Latin America while emphasizing the place of *habitus* and 'invented tradition'.
[87] Hay (1990). See Kim (2003: 3, 6) for 'stories that must never be told'.

some who would wish to differentiate religious experience from many other forms of experience. Certainly, such events influence and help transform a person's identity in processes deeply that are touched by emotion and that create new mood bases for ongoing life. Because life is, quite obviously, lived amid physical contexts and sensory media, albeit in imaginative ways, we now turn to an analysis of sacred places, worship, and music.

10

Sacred Place, Worship, and Music

Throughout this study we have combined social values and human emotions within the idea of embodiment to bring the nature of human identity to sharp focus. We have said much about transformations in values and emotions that generate a sense of what we have called superplausibility. That embodiment of identity properly brings us to a consideration of its environments, to sacred places, holy lands, and to their sensory media. Yet, as we do so, we soon appreciate that, while embodiment takes us to 'real' sites and the manufacture of much sacred material culture, the religious imagination and its managed emotions frequently frame them with the vision of transcending and idealized realms. Just as earlier chapters have referred to the virtual relationships between devotee and deity, so it is with 'holy lands', whose 'discovery' often offers new opportunity for spiritual exploration. It is as though the animal drive to investigate new potential habitats has also been extended in a virtual direction. One existential paradox implicit in the power-driving revelation and the spirit worlds of the previous chapter lies in the curious fact that humans not only settle geographical domains but create imaginary worlds and then select certain places as portals from the one to the other. This chapter takes this double action as the basis for defining 'sacred places' and for analysing the worship occurring in them, as sound and silence interplay in nurturing religious identity by fostering hope and contextualizing a sense of otherness. This is not to deny that sacred places may be created within individual lives, but it emphasizes the social nature of foundational religious behaviour.

It would be easy to approach these themes through the setting of great architecture, like that of Durham Cathedral, whose 900-year-old building holds the relics of the seventh-century saints Cuthbert and Bede, where daily praise is still offered to God by professional clergy, musicians, local worshippers, and visitors from across the world. Instead, let us take a small brick and corrugated-iron roofed chapel but a few miles away, located at a terraced-street corner of a former mining village and only slightly larger than its neighbouring houses, where, over the years, hundreds have found God. Just as some science fiction offers portals into other dimensions, so, for many, this unprepossessing building has been their portal to heaven—their arena of emotional experience and home of fostered moods. In millions of such places across the world, albeit under different myths and theologies, the living find meaning and, even when meaning falters, find hope. They sense the presence of their God, sometimes of their dead, and often have their downcast hearts uplifted. There, the errors of their lives are presented for forgiveness, their worries over today's problems are allayed, fears for the future condense in voiced and unvoiced prayers in song, and they experience peace. This gathering of neighbours, animosities included, finds a shared sound that contradicts gossip and partial speech, and, at least for a moment, their hymnody creates a unity.

Such places develop an allure, a power of anticipated gathering, an excitement grounded in the memories of previous 'blessings' when hope was restored. Here, too, the words of other people, often people just like themselves, take on a power generated by the sacred texts that link their locality with the great traditions of the centuries.[1] Even the voice of little people may come to be the voice of gods or ancestors, whether in preaching or in séance. The gates of glory open and hope surges anew. Such experiences, rooted in emotions and fostering spirituality's moods, have made the rites of otherness the basis of success for what we call religion. In secularized worlds, however, who can estimate the emotional loss of such spiritualities upon individual identity or community integration, or their potential replacement in aesthetic endeavours? Here, however, our concern is with religion's presence and not its absence, and our focus is upon worship's lineaments in structures and sound as they affect emotion and identity. For this we draw heavily from all that has already been said about embodiment, about ritual intensification, superplausibility, and transcendence.

---

[1] Augé ([1992] 1995: 94). If, as Augé argues, words and text link individuals to their surroundings in the apparently nondescript 'space of non-places', then sacred texts will do so even more potently within the context of sacred places.

MUSICAL KNOWING: EMBODIMENT'S UNDERSTANDING

We begin with music as the best symbol of the embodiment of culture, for music has the capacity to unite not only the cognitive and affective dimensions of human experience but also the social bonds of the participating community. Were 'music' granted a life of its own, much as some speak of the 'gene' as a 'virus', it could be described as an ever-expanding entity within human populations in quite remarkable ways. The discovery of electricity and invention of recording systems has, for example, provided millions with the opportunity of choosing music to create specific moods and enabling religious devotees to bring the music of communal worship into their private realm. This integration of private and public domains further increases the effect of religion's corporate activity.

At the communicative level, music, even when it is not the medium for religious texts, often seems to 'say' something, an issue that allows us to continue Chapter 3's discussion of Ernst Bloch on hope, pursued through a seamless weaving of emotion and ideology. His approach to music as a 'venturing beyond' captures the human exploratory drive in more philosophical and religious directions and, especially, for their union in acts of worship.[2] In a clear demonstration of the nature of embodiment, Bloch, for example, saw in Albert Schweitzer's analysis of J. S. Bach's music an understanding 'based completely on the practice of playing Bach', one that even integrated 'the visual pattern of the notes' with 'the overheard gesture of action and emotion'. In other words, a certain musical 'understanding' emerged from a combination of seeing the written music and the muscular familiarity of playing it, let alone the theological insight Bach possessed. As for emotion, Bloch saw in Schweitzer's performance of Bach just how he brought out 'the figures of weariness, of pain, both agonizing and proud, of joy, both lively and transfigured, of fear, of jubilation'. This view of human knowing and acting adds all the more to the 'unparalleled scale of expression in Bach's work' as it 'ranges from fear of death', to a longing for death and for consolation, and expresses 'confidence, peace, victory'. Bloch's use of the 'scale of expression' is telling, for it highlights the role of music in the

---

[2] Solomon (2002: p. xv) begins his study of 'naturalized spirituality' with experience of music in relation to emotion and 'passions'.

performance of the human repertoire of emotions, as now one, now another, interplays to intensify each other and make all more than the sum of their parts. Indeed—'love apart'—he emphasizes that 'the leap between the extremes' is at its greatest 'in the realm of religious emotion'.[3]

While it would be possible to explore this emotional–religious spectrum across the gamut of musical styles from antiquity to today, considering how instruments are chosen to excite and depress human responses, but one example must suffice—namely, Bruckner's Eighth Symphony, described by him as 'the annunciation of death'. In this 'music of profound tragedy', and at its *Totenuhr*, after the other instruments fall silent, the 'horns and trumpets repeat' a key rhythm 'on a stark monotone'. Then the drums roll, and 'shattered fragments' are 'repeated over and over again' until its final and quiet end. The scene has been one 'of a man dying in a room' where the 'clock ticks on even when his life has passed away'.[4] Even without hearing or even knowing this music, readers are likely to create a cameo sound-world of their own to evoke a sense of the scene. Far from this concert-hall formality, musical instruments also create or re-create sound-worlds in which people may come to live for the duration of ritual. Bettina Schmidt, for example, shows 'how music opens a path to Caribbean religion, for people of Caribbean as well as non-Caribbean descent' in New York, not least through the emotions evoked by drumming, which is believed to be part of spirit-contact rites of *Santeria* and *Vodou* traditions.[5] Many comparative examples could be invoked to demonstrate the power of music to create shared emotion and open the world of ordinary sense to supernatural domains, whether in monastic plainsong or the harmonic congregational hymnody that flowed from the Reformation and played a dramatic role, for example, in later Methodism and in many forms of Protestant revivalism.[6] This dynamic capability of music to generate a sense of otherness gains from Ernst Bloch's insight into music as expressing such a 'subject-based Outside'. It is not accidental that many sacred places that provide a natural home for music are also often associated with the dead, who comprise a distinctive form of the other. Bloch speaks of our human 'elective affinity' with death, through which we 'certainly do hear dying in music', for 'death-space borders

---

[3] Ernst Bloch ([1959] 1986: 1065).
[4] Sadie ([1975] 1996: 113).
[5] Schmidt (2008: 30).
[6] Ortiz (1997). The book is subtitled 'using music to change your life'.

mediatedly on music'.[7] This, for him, sets music aside as 'the best access to the hermeneutics of emotion, especially the expectant emotions'.[8]

EXPECTANT EMOTIONS: HOMECOMING AND PEACE

'Expectant emotions'! This commandingly paradoxical phrase catches the very substance of this chapter, which takes worship as the prime expression of this study's integrated motifs of meaning, hope, reciprocity, and otherness in generating religious identity. But, to speak of 'expectant emotions' is to prompt the paradox that, while 'emotion' usually refers to an immediate yet quickly passing experience of strong feeling, 'expectant' indicates anticipation of a future moment when such an experience will be gained. While acknowledging that it is unwise to press Bloch to any technical strictness of definition, it is worth considering the ideas clustering around his evocative phrase. For we all set about many kinds of activities that we hope will result in emotional experiences, and excitement inheres in such preparatory behaviour, reinforced by previous planning that resulted in particular emotions. Few actual moments of emotion come unprepared, and, even if they do surge as new experiences, they will seldom arrive announced on future occasions. This interplay of dramatic novelty followed by anticipated pleasure is fully exploited in religions and has been astutely analysed in Lindsay Jones's discussion of sacred architecture's 'allurement or magnetism or invitation' that attracts people to them and provides a sense that expectations may be met there.[9] He explores this attraction through motifs such as homecoming, one of the most enduring of all human idioms of identity, whether in Homer's *Odyssey*, the biblical myths of God's chosen people travelling towards their promised land,[10] or even the ascension of Christ.[11] The dynamics of personal emotion of repentance also has its place in the homecoming motif of the prodigal son.[12] Many aspects of emotion explored in this study have to do with degree of experience. Chapter 1, for example, considered

---

[7] Ernst Bloch ([1959] 1986: 1097).   [8] Ernst Bloch ([1959] 1986: 1070).

[9] Lindsay Jones (1993: 79).

[10] See Douglas J. Davies (2004: 108–17) for a variety of 'homecoming' from Gilgamesh to modern Mormons.

[11] Barth (1956: 181).   [12] Nouwen ([1992] 1994).

how the intensity of a feeling helped describe it as an 'emotion', and such intensity is valuable again here in terms of emotions of place typified in this notion of home. Of course, each society will have its own sense of what home means, with nuanced differences among traditionally nomadic, modern mobile, and long-settled urban residents. Even so, we can anticipate certain experiences associated with what William James once astutely described by 'coming "to feel at home" in a new place or with new people': for him it involved the disappearance of the 'feeling of strangeness'.[13] Evolutionary thoughts drove his discussion, as he invoked 'natural selection' as framing the 'emotional effect of expectation' upon a person in a new place or with new people. Novelty, he argued, 'ought to irritate' until such time as a sense of peril declined and the advantage of a context emerged. More widely speaking, home has to do with the mutual commitment of support from familial others in familiar territory. It is also embedded in language, our mother-tongue, and with the issue of taste, not only in matters of food but also in many other aesthetic preferences.

These combined factors generate the sense of security, of being safe, and of sanctuary, with the very idea of sacred place often carrying this sense of a safe place in which to beseech deity or ancestor to grant proximate safety in life's forthcoming ventures or, indeed, in the ultimate safety of salvation of various kinds. Survival and sanctuary become mutually creative and prompt the sense of peace, itself an intriguing concept within a bio-cultural approach to emotions, religious identity, and physical space. Here we encounter the paralleling of the physical universe of silence with an interior sense of calm. One of the most frequent descriptions made by many people of established sacred sites is that they have 'an atmosphere' about them, often qualified in terms of being 'peaceful'. One aspect of such peace is associated with the successful completion of ritual acts reminiscent of Aquili's work on the satisfaction achieved through ritual performance alluded to in Chapter 2. To engage in ritual in a recognized place of power is satisfying; it is an end in itself. There is nothing more to be done except to await the future allurement of peace. In many prophetic-guru traditions, as with the Sikhs described below, the allurement of place and the peace it offers is given secondary place over the call to an inner engagement with peace developed through meditative or physical practices. The place of peace is to be within the heart or self. The importance of sensed changes within one's interior emotions and moods has, obviously, been developed by all traditions, not least in the many secular

[13] James ([1879] 1956: 78).

or semi-secular therapeutic practices of contemporary life, which, for example, see illness-inducing stress as needing to be offset through various coping strategies to bring peace. Nevertheless, whether in traditionally religious or innovative modernity, there often emerges a dialectic between particular centres that provide such activities and the individual self, as the arena of creating resolution of turmoil.[14] A rather different interplay of sources and locations of healing power has been identified by Matthew Wood, whose notion of 'non-formativeness' highlights the way some contemporary people draw different ideas and practices from a variety of sources in such a way that no single leader, authority, or tradition becomes dominant over their life, as they seek to engage with 'power' amid their daily life.[15] One crucial qualification of the nature of the networks, workshops, and groups underlying the desired freedom of the agent in drawing from different power sources to obtain 'peace' as we are discussing it here lies in the issue of sacred place. The sheer facticity of long-established sacred places, often owned by established religions, needs to be set alongside the inevitable lack of such places for new or invented traditions. This is one reason, for example, why a site such as Glastonbury or Stonehenge can become contested as symbolic places capable of framing 'new' groups, which, in their own terms, often align themselves with 'ancient' traditions. Identity is aligned with sacred place, even if it has to be contested. In this sense, 'peace' is hard won and shows the vitality of place in alluring devotees towards a desired emotional goal.

The ability of a religious tradition to build, maintain, and retain key sacred places over long periods of time is a significant factor in their capacity to endure. Such sites, and the emotions aligned with them, often have the capacity to be replicated. Rome is 'repeated' in some sense in Catholic churches the world over; so, in a sense, is Mecca in Islamic worship and Amritsar's Golden Temple in Sikh *gurudwaras*. Meanwhile, Jerusalem stands as the longed-for centre for Diaspora Jewry. Many local sacred places are validated by the central sites of their tradition, and this in complex ways. In sacramental forms of Christianity, for example, the theme of 'peace' as an attribute of emotional identity is allied with Eucharistic ritual and the belief that the divine becomes present to the faithful through the rite of eating bread and drinking wine. It is no accident that the Eucharist is an event of symbolic ingestion, its elements comprising a kind of comfort food. This is evident in

---

14 McGuire with Kantor (1998: 105–29).
15 Wood (2007: 159).

the classic Christian integration of 'peace' motifs, with an identity within a Christian community conceived of as being 'the body of Christ' sustained through eating and drinking his 'body' and 'blood'. This is encapsulated in the sophisticated theological Gospel of John, where peace passes from the customary greeting of *Shalom* ('peace') to a description of 'the absence of fear and perturbation of heart' as something that 'is the gift of Christ alone'.[16] In the religious mapping of several streams of early Christianity there is an active drive to establish peace as an ethically bonded emotion characterizing the identity of the Christian community independent of place. Believers are said to have peace rather than enmity with the God whose attribute is peace; the 'peace of Christ' is to rule believers' hearts not least because the antagonistic division between Jew and Gentile has been broken down through Christ's work.[17] One element of subsequent liturgy involved the exchange of a 'kiss of peace', while one popular form of blessing, also derived from an Epistle, refers to the peace of God, which is said to pass all understanding and to keep the believer's 'heart and mind in Christ Jesus'.[18] Whatever might have been the necessity of locating peace within the individuals who constituted the early community, quite apart from any settled place of meeting, it is now the case, some two thousand years later, that each church with its altar or table for Eucharistic activity offers an allure for peace. To mention such altars is to highlight the fact that such allurement sites frequently become decorated with objects of material culture that firmly embed theological ideas. Whether in an Indian temple and its deities, which are awakened, fed, and worshipped each day, or in the Sikh *Guru Granth* as the scriptural materialization of Guru and community ideals, which is similarly brought into the worship site after its nocturnal rest, we find these devotional foci consisting in and surrounded by symbolic objects. When it comes to symbolic multivocality expressed in material culture, few objects excel the tabernacle in strongly sacramentally focused churches, for this is a container, often ornamented, veiled, and attended by a lighted lamp, in which are kept consecrated sacramental elements, usually the consecrated bread or host, reckoned to consist in the very substance of Christ. The symbolic presence of the deity within this object and within a church offers a fine example of a portal

---

[16] Barrett (1955: 391).
[17] Romans 5: 1; 15: 33. Ephesians 2: 14. Colossians 3: 15.
[18] Philippians 4: 7.

between earthly and heavenly domains or, in the classic terms of the history of religions, an *axis mundi*.[19]

DIVERSE LOCALIZATIONS

But the material culture of religion and its symbolic load can take quite different directions, as when, for example, a relatively short-lived American evangelical group, the Promise Keepers, founded by an American Football coach to intensify a Christian male identity, utilized football stadiums as sites for its revival-like activities. Its encouragement of emotional expression between men was facilitated by an environment where men would, in sporting contexts, also be freer to demonstrate emotion in general.[20] These cases of sacramental Catholicism and emotive Protestantism typify Harold Turner's valuable distinction between the 'temple' and the 'meeting house' as archetypal elements of Christianity, which he believed operated in a kind of dynamic interaction between each other.[21]

Quite different from these diverse cases is the recent impact of the notion of cyberspace as a virtual point of accessing information and for interacting with other persons or, indeed, with groups and institutions. Many religious groups have rapidly seen the opportunities of this medium as a means of engaging millions of individuals at speeds and over distances that were unimaginable only one generation ago. Cyber-worship is already accessible, and groups are eagerly fostering the possibilities associated with it.[22] Just how issues of religious identity and emotional responses will be affected in the longer term by this new world of communication and interaction awaits to be seen. Certainly it has allowed some disaffected group members to establish contact with likeminded people far beyond their normal contact, just as it allows people to canvass prayer from otherwise unknown people.[23] Whatever is the case, it is likely that emotions engendered in real time and virtual relationships will bear heavily upon each other. In terms of embodiment, the topic of cyber-faith experience raises the theme of otherness in quite a distinctive way, in that cyberspace offers a certain form of otherness that is

---

[19] Eliade (1979: 42, 50).   [20] Bartkowski (2004: 79–82).
[21] Harold W. Turner (1979: 12). The 'temple' and the 'meeting house' were typified, respectively, as the *domus dei* (house of god) and *domus ecclesiae* (house of group assembly).
[22] e.g. Babin and Zukowski (2002).   [23] Mayer (2003: 44).

immediately accessible online. The constancy of electronic contact that many people maintain with each other is but one reflection of the fact that they have a sense that the other is available to them, much as some religious devotees have a sense of the accessibility of the divine at any time and in any place. Just how issues of transcendence relate to the online other remains to be seen.

Peaceful sound

Certainly, cyber-sources possess great capacity to refer to and participate to some degree in traditional sacred places and, in so doing, raise the interesting issues of silence and peace. When considering the sensory nature of real sanctuaries, for example, we soon encounter the interplay of sound and silence, through chant, hymnody, musical instruments, and the mere fact of being present in a place. George Steiner, whose emphasis on otherness has already been appreciated, is valuable here, as he sets the question 'what is music?' alongside the question 'what is man?'[24] He dwells on this while sketching his ideal world, where there would be many concerts but no music critics, for, to him, 'the universality of music... declares man's humanity'.[25] He equates 'the energy that is music' with the 'energy that is life', seeing both as resonating within our physical embodiment to give us a 'somatic and spiritual' knowing of what we are.[26] With an elastically elegant style, Steiner indicates how musical performance takes us into a special kind of time—he calls it 'the only *free time* granted us prior to death'—and speaks of the power in music and of the 'tone-relations which make us strangers to ourselves or, on the contrary, impel us homeward'.[27] Steiner works around this theme of life energy to its central point concerning our 'irreducible subjectivity', to that which we encounter by intuition, to that kind of immediate knowledge that seems to be instinctive. Albeit in different terms, he is speaking of 'intensive living'. In terms of reciprocity theory, such music belongs to the inalienable categories of human endeavour in the context of worship, even though, at other times, it may belong to a market economy. Many great Christian cathedrals, for example, admit people

---

[24] George Steiner (1989: 5).
[25] George Steiner (1989: 195).
[26] George Steiner (1989: 196).
[27] George Steiner (1989: 197).

without charge when attending for worship, when they may share in some of the greatest music of the world performed at a professional level. Hours later, at a concert in the same place by the same musicians, they would have to pay a fee. The economic difference between the two events is qualified by worship, and it pinpoints the nature of the other and of reciprocity: there is a passage from payment to offering, from money as definer of status to praise as its defining base.

TONE, SOUND, AND SPEECH

Whether within the self, in some sacred place, or even in a cyber-sanctuary, emotions are often associated with the capacity for music in the evocation of feeling. Through hymns and chants, the bio-cultural nature of emotion becomes clear. As theological ideas inform musical modes to create desired moods, some would clearly identify particular keys with moods, with major keys allied with brightness of spirit and minor keys inducing a degree of meditative depth. Moreover, singing seems to convey a sense of transcend-ence over immediate circumstances, as in community singing, when all act as one and each individual senses the greater whole and an encounter with the divine. Sometimes the very history of a group becomes embedded within such singing, and within patterns of speech in preaching, as has been analysed, for example, in African-American forms of Baptists.[28]

As the contemporary world expands, so does music. Singing is dynamically present at sporting events, especially in football stadiums, where fans have their own anthems and where creativity in developing songs is considerable. These mark club identities and may be sung in times of exuberance; just as other songs bring out emotions of sadness at times of death or memorial. Singing is highly integrative of human brain activities as well as integrative of individuals in a group. It causes the body to be exercised, as breathing increases and individuals are alerted to the activities of others. It is not surprising that social commentators periodically ask whether sport is its own form of religion.

One way of appreciating the potential root of this alliance of music, emotion, and religion concerns the tone of voice associated with joy or sorrow in many societies. Death, for example, often prompts restrained and

[28] Pitts (1993: 132–54).

low speech tones, which express the loss of vitality in bereaved persons and evoke a supportive response from others. This is regularly witnessed in the media, when commentators adopt tones quite unlike their sharper media style when in masterly control of events. Here sincerity and authenticity emerge, as individuals wish not to make their mark through clever comment but simply to share a common plight. Ordinary contexts reflect similar responses, as one example will suffice, taken from an interview situation concerning a person telling how he had ceased to be active in his Christian church membership. He recalled the death of twins in his family and of how he became 'disoriented and disillusioned' and 'had the wind knocked out of' him, not least by a funeral service for the twins, who had died so very young that 'no one knew them'. The sociologist tells how, as this person described his experience, 'there was a palpable change in tone within the interview', as 'deep and unresolved emotions' were touched upon.[29] Such tonal shifts even occur in established media anchor men and women when they have to report some striking death or tragedy.

At the opposite end of the emotional spectrum, interviews with sportsmen and women just after they have won some impressive victory are usually marked with enthusiasm and celebratory feelings of triumph. They, too, want to involve others in their victory, and their tone manages to do this very successfully. One of the most intriguing contexts of emotional expression is that of actors winning some prestigious film award, when those whose profession is rooted in the control and production of specific emotions become uncontrolled, reduced almost to an infantile state of amazed surprise at winning. Such a response is, presumably, aimed to convey a sense of personal authenticity as well as a degree of apparent humility in the presence of peers. Against such backgrounds, it is easier to see the part played by emotion within religious contexts, where a social performance merges with the life context of people and where conventions of wider social life also make their mark. The role of established ritual along with favoured speech forms and styles of music all conduce to creating and managing particular emotional patterns. Such a profile is even likely to change within a particular ritual, as subdued feelings pass into boisterous moments as the context adds its own significance to the performance.

---

[29] Richter (2000: 28).

MOVING TOWARDS

Beyond music and singing, another aspect of embodiment affecting emotion and location is the very act of walking: humanity's original exploratory medium. To walk to a place offers a variety of emotional possibilities *en route*, not only in walking with or meeting others, or in tiredness and fatigue that may highlight or even call into question the value of the venture, but also in the sense of achievement of the goal achieved and the rest and sense of hospitality and safety afforded by the destination. While such destinations reinforce Augé's assertion that 'Gods need shrines, as sovereigns need thrones and palaces, to keep them above temporal contingencies',[30] his analysis also helps to make sense of those traditions such as early Sikhism and much Protestantism that both address a transcendent deity and forge a link between that deity and the very person of the devotee and to devalue physical pilgrimage to a place where the divine might the better be found. So it is that the fact of pilgrimage, with its allied experiences of exertion, the joy of arrival, and its place in memory ever ready for recall, stands in sharp contrast to those more static perspectives that favour an inner journey to a trans-formed self. Historically, for example, it has been argued that the second–third-century figure Origin did much to change Christian attitudes to the Holy Land from being 'forward looking in literalist restorationist terms to being essentially backward looking', a perspective that would root salvation in other than geographical terms and yet could foster pilgrimage to a place of past significance, especially once the new Emperor Constantine had become Christian.[31] This meant, and for millions to this day still means, that the personal journey of faith to the heavenly Jerusalem can be inspired by physical pilgrimage to the earthly Jerusalem that was the site of so many key events in the history of the Jewish–Christian foundations of their belief. Though quite different theological motivations may apply, we find what are likely to be very similar emotional anticipations underlying the pilgrimage journeys of Muslims, Sikhs, and Hindus. Such anticipation underlies the preparation for specific acts of worship or particular festivals and their associated emotional tones. The use of body-washing, fasting, prayer, dress, or pilgrimage to a particular site conduces to what will befall the devotees in

[30] Augé ([1992] 1995: 60).
[31] Inge (2003: 95).

the final context, where music and spoken or sung sacred narratives all help frame the ritual arenas in which desired emotions may be felt. 'Expectant emotions' exist prior to the key emotion and, to coin an apparently contradictory phrase, can be viewed as 'preparatory shadows' of the anticipated event. Then, religious ritual, being by definition repetitive, allows many opportunities for distinctive emotional arousal to take place, with memory motivating future participation. Memory, itself, is for many integral to human culture in its forward drive: 'for the cord of culture—and religion—is memory.'[32]

PLACE AND TIME

What, then, of the locations of emotion-engendered rites? Certainly, sacred places are not simply physical structures but entertain a range of sound and silence over the course of a day or year. Many temples in Hinduism and churches in Christianity, for example, are open for devotees at times when silence predominates and when people may come into that place to use the silence as the basis for their own devotion and meditation. At other times of day, priests engage in verbal, chanted, or sung rituals in which many participate. Monasteries in Buddhism and Christianity exemplify the interplay of silence and music, as collective worship and private meditation divide each day. Invariably there are festivals at fixed points in the year when the tone of such collective sound explores the repertoire of emotions, as in the discipline of Islam's Ramadan ending in the festival of Id al-Fitr, with its celebratory overtones reminiscent of Christianity's Lent followed by Easter. So, too, with ceremonies performed as part of the human life cycle, with marriages and births evoking joyful emotions while funerals strike the note of sadness.

Among Jews, the annual Day of Atonement, Yom Kippur, beginning in the evening of one day—9 *Tishri*—and ending at sunset the following day, exemplifies a period of particular emotion. It marks the need for people to make atonement with God and with each other for the sins they have committed. In ancient Israel the day of atonement was marked by crucial sacrificial ritual performed by priests in the Temple at Jerusalem. After the destruction of that temple by the Romans in 70 CE, the Day of Atonement shifted into the local congregations of Jews, with the day itself coming to

[32] Daniel Bell ([1980] 1991: 354).

serve as a kind of temple and with fasting and abstinence serving as a form of sacrifice. The period closes with the blowing of the *Shofar* or ram's horn, which has been interpreted as a sound to wake from sleep and live a repentant life.

Sound may also extend beyond the immediate place of worship as a reminder of its existence and of what is done there. Such prompts help manage the religious emotions of believers. It became customary in Islam for a *muezzin* to chant the *adhan* or call to prayer five times a day. In Islamic societies this call from the minaret, often aided by a public-address system, marks a religious territory and evokes appropriate attitudes among the faithful, reminding them that God is great and that they should come to prayer and to what makes for their well-being rather than sleep. As characteristic is the use of bells within many Christian traditions, whether in calling the faithful to a religious service or to mark a moment within it, as in traditional Catholic countries, where the bell at the consecration announces the mystery in which the bread and wine used in the Mass becomes the very body and blood of Christ. Sometimes a 'passing bell' marked someone's death. One form of bell-ringing largely restricted to Britain is that of change-ringing, in which bells are rung not in an almost arbitrary fashion but in quite complicated patterns or changes. Such peals easily evoke a sense of joy within a communal group. The sound of many bells ringing in harmony can be as symbolic of an integrated community as the single toll of the passing bell indicating the death of an individual. This contrast between life and death is, for example, fully reflected in the British tradition of ringing a peal of bells from church towers in which half the bells sound in their usual way while the other half are muffled. The contrast between the clear and the dulled tones marks the transition from life to death that someone has just undertaken. Also marking both place and time are cemeteries, which stand 'on the borders of two worlds', as described by Judge Joseph Story when giving the inaugural address at the dedication of the new Mount Auburn Cemetery in Boston, USA, in 1831. He encouraged the value of the 'melancholy reflection' that such a 'rural cemetery' could help us 'cultivate' to our advantage, with Schantz commenting that such an attitude to cemeteries 'was calculated to work changes in the emotional life of the human soul'.[33]

---

[33] Schantz (2008: 71–2).

MOVING MEMORY

This case highlights the fact that, in addition to the movement of the body to religiously significant places, another aspect of emotion and identity concerns 'movement within' the self, in terms of both memory and imagination. Such movements take place 'in time' as we age and watch others age and die, all in place-tied contexts. As human beings we move within environments that societies define as having sites of greater and lesser spiritual significance. Human environments are typified by relatively small sites deemed to be of spiritual depth set amid large expanses deemed much more ordinary. This spatial orientation of sacred sites helps focus ideas of experiential power and of the need, periodically, to move physically to those sites. Such a journeying to sites of power is well known in a spectrum of behaviour from major pilgrimages undertaken once in a lifetime, as with the Hajj for some Muslims, to the weekly visit to synagogue, church, or mosque in the more immediate locality of believers. It is often not enough simply to travel to such sites; it is 'entering into' or 'exploring' aspects of one's inner life while being there that counts, a factor closely linked to our discussion in Chapter 7 of the role of the interior dialogue within human identity. Indeed, these very idioms of entering and exploring one's inner life reveal the appeal of images of movement to our very sense of experience. It has become common to speak of 'inner journey' as a description of processes of self-reflection. This is not surprising, since much social life involves this spatial variation of emotions. As Augé argues, for practically any French town, 'the town centre is an active place' that 'comes to life' on market day or at some other event.[34] This life of a place often exists as part of its local history, but the sheer attractive or evocative power of some natural sites should not be ignored in and of itself. Gatherings in many parts of the world at the precise time of the New Year mark key cultural sites of allurement, just as do religious festivals as our workings of theological beliefs and mythological traditions.

---

[34] Augé ([1992] 1995: 66) argues with Michel de Certeau over defining place, space and non-place. Cf. Inge (2003: 1–32) for a synopsis of 'Place in Western Thought and Practice'.

SENSING MYSTERY, SIGNALLING OTHERNESS

At this pivotal point in this chapter, it is time to recall Rudolph Otto's early twentieth-century study of the intensity of interior emotion of devotees: he wished 'to give it a name of its own . . . "creature-consciousness" or creature feeling.'[35] He then utilized Latin concepts to describe a strongly nuanced sense of such feeling in the ideas of the *sensus numinis*, an awareness of the holy, in which a person encountered a *mysterium tremendum et fascinans*. This *mysterium* or mystery was not only remarkable, greatly impacting upon a person's awareness, but also had an attractive or fascinating force. Once encountered, this *fascinans* element is likely to give a memory that would feed into, or have some close affinity with, Jones's notion of allurement and Bloch's 'expectant emotions' discussed above. The dynamic nature of worship within sacred places, especially where music, chanted narrative, or hymn singing occurs, is, in more recent psychological terms, explicable in terms of pattern association memory, where one stimulus—for example, music or silence—is encountered alongside another—say, a sense of self-transcendence, joy, fear, or guilt. At future events any one stimulus, say music, is able to help 'retrieve the second stimulus'.[36] Religious interpretations of such experience usually speak of the deities, spirits, or ancestors making their presence felt. Still, however singing is interpreted, few group activities are as dynamic in their capacity to unite a group in a transcendent unity, allowing the participant a sense of contact with the divine other.

This otherness has surfaced constantly in preceding chapters, whether in Schleiermacher's reference to God or Durkheim's to society. This familiar strangeness takes us beyond our self while deeply affirming self-identity, echoing a wide spectrum of human experience, especially within worship practised daily by millions in acts of piety towards deities and ancestors. Such divine addresses prompt philosophers to theorize over the nature of religious language and prayer, while the faithful, at famous events such as the Mexican Day of the Dead, unselfconsciously invite their deceased kin to return to the world of the living for appropriate festivities.[37] Millions more visit the graves of their dead and 'speak to them', an act that is not strange, especially when

---

[35] Otto ([1917] 1924: 10).
[36] Rolls (2005: 466).
[37] Carmichael and Sayer (1991).

we know that a significant number of people gain a sense of the presence of their dead kin sometime after their funeral. There are many ways in which we might describe and interpret these facts. For the devotee, the act of communication with these others is due simply to the spirits' existence. The divine becomes a reality in the here and now and gives a deep sense of the meaning of life. This key feature of much worship holds profound significance for human identity and the role of emotions in its composition. Excitement, anticipation, and hope over future events as well as sadness over past failure or guilt parallel desires for some future benefit, gift, advantage, or healing. Fear in its many forms may also enter this encounter with otherness, as may a sense of dependence or love. Such awareness affirms the devotees' existence and marks their identity. The very otherness of the supernatural enhances the presence of the living to themselves.

While this sense of encountering an other is obviously related to experiences of ordinary relationships in daily life, it assumes added significance when intensified by custom. While the philosopher of religion may argue that prayer to the gods is just like talking to another human being, it is precisely the invisibility of the other that makes the event so affirming of the devotee. And this is where the role of sacred places and times becomes significant. Human nature demands that we be in one place at one time and often that we do particular things in those places. One of the many potential functions of sacred sites is to allow time for people to focus on the otherness of their life experience. Places come to frame experience, as people associate their memories with them and as future visits prompt such memories and trigger emotions. Such a sedimentation of emotional memories easily provides a basis for future allurement.

The example of Mount Athos, with its tradition of monks engaged in salvation-oriented living, is especially instructive, because its spatial sacrality is intimately aligned with what is taken as a historically based theology that is, essentially, mythological.[38] This offers a clear example of 'living in myth', a meaning-making process grounded in hope, with a social and ritual life pursued through the reciprocity of self with the other. In less technical terms, this may be spelled out as 'the Holy Mountain', where the eremitic and cenobitic forms of monastic life, the former living in solitude and the latter in community, inhabit a territory defined as 'the Garden of the Virgin'.

---

[38] In this I follow René Gothóni's basic account (1987: 73–85): its particular Structuralist analysis could, however, be differently rendered.

It follows a complex tradition that Mary, the mother of Jesus, had been travelling to Cypress to visit Lazarus when her ship was blown off-course to Athos. A local deity's voice bade its pagan inhabitants to go to meet her, and in so doing they were converted and baptized. Mary found the place so beautiful that she asked Jesus to grant it to her, which he did as her inheritance and garden and a place of refuge for those pursuing salvation. All other women and even female animals are forbidden in this space, where life and its thoughts are to be focused on God and not to include the temptations of women and reminders of them. Its monasteries, typically, have their chapel at their centre as a symbolic Ark of Noah, into which they are called by a sounding board to be saved from worldly destruction. In Gothóni's analysis of Athos, time as well as space are ordered in such a way as to define an environment of difference from the wider world. Being a monk is to partake of a sacred time, not least in its round of daily worship, work, and rest, and not of the profane world of the laity. The role of the 'Jesus prayer'— 'Lord, Jesus Christ, have mercy upon me a sinner'—is also important, for ever marking the fall of Adam and of all men and of the need for constant repentance.

This theologically resonating ritual world offers a good example of the control of both behaviour and belief and is a reminder of Mary Douglas's notion of the purity rule mentioned in Chapter 2. Its preoccupation with issues of social control and of a centre of society readily raises the notion of power. In terms of this chapter, 'society' can be aligned with those places from which an individual or the group to which he belongs derives a core of identity, such as the geographical territory of Mount Athos and the architectural focus on each monastery's chapel. Places become powerful because they confer identity and, with it, a degree of existential safety. To speak of 'existential' safety is to highlight the psychological and philosophical aspects of identity, but this should not lead us to ignore the importance of physical contexts within which such existential safety obtains. Examples are legion. Michael Jackson, one of the most famed of all twentieth- and twenty-first-century popular musical celebrities, who possessed hundreds of millions of fans and who died suddenly in June 2009, was said to have described himself as the most lonely of people, and was described as being most at home when performing on stage. If that was, indeed, the case, then it would be easy to see the stage as his home, the place of deepest identity conferral and of power. Beyond the stage, a place that comes alive with performance but otherwise lies silent, lie many locations of enduring power. The home is one of these, especially in societies where families are long resident and where many generations have lived and died. The role of formal family shrines in Japanese homes or of pictures of family members in homes across the world are testimony to the power of the home. Displacement of populations for military or economic reasons disrupts such a centred sense of identity within the power field of life and can easily lead to an accentuation of other foci of identity-power conferral, as in impromptu community centres, places of worship, or festivals, as exemplified in Toulis's research on Jamaican immigrants to Britain presented in the previous chapter.

Power of place thus reflects the individual–society bond while conferring a sense of safety upon the individual. Just where a person locates that power place will depend upon his perception of his society or some subgroup within it; groups are often subsumed by civic buildings and the attitudes they attract. On the international scene this applies in a distinctive sacred-secular sense to the USA, a country viewed by many Americans as divinely blessed and possessing a Manifest Destiny to lead the world in the salvation-like direction of democracy. Writing before the terrorist attacks on the Twin Towers in New York, Daniel Bell already thought that 'God's gift of insulated space' and 'the unique freedom' of the USA from military threats and invasion had already disappeared as a result of 'internecine conflict' in social violence, and the existence of intercontinental ballistic missiles, which ensured that there are 'no hiding places in any part of the globe'.[39] When such potential uncertainties arise, they allow anxiety and fear to motivate even closer commitment to potential sites of succour and hope, whether courts of law, civic and military centres, castles, royal palaces, or places of worship—all of which may appeal as places of power that proffer protection. This suggests that power should not be viewed as either secular or sacred, a polarity that is often ideologically driven, but always appreciated in terms of local historical-cultural contexts and the emotional identity of a people. So, too, with peace when used of a society: it is capable of many meanings, or of implementation at one level but not at another, as Paul Heelas has reminded us.[40] For, as the twenty-first century advances, there are many American and European towns that are peaceful while soldiers from them are fighting a war elsewhere. What

---

[39] Daniel Bell ([1980] 1991: 260–2)—a valuable essay on 'The End of American Exceptionalism'.
[40] Heelas (1989: 225).

is more, many societies have and continue to fight over sacred sites that they would otherwise deem as places of peace.

Still, the long existence of sacred sites is one of the most remarkable aspects of humanity, and, though archaeologists are not always sure of the function of many ancient structures, it is often presumed that they had some ritual or religious purpose, often thought of as a connection with their dead. While the emergence of human self-consciousness can, at least, be assumed to have involved an awareness of the power of emotion, it might also be assumed to have paralleled this issue of otherness. While it is too risky to speak of that otherness emerging from experiences of the dead or from ancestors or deity-based rites, even if many ancient sites are associated with burials or funerals, what is clear is that human beings have found specific places that answer some deep need of and for location. In the contemporary world, it is not too excessive to identify those places with aspects of the sense of otherness that helps confer an identity upon devotees. This makes it perfectly understandable why individuals often become attached to particular temples, churches, and other sites, for they are places of personal strengthening and affirmation. In some Christian churches, for example, some individuals like to sit in the same place time after time, the familiarity predisposing them, we may assume, to gain their desired experience in line with previous experiences encountered there. But sacred sites often retain a sense of power, even when no longer central to most people's lives. William Watson, not one of the better-known poets of the early twentieth century, could write of a Christian church in lines that half-betoken a secularized society.

> Outwardly splendid as of old—
> Inwardly sparkless, void and cold—
> Her force and fire all spent and gone—
> Like the dead moon, she still shines on.[41]

Does allurement remain here? Whose is the sun granting reflected light? Perhaps it is precisely the 'light' of an emotional hope brought by visitors. Still, such places often continue to offer 'sanctuary' in an absence of fear. It is interesting, for example, to witness the centuries-long Christian practice of sanctuary that allowed people fleeing from the law to take refuge in certain places of worship for various periods of time and under particular

---

[41] Watson (1919: 128).

circumstances.[42] On a wider basis, it is worth considering how safety and worship may be related and why, for example, attacks upon places of worship or the killing of worshippers at such sites are uniformly regarded as particularly heinous crimes. While one obvious sociological explanation of this would be that places of worship enshrine key social values, so that any attack upon them can be conceived as an act against society and of ritual impurity, a more psychological view might focus on the needs of people as they come to experience the otherness of their existence. When they do so, they often engage in bodily activities such as kneeling or prostrating themselves, or praying with their eyes closed or focused on one central object, actions that easily render them vulnerable to attack or exploitation at the hands of others. To experience otherness would seem to demand a safe place in which fear of others would play no part. Indeed, the emotional tone of worship, especially when thinking of it as a collective activity, is one of communal unity. The sight of hundreds of Muslim men prostrated in prayer is one of the more remarkable human sights. Many other large-scale events could also be cited, whether in pilgrimage at Mecca, or with Greek Christians celebrating Easter in Corfu, beginning in darkness and ending in person-to-person lighting of candles in an exponential wave of light. India's three-yearly Kumbhamela, a festival involving devotees immersing themselves in sacred rivers, attracts millions of devotees and may well be the largest collection of human beings ever known. The fact that such enormous gatherings may bring danger to individuals because of crowd surges does not seem to influence devotees, as in the fear of an enemy attack. In terms of interpretation, it would seem that, at such times, the devotee is much influenced by the power of society, and gains a sense of the meaningfulness of life shared by so many.

We mentioned above that the devotee might explain what we have called otherness in simple terms of the actual existence of the other as God, spirit, or ancestor. For those who do not accept the existence of such supernatural entities, the nature of otherness can be approached in different ways. Sociologically, Durkheim's idea of *Homo duplex*, introduced in Chapter 1, could explain otherness as society present within an individual. This complex idea is exemplified by language, which is social and, initially, exists outside of us before becoming part of our internal identity as we learn to speak. Subsequently, we use that social tool of language as a basic means of thinking about ourselves as well as of coping with many kinds of social situations. It is often

---

[42] Note also the cities of refuge established in ancient Israel (Deuteronomy 4: 41–3; 19: 1–13).

that very tool of language, of 'society within us', that we deploy in worship. But language is extremely complex. It poses some crucial questions to us about ourselves in the sense that we can speak it without thinking: words simply seem to pour from our mouths without our having any sense of how we manage to do that. The very nature of our embodiment allows us to learn to speak and then to do it with such ease that it becomes first nature to us.

When we ponder this ease of speaking, we appreciate its remarkable nature and sense what we referred to earlier as a 'familiar strangeness', a notion that itself helps us understand the issue of sacred place and worship in terms of 'perceptual ineffability'. This technical term of Diana Raffman was used by Iain Edgewater in his discussion of music and emotion and developed into what he called the 'suggestion of significance'.[43] Raffman argued that listening to music could, as it were, challenge the listener to understand its significance, to ask just what music might mean. This extremely difficult task seems to challenge the mind and gives the sense that there is something about music or something going on in it that we simply cannot explain in words—hence the notion of 'ineffability'. 'Perceptual ineffability' thus refers to our inability to explain something that we think we ought to be able to explain. We become aware of something lying just beyond our grasp, as when we can speak but are unaware of just how we do it. This is the idea that Edgewater then picks up as a 'suggestion of significance': in other words, we hear music and we know it means something to us but we are hard pressed to know just what it means. He saw this capacity as important for religion, as also in politics or patriotism, because it could be harnessed to doctrines or ideologies as people linked music with religious words attached to or performed in sacred settings. These ideas allow us to think again about such things as hymns or chanted scriptures. From one perspective they make music easier, in the sense that the actual words give us an immediate meaning: they say something or speak to us, but do so with the added value of music and its power to imply a hidden meaning of its own. This perspective on 'suggestions of significance' may also be relevant to the kind of complex ritual situation involving both 'intimacy' and 'silence', as described by Pink Dandelion for contemporary Quakerism, in which there may or may not be a traditional belief in God as an other but where silence is prized as a group activity.[44] Here we encounter just the sort of idea that reveals a

---

[43] Edgewater (1999: 172), citing Raffman (1988: 688).
[44] Dandelion (2005: 116, 124).

complex historically rooted and culturally framed experience identified as intimacy and yet open to quite different ideological interpretations by a group of people all sitting together on their individual chairs in silence.

Here issues of psychology and the embodied nature of emotions, on the one hand, and philosophical arguments, on the other, offer interesting paths for future exploration. Edgewater, for example, offers suggestions as to how brain studies may yet show how the ways the brain processes musical information may link with the capacity for religiosity and altered states of consciousness.[45] This might illuminate the experience of otherness, for the very fact that a person has the neural and psychological capacity to experience some quite different emotional states in his life easily gives a sense of there being other forces around him or within him ready to exert an influence on him if the right circumstances prevail. Widespread reference to powers identified with ancestors, ghosts, spirits, or deities seem to attest to such an awareness and cultural response.

From quite a different perspective, we turn again to Steiner's philosophical discussion of otherness aimed largely at literary-influenced culture theorists, especially those known as postmodern, on the issue of otherness. For him 'there is language, there is art', because there is the 'other',[46] where the 'other' initially means other people and things but soon moves to entertain the issue of the existence of God, seeming to say that belief in God is a fundamental means of speaking at all, of making sense of things, of holding 'a rendezvous with intelligibility'.[47] In philosophical terms, the intellectual life of human beings also requires an explanation of and for emotional sensibility and its spectrum of possibility stretching from near solipsism, with its own dual potential for creative narcissism or destructive nihilism, to submissive devotionalism to an ultimate deity—a span holding its own potential for negative despotism or creative altruism. The sense of the world around us, and of the forces acting upon us or with which we may interact, provides the very basis for our sense of self and capacity to live. Art historian James Elkins, for example, speaks of his engagement with art as 'among the experiences I rely on to alter what I am'.[48] Paralleling this, as intimated at the outset of this chapter, Steiner sees a power in music and speaks of 'the energy that is music' putting us into 'felt relation to the energy that is life', to an 'experienced immediacy', which is the 'verbally inexpressible but wholly palpable, primary fact of being'.[49]

---

[45] Edgewater (1999: 173).
[46] George Steiner (1989: 137).
[47] George Steiner (1989: 137).
[48] Elkins (1996: 41).
[49] George Steiner (1989: 196).

Philosophically speaking, it is interesting to compare Steiner's approach to music with Darwin's, who notes that 'music has a wonderful power' to recall 'strong emotions', but then roots its significance not in existential or philosophical domains but in the evolutionary past of 'emotions which were felt during long-past ages' when our 'progenitors courted each other by the aid of vocal tones'.[50] It is interesting that Darwin moved directly from his brief note on music to a section that is only slightly longer on Devotion, a topic that is relevant to this chapter. There his prime concern is with posture and bodily action and, for example, with upturned eyes, hands placed together, and kneeling in worship. He describes these learned behaviours of 'devotion' as a 'state of mind . . . related to affection, though mainly consisting of reverence, often combined with fear', but he doubts whether they 'affected the hearts of men, whilst they remained during past ages in an uncivilized condition'.[51] For Darwin, as for the newly emerging group of anthropologists of the nineteenth century, religion was, itself, something that emerged within developing humanity.

While musical environments for the self are, then, often seen as grounded in our animal origin, the emergence of sensibilities classed as religious or devotional are aligned with human cultural development. What is historically obvious is that musical sounds, their verbal correlate in song, and physical movement have all combined in ritual ways that make them inseparable within most religious traditions. The capacity of music in its emotional dynamism to evoke a sense of 'being' is hard to separate from theological and mythological narratives of existence. While nobody can be sure how any individual will respond emotionally to the musical mapping of his world, one potential benefit of places of worship as musical environments is that they provide a spatial context in which a diversity of emotion may be schooled and performed. Here, as in the previous chapter, Wilfred Cantwell Smith's deconstruction of the very word 'religion' into 'faith' and 'cumulative tradition' is valuable, if we see 'faith' as the individual appropriation of 'cumulative tradition', including its musical base.[52]

---

[50] Darwin ([1872] 1998: 216).
[51] Darwin ([1872] 1998: 216–18).
[52] Wilfred Cantwell Smith (1963: 61 ff.). This faith-cumulative tradition of complementarity offers one creative way of approaching the deconstruction debate that Lindsay Jones pursues with Hans-Georg Gadamer and others over the impossibility of knowing the intentions of the originators of architecture or art as opposed to the sense we make of it today (Lindsay Jones 2000: 135–47).

SUMMARY

Just how individuals personalize their own tradition will vary greatly according to temperament, circumstance, and the emotional resources of their tradition, and it is unlikely that any group will prove successful in the long term without a variety of cues for diverse emotions and environments for their appropriation and practice. All of this is likely to enhance this sense of otherness, which, as fraught with conceptual difficulties as it is, remains quite fundamental when pondering human life across the world. Critics, of course, might take a different stance on allurement, as when the 'box-like' Methodist chapels of Britain's Industrial Revolution were described as 'great traps for the human psyche' in which some 'transforming power' was manifest in the 'emotional dramas' of conversation or repentance after backsliding.[53] Whichever descriptor is preferred, sacred places are inescapably aligned with the emotional identities of religious traditions and their changes over time. The allurement of place that pervades this chapter, along with its allied symbolic objects and ritual activities, has allowed us to grasp something of the complexity of emotions within a devotee's embodiment and religious career. It has also touched not only on the crucial process of the individual's appropriation of established cultural practice but also on the profound theme of otherness that influences much religious awareness, not least as captured and mediated by music. Above all, perhaps, allurement has added a sense of the material and spatial nature of human embodiment as the basis for developing a religious identity.[54]

[53] Thompson ([1963] 1968: 404–5) uses strong sexual analogy of 'ritualized psychic masturbation' to describe some religious emotions of that period.

[54] Cf. Vokes (2007: 285–303). His use of 'actor-network' theory (citing Latour 1993) would have considerable application to the material and auditory culture of this chapter and religious identity.

11

Sensory Identity: Wisdom, Wonder, and Worship

The previous chapters have integrated a number of established and more recent ideas describing the dynamic effect of emotions upon the embodied nature of religious identity. We have seen how simple 'named' emotions become complexly nuanced as human imagination creates world views within religious traditions and then, through ritual and ethical schemes, fashions and manages the ensuing identities of devotees. We have seen how the sensory dynamics of emotion—whether in the interplay of rupture and rapture, crisis and cure, or the transformation of perceived faults of identity—are resolved in an awareness of hopeful meaningfulness. We have also seen how embodied creativity contributes to such resolution, something that Jenkins and Valiente describe in terms of 'the degree of intentionality and agency of the body in creating experience'. By emphasizing the body's own way of 'creating experience', amid 'social domains of power', they compensate for the frequent overemphasis on cultural influences upon the body; they affirm the body's own capacity to create cultural and interpersonal responses.[1]

In a telling example, their analysis of 'el calor (the heat)' among refugee women from El Salvador draws on a variety of scholars who speak of the body disclosing aspects of its feeling rather than having cultural idioms thrust upon it. Their Salvadorean case associated calor mostly with negative sensations of fear, dread, fright, worry, despair, misery, agony, and death, and they interpreted it as the outcome of 'emotional engagement with social and political realities'.[2] Nevertheless, by speaking of 'evanescent disclosures of inexhaustible bodily plenitude', they suggest that there is much more going on in and through bodily processes and the experiences aligned with them than can ever

---

[1] Jenkins and Valiente (1994: 164).
[2] Jenkins and Valiente (1994: 170, 172).

be caught in the limited number of cultural concepts available for their description. The findings of cognitive psychology cited in previous chapters would seem to underscore their view, while, from a philosophical standpoint, the case has been well made that 'transformative wisdom' resides in a 'process of *understanding through embodiment*', as David Michael Levin described the 'process of ritual embodiment'.³ Levin's work, not least in its engagement with Heidegger's philosophy of 'being' and feeling, is important for the way in which our sensation of existence engages with 'the ontological gift' of human being.⁴

Mutual understanding within religious groups often depends upon a sensed bodily awareness of the significance of motifs such as the 'heat' in the Salvador case. That ethnography complements a comparative case where a kind of 'heat' is associated with salvation through the Mormon idiom of a 'burning in the breast'. This motif appeared in a formal revelation dated to 1829 in which the prophet Joseph Smith's assistant, Oliver Cowdery, is told by God that, over a certain issue, he needs to 'study it out in your mind' and then ask God if his decision is correct. If it is, then God will 'cause that your bosom shall burn within you'; if not correct, then Oliver will simply experience 'a stupor of thought'.⁵ These texts present an interesting folk model of human life as a mind–body interplay of rational and emotional factors and reflect the Mormon mind–body dualism inherent in its ultimate doctrine of human nature. This 'burning in the breast' motif became common parlance within Mormonism and exemplifies a group-sanctioned sensation, one located in the chest, allied with heat, and identified as a form of divine approval. In denoting an emotional experience pertaining to salvation, this 'burning' comes into its own as a common means of communicating one's authentic sincerity.

Religious traditions thrive to the degree that they offer such emotion-signalling idioms, intensified by narrative and rite, and help create a person's identity. Salvation, in turn, becomes a process of adaptation to cultural environments, with their negative forces resolved in a form of 'closure', all enhanced by grammars of emotional and mood-related discourses embedded in spatial and musical dimensions to the ritual. Secular explanations, too, also indicate that meaning is also achievable by other routes, even if it remains to

---

³ Levin (1985: 214, 211, 220; emphasis in original).
⁴ Levin (1985: 50).   ⁵ Doctrine and Covenants 9: 8–9.

be seen how successfully secularity may achieve hope-engendering moods and motivations for mass populations.[6]

We have seen that some anthropologists have long encouraged such a focus on emotional and sensory aspects of social life, with Emiko Ohnuki-Tierney, for example, urging widespread interest in 'the emotive and sensory dimensions of human perception', especially over areas of cultural life that are only vaguely classified in explicit terms. For example, her Sakhalin study subtly revealed that 'vision . . . does not generally play a significant role in the Ainu perception of the universe' but that the 'olfactory sense is especially important during shamanistic rites'.[7] I have also pressed a similar point on 'the question of mood or a sense of embodiment', both when studying Mormons and when engaging in Christian pastoral theology.[8] Such theoretical interests in emotional aspects of body symbolism help develop the long-standing interplay between individual and society that dominates sociological and psychological thought and is foundational for any critical understanding of emotion, identity, and religion, as also for the depth of meaning that drives religious individuals and the key narratives through which religious identities are formed and the process of the salvation of the imagination proceeds. Folk narratives continue to channel distinctive emotions, and, as the twenty-first century moves into its second decade, many political issues of peace and hostility are influenced by myths of Jewish origin and homeland, their Christian appropriation, and their interplay with Islamic ideals. So, too, with Hindu and Sikh opinions over lands and culture, not to mention the ideological-religious claims of Native Americans, Australians, and New Zealanders, and, albeit at a different level of intensity, the claims of Pagan and of Secularist groups.

Running in parallel, scientific discoveries have generated their own accounts of human identity, even if their narrative power often appears weak when facing traditional religious narratives whose dynamism lies in the focal leaders who easily embody the core values of these stories. Values and principles need a personalized focus. The physical and mental laboratories of biological and mathematical sciences, by contrast, not to mention the

---

[6] Comte-Sponville ([2006] 2007)—an atheist who bemoans the shallow emotion of secular funerals.

[7] Ohnuki-Tierney (1981: 149, 97). Similar modes of embodied knowledge are also of fundamental importance in W. E. H. Stanner's analysis of 'transitive and intransitive conduct' (1960a: 124).

[8] Douglas J. Davies (1987: 154; 1986: 21–31).

enormities of space–time science and astronomy, often lack the persuasive power of religious 'ideas' because they lack ritualized arenas. However, they do possess rare figures such as Darwin and Einstein, who, in some measure, serve as embodiments of concepts, even if most people do not understand the subtlety of their theories. For those few scientists whose lives are shaped by laboratory or mental science, identity transformation is possible through those lived experiences where experimentation ritualizes the scientific method. To repeat, it is in and through embodiment that abstract principles or values become potent.

What is involved here is the way people engage with truth and understand that engagement in relation to their own life's venture and to the widespread human sense of positive and negative factors underlying existence. One way of approaching this is through Chapter 3's allusion to Jung's stress on the moral opposites between forces conceived as good and as evil and often reckoned inaccessible to conscious awareness. I am not rehearsing this because of any Jungian agenda but simply as one way of dealing with the widespread sense of positive and negative forces in life. Jung provides a convenient foil for this when taking this dividedness further in his psycho-philosophical argument over a process of salvation involving both a growing awareness of these opposites as explicitly taught by most religious traditions, and the further insight into how they may be engaged by the self in ways not necessarily fostered by those traditions. This more developed sense of engagement with our human internal opposition is likely to involve the need to transcend institutional teachings and the very safety that large institutions confer. As a corollary, Jung emphasized the potential consequence of this shift in the 'devastating effect of getting lost in the chaos' outside such organizations,[9] a 'lostness' that is a powerful aspect of the human emotion of fear. To sense oneself beyond and outside the community that confers one's sense of identity is to know the fragile dynamics of identity as well as identity's potential. For Jung, the capacity for such self-knowledge is hard, necessitating a facing of one's internal oppositions without seeking to escape by projecting them onto external demonic or saviour figures.[10] Such self-knowledge may, in turn, involve repositioning institutional teaching in such a way that 'even a moderately alert intellect' will come to disbelieve dogma and

---

[9] Jung ([1953] 1968: 74).

[10] There is something subtly profound in the distinction between Jung on 'insight' and Sigmund Freud's use of 'archaeology' as a metaphor for his psychoanalytical method of unearthing or digging up a person's past life. Cf. Kuspit (1989: 136).

see it as 'absurd'.[11] At this point Jung offers no formula for gaining such insight or achieving 'wholeness'. Rather, he does what is anathema to many scholars by acknowledging that 'wholeness is in fact a charisma that cannot be manufactured'; we can 'only grow into it and endure whatever its advent may bring'.[12] This approach is potentially valuable for those engaging in the study of religion, many coming from established religious positions who undergo various kinds of questions, doubts, and avenues of self-repositioning in relation to doctrinal worlds.

Emotional intimacy, distance, and faith

From quite a different theoretical perspective, we alluded at the outset of this study to Bourdieu's use of *doxa* to describe the tacit forms of life acceptance of the ways things are, and we return to it again because his account of the 'field of opinion' is valuable as we conclude our study. It highlights potential changes to *doxa* following 'the confrontation of competing discourses'.[13] In other words, some critically reflexive sense of ourselves, of others, and of differing interpretations of the world challenges our own sense of identity. This echoes our discussion of 'superplausibility' in Chapter 9. The distinguished sociologist Armand Mauss had just such an experience of critical study and change in mind when addressing fellow Mormons in this way.

Abandon certainty all ye who enter herein! Never again will you enjoy the immunity to doubt and ambiguity that went with your previous life. But then the ability to live with perpetual ambiguity is also the trait that distinguishes adults from adolescents.[14]

In Bourdieu's terms, *doxa* now gives way to the tension between *orthodoxy* and *heterodoxy*: in the Mormon case this would be interpreted in terms of an explicit acceptance or rejection of religious teaching. Mauss's words become even more poignant, however, when couched in terms of emotional factors triggered by the surprise that knowledge may trigger. This can be understood at many levels, not only if a formerly and tacitly accepted knowledge base is challenged in serious doubt or radically and explicitly reinforced in a distinctive conversion, but also in life experiences such as that of bereavement. There, for example, no matter how much a person 'knows' *about* grief or is professionally involved in death, he or she is often surprised by the experience

---

11 Jung ([1953] 1968: 20).   12 Jung ([1953] 1968: 30).
13 Bourdieu ([1972] 1977: 168).
14 Mauss (1990: 9), cited in Givens (2007: 239).

of grief when it is personally encountered for the first time. The context of personal bereavement brings the individual to live within a cluster of emotions, as the sense grief is 'learned', as we say, 'by experience'. This example shares its own family resemblance with other forms of emotional experience, not least with some religious experiences. Aspects of religious conversion, the gaining of insight, shared experience, or a sensed encounter with the divine, or of having 'lost faith'—all of these may 'come to' an individual with such a sense of immediate authenticity that they are an end in themselves. But, just as a moment of hope and the possibility of a future life often follow a period of grief, so there may come a time when a certain distance is gained from those experiences and the individual may wish to consider or reconsider them in a new and critical fashion. To develop Mauss's words, what does it mean to be an adult in terms of religious emotion? Three potential pathways present themselves.

The first happily describes religious emotions locating the 'truthfulness' of each within their own particular group but, ultimately, adopting a critical distance from all of them in favour of a cultural relativism. This critical attitude, grounded in religious agnosticism, atheism, or secularism, is granted dominance, and the individual gains his own sense of 'adulthood' from some other source. The second regards religious emotions in terms of particular actions of the deity, gods, ancestors, nature, or some other powers. This view is grounded in religious belief and, within itself, either argues that the supernatural source is unique to its own group, with other groups being deceived in some emotional way, or that the supernatural source influences different traditions in appropriately different ways. The third also happily describes religious emotions as culturally given, but, while not accepting their supernatural origin in any traditional sense, accepts their importance for individuals living 'within' the mythical narratives framing them. This position acknowledges the culturally relative factors that name, create, and stimulate these emotions, and yet is content to experience them, personally, on the assumption that humans are feeling persons whose 'adulthood' requires emotional fulfilment. It understands that human embodiment is always context and group grounded, and that this applies equally to emotions and to moods of salvation.[15]

---

[15] See Schneider's discussion (1993: 3) on 'The Logic of Enchantment'. 'Enchantment' has shifted from nature to the study of culture—enchantment being a sense that, if certain things were to be proved to be the case, then 'our image of how the world operates would be radically transformed'.

This is an important issue at this point, for the theoretical reason that many experience both the naive world view and a critical-analytical world view but are not always sure how to relate them. It is an issue often posed between the stance of being religious and of studying religion, and of whether to accord primacy to one or the other. This dilemma is accentuated in this study through the use of neuroscience-type accounts of emotion that can easily lead to the question of the 'real' nature of emotional aspects of life. Is the 'real' nature of things what goes on in the inaccessible depths of mental processes or in what we are able to think and feel at a more conscious level? The same option can be couched in terms of whether it is the cognitive-scientific theory of religious perception or a theological account of the way things are that should take primacy. The stance adopted here abandons the opposition as a false move and accepts the value of each in its place. As human beings we must act in order to live, just as much as we sometimes feel obliged to be critically self-analytical of how we live.

The phenomenologists have long understood these positions when distinguishing between the everyday life world in which we simply live in an uncritical flow of customary action characterized by a tension of consciousness appropriate to it and, by contrast, a critical analysis of life that breaks down 'wholes' into their constituent parts. When we are simply 'living', it makes sense to accept what is there, knowing full well that if we stop to subject our action to analysis we immediately destroy its immediate nature. It is hard to sing and to be critically evaluative of the lyrics at the same time. Similarly, when we stop to analyse a text, it loses its capacity to speak to us as an integrated whole. To appreciate the differences inherent in these different forms of 'tensions of consciousness'—one grounded in the method of philosophical doubt and the other in an acceptance of the everyday world—is to begin to understand the nature of being human. To practise each of them as may be appropriate to context is to develop a genuine life skill and to begin to become wise. Seldom is this distinction more germane than when discussing the integrated domains of sacred place, worship, and music as they conduce to distinctive moods of salvation. Practical analogies are helpful here, as in the case of learning to drive or to play a racquet sport. The beginner is taught itemized skills such as how to change gear or hold a racquet, and this is done with verbal instruction and in a logical-rational way. This often induces immediate difficulties, because learners become very self-conscious and 'think' about carrying them out, with such thinking getting in the way of the action. It is only when the behaviour takes on a life of its own and people 'stop thinking about it' that competence begins. Indeed, accomplished performers speak of times when they transcend themselves and accomplish great things, with psychologists even using the notion of 'flow' to describe these moments of what seems like a perfect integration of thought and action in physical movement.[16] It is because of such emotional experiences that Jehangir Khan, for example, one of the greatest twentieth-century squash players, could speak of sport as helping 'to give meaning to life' as it fosters integration of personality.[17]

Much the same can be said of worship when individuals learn units of worship in posture, words, and music, and in how to behave within a building, all before these elements combine in their own form of 'flow' such that a sense of transcendence may be experienced. It is likely to do so when a person is simply given to the act and is not pondering and analysing his own activities. Music is especially important in fostering this kind of awareness. The sense of oneness with the world often associated with mystics and described as an oceanic experience affords a similar sense.[18] The practice of ritual, when it takes this form, gives a person a sense of the truthfulness of things. It is satisfying and is grounded in an intuition of the self and its existence that cannot be denied. Such a mood of salvation is its own form of truth. But such periods do not last for ever.

For those who may stop to ponder their ritual behaviour, the challenge may arise as to which of these outlooks is 'true', the analytically reductionist or the experienced performance view. One possibility is that there is a kind of 'truth' in each of them, but this problem of options is often aggravated by the theological or philosophical presupposition that there is only 'one' truth behind any matter. Such a priority-demanding view sits uneasily with what it sees as the liberal view that there can be different forms of 'truth' relevant to different life contexts. The study of religion, whether from a humanities or social-science base, does, however, seem to offer this realistic option of intuitive and analytical competences. One could argue further to say that the ability to see this option and to practise it involves the development of a

---

[16] Cf. Csikszentmihalyi ([1974] 1991), discussed and criticized by Victor Turner (1982: 56–9), who sees in the potentially spontaneous nature of 'flow' something analogous to 'grace' as a theological concept; see Stålhandske (2005: 280) for an analogous link with a 'transitional mode' connecting 'the absorbing sensuality of bodily perception and the distancing mediation of language and culture'.

[17] Khan et al. (1990: 88).

[18] Rieff (1966: 153) comments on the 'dry land' version of the 'oceanic' experience when citing Reich's notion of the 'meadow experience' of feeling at one with nature.

distinctive competence all of its own. At its most stark, it advocates the feasibility of being able to live in a myth whilst also, before or after the event, acknowledging the nature of that myth as myth. This, in itself, involves profound issues of self-identity, of the management of one's own emotion, and of a community that understands such a world view. It demands both a sense of distance from the self and honesty with the self about the nature of human life and thought and, in particular, of the way emotions function in generating meaning and hope. Some have argued that one of the goals of European Enlightenment intellectualism has been to create philosophical heroes who discover how to become thinkers who stand on their own having seen through the inadequate theories of others.[19] This stance easily includes anthropologists who, having interpreted the beliefs of some native group in symbolic ways, have then to appreciate the impact of similar forms of analysis on their own faith. One notable case is that of Evans-Pritchard: 'by disenchanting the natives' faith, he became disenchanted with, and lost his own Catholic faith.'[20] This trajectory can be found in many contexts; even Cicero, two millennia earlier, preferred not to engage in public discussion on the false nature of the objects of human worship lest it 'destroy the established religion'.[21]

Reflexive naivety

Here, however, we inevitably encounter potentially bitter debates, with people disagreeing quite strongly over just what an 'honest' understanding of life means. The approach offered throughout this study has been rooted in the notion of core values, core culture, and allied emotions introduced in the very first chapter. This perspective views human life as embedded within a particular society, with its subdivisions of family, work, leisure, voluntary groups, and activities all playing a part in constituting our identity. Similarly important are memories, the role they play in the groups to which we belong, and the hope they may foster. The assumption we have made is that for most people 'inclusion', or life nearer the core, is more fulfilling than relative exclusion at the margin—always accepting that specific individuals may, for

---

[19] Argyrou (2002: 82–91).
[20] Argyrou (2002: 69), citing Morris (1987: 72).
[21] Ross (1972: 237).

whatever reasons, not function in this way and may prefer life at the boundaries of worlds of meaning.

Applying that model to religious life, we have described 'salvation' in similar terms of participation and recognition, with damnation pertaining in expulsion and alienation. One popular expression of these deep issues lies in the common use of the terms 'respect' and 'dignity', which mark the quality of identity and the worth ascribed to persons. Here I use the idea of 'salvation' in a general and technical sense that is much broader than any specific formula of salvation existing within any particular religion. Such a view of salvation allows immediate access to ideas of spirituality, a term that originated within specific world religions and then expanded into discussions ranging from innovative meditative practices, 'new-age' attitudes, and ecological concerns over the world's future to attitudes framing medical and clinical practice. In all of these, 'spirituality' was an index of a sense of the depth of meaning in life coupled with particular forms of activity. It, too, involves moods of distinctive kinds.

Spirituality

Spirituality now regularly serves as a term alluding to a self-aware acknowledgement of emotional experiences enhancing the meaning of life, especially where no explicit commitment is made to established religious traditions. In so doing it largely supplants the traditional role of the word 'religion' but tends to leave the realm of 'morality' in need of some explicit recognition, for few who claim to possess a 'spirituality' would wish to ignore some form of 'morality'. And it is precisely in this connection that 'ethics' has come to assume a distinctive significance of its own. It seems that, in contexts where traditional forms of religion, or at least of Christianity, have declined in a general context of secularization, it has been replaced by the partnership of 'spirituality' and 'ethics'. In such contexts, moods of salvation become moods of spirituality complemented by appropriate ethical considerations. The significance of ethics within this study lies precisely in its inherent grounding in the relationship between forms of reciprocity in the face of alterity.

To speak of secularization is, sociologically, to emphasize the decline of influence of formal religious institutions upon decision-making and the functioning of public life, with, perhaps, the localization of religious concerns to the private arena. It need not imply any necessary loss of feeling as such, but does imply its reformatting. Indeed, the spread of spirituality-terminology from traditional religious channels into wider areas of life, some of which might even be described as secular, highlights the importance of the value-framing of emotional dimensions of existence.[22] For, while it is easy to debate the precise meaning and the many meanings of 'spirituality' in terms of the ideas it carries in particular contexts, there can be no ignoring the intention of these contexts to affirm the emotional dimension of life. Moreover, there also seems to be a major concern to frame that emotional domain with some kind of moral perspective, one of the most significant of which has been an ethics of ecology and of saving the planet.[23] Indeed, this particular 'mood of salvation' often shares roots embedded in individual and in wider social-political life. When taken beyond the ecological domain, 'ethics' has become a foundational aspect of the development of institutional life, with practically every large institution developing its own 'ethics committee'. One of the most significant features of secular society is the emergence of spirituality and ethics as key factors in the management of the existential domains of life. It is as though spirituality and ethics offer a close parallel of the religion and ethics partnership in traditional religious societies. Secularists do not, quite properly, wish their perspective on life to be viewed as inferior to that of the traditional religions, best exemplified in Comte-Sponville's work on atheist spirituality.[24] Here, as ever, the question of terminology poses problems. How may atheists or secularists ensure that their views are assumed not to focus only on rational argument but also to engage with the depths of human experience and the emotions aligned with them? Some may, for example, even consider 'spirituality' too risky a loanword and seek an alternative emphasis upon human significance by emphasizing 'morality' as an emotion-allied term. Once again, the theme of hope as driving a mood of salvation comes into question, especially if, as some argue, 'an atheism without hope will degenerate into nihilism'.[25] One way of circumventing the hazards of inherited terminology is, at this point, to invoke the concept of wisdom.

---

[22] Cottingham (2005); Cook, Powell, and Sims (2009).
[23] Sheldrake and Fox ([1996] 1997).
[24] Comte-Sponville ([2006] 2007).
[25] Geoghegan (1996: 95), a comment on Ernst Bloch's view of Marxism, Utopianism, and Christianity.

Wisdom

From Chapter 1, then, we have pursued the idea of core values of a group. We have seen how in some Indian traditions, notably in some schools of Hinduism, Buddhism, and Sikhism, the foundational notion of illusion (*maya*) drives entire schemes of religious thought and practice, as devotees seek to move from evil in the sense of illusion's captive snare, from the way 'reality' is veiled from view, in order to achieve enlightenment. Here wisdom lies in the prime goal of a transitive 'seeing-through' the way things appear to be in order to see them as they 'really' are. This fosters both a philosophical programme of reflection alongside meditative practice and a control of certain emotions in order that others may arise. What this approach does in and of itself is to provide a religious framework for understanding the relative nature of existence. This mirrors Loyal Rue's 'formal definition of wisdom' as 'living in harmony with reality', or Evens's more open-ended view of wisdom as a practice with 'the capacity to improvise radically'.[26]

The Jewish–Christian–Islamic traditions took a different path to knowledge, originating in ideas of divine revelation of information, the core of which appeared as laws or principles of action, to be received and obeyed. As we saw in Chapter 3, while this approach to 'evil' does not regard the world as an illusion, it portrays it as fractured or disrupted by sin, a state depicted as 'fallen'. Even so, within this broad tradition, which emphasized the cultivation of devotional attitudes to the divine and obedience to divine teaching, there also emerged esoteric and mystical traditions seeking distinctive forms of knowledge of the divine. As we have also seen in previous chapters, many native traditions of knowledge acquisition have their own forms of mystical and secret knowledge, often controlled by older people and imparted to new generations as and when deemed appropriate. What should not be ignored, however, is the way human creativity may exceed its prevailing cultural and traditional base. Kees Bolle, for example, has argued for the way some mystics may take 'steps beyond an accepted tradition'.[27]

A more social-scientific way of describing these schemes is to see them as all dealing with the idea of wisdom interpreted as the nature of understanding of, and the quality of participation in, the core values of a group. To highlight wisdom is, as we have just indicated, to invoke a word that also comes with an

---

[26] Rue (2005: 135); Evens (2008: 255).
[27] Bolle ([1968] 1993: 151).

enormous history of meaning in the overlapping worlds of religion and philosophy. Scholars are familiar with what is often called 'wisdom literature', associated with ancient Near Eastern and biblical literature, as well as, for example, classical philosophy, as in the case of Aristotle. Such materials concern human life and how best to live it; how best to organize life in society for its advantage.

For our purposes, the key to wisdom lies both in 'understanding' and 'participating' in social life, on the one hand, and in the sense of a certain 'knowing-naivety', on the other.[28] Wisdom is the consequence of insight into human life. The existentialist Paul Tillich describes wisdom as 'insight into the meaning of one's own life, into its conflicts and dangers, into its creative and destructive powers, and into the ground of which it comes and to which it must return'.[29] Something similar was sketched by Mary Douglas when analysing the Pangolin Cult of the Lele people; she spoke of how 'they confront ambiguity in an extreme and concentrated form', in ways that make the cult 'capable of inspiring a profound meditation on the nature of purity and impurity and on the limitation on human contemplation of existence'. Indeed, she sees this in numerous other groups too, where initiates are invited 'to turn round and confront the categories on which their whole surrounding culture has been built up and to recognise them as the fictive, man-made, arbitrary creations that they are'.[30]

In the theoretical terms developed earlier in this study, such a 'turn round' invites a form of superplausibility, not simply knowledge in the sense of an accumulation of information but the outcome of pondering information in the light of experience. When fourth-century BCE Aristotle analysed what he called 'practical wisdom', he gave due weight to the importance of experience as the arena within which the general principles developed by 'theoretical wisdom' have to be worked out, arguing that youths may become mathematicians and deal well with abstract principles: 'no young man is ever considered to have practical wisdom', for he lacks that experience, which time alone can furnish.[31] Aristotle is clear that the ability to act lies at the heart of practical wisdom[32] and that emotions play their part in it.[33] For its part, the biblical outlook roots wisdom in an experiential familiarity with the divine and in

---

[28] For an extensive discussion of similar issues, see Evens (2008), whose major study of anthropology explores human responsibility through a variety of relationships with the other, all through the idiom of sacrifice, self-sacrifice, and idolatry.

[29] Tillich (1963: 143).   [30] Douglas (1966: 169–70).   [31] Aristotle (1963: 128).

[32] Aristotle (1963: 156).   [33] Aristotle (1963: 57).

enacted implementation of the knowledge gained. So, while 'the fear of the Lord is the beginning of wisdom', subsequent action is its proper complement.[34] For both Aristotelian and biblical sources, wisdom is the desirable outcome of engaged persons embedded in their culture.

Insight and 'through sight'

Taking that position a step further, we can argue that wisdom involves the kind of insight into the rationale of a culture's meaning-making process that leads to a 'seeing-through' in the two ways offered by the verb itself. In its transitive form, we come to see or understand things by means of our culture. This recalls Chapter 1 and the way society provides a classification of our world. In its intransitive form, however, we can be said to 'see through' a culture in the sense that we understand that this perspective is but one among many others: it is not the last word on 'reality'. In the more technical terms of the phenomenology of religion, this reflexive approach acknowledges the different universes of meaning that exist in the world and the different 'tensions of consciousness' and, we might add, the different emotional patterns found in each of them.

Knowledge of more than one society and religion can be a trigger for this process of knowing, as can the life experience that age brings with it. Just how a person will respond to this kind of insight or 'through sight' is hard to predict. Some may think that they have been deceived by their home society and come to adopt a position of cynical cultural relativism in which nothing matters and they may now wish to stand at the very margin of or even outside their original world view as critics. Others, as intimated in the 'knowing-naivety' model mentioned above, accept that 'everything is relative' but that life has to be lived in some social context and commit to a practical wisdom of living by one particular cultural scheme of things.[35] By analogy: a person who is raised in an isolated community and speaks only one language comes to find out that other languages and societies also exist. This makes his own language 'relative' and no more or less important than any other human tongue. But if such a person is to live a social life at all, it will have to be in and through one language at any one time and place. So he will commit to living in and through one language, even though he may know several

[34] Psalm 111: 10; Proverbs 1: 7.
[35] I intend cultural relativism to apply to distinctive ideas about life present in the broad cultural values of societies and not to empirical issues of science.

languages and will certainly know that his native language is not the 'best' language in any ultimate sense. In terms of this study we can add to this analogy that a person knowing different languages will also know, to some degree, how each manages and fosters different schemes of emotion, and that to adopt one language is to acknowledge acceptance of its emotional scheme. Here again there is a conscious commitment to a way of life: practical wisdom drives it.

'Through sight': ethics, emotions, and reflexive moods

Because this kind of practical wisdom will entail not only some emotional response but also an ethical perspective, it is worth asking after the 'emotional-ethics' of wisdom: what might such an ethics be? Given that we are now concluding this study, we prefer to make suggestions for the future rather than argue a new case at length. Accordingly, it seems that the best answer is 'compassion': a concept that bonds emotion and life rules. This is, of course, a complex identification, since 'compassion' mirrors a distinctive Buddhist perspective while also matching concepts from other religious traditions—for example, Christian notions of love or Jewish notions of mercy. The Buddhist background, in particular, expresses some 2,500 years of human thought and practice in a tradition that pays great attention to life directives as well as to emotions. Peter Harvey has explored this area quite extensively in his study of Buddhist ethics, drawing our attention to 'the development of heart-felt feelings of loving kindness and compassion' that are intimately linked with 'one who has thoroughly seen through the delusion of the "I am" conceit'.[36]

There is a sense in which the broad Indian critique of human life is not unlike an academic critique of cultural life as a social construction of 'reality', with the 'through sight' of cultural relativism resembling the Buddhist 'seeing through' 'the "I am" conceit'. What is interesting is that one might argue that Buddhism turned an existential critique into 'a religion' whose ritual practice contextualizes 'through-sight', directing it away from cynicism, nihilism, or anguished relativism. What Buddhism has developed, and what scholarly traditions easily lack, then, is a life practice of emotional education to serve as the medium within which to come to terms with the intellectual insights over the provisional and fragile worlds of culture. The way academic life

---

[36] Harvey (2000: 103–5).

developed in 'the West', though the pattern is essentially universal, involves a separation between scholar and subject matter. Instead of the knowledge of a particular subject or pattern of subjects being part of a vocation, an entire way of life, it becomes partial, a job. Furthermore, issues of the deconstruction of power-laden narratives of existence and an almost overburdening of the self with reflexive analysis of motives—conscious or unconscious—have often reinforced a loss of nerve. Yet each of us must live and decide for ourselves just where to locate our thinking, living, and social participation. How we do this remains a challenge as we consider what we make of ourselves, both in the sense of the person we become over time and in the way we evaluate what we become. In this, our study's theme of identity comes to sharp focus and, with it, the role of religion in forging emotional patterns. Contemporary life presents a great variety of world views and emotional sets within which individuals may so make themselves at home. In final conclusion we offer four diverse perspectives that suggest how emotions may suffuse core values and be stimulated by them in terms of religious identity.

Psychological reflections

The first perspective is psychological. Set against the background of Albert Schweitzer's 'reverence for life' motif documented in Chapter 4, it highlights Philip Rieff's insightful psycho-social study of culture, focused on American ideological shifts of the later 1950s and 1960s. He described a scene in which psychoanalysis, as a 'secular paradigm of religious self-knowledge', was likely to generate an ideal type of 'therapeutic' personhood that made gods into neuroses. He anticipated a future in which psychology would 'cease to be a post-religious discipline' and simply come to 'supply the language of cultural controls by which the new man will organize his social relations and self-conceptions'.[37] It is interesting that, some fifty years later, the direction taken by cognitive psychology and evolutionary biology is far from Rieff's antici-pated psychological engagement in a 'binge of inwardness'. For, despite the renewed interest in emotions, one is far more aware of outward-directed commitments, whether within small-scale groups or the more bureaucratized human concerns of work or wider community-based ethical-spirituality.[38] Here much depends on both the 'ritual' and 'sacred narratives' of these

---

[37] Rieff (1966: 171). [38] Rieff (1966: 174).

contexts and on what Darwin called the 'power of the imagination and of sympathy' that allows us to put ourselves into the position of another person.[39] Certainly, Darwin was aware of our capacity to sympathize with someone about to undergo some great suffering and, indeed, 'to sympathize with ourselves' when recalling our feelings of a former time and place.[40] This important observation highlights the human capacity for reflection, when memories are given new emotional force and are, as it were, felt again. Since Rieff, the impact of ecological concerns, as unexpected as it may have been, has prompted a spectrum of sympathies beyond the self that has overshadowed the temptation to that binge of inwardness of rich people in safe society, and ethics has resurged as the reasoned basis for action, seeking to applaud the will as a motive force in human behaviour, albeit not without an emotional driver in fear for the future of life on earth.

Theological wonder

The second perspective on emotional rationality in religiously formed and embodied identities can be typified by Andrew Louth's comparison of understanding within theology, the humanities, and sciences on the basis of the notion of 'mystery'. His *Discerning the Mystery* found considerable value in Josef Pieper's emphasis on 'the sense of wonder' as a 'receptive attitude to reality': 'Wonder shakes a man, it disturbs him.'[41] Louth aptly uses this perspective to dwell on the way Western philosophy, following Descartes, transformed wonder into doubt or, as he put it, 'wonder becomes reduced to doubt'—typifying what might be defined as one mood of philosophy. Louth wants to join Pieper in following a different path that accepts a Cartesian method of doubt as a trigger for philosophy in its full sense of *philo-sophia*, the love of wisdom, and 'the quest for wisdom'. For Louth the pivotal point of the humanities has to do with the nature of individuals, with 'the mystery of the person', and, as a priest and Orthodox theologian, he argues that 'theology holds before us, and holds us before, the ultimate mystery of God'.[42]

---

[39] Darwin ([1872] 1998: 306). Darwin even speaks of sympathy as 'a separate and distinct emotion' (1998: 215).

[40] Darwin ([1872] 1998: 215).   [41] Louth ([1983] 2003: 143).

[42] Louth ([1983] 2003: 146).

In the light of preceding chapters, we could explain this theological approach in terms of cognitive psychology and say that the theologian's invocation of mystery is an expression of a partial self-conscious awareness of human systems of intuition, of 'aggregate relevance'.[43] Theologians would, generally, be unhappy with such a purely cognitivist interpretation, deeming it reductionist, precisely because of their overarching belief in a God. Louth would insist, too, that wonder in mystery is a matter not simply of philosophical or theological ratiocination but of religious practice. Indeed, he invokes not only the importance of 'performance', citing Gadamer in the process, but also John Henry Newman on 'anticipations and presumptions' aligned with the nature of faith, involving 'the practice of love, humility and trust in God'.[44] Here we are faced with the obvious differences between those with a theistic world view and those of a naturalist perspective. Indeed, Louth notes that 'Newman's doctrine of faith can be seen . . . as a response to the rationalism of the Enlightenment'.[45] But Newman's life spanned almost the entire nineteenth century, and a great deal of knowledge on human nature has emerged since then. But wonder remains as a challenge to theists and to naturalists embedded in their proper response as self-aware persons alert to the puzzlement of their own processes of engagement with the world around them and within them. This is an important issue, because it is too easy to follow a cognitive psychological argument on mental inference processes that are inaccessible to conscious awareness without giving some credit to the centuries of theological-philosophical reflection upon the experiences and intuitions that intellectual believer-practitioners have pondered.

Philosophical mood concluded

A third scenario brings us back to meaning-making, to the interplay of belief and doubt within religious life, and to an 1879 essay of William James, whose three points reinforce our focus on embodiment and emotions and provide a different engagement with *philosophia* from that of Louth. The first concerns the contemporary issue of how rational and emotional aspects of life are related within human emotions. Here he stresses the integration of mind and body, or the unity of thought and feeling, rather than any division between them. He exemplifies this when answering the question of why philosophers

---

[43] See Boyer (2001: 342), for religion as the result of 'aggregate relevance'.
[44] Louth ([1983] 2003: 137, 139, 140).
[45] Louth ([1983] 2003: 140).

philosophize at all? For, after noting the simple fact that philosophers want to know the answers to problems, he asks how it is they know when they have the right answer. To resolve this he invokes emotional ideas, arguing that philosophers come to possess 'a strong feeling of ease, peace', and 'rest' as they shift from a 'state of puzzle and perplexity' to a 'rational comprehension' that is 'full of lively relief and pleasure'. This stress on the intimacy of thought and feeling is often invoked by those who discover some idea as having 'come' to them, and who may also speak of solutions to problems as being 'beautiful'. As for James, he refers to 'the Sentiment of Rationality' as a form of awareness or feeling associated with times when a thinker is fully engaged in thinking and is devoid of stress or complexity. This offers a good case of a feeling that, hitherto, may have been experienced but left nameless.[46] His second point deals with 'more mystical minds', as they engage with the great questions of existence and, 'when logic fails', experience a kind of ecstasy that James describes as 'ontological emotion'.[47] His later study of *The Variety of Religious Experience* provided many descriptions of religious experiences that seemed to overwhelm a person's view of the world, if only for a short time, but that significantly affected their subsequent outlook. His third theme, after the sentiment of rationality and ontological emotion, lay in a brief account of faith as 'belief in something over which doubt is still theoretically possible' but which still influences a person's 'readiness to act'. Echoing part of our discussion in Chapter 4, he speaks of trust as he sees in faith a 'moral quality' resembling 'courage in practical affairs'. Indeed, he sees the need to act on trust as an 'essential function' in ordinary life, arguing that, for many people, 'faith is synonymous with working hypothesis'. Then, with time, 'faith creates its own verification', in the sense that, 'the longer disappointment is delayed, the stronger grows his faith in his theory'.[48]

Poetic closure

For our fourth and final perspective on emotions, core values, and identity, we combine a poetic turn and an existential vignette—a poem because it is the closest linguistic form to music and embodied 'knowing', and a sketched case study as a constant reminder of empirical realism.

---

[46] James ([1879] 1956: 63–4).
[47] James ([1879] 1956: 74).
[48] James ([1879] 1956: 90–7).

The great Bengali poet Rabindranath Tagore offers a meaning-making and emotion-inducing text carrying its own direction of otherness, with brevity as opposed to prolixity typifying its creativity of hopeful wisdom.

> When I stand before thee at the day's end thou shalt see my scars
> and know that I had my wounds and also my healing.[49]

Whether depicting a lover and the beloved, a devotee and deity, or the self in self-reflection, something here symbolizes the complex notion of 'closure', a concept whose family likeness with the 'mood of salvation' pervades previous chapters and is now captured in a last case cameo of Susan Sharp.[50] Her narrative scene reveals the emotional turmoil of family rupture. A woman ponders the life of a criminal cousin with learning difficulties who, having suffered numerous losses in his life, had killed his own adoptive mother and now awaits capital punishment on death row. This woman had, herself, suffered two heart attacks and, now, 'coming face to face with her own mortality . . . began looking for healing in her relationships'. She also reflected on her brother's recent death and spoke of him as having wanted 'closure' over the family murder before he died. This, she tells us, he had achieved: 'Before he died, he was able to forgive his cousin without accepting that it was OK to murder'.[51] 'Closure' comes with the brother being 'able to forgive' the murderer-cousin. For them 'closure' links emotion and meaning in a satisfactory endpoint to a narrative-embedded episode that combined issues of otherness and deeply negative reciprocity, a situation resembling a 'mood of salvation'. Such a case of emotion-laden identities and prime cultural values provides as good a scene as any at which to conclude our study of the ever-changing dynamics of identity, emotion, and religion.

[49] Tagore ([1916] 1921: 83).
[50] 'Closure' is discussed in Chapter 4, citing Fiske (2004: 88, 164), drawing on Webster and Kruglanski (1994).
[51] Sharp (2005: 135).

References

Abbink, Jon (2000). 'Restoring the Balance: Violence and Culture among the Suri of Southern Ethiopia', in Göran Aijmer and Jon Abbink (eds), *Meanings of Violence*. Oxford: Berg, 77–100.

Aberbach, David (1996). *Charisma in Politics, Religion and the Media: Private Traumas, Public Ideals*. London: Macmillan.

Alter, Robert (1981). *The Art of Biblical Narrative*. New York: Harper-Collins, Basic Books.

Anand, Mulk Raj (1989) (ed.). *Sati*. Delhi: B. R. Publishing Corp.

Andrade, Roy d' (1995). *The Development of Cognitive Anthropology*. Cambridge: Cambridge University Press.

Aquili, Eugene G. d', and Charles D. Laughlin, Jr (1979). 'The Neurobiology of Myth and Ritual', in Eugene G. d'Aquili, Charles D. Laughlin Jr, John McManus, et al. (eds), *The Spectrum of Ritual: A Biogenetic Structural Analysis*. New York: Columbia University Press, 152–82.

Aquili, Eugene G. d', Charles D. Laughlin Jr, John McManus, et al. (1979). *The Spectrum of Ritual: A Biogenetic Structural Analysis*. New York: Columbia University Press.

Arend, Walter (1933). *Die typischen Scenen bei Homer*. Berlin: Weidmannsche Buchhandlung.

Argyrou, Vassos (2002). *Anthropology and the Will to Meaning*. London: Pluto Press.

Aristotle (1963). *Ethics*, ed. and trans. John Warrington. London: Dent.

Augé, Marc ([1992] 1995). *Non-Places*. London and New York: Verso.

—— ([1998] 2004). *Oblivion*. Minneapolis: University of Minnesota Press.

Augustine ([413–426] 1945a). *The City of God*, trans. John Healey, ed. R. V. G. Tasker. London: J. M. Dent & Sons Ltd.

—— ([413–426] 1945b). *The Confessions of St Augustine*, trans. F. J. Sheed. London: Sheed and Ward.

Baal, J. van, and W. E. A. van Beek (1985). *Symbols for Communication*. Assen: Van Gorcum.

Babin, Pierre, and Angela Ann Zukowski (2002). *The Gospel in Cyberspace: Nurturing Faith in the Internet Age*. Chicago: Loyola Press.

Bainton, Roland H. ([1951] 1958). *The Travail of Religious Liberty*. New York: Harper and Brothers Publishers.

Baldwin, Stanley ([1925] 1939). 'Truth and Politics', in *On England and Other Addresses by Stanley Baldwin*. Harmondsworth: Penguin Books, 83–98.

Barrett, C. K. (1955). *The Gospel of St John: An Introduction with Commentary and Notes on the Greek Text.* London: SPCK.

Barth, Karl (1956). *Church Dogmatics,* iv. *The Doctrine of Reconciliation,* ed. G. W. Bromiley and T. T. Torrance. Edinburgh: T & T Clark.

Bartkowski, John P. (2004). *The Promise Keepers: Servants of God and Godly Men.* New Brunswick, NJ: Rutgers University Press.

Barton, D. (1977). *Dying and Death: A Clinical Guide for Care Givers.* Baltimore: Williams and Wilkins Co.

Batson, C. D., and W. L. Ventis (1982). *The Religious Experience,* Oxford: Oxford University Press.

Bell, Charles (1864). *The Anatomy and Philosophy of Expression.* 4th edn. London: Henry G. Bohn.

Bell, Daniel ([1980] 1991). *The Winding Passage: Sociological Essays and Journeys.* London: Transaction Publishers.

Bentley, James (1978). *Ritualism and Politics in Victorian Britain.* Oxford: Oxford University Press.

Berlin, Isaiah (1997). *The Proper Study of Mankind: An Anthology of Essays,* ed. Henry Hardy and Roger Hausheer. London: Chatto and Windus.

Bettelheim, Bruno (1982). 'Freud and the Soul', *New Yorker,* 1 Mar., pp. 52–93.

Bird, Steve (2009). Article in *The Times,* 21 Sept., p. 9.

Blatty, William Peter ([1971] 1972). *The Exorcist.* London: Corgi Books.

Bloch, Ernst ([1959] 1986). *The Principle of Hope,* trans. Neville Plaice, Stephen Plaice, and Paul Knight. Oxford: Basil Blackwell.

Bloch, Maurice (1992). *Prey into Hunter.* Cambridge: Cambridge University Press.

—— (2004). 'Ritual and Deference', in Harvey Whitehouse and James Laidlaw (eds), *Ritual and Memory.* New York and London: Altamira Press.

Bolle, Kees W. ([1968] 1993). *The Freedom of Man in Myth.* Nashville, TN: Vanderbilt University Press.

Bonhoeffer, Dietrich ([1949] 1955). *Ethics,* trans. Neville Horton Smith. London: SCM Press.

Book of Mormon ([1830] 1981). Salt Lake City, UT: Church of Jesus Christ of Latter-Day Saints.

Borella, Jean ([1996] 1998). *The Sense of the Supernatural,* trans. G. John Champoux. Edinburgh: T & T Clark.

Børresen, Kari Elisabeth (1995). 'Women's Studies of the Christian Tradition: New Perspectives', in Ursula King (ed.), *Religion and Gender.* Oxford: Blackwell, 245–55.

Bourdieu, Pierre ([1972] 1977). *Outline of Theory of Practice.* Cambridge: Cambridge University Press.

Bourke, Joanna (2006) *Fear: A Cultural History.* London: Virago Press.

Bowker, John (1973). *The Sense of God.* Oxford: Oxford University Press.

Bowker, John (1978). *The Religious Imagination and the Sense of God*. Oxford: Oxford University Press.

Boyer, Pascal (2001). *Religion Explained: The Human Instincts that Fashion Gods, Spirits and Ancestors*. London: William Heinemann.

Bronstein, Leo (1991). *El Greco*. London: Thames and Hudson.

Brown, Dan (2009). *The Lost Symbol*. London: Bantam Press.

Brown, Hugh B. (1965). *The Abundant Life*. Salt Lake City, UT: Bookcraft.

Brown, S. Kent, Richard Neitzel Holzapfel, and Dawn C. Pheysey (2006). *Beholding Salvation: The Life of Christ in Word and Image*. Salt Lake City, UT: Deseret Book Company.

Bryman, Alan (1992). *Charisma and Leadership in Organizations*. London: Sage.

Buckley, Thomas, and Alma Gottlieb (1988) (eds). *Blood Magic: The Anthropology of Menstruation*. Berkeley and Los Angeles: University of California Press.

Burkert, Walter (1998). *Creation of the Sacred: Tracks of Biology in Early Religions*. Cambridge, MA: Harvard University Press.

Butler, Samuel ([1872] 1939). *Erewhon or Over the Range*. London: Jonathan Cape.

Calvin, John ([1536] 1838). *Institutes of the Christian Religion*, trans. John Allen. London: T. Tegg and Son.

Cannon, W. B. (1929). *Bodily Changes in Fear, Hunger and Rage*. 2nd edn. New York Appleton and Co.

Cannon, W. B. (1942). '"Voodoo" Death', *American Anthropologist*, NS 44: 169–81.

Carmichael, E., and C. Sayer (1991). *The Skeleton at the Feast: The Day of the Dead in Mexico*. London: British Museum Press.

Cartledge Mark J. (2006) (ed.). *Speaking in Tongues: Multi-Disciplinary Perspectives*. Milton Keynes: Paternoster.

Cavell, Stanley (1995). *Philosophical Passages: Wittgenstein, Emerson, Austin, Derrida*. Oxford: Blackwell.

Certeau, Michel de, Luce Giard, and Pierre Mayol ([1994] 1998). *The Practice of Everyday Life*, ii. *Living and Cooking*, trans. Timothy J. Tomasik. Minneapolis: University of Minnesota Press.

Chakrabarti, S. C. (1974). 'Human Sacrifice in the Vedas', paper presented at All India Oriental Conference, University of Jammu, 1974.

Chalmers, Thomas (1827). *On the Respect due to Antiquity: A Sermon Preached on Friday May 11th 1827, at the Opening of the Scotch National Church London*. Glasgow: Printed for William Collins.

Chang, Maria Hsia (2004). *Falun Gong: The End of Days*. New Haven: Yale University Press.

Chapple, Elliot, and Carleton Stevens Coon (1947). *Principles of Anthropology*. London: Cape.

Chesnut, Andrew R. (1997). *Born Again in Brazil: The Pentecostal Boom and the Pathogens of Poverty*. New Brunswick, NJ: Rutgers University Press.

Cicero, Marcus Tullius ([BC 44] 1972). *The Nature of the Gods*, trans. Horace C. P. McGregor. Harmondsworth: Penguin.

Clark, Ronald W. (1984). *The Survival of Charles Darwin: A Biography of a Man and an Idea*. London: Weidenfeld and Nicolson.

Cline, Sally (1995). *Lifting the Taboo: Women, Death and Dying*. London: Abacus.

Coelho, Paulo ([1988] 1995). *The Alchemist*. London: Harper Collins.

Coleridge, Samuel Taylor ([1810] 1907). 'Fragment of an Essay on Taste', in *Coleridge's Essays and Lectures on Shakespeare and Some Other Old Poets and Dramatists*. London: J. M. Dent and Co.

Collins, Harry (2010). 'It's there—or is it?' *The Times Higher Education Supplement*, 25 Feb., pp. 42–4.

Colson, Charles W. (1976). *Born Again*. London: Hodder and Stoughton.

Comte-Sponville, André ([2006] 2007). *The Book of Atheist Spirituality*, trans. Nancy Huston. London: Bantam Books.

Constable, John (1968). *John Constable's Correspondence*, vi. *The Fishers*, ed. R. B. Beckett. Ipswich: Boydell Press.

Cook, Chris, Andrew Powell, and Andrew Sims (2009). *Spirituality and Psychiatry*. London: RCPsych Publications.

Coon, Carleton S. (1950). *A Reader in General Anthropology*. London: Jonathan Cape.

Corrigan, John (2002). *Business of the Heart*. Berkeley and Los Angeles: University of California Press.

—— (2004a) (ed.). *Oxford Handbook of Religion and Emotion*. Oxford: Oxford University Press.

—— (2004b) (ed.). *Religion and Emotion*. Oxford: Oxford University Press.

—— (2008) (ed.). *The Oxford Handbook of Religion and Emotion*. Oxford: Oxford University Press.

Cottingham, John (2005). *The Spiritual Dimension: Religion, Philosophy and Human Value*. Cambridge: Cambridge University Press.

Covell, Stephen G. (2008). 'The Price of Naming the Dead: Posthumous Precept Names and Critiques of Contemporary Japanese Buddhism', in Jacqueline I. Stone and Mariko Namba Walter (eds), *Death and the Afterlife in Japanese Buddhism*. Honolula: University of Hawai'i Press, 293–324.

Craib, Ian (1998). *Experiencing Identity*. London: Sage.

Cranmer, Thomas (1907). *The True and Catholic Doctrine and Use of the Lord's Supper*. London: Thynne and Jarvis.

Cross, F. L. (1977) (ed.). *The Oxford Dictionary of the Christian Church*. Oxford: Oxford University Press.

Cross, F. L. (1997) (ed.). *The Oxford Dictionary of the Christian Church.* 3rd edn. ed. E. A Livingstone. Oxford: Oxford University Presss.

Csikszentmihalyi, Mihaly ([1974] 1991). *Flow: The Psychology of Optimal Experience:* New York: Harper Perennial.

Csordas, Thomas J. (1990). 'Embodiment as a Paradigm for Anthropology: The 1988 Stirling Award Essay', *Ethos*, 18: 5–47. Repr. in Csordas (2002), 58–87.

—— (1994) (ed.). *Embodiment and Experience: The Existential Ground of Culture and Self.* Cambridge: Cambridge University Press.

—— ([1990] 2002). *Body/Meaning/Healing.* New York: Palgrave-Macmillan.

Dandelion, Pink (1996). *A Sociological Analysis of the Theology of Quakers.* Lewiston: Edwin Mellen Press.

—— (2005). *The Liturgies of Quakerism.* Aldershot: Ashgate.

Darwin, Charles ([1872] 1998). *The Expression of the Emotions in Man and Animals.* 3rd edn, with an Introduction, Afterword, and Commentaries by Paul Ekman. London: Harper-Collins Publishers.

Das, Veena (1997). 'Language and Body: Transactions in the Construction of Pain', in Arthur Kleinman, Veena Das, and Margaret Lock (eds), *Social Suffering.* Berkeley and Los Angeles: University of California Press.

Davies, Douglas J. (1976). 'Social Groups, Liturgy and Glossolalia', *Churchman*, 90/3: 193–205.

—— (1984a). *Meaning and Salvation in Religious Studies.* Brill: Leiden.

—— (1984b). 'The Charismatic Ethic and the Spirit of Post-Industrialism', in David Martin and Peter Mullen (eds), *Strange Gifts.* London: SPCK.

—— (1986). *Studies in Pastoral Theology and Social Anthropology.* Birmingham: Institute for the Study of Worship and Religious Architecture, Birmingham University.

—— (1987). *Mormon Spirituality: Latter Day Saints in Wales and Zion.* Nottingham: Nottingham University Series in Theology.

—— (1996). 'The Social Facts of Death', in Glennys Howarth and Peter C. Jupp (eds), *Contemporary Issues in the Sociology of Death, Dying and Disposal.* Basingstoke: Macmillan, 17–29.

—— (1997a). *Death, Ritual and Belief.* London and Washington: Cassell.

—— (1997b). 'Contemporary Belief in Life after Death,' in Peter C. Jupp and Tony Rogers (eds), *Interpreting Death: Christian Theology and Pastoral Practice.* London: Cassell, 131–42.

—— ([1997] 2002). *Death Ritual and Belief.* 2nd rev. edn. London: Continuum.

—— (2000). *The Mormon Culture of Salvation.* Aldershot: Ashgate.

—— (2002). *Anthropology and Theology.* Oxford: Berg.

Davies, Douglas J. (2004). 'Time, Place and Mormon Sense of Self', in Simon Coleman and Peter Collins (eds), *Religion, Identity and Change: Perspectives on Global Transformations*. Aldershot: Ashgate, 107–18.

—— (2006). 'Inner Speech and Religious Traditions', in James A. Beckford and John Wallis (eds), *Theorising Religion: Classical and Contemporary Debates*. Aldershot: Ashgate, 211–23.

—— (2010). *Jesus, Satan and Joseph Smith: Atonement, Evil and the Mormon Vision*. Aldershot: Ashgate.

—— and Mathew Guest (2007). *Bishops, Wives and Children: Spiritual Capital across the Generations*. Aldershot: Ashgate.

—— and Alister Shaw (1995). *Reusing Old Graves: A Report on Popular British Attitudes*. Crayford: Shaw and Sons.

Davies, Jon (1995). *The Christian Warrior in the Twentieth Century*. Lewiston, NY: Edwin Mellen.

Davies, Paul (1995). *Are We Alone?* Harmondsworth: Penguin.

Dearden, Harold (1925). *The Science of Happiness*. London: William Heinermann.

Default, K., and R. N. Martocchio (1985). 'Hope: Its Fears and Dimensions', *Nursing Clinics of North America*, 20/2 (June), 379–91.

Delaney, Carole (1988). 'Mortal Flow: Menstruation in Turkish Village Society', in Thomas Buckley and Alma Gottlieb (eds), *Blood Magic: The Anthropology of Menstruation*. Berkeley and Los Angeles: University of California Press, 74–93.

DeMar, Gary (2001). *End Times Fiction: A Biblical Consideration of the Left behind Theology*. Nashville: Thomas Nelson Publishers.

Derbes, Anne (1996). *Picturing the Passion in Late Medieval Italy: Narrative Painting, Franciscan Ideologies and the Levant*. Cambridge: Cambridge University Press.

de Souza, Ronald (1990). *The Rationality of Emotion*. Cambridge, MA: MIT Press.

Dillenberger, John (1986). *A Theology of Artistic Sensibilities*. London, SCM Press.

Dixon, Thomas (2003). *From Passions to Emotions*. Cambridge: Cambridge University Press.

Doctrine and Covenants (1981). Salt Lake City, UT: Corporation of the President of the Church of Jesus Christ of Latter-Day Saints.

Douglas, Mary (1966). *Purity and Danger*. London: Routledge and Kegan Paul.

—— (1970) (ed.). *Witchcraft Confessions and Accusation*. London: Tavistock.

Durkheim, Émile ([1897] 1970). *Suicide: A Study in Sociology*. London: Routledge and Kegan Paul.

—— ([1902] 1984) *The Division of Labour in Society*, trans. W. D. Halls. Basingstoke: Macmillan.

—— ([1912] 1976). *The Elementary Forms of the Religious Life*. London: Allan Lane.

Ebersole, Garry (2004). 'The Function of Ritual Weeping Revisited: Affective Expression and Moral Discourse', in John Corrigan (ed.), *Religion and Emotion*. Oxford: Oxford University Press, 185–222.

Edgewater, Iain D. (1999). 'Music hath charms...: Fragments toward Constructionist Biocultural Theory with Attention to the Relationship of "Music" and "Emotion"', in Alexander Laban Hinton (ed.), *Biocultural Approaches to the Emotions*. Cambridge: Cambridge University Press, 153–81.

Edwards, Felicity (1995). 'Spirituality, Consciousness and Gender', in Ursula King (ed.), *Religion and Gender*. Oxford: Blackwell, 176–91.

Ehrman, Bart D. (2003). *Lost Scriptures: Books that did not Make it into the New Testament*. Oxford: Oxford University Press.

Eisler, Riane (1987). *The Chalice and the Blade: Our History, our Future*. New York: Harper and Row.

Ekman, Paul (1965). 'Introduction', in Charles Darwin, *The Expression of the Emotions in Man and Animals* [1872]. Chicago: Chicago University Press.

Eliade, Mircea (1979). *A History of Religious Ideas*, vol. i. London: Collins.

Elkins, James (1996). *The Object Stares back: On the Nature of Seeing*. Harvest book. London: Harcourt, Inc.

Elliott, Matthew (2005). *Faithful Feelings: Emotion in the New Testament*. Leicester: Inter-Varsity Press.

Evans-Pritchard, E. E. (1937). *Witchcraft, Oracles and Magic among the Azande*. Oxford: Clarendon Press.

Evens, T. M. S. (2008). *Anthropology and Ethics: Nondualism and the Conduct of Sacrifice*. Oxford: Berghan Books.

Farmer, Paul (1997). 'On Suffering and Structural Violence: A View from Below', in Arthur Kleinman, Veena Das, and Margaret Lock (eds), *Social Suffering*. Berkeley and Los Angeles: University of California Press.

Fernandez, James W. (1995). 'Meaning Deficit, Displacement and New Consciousness in Expressive Interaction', in Anthony P. Cohen and Nigel Rapport (eds), *Questions of Consciousness*. London: Routledge, 21–40.

Fessler, Daniel M. T. (1999). 'Towards an Understanding of the Universality of Second Order Emotions', in Alexander Laban Hinton (ed.), *Biocultural Approaches to the Emotions*. Cambridge: Cambridge University Press, 75–116.

Finaldi, Gabriele (2000). *The Image of Christ: The Catalogue of the Exhibition Seeing Salvation*. London: National Gallery, Yale University Press.

Fine, Ben (2010). *Theories of Social Capital: Researchers Behaving Badly*. London: Pluto Press.

Fisch, Joerg ([2005] 2006). *Burning Women: A Global History of Widow-Sacrifice from Ancient Times to the Present*, trans. Rekha Kamath Rajan. London, New York, and Calcutta: Seagull Books.

Fiske, Susan T. (2004). *Social Beings: A Core Motives Approach to Social Psychology.* Hoboken, NJ: John Wiley & Sons.

Flanagan, Kieran (1991). *Sociology and Liturgy: Re-presentations of the Holy.* London: Macmillan.

Foster, James (1752). *Discourses on all the Principal Branches of Natural Religion and Social Virtue.* London: Mr Noon in Cheapside et al.

Foxe, John ([1563] n.d.). *Foxe's Book of Martyrs: Being an Authentic Account of the Sufferings and Deaths of Primitive and Protestant Martyrs in Various Countries.* London: Milner and Company.

Freud, Sigmund ([1927] 1973). *The Future of an Illusion,* trans. W. D. Robson-Scott. London: Hogarth Press.

—— (1930). *Civilization and its Discontents.* London: Routledge.

—— ([1964] 1977). *New Introductory Lectures in Psychoanalysis,* vol. ii. London: Pelican Books.

Freze, Michael (1989). *They Bore the Wounds of Christ: The Mystery of the Sacred Stigmata.* Huntington, IN: Our Sunday Visitor Publication Division.

Friedrich, Paul (1997). 'The Prophet Isaiah in Pushkin's "Prophet"', in John Leavitt (ed.), *Poetry and Prophecy: The Anthropology of Inspiration.* Ann Arbor: University of Michigan Press, 169–200.

Fromm, Erich ([1942] 1960). *Fear of Freedom.* London: Routledge & Kegan Paul.

Gadamer, Hans-Georg ([1960] 1989). *Truth and Method.* London: Sheed and Ward.

Galanter, Marc (2005). *Spirituality and the Healthy Mind.* Oxford: Oxford University Press.

Geertz. Clifford ([1966] 1973). 'Religion as a Cultural System', in Michael Banton (ed.), *Anthropological Approaches to the Study of Religion.* London: Tavistock.

Gennep, Arnold van ([1908] 1960). *The Rites of Passage,* trans. M. K. Vizedom and G. Caffee. London: Routledge and Kegan Paul.

Geoghegan, Vincent (1996). *Ernst Bloch.* London and New York: Routledge.

George, Andrew (1999). *The Epic of Gilgamesh,* trans. and intro. Andrew George. New York: Barnes and Noble.

Gereboff, Joel (2008). 'Judaism', in John Corrigan (ed.), *Oxford Handbook of Religion and Emotion.* Oxford: Oxford University Press, 95–110.

Gibson, Margaret (2008). *Objects of the Dead.* Melbourne: Melbourne University Press.

Gilhus, Ingvild Saelid (1997). *Laughing Gods, Weeping Virgins, Laughter in the History of Religions.* London: Routledge.

Girard, René (1977). *Violence and the Sacred.* London: Johns Hopkins University Press.

Givens, Terryl L. (2007). *People of Paradox: A History of Mormon Culture*. Oxford: Oxford University Press.

Glaser, B. G., and A. L. Strauss (1965). *Awareness of Dying*. Chicago: Aldine Publishing Co.

Glassman, Hank (2008). 'At the Crossroads of Birth and Death', in Jacqueline I. Stone and Mariko Namba Walker (eds), *Death and the Afterlife in Japanese Buddhism*. Honolulu: University of Hawai'i Press, 175–207.

Glick, Leonard B. (2005). *Marked in your Flesh*. Oxford: Oxford University Press.

Goldschmidt, Walter (1990). *The Human Career: The Self in the Symbolic World*. Oxford: Blackwell.

Gorringe, T. J. (2004). *Furthering Humanity: A Theology of Culture*. Aldershot: Ashgate.

Gothóni, René (1987). 'Monastic Life on Mount Athos: A Reflection of Cosmic Order', *Studia Fennica*, 32: 73–85. (Suomalaisen Kirjallisuuden Seura.)

Good, Mary-Jo D., Paul E. Brodwin, Byron J. Good, and Arthur Kleinman (1992) (eds). *Pain as Human Experience: An Anthropological Perspective*. Berkeley and Los Angeles: University of California Press.

Grabbe, Lester L. (1995*). Priests, Prophets, Diviners, Sages: A Socio-Historical Study of Religious Specialists in Ancient Israel*. Valley Forge, PA: Trinity Press International.

Greenwood, Susan (2000). *Magic, Witchcraft and the Otherworld: An Anthropology*. Oxford: Berg.

Guest, Mathew (2007). *Evangelical Identity and Contemporary Culture: A Congregational Study in Innovation*. Milton Kenes: Paternoster Press.

Haecker, Theodor (1947). *Virgil Father of the West*, trans. Arthur Wesley Wheen, London: Sheed and Ward.

Halbwachs, Maurice ([1941, 1952] 1992). *Maurice Halbwachs on Collective Memory*, ed., trans., and intro. Lewis A. Coser. Chicago: University of Chicago Press.

Hall, John R., with Philip D. Schuyler (2000). *Apocalypse Observed: Religious Movements and Violence in North America, Europe, and Japan*. London: Routledge.

Hallam, Elizabeth, and Jenny Hockey (2001). *Death, Memory and Material Culture*. Oxford: Berg.

Hanley, E. (2005). 'Holistic Philosophy and Spiritual Wellbeing in People Facing Life-Threatening Illness'. Unpublished M.Litt. thesis, Durham University.

Hardman, Charlotte E. (2000). *Other Worlds: Notions of Self and Emotion among the Lohorung Rai*. Oxford: Berg.

Harvey, David (2000). *Spaces of Hope*. Edinburgh: Edinburgh University Press.

Harvey, Peter (2000). *An Introduction to Buddhist Ethics*. Cambridge: Cambridge University Press.

Havergal, M. V. G. (1890). *Frances Ridley Havergal: By her Sister M.V.G.H.* London: Nisbet & Co.

Hay, David (1990). *Religious Experience Today.* London: Mowbray.

Heath, Geoff (2003). *Believing in Nothing and Something.* Chesterfield: Bowland Press.

Heelas, Paul (1989). 'Identifying Peaceful Societies', in Signe Howell and Roy Wallis (eds), *Societies at Peace: Anthropological Perspectives.* London: Routledge, 225–43.

Heidel, Alexander ([1946] 1963). *The Gilgamesh Epic and Old Testament Parallels.* Chicago: University of Chicago Press.

Heiler, Friederich ([1918] 1932). *Prayer.* Oxford: Oxford University Press.

Hertz, Robert ([1905–6] 1960). 'A Contribution to the Study of the Collective Representation of Death', in R. Needham and C. Needham (eds), *Death and the Right Hand.* New York: Free Press.

Hindmarsh, D. Bruce (2005). *The Evangelical Conversion Narrative: Spiritual Autobiographies in Early Modern England.* Oxford: Oxford University Press.

Hinnells, John R. (2005). *The Zoroastrian Diaspora: Religion and Migration.* Oxford: Oxford University Press.

Hinton, Alexander Laban (1999) (ed.). *Biocultural Approaches to the Emotions.* Cambridge: Cambridge University Press.

Hirschon, Renée (1978). 'Open Body/Closed Space: The Transformation of Female Sexuality', in Shirley Ardener (ed.), *Defining Females: The Nature of Women in Society.* London: Croom Helm.

Hocart, A. M. (1933). *The Progress of Man.* London: Methuen.

—— ([1935] 1973). *The Life-Giving Myth and Other Essays,* ed. Rodney Needham. London: Tavistock Publications in association with Methuen.

Hovenden, Gerald (2002). *Speaking in Tongues: New Testament Evidence in Context.* Sheffield: Sheffield Academic Press.

Huffington, Ariana Stassinopoulos (1988). *Picasso, Creator and Destroyer.* New York: Simon and Schuster.

Hutchins, Christina K (2002). 'A Place and a Moment: One Poem about Becoming', in Darren J. N. Middleton (ed.), *God, Literature and Process Thought.* Aldershot: Ashgate, 229–46.

Huxley, Aldous ([1932] 1994). *Brave New World.* London: Vintage.

—— ([1925] 1951). *Those Barren Leaves.* Harmondsworth: Penguin.

Hyde, John, Jr (1857). *Mormonism: Its Leaders and Designs.* New York: W. P. Fetridge and Company.

Inge, John (2003). *A Christian Theology of Place.* Aldershot: Ashgate.

Ingoldsby, Mary F. (1978). *Padre Pio: His Life and Mission.* Dublin: Veritas Publication.

Irwin, Margaret ([1960] 1962). *That Great Lucifer: A Portrait of Sir Walter Raleigh.* Harmondsworth: Penguin, with Chatto and Windus.

Jackson, Brian (2007). 'Jonathan Edwards Goes to Hell (House): Fear Appeals in American Evangelism', *Rhetoric Review*, 26/1: 42–59.

James, William (1902). *The Varieties of Religious Experience*. London: Longmans.

—— ([1904] 1950). 'The Moral Equivalent of War' (Association for International Conciliation), in *William James*, ed. and with a commentary by Margaret White. Harmonsdworth: Penguin.

—— ([1910] 1950). 'Remarks at the Peace Banquet' (Universal Peace Congress), in *William James*, ed. and with a commentary by Margaret White. Harmondsworth: Penguin.

—— ([1879] 1956). 'The Sentiment of Rationality', in his *The Will to Believe and Other Essays in Popular Philosophy*. New York: Dover Publications, 63–110.

Jankowiak, William (1995) (ed.). *Romantic Passion*. New York: Columbia University Press.

Juaregui, J. A. (1995). *The Emotional Computer*. Oxford: Blackwell.

Jenkins, Janis H., and Martha Valiente (1994). 'Bodily Transactions of the Passions: El Calor among Salvadoran Women Refugees', in Thomas J. Csordas (ed.), *Embodiment and Experience: The Existential Ground of Culture and Self*. Cambridge: Cambridge University Press.

Jevons, F. B. (1896). *Introduction to the History of Religion*. London: Methuen.

Johnson, Luke Timothy (1998). *Religious Experience in Earliest Christianity*. Minneapolis, MN: Fortress Press.

Jones, Dan (2009). *The Lost Symbol*. London: Bantam Press.

Jones, Lindsay (1993). 'The Hermeneutics of Sacred Architecture: A Reassessment of the Similitude between Tula, Hidalgo and Chichen Itza', Part 1, *History of Religions* 32/3.

—— (2000). *The Hermeneutics of Sacred Architecture, Experience, Interpretation, Comparison*. Cambridge, MA: Harvard Centre for the Study of World Religions, Harvard University Press.

Jordanova, L. J. (1980). 'Natural Facts: A Historical Perspective on Science and Sexuality', in Carol McCormack and Marilyn Strathern (eds), *Nature, Culture and Gender*. Cambridge: Cambridge University Press, 42–69.

Jung, C. G. ([1953] 1968). *Psychology and Alchemy*, trans. R. F. C. Hull. 2nd edn. London: Routledge.

Jupp, Peter C. (2006). *From Dust to Ashes: The British Way of Death*. London: Palgrave Macmillan.

Justice, Christopher (1997). *Dying the Good Death: The Pilgrimage to Die in India's Holy City*. Albany, NY: New York State University Press.

Kapferer, Bruce (1995). 'From the Edge of Death: Sorcery and the Motion of Consciousness', in Anthony P. Cohen and Nigel Rapport (eds), *Questions of Consciousness*. London: Routledge, 134–52.

Kaplan, E. Ann (2005). *Trauma Culture: The Politics of Terror and Loss in Media and Literature*. New Brunswick, NJ: Rutgers University Press.

Karant-Nunn, Susan C. (2010). *The Reformation of Feeling: Shaping the Religious Emotions in Early Modern Germany*. Oxford: Oxford University Press.

Keane, A. H. (1908). *The World's Peoples: A Popular Account of their Bodily and Mental Characters, Beliefs, Traditions, Political and Social Institutions*. London: Hutchinson.

Kelly, Henry Ansgar (2006). *Satan: A Biography*. Cambridge: Cambridge University Press.

Kerr, Fergus (1997). *Immortal Longings: Visions of Transcending Humanity*. London: SPCK.

Khan, Jahangir, with Rahmat Khan and Richard Eaton (1990). *Advanced Squash*. London: Stanley Paul.

Kierkegaard, Søren ([1842] 1941). *Fear and Trembling and The Sickness Unto Death*, trans. with Introduction and Notes by Walter Lowrie. Princeton, NJ: Princeton University Press.

—— ([1843] 1944). *Either/Or*, trans. David F. Swenson and Lillian Marvin Swenson. Princeton, NJ: Princeton University Press.

—— ([1844] 1980). *The Concept of Anxiety*, ed. and trans. Reidar Thomte and Albert B. Anderson. Princeton, NJ: Princeton University Press.

Kim, Chongho (2003). *Korean Shamanism: The Cultural Paradox*. Aldershot: Ashgate.

Kimball, Edward E. (1982). *The Teachings of Spencer W. Kimball*. Salt Lake City, UT: Bookcraft.

King, Ursula (1995) (ed.). *Religion and Gender*. Oxford; Blackwell.

Kirkpatrick, L. A., and P. R. Shaver (1990). 'Attachment Theory and Religion: Childhood Attachments, Religious Beliefs and Conversion', *Journal for the Scientific Study of Religions*, 29: 305–34.

Kleinman, Arthur (1992). 'Pain and Resistance: The Delegitimation and Relegitimation of Local Worlds', in Mary-Jo Good, D. Good, et al. (eds), *Pain as Human Experience: An Anthropological Perspective*. Berkeley and Los Angeles: University of California Press, 169–97.

—— Veena Das, and Margaret Lock (1997). *Social Suffering*. Berkeley and Los Angeles: University of California Press.

Kraemer, David (2000). *The Meanings of Death in Rabbinic Judaism*. London and New York: Routledge.

Kunin, Seth (2009). *Juggling Identities: Identity and Authenticity among the Crypto-Jews*. New York: Columbia University Press.

Kuspit, Donald (1989). 'A Mighty Metaphor: The Analogy of Archaeology and Psychoanalysis', in Lynn Gamwell and Richard Wells (eds), *Sigmund Freud and Art: His Personal Collection of Antiquities*, with an introduction by Peter Gay. London: Thames and Hudson, 133–51.

Laidlaw, James (2004). 'Introduction', in Harvey Whitehouse and James Laidlaw (eds), *New Ritual and Memory*. York: Altamira Press, 1–9.

Lake, Tony ([1980] 1983). *Lonelines*. London: Sheldon Press.

LaHaye, Tim, and Jerry B. Jenkins (2001). *Desecration: Antichrist Takes the Throne*. Wheaton, IL: Tyndale House Publishers.

Lampedusa, Tomasi di ([1958] 2007). *The Leopard*, trans. Archibald Colquhoun. London: Vintage Books.

Latour, B. (1993). *We Have Never Been Modern*, trans. C. Porter. Cambridge, MA: Harvard University Press.

Law, William ([1728] 1893). *A Serious Call to a Devout and Holy Life*. London: Brockenhurst.

Lawton, J. (2000). *The Dying Process: Patients' Experiences of Palliative Care*. London: Routledge.

Leenhardt, Maurice ([1947] 1979). *Do Kamo: Person and Myth in the Melanesian World*. Chicago: University of Chicago Press.

Leeuw, Gerardus van der ([1933] 1967). *Religion in Essence and Manifestation*, trans. J. E. Turner (1938). Gloucester, MA: Peter Smith.

Levenson, Jon D. (1993). *The Death and Resurrection of the Beloved Son: The Transformation of Child Sacrifice in Judaism and Christianity*. New Haven: Yale University Press.

Lévi-Strauss, Claude (1949). *Les Structures élémentaires de la parenté*. Paris: La Haye, Mouton.

—— (1963). *Structural Anthropology*. London: Allen Lane.

Levin, David Michael (1985). *The Body's Recollection of Being*. London: Routledge and Kegan Paul.

Lewis, I. M. (1971). *Ecstatic Religion: An Anthropological Study of Spirit Possession and Shamanism*. Harmondsworth: Penguin.

Liddell, H. G., and R. Scott (1855). *Greek–English Lexicon*. 5th edn. Oxford: Oxford University Press.

—— (1861). *A Greek–English Lexicon*, Oxford: Oxford University Press.

Lienhardt, Godfrey (1961). *Divinity and Experience: The Religion of the Dinka*. Oxford: Clarendon Press.

—— (1970). 'The Situation of Death: An Aspect of Anuak Philosophy', in Mary Douglas (ed.), *Witchcraft Confessions and Accusation*. London: Tavistock, 279–91.

Linnaeus ([1741] 1762). 'An Oration Concerning the Necessity of Travelling in one's own Country', in Benjamin Stillingfleet (ed.), *Miscellaneous Tracts Relating to Natural History, Husbandry, and Physick*. 2nd edn. London, Pall Mall: R. and J. Dodsley.

Linger, D. T. (1992). *Violent Encounters: Meanings of Violence in a Brazilian City.* Stanford: Stanford University Press.

Liveris, Leonie (1999). *Memories Eternal: The First 100 Years of Karrakatta Cemetery 1899–1999.* Claremont, Western Australia: Australia Metropolitan Cemeteries Board.

Louth, Andrew ([1983] 2003). *Discerning the Mystery: An Essay on the Nature of Theology.* Oxford: Clarendon Paperbacks.

Lukes, Steven (1973). *Émile Durkheim: His Life and Work: A Historical and Critical Study.* London: Allen Lane.

Lyon, M. L., and J. M. Barbalet (1994). 'Society's Body: Emotion and the "Somatization" of Social Theory', in Thomas J. Csordas (ed.), *Embodiment and Experience.* Cambridge: Cambridge University Press, 48–68.

Lysaght, Karen D. (2005). 'Catholics, Protestants and Office Workers', in Kay Milton and Svasek Marusks (eds), *Mixed Emotions: Anthropological Studies of Feeling.* Oxford: Berg, 127–43.

McCauley, Robert N., and E. Thomas Lawson (2002). *Bringing Ritual to Mind: Psychological Foundations of Cultural Forms.* Cambridge: Cambridge University Press.

MacCormack, Carol, and Marilyn Strathern (1980). *Nature, Culture and Gender.* Cambridge: Cambridge University Press.

McGuire, Meredith B., with Debra Kantor (1998). *Ritual Healing in Suburban America.* New Brunswick, NJ: Rutgers University Press.

McKay, David O. (1953). *Gospel Ideals,* ed. G. Homer Durham. Salt Lake City, UT: Improvement Era.

McMahon, Ciarán (2008). 'The Origin of the Psychological "Interior": Evidence from Imperial Roman Literary Practices and Related Issues', *Journal of the History of the Behavioural Sciences,* 44/1: 19–37.

Malinowski, Bronislaw ([1948] 1974). *Magic, Science and Religion.* London: Souvenir Press.

Malthus, Thomas ([1798] 1960). *An Essay on the Principle of Population,* with an Introduction by Anthony Flew. Harmondsworth: Penguin.

Marett, R. R. (1933). *The Sacraments of Simple Folk.* Oxford: Clarendon Press.

Mariña, Jacqueline (2008). 'Rudolph Otto and Friedrich Schleiermacher', in John Corrigan (ed.), *The Oxford Handbook of Religion and Emotion.* Oxford: Oxford University Press.

Martin, Dale B. (2004). *Inventing Superstition: From the Hippocratics to the Christians.* Cambridge, MA: Harvard University Press.

Marvin, Carolyn, and David Ingle (1999). *Blood Sacrifice and the Nation: Totem Rituals and the American Flag.* Cambridge: Cambridge University Press.

Maschio, Thomas (1994). *To Remember the Faces of the Dead.* Madison: University of Wisconsin Press.

Mauss, Marcel ([1925] 1966). *The Gift, Forms and Functions of Exchange in Archaic Society,* trans. Ian Cunnison. London: Routledge and Kegan Paul.

—— ([1933] 1979). *Sociology and Psychology: Essays by Marcel Mauss,* trans. Ben Brewer. London: Routledge and Kegan Paul.

Mauss, Armand (1990). 'Alternative Voices: The Calling and its Implications', *Sunstone,* 14/2 (Apr. 1990).

Mayer, Jean-François (2003). 'Religion and the Internet', in James A. Beckford and James T. Richardson (eds), *Challenging Religion: Essays in Honour of Eileen Barker.* London: Routledge, 36–46.

Melling, Philip (1999). *Fundamentalism in America: Millennialism, Identity and Militant Religion.* Edinburgh: Edinburgh University Press.

Mellor, Phillip (2004). *Religion, Realism and Social Theory: Making Sense of Society.* London: Sage.

Mestrovic, Stjepan G. (1992). *Durkheim and Postmodern Culture.* New York: Aldine de Gruyter.

Miller, Daniel (2008). *The Comfort of Things.* Cambridge: Polity.

Milton, John ([1667] 2000). *Paradise Lost.* Harmondsworth: Penguin.

Morris, Brian (1987). *Anthropological Studies of Religion.* Cambridge: Cambridge University Press.

Moscovici, Serge (1993). *The Invention of Society.* Cambridge, MA: Polity.

Muers, Rachel (2004). 'New Voices, New Hopes?' in Pink Dandelion, Douglas Gwyn, Rachel Muers, Brian Phillips, and Richard E. Sturm (eds), *Towards Tragedy/Reclaiming Hope, Literature, Theology and Sociology in Conversation.* Aldershot: Ashgate. pp. 109–23.

Nandy, Ashish (1989). 'The Sociology of Sati', in Mulk Raj Anand (ed.), *Sati.* Delhi: B. R. Publishing.

Needham, Rodney (1972). *Belief, Language and Experience.* Oxford: Blackwell

—— (1980). *Reconnaissances.* Toronto: University of Toronto Press.

—— (1981). *Circumstantial Deliveries.* Berkeley and Los Angeles: University of California Press.

Newport, Kenneth G. C. (2006). *The Branch Davidians of Waco.* Oxford: Oxford University Press.

Neyrey, Jerome H. (1998). *Honor and Shame in the Gospel of Matthew.* Louisville, KY: Westminster John Knox Press.

Nouwen, Henri J. M. ([1992] 1994). *The Return of the Prodigal Son: A Story of Homecoming.* London: Darton Longman and Todd.

Oberoi, Harjot (1997). *The Construction of Religious Boundaries.* Delhi: Oxford University Press.

Obeyesekere, Gananath (1968). 'Theodicy, Sin and Salvation in a Sociology of Buddhism', in E. R. Leach (ed.), *Dialectic in Practical Religion*. Cambridge: Cambridge University Press.

—— (1981). *Medusa's Hair: An Essay on Personal Symbols and Religious Experience*. Chicago: University of Chicago Press.

Ohnuki-Tierney, Emiko (1981). *Illness and Healing among the Sakhalin Ainu*. Cambridge: Cambridge University Press.

Ortiz, John M. (1997). *The Toa of Music: Using Music to Change your Life*. Dublin: Newleaf.

Otto, Rudolph ([1917] 1924). *The Idea of the Holy*, trans. John W. Harvey. Oxford: Oxford University Press.

Page, I. E., and John Brash (n.d. but 1891 Preface). *Scriptural Holiness as Taught by John Wesley*. London: C. H. Kelly.

Parish, Steven M. (2004). 'The Sacred Mind: Newar Cultural Representations of Mental Life and the Production of Moral Consciousness', in John Corrigan (ed.), *Religion and Emotion*. Oxford: Oxford University Press, 149–84.

Park, Chang-Won (2010). *Cultural Blending in Korean Death Rites*. London: Continuum.

Parkes, Colin Murray (2006). *Love and Loss: The Roots of Grief and its Consequences*. London and New York: Routledge.

Parkes, Colin Murray, Joan Stevenson-Hinde, and Peter Marris (1991). *Attachment across the Life Cycle*. London: Routledge.

Parkin, Robert (1996). *The Dark Side of Humanity: The Work of Robert Hertz and its Legacy*. Abingdon: Harwood Academic Publishers.

Parrinder, Geoffrey (1974). *The Bhagavad Gita: A Verse Translation*. London: Sheldon.

Parsons, Talcott (1965). 'Introduction', in Max Weber, *The Sociology of Religion*, trans. Ephraim Fischoff. London: Social Science Paperbacks in association with Methuen & Co., [1922] 1965, pp. xix–lxvii.

Pattison, Stephen (2000). *Shame, Theory, Therapy, Theology*. Cambridge: Cambridge University Press.

Peters, Erskine (1996). 'Spirituals, African American', in Jan Harold Brunvand (ed.), *American Folklore: An Encyclopedia*. New York: Garland Publishing, 682–4.

Pitts, Walter F., Jr (1993). *Old Ship of Zion: The Afro-Baptist Ritual in the African Diaspora*. New York: Oxford University Press.

Plato (1974). *The Republic*, ed. Desmond Lee. 2nd edn. Harmondsworth: Penguin Books.

Prideaux, Sue (2005). *Edvard Munch: Behind the Scream*. New Haven: Yale University Press.

Properzi, Mauro (2010). 'Emotions in Mormon Canonical Texts'. Unpublished Ph.D. thesis, University of Durham.

Radcliffe-Brown, A. R. ([1922] 1964). *The Andaman Islanders*. Glencoe: Free Press.

Radin, Paul ([1927] 1957). *Primitive Man as Philosopher*. New York: Dover.

Raffman, Diana (1988). 'Towards a Cognitive Theory of Musical Ineffability'. *Review of Metaphysics*, 41/4: 685–706.

Rappaport, Roy (1999). *Ritual and Religion in the Making of Humanity*. Cambridge: Cambridge University Press.

Ratzinger, Joseph (2007). *Jesus of Nazareth*, trans. Adrian J. Walker. London: Bloomsbury.

Reynolds, Vernon, and Ralph Tanner ([1983] 1995). *The Social Ecology of Religion*. Oxford: Oxford University Press.

Richter, Philip (2000). 'Gone but not Quite out of the Frame: The Distinctive Problems of Researching Religious Disaffiliation', in L. J. Francis and Y. J. Katz (eds), *Joining and Leaving Religion: Research Perspectives*. Leominster: Gracewing, 21–31.

Rieff, Philip (1966). *The Triumph of the Therapeutic*. Harmondsworth: Penguin Books.

Ritson, Joseph (1909). *The Romance of Primitive Methodism*. London: Edwin Dalton, Primitive Methodist Publishing House.

Roberts, B. H. (1930). *A Comprehensive History of the Church of Jesus Christ of Latter-day Saints*. 6 vols. Salt Lake City: Deseret News Press.

Robbins, Joel (2004). *Becoming Sinners: Christianity and Moral Torment in a Papua New Guinea Society*. Berkeley and Los Angeles: University of California Press.

Rolls, Edmund (2005). *Emotion Explained*. Oxford: Oxford University Press.

Rosaldo, Michelle (1980). *Knowledge and Passion: Ilongot Notions of Self and Social Life*. Cambridge: Cambridge University Press.

Ross, J. M. (1972). *Cicero: The Nature of the Gods*. Harmondsworth: Penguin Books.

Rostas, Susanna, and André Droogers (1993) (eds). *The Popular Use of Popular Religion in Latin America*. Amsterdam: Centre for Latin American Research and Documentation.

Rue, Loyal (2005). *Religion is not about God*. New Brunswick, NJ, and London: Rutgers University Press.

—— (2007). *Religion is not about God*. New Brunswick, NJ, and London: Rutgers University Press.

Rustomji, Nerina (2009). *The Garden and the Fire: Heaven and Hell in Islamic Culture*. New York: Columbia University Press.

The Sacred Writings of the Sikhs (1960). Introduction by Radhakrishnan, trans. Trilochan Singh et al. London: George Allen and Unwin.

Sadie, Stanley ([1975] 1996). *Bruckner*. Oxford: Oxford University Press.

Sagan, Eli (1974). *Cannibalism: Human Aggression and Cultural Form*. New York: Harper Torchbook.

Samarin, William (1972). *Tongues of Men and Angels: The Religious Language of Pentecostalism*. New York: Macmillan.

Sanday, Peggy Reeves (1986). *Divine Hunger: Cannibalism as a Cultural System*. Cambridge: Cambridge University Press.

Sanders, George R. (1995). 'The Crisis of Presence in Italian Pentecostal Conversion', *American Ethnologist,*. 22/2: 324–40.

Sanders, N. K. ([1960] 1978). *The Epic of Gilgamesh*. Harmondsworth: Penguin Classics.

Schantz, Mark S. (2008). *Awaiting the Heavenly Country: The Civil War and America's Culture of Death*. Ithaca, NY, and London: Cornell University Press.

Schechner, Richard ([1977] 1988). *Performance Theory*. Rev. and expanded edn. New York: Routledge.

Schimmel, Solomon (2002). *Wounds not Healed by Time: The Power of Repentance and Forgiveness*. Oxford: Oxford University Press.

Schleiermacher, Friedrich ([1821–2] 1928). *The Christian Faith*. Edinburgh: T & T Clark.

—— (1830). *The Christian Faith*. 2nd rev. edn. Edinburgh: T&T Clark.

—— (1885). *Selected Sermons of Schleiermacher*, trans. Mary F. Wilson. London: Hodder and Stoughton.

Schmidt, Bettina (2008). *Caribbean Diaspora in the USA: Diversity of Caribbean Religions in New York City*. Aldershot: Ashgate.

Schneider, Mark A. (1993). *Culture and Enchantment*. Chicago: Chicago University Press.

Schuger, Deborah K. (2004). 'The Philosophical Foundations of Sacred Rhetoric', in John Corrigan (ed.), *Oxford Handbook of Religion and Emotion*. Oxford: Oxford University Press, 115–32.

Schweitzer, Albert ([1907] 1974). 'Overcoming Death', in *Reverence for Life*, trans. Reginald Fuller, London, SPCK, 67–81.

—— ([1931] 1933). *Albert Schweitzer: My Life and Thought*, trans. C. T. Campion. London: Allen and Unwin.

—— ([1936] 1962). 'The Ethics of Reverence for Life', *Christendom*, 1/2 (Winter 1936), 225–39, in Henry Clark, *The Ethical Mysticism of Albert Schweitzer*. Boston: Beacon Press, 180–94.

Seale, Clive (1998). *Constructing Death: The Sociology of Dying and Bereavement*. Cambridge: Cambridge University Press.

Sennett, Richard (2003). *Respect: The Formation of Character in a World of Inequality*. London: Penguin.

Service, Robert (2004). *Stalin: A Biography*. London: Pan-Macmillan.

Sharp, Susan F. (2005). *Hidden Victims: The Effects of the Death Penalty on Families of the Accused*. New Brunswick and London: Rutgers University Press.

Shaw, George Bernard (1967). *Shaw on Religion*. London: Constable.

Sheldrake, Rupert, and Matthew Fox ([1996] 1997). *Natural Grace: Dialogues of Science and Spirituality*. London: Bloomsbury.

Sinkewicz, Robert E. (2006). *Evagrius Ponticus: Greek Ascetic Corpus*. Oxford: Oxford University Press.

Smith, Christian, with Patricia Snell (2009). *Souls in Transition: The Religious and Spiritual Lives of Emerging Adults*. Oxford: Oxford University Press.

Smith, Joseph Fielding, Jr (1954–6). *Doctrines of Salvation: Sermons and Writings of Joseph Fielding Smith*, ed. Bruce R. McConkie. Salt Lake City, UT: Bookcraft.

Smith, Paul Thomas (1992). 'John Taylor', in Daniel L. Ludlow (ed.), *Encyclopedia of Mormonism*. New York: Macmillan, 1438–41.

Smith, Wilfred Cantwell (1963). *The Meaning and End of Religion*. New York: Macmillan.

Smith, William Robertson (1889). *Lectures on the Religion of the Semites*. London: Adam and Charles Black.

Solomon, Robert C. (2002). *Spirituality for the Sceptic: The Thoughtful Love of Life*. Oxford: Oxford University Press.

—— (2007). *Spirituality for the Skeptic*. Oxford: Oxford University Press.

Spencer, Herbert ([1852]) 1891). *Essays Scientific, Political and Speculative*. London: Williams and Norgate.

Sperber, Dan (1975). *Rethinking Symbolism*, trans. Alice L. Morton. Cambridge: Cambridge University Press.

Spurgeon, Charles H. (1876). *Lectures to my Students*. London: Passmore and Alabaster.

Stålhandske, Maria Liljas (2005). *Ritual Invention: A Play Perspective on Existential Ritual and Mental Health in Late Modern Sweden*. Uppsala: Uppsala University.

Stanley, Gail (2008). 'Genes', in *Rowing Home: A Journey through Grief*. Newcastle upon Tyne: Cruse Bereavement Care, 39.

Stanner, W. E. H. (1959–60a). 'On Aboriginal Religion 1: The Lineaments of Sacrifice, Mime, Song, Dance, and Stylized Movements', *Oceania*, 30/1: 108–27.

—— (1959–60b). 'On Aboriginal Religion 2: Sacramentalism, Rite and Myth', *Oceania*, 30/4: 245–78.

Steiner, Franz ([1956] 1967). *Taboo*. Harmondsworth: Penguin.

Steiner, George ([1968] 1972). *Extraterritorial: Papers on Literature and the Language Revolution*. Harmondsworth: Penguin Books.

—— (1989). *Real Presences: Is There Anything in What We Say?* London: Faber and Faber.

Stevens, MaryAnne (1992) (ed.). *Alfred Sisley*. London: Royal Academy of Arts.

Storr, Anthony ([1988] 1977). *Solitude*. London: Harper Collins.

Strathern, Marilyn (1980). 'No Nature, No Culture: The Hagen Case', in Carol MacCormack and Marilyn Strathern (eds), *Nature, Culture and Gender*. Cambridge: Cambridge University Press, 174–222.

Stringer, Martin (1999). *On the Perception of Worship*. Birmingham: Birmingham University Press.

Stroebe, Wolfgang, and Stroebe, Margaret (1987). *Bereavement and Health*. Cambridge: Cambridge University Press.

Svasek, Maruska (2005). 'Introduction: Emotions in Anthropology', in Kay Milton and Svasek Maruska (eds), *Mixed Emotions: Anthropological Studies of Feeling*. Oxford: Berg, 1–23.

Sykes, Stephen (1971). *Friedrich Schleiermacher*. London: Lutterworth Press.

Tagore, Rabindranath ([1916] 1921). *Stray Birds*. New York: Macmillan.

Tambiah, S. J. (1968). 'The Ideology of Merit and the Social Correlates of Buddhism in a Thai Village', in E. R. Leach (ed.), *Dialectic in Practical Religion*. Cambridge: Cambridge University Press.

Tanabe, George J. (2008). 'The Orthodox Heresy of Buddhist Funerals', in Jacqueline I. Stone and Mariko Namba Walter (eds), *Death and the Afterlife in Japanese Buddhism*. Honolula: University of Hawai'i Press, 325–48.

Taylor, Charles (2007). *A Secular Age*. Cambridge, MA, and London: Belknap Press, Harvard University Press.

Taylor, Christopher (1999). *Sacrifice as Terror: The Rwandan Genocide of 1994*. Oxford: Berg.

Thomas à Kempis (n.d.). *Of the Imitation of Christ*. London: Thomas Nelson and Sons.

Thompson, E. P. ([1963] 1968). *The Making of the English Working Class*. Harmondsworth: Pelican Books.

Tillich, Paul (1963). *The Eternal Now: Sermons*. London: SCM Press.

Toulis, Nicole Rodriguez (1997). *Believing Identity: Pentecostalism and the Mediation of Jamaican Ethnicity and Gender in England*. Oxford: Berg.

Tovey, Phillip (2004). *Inculturation of Christian Worship: Exploring the Eucharist*. Aldershot: Ashgate.

Turcan, Robert ([1998] 2000). *The Gods of Ancient Rome*. Edinburgh: Edinburgh University Press.

Turnbull, Colin (1972). *The Mountain People*. London: Pan Books.

Turner, Harold W. (1979). *From Temple to Meeting House: The Phenomenology and Theology of Places of Worship*. The Hague: Mouton Publishers.

Turner, Victor (1969). *The Ritual Process*. London: Routledge and Kegan Paul.

—— (1974). *Dramas, Fields and Metaphors*. Ithaca, NY: Cornell University Press.

Turner, Victor (1982). *From Ritual to Theatre: The Human Seriousness of Play.* New York: PAJ Publications.

—— (1992). *Blazing the Trail.* Tucson, AZ: University of Arizona Press.

Tylor, E. B. ([1871] 1958). *Primitive Culture.* New York: Harper.

Tyson, Ruel W., Jr., James L. Peacock, and Daniel W. Patterson. (1988). *Diversities of Gifts: Field Studies in Southern Religion.* Urbana, IL, and Chicago: University of Illinois Press.

Vokes, Richard (2007). '(Re)constructing the Field through Sound: Actor-Networks, Ethnographic Representation and "Radio Elicitation" in South-Western Uganda', in Elizabeth Hallam and Tim Ingold (eds), *Creativity and Cultural Improvisation.* Oxford: Berg, 285–303.

Wach, Joachim (1951). *Types of Religious Experience Christian and Non-Christian.* Chicago: University of Chicago Press.

Walter, Mariko Namba (2008). 'The Structure of Japanese Buddhist Funerals', in Jacqueline I. Stone and Mariko Namba Walter (eds), *Death and the Afterlife in Japanese Buddhism.* Honolula: University of Hawai'i Press, 247–92.

Watson, William (1919). *New Poems.* London: John Lane, The Bodley Head.

Weber, Max ([1904–5] 1976). *The Protestant Ethic and the Spirit of Capitalism.* London: Allen and Unwin.

—— ([1915] 1991). 'Religious Rejections of the World and their Directions', in *Max Weber: Essays in Sociology,* ed. H. H. Gerth and C. Wright Mills. London: Routledge, 323–59.

—— ([1922] 1965). *The Sociology of Religion,* trans. Ephraim Fischoff. Introduction by Talcott Parsons. London: Methuen.

Webster, D. M., and A. W. Kruglanski (1994). 'Individual Differences in Need for Cognitive Closure', *Journal of Personality and Social Psychology,* 67: 1049–62.

White, Erin (1995). 'Religion and the Hermeneutics of Gender', in Ursula King (ed.), *Religion and Gender.* Oxford Blackwell, 77–100.

Whitehouse, Harvey (2000). *Arguments and Icons: Divergent Modes of Religiosity.* Oxford: Oxford University Press.

—— (2004a). *Modes of Religiosity.* New York: Altamira Press.

—— (2004b). 'Rites of Terror: Emotion, Metaphor, and Memory in Melanesian Initiation Cults', in John Corrigan (ed.), *Religion and Emotion.* Oxford: Oxford University Press, 133–48.

—— and Laidlaw (2004) (eds). *Ritual and Memory, Towards a Comparative Anthropology of Religion.* New York and London: Altamira Press.

Whittle, Brian, and Jean Ritchie (2005). *Harold Shipman: Prescription for Murder.* London: Time Warner Books.

Widtsoe, John A. (1978) (ed.). *Discourses of Brigham Young.* Salt Lake City, UT: Church of Jesus Christ of Latter-Day Saints.

Williams, Duncan Ryuken (2008). 'Funerary Zen: Soto Death Management in Tokugawa', in Jacqueline I. Stone and Mariko Namba Walter (eds), *Death and the Afterlife in Japanese Buddhism*. Honolula: University of Hawai'i Press, 207–46.

Wood, Matthew (2007). *Possession, Power and the New Age: Ambiguities of Authority in Neoliberal Societies*. Aldershot: Ashgate.

Woodruff, Wilford (1946). *The Discourses of Wilford Woodruff*, ed. G. Homer Durham. Salt Lake City, UT: Bookcraft.

Wynn, Mark (2005). *Emotional Experience and Religious Understanding*. Cambridge: Cambridge University Press.

Young, Allan ([1996] 1997). 'Suffering and the Origins of Traumatic Memory', in Arthur Kleinman, Veena Das, and Margaret Lock (eds), *Social Suffering*. Berkeley and Los Angeles: University of California Press, 245–60.

Zaehner, R. C. (1970). *Concordant Discord*. Oxford: Clarendon Press.

Zeki, Semir (1999). *Inner Vision: An Exploration of Art and the Brain*. Oxford: Oxford University Press.

Index